Humana Festival '96
The Complete Plays

Humana Inc. is one of the nation's largest
managed health care companies
with more than 3.5 million members in its health care plans.

The Humana Foundation was established in 1981
to support the educational, social, medical and cultural development
of communities in ways that reflect
Humana's commitment to social responsibility
and an improved quality of life.

Smith and Kraus *Books For Actors*

CONTEMPORARY PLAYWRIGHTS SERIES

Christopher Durang Vol. I: 27 Short Plays
Christopher Durang Vol. II: Complete Full-Length Plays, 1975-1995
Horton Foote Vol. I: 4 New Plays
Horton Foote Vol. II: Collected Plays
John Guare: The War against the Kitchen Sink
A.R. Gurney Vol. I: 9 Early Plays
A.R. Gurney Vol. II: Collected Plays, 1977-1985
Israel Horovitz Vol. I: 16 Short Plays
Romulus Linney: 17 Short Plays
Jane Martin: Collected Plays, 1980-1995
Terrence McNally Vol. I: 15 Short Plays
Terrence McNally Vol.II: Collected Plays
William Mastrosimone: Collected Plays
Marsha Norman: Collected Plays
Eric Overmyer: Collected Plays
Lanford Wilson: 21 Short Plays
Lanford Wilson: Collected Plays, 1965-1970
20 One-Acts from 20 Years at the Humana Festival, 1975-1995
Humana Festival '93: The Complete Plays
Humana Festival '94: The Complete Plays
Humana Festival '95: The Complete Plays
Women Playwrights: The Best Plays of 1992
Women Playwrights: The Best Plays of 1993
Women Playwrights: The Best Plays of 1994
Women Playwrights: The Best Plays of 1995
EST Marathon '94: One-Act Plays
EST Marathon '95: One-Act Plays
EST Marathon '96: One-Act Plays
Act One Festival '94: One-Act Plays
Act One Festival '95: One-Act Plays

If you require pre-publication information about upcoming Smith and Kraus books, you may receive our semi-annual catalogue, free of charge, by sending your name and address to *Smith and Kraus Catalogue, P.O. Box 127, One Main Street, Lyme, NH 03768. Or call us at (800) 895-4331, fax (603) 795-4427.***Smith and Kraus** *Books For Actors*

Humana Festival '96
The Complete Plays

Edited by Michael Bigelow Dixon
and Liz Engelman

Contemporary Playwrights Series

SK
A Smith and Kraus Book

A Smith and Kraus Book
Published by Smith and Kraus, Inc.
One Main Street, PO Box 127, Lyme, NH 03768

Manufactured in the United States of America

Cover and Text Design by Julia Hill
Cover artwork: photography © Franco Donaggio, graphic design Choplogic/Walter McCord and Mary Cawein

First Edition: November 1996
10 9 8 7 6 5 4 3 2

Library of Congress Cataloguing-in-Publication Data
Contemporary Playwrights Series
ISSN 11067-9510

Contents

FOREWORD by Jon Jory vii

EDITORS' NOTE by Micheal B. Dixon and Liz Engelman viii

THE BATTING CAGE by Joan Ackermann 1

GOING, GOING, GONE: An Article by Anne Bogart 39

CONTRACT WITH JACKIE by Jimmy Breslin 47

FLESH AND BLOOD by Elizabeth Dewberry 57

TRYING TO FIND CHINATOWN by David Henry Hwang 103

REVERSE TRANSCRIPTION by Tony Kushner 113

WHAT I MEANT WAS by Craig Lucas 127

JACK AND JILL by Jane Martin 135

CHILEAN HOLIDAY by Guillermo Reyes 189

MISSING MARISA AND KISSING CHRISTINE by John Patrick Shanley 239

ONE FLEA SPARE by Naomi Wallace 279

HUMANA FESTIVAL HISTORY compiled by Joel A. Smith 331

Acknowledgements

Thanks to the following persons for their invaluable assistance in compiling this volume of plays:

Spencer Parsons
Erin Watson
Charles Forbes
Jenny Sandman
Joel A. Smith
Val Smith
Alexander Speer

William Craver
Peter Franklin
Mary Harden
Joyce Ketay
George Lane
Carl Mulert
Esther Newberg
Ruth Nightengale
Bruce Ostler

Foreword

One thing about these plays, they are heartfelt. Rightly or wrongly they seem to be open windows on their authors' lives. I like that, don't you? Somehow as the century winds to a close we cooled on cool detachment. For a time the theatre seemed determined to hide its naiveté, its sentiment, its longing for intimate connections and stand outside the party with an ironic glint in its eye and a wry, somewhat condescending smile for the human behaviors of those who simply didn't know any better.

These plays are smart without forgetting to care as they probe connection, missed connection and the longing for connection. Anne Bogart examines the physics of intimacy ending in a universal dance. Joan Ackermann shows the comedy in the heart of depression as the characters learn they have to step up to the plate. John Patrick Shanley does a nineties twist on strangers meeting between trains. Jane Martin shows that in matters of the heart timing is everything. I could go on, but in this delicious constellation of plays there is, without exception, the drive for intimacy and being known. They are documents of stumbling, careening, crawling toward connection and there is a wise simplicity in them that as a producer of new work I haven't seen so clearly in a long time. As such, I'm going to call them valentines of the human condition and risk the satirical thrust of those too wise to care.

Jon Jory
Producing Director
Actors Theatre of Louisville

Editors' Note

1996 marks the 20th anniversary of the Humana Festival of New American Plays. Thanks to the generosity and vision of the Humana Foundation, the festival has introduced to the American repertoire more than 200 plays by 130 playwrights. That's an impressive body of work, created by an astounding range of playwrights, whose passion and perspective, craft and style, humor and provocation bespeak the nonconformist spirit of American playwriting. To honor all 130 playwrights—and to document their achievement for scholars and artists—we have included an annotated history of the Humana Festival in the endpages of this volume.

This year's plays reinforce the Humana Festival's reputation for great variety in style, subject and authorship. But even more, as editors, the plays remind us that drama is a genre of experiment and revision. For instance, this book includes what Tony Kushner suggested might be his only foray into the ten-minute form, *Reverse Transcription,* which he ironically subtitled "A Ten-Minute Play That's Nearly Twenty Minutes Long." For Anne Bogart, "scripted text" remains part of her ongoing experiment with "performance text"; so she contributed an article that illuminates her process. And while most of the plays are printed here precisely as they were performed in the Humana Festival, several authors took the publishing opportunity to add some finishing touches. Guillermo Reyes even created a new character for who makes his first appearance in this book!

Even now, in printed form, the plays are not necessarily "finished." As John Patrick Shanley reminds us in a prefatory note to his script, the plays remain "in process" and playwrights reserve the right to revise for future production. Just as human change is essential to dramatic action, so too are script changes essential to playwriting. This book then stands as a record of this year. Who knows what will happen to these plays in the future? We only know this is the one place you can find out what happened at the Humana Festival in 1996.

Michael Bigelow Dixon & Liz Engelman

Humana Festival '96
The Complete Plays

The Batting Cage
by Joan Ackermann

BIOGRAPHY

Joan Ackermann is co-artistic director of Mixed Company in Great Barrington, Mass., a year-round theatre now in its fourteenth year. Her plays include *Zara Spook and Other Lures* (1990 Humana Festival of New American Plays), *Stanton's Garage* (1993 Humana Festival), *Don't Ride the Clutch, Yonder Peasant, Bed and Breakfast, The Light of His Eye, Rescuing Greenland and Off the Map*. Her new play, *The Batting Cage*, was commissioned by Actors Theatre of Louisville for the 1996 Humana Festival. She recently wrote a TV pilot for Steven Spielberg and two screenplays under contract. A special contributer to *Sports Illustrated* for six years, she has also written for *Time, the Atlantic, Esquire, GQ, Audubon, New York Magazine* and many others.

ORIGINAL PRODUCTION

The Batting Cage was first performed at the 1996 Humana Festival of New American Plays, March, 1996. It was directed by Lisa Peterson with the following cast:

Julianna	Veanne Cox
Wilson	Babo Harrison
Bobby	Justin Hagan
Peg	Carol Morley

and the following production staff:

Scenic Designer	Paul Owen
Costume Designer	Jeanette deJong
Lighting Designer	Mimi Jordan Sherin
Sound Designer	Martin R. Desjardins
Properties Master	Mark J. Bissonnette
Production Stage Manager	Debra Acquavella
Assistant Stage Manager	Cind Senensieb
Dramaturg	Liz Engelman
New York Casting Arrangements	Laura Richin Casting

CHARACTERS

JULIANNA
WILSON
BOBBY
PEG

PLACE

A Holiday Inn hotel room in St. Augustine, Florida. The present.

THE BATTING CAGE

ACT ONE

A Holiday Inn hotel room. Two double beds, a table, chairs, at least one paint-
ing, sliding glass door that leads out to balcony, door that leads into bathroom
off a small changing room with bar for hanging clothes.

Scene One

Wilson enters the room. Her hair uncombed, she wears severe black glasses, a
baggy pair of worn dark khaki shorts, a dark blue polo shirt, dirty cross-train-
er sneakers. She looks around, puts down her suitcase, an old maroon Samsonite
case, and lies on the bed closer to the balcony. Gets up and goes to the main light
switch. With a pocket screwdriver she takes off the plate, rewires inside and
installs a dimmer switch. Turns the light up to full and then down to half
brightness. Lies down again on her stomach. Julianna enters carrying two suit-
cases. She is pretty, slim, wearing a pretty dress, heels, sunglasses, and a hat. She
puts down her suitcases and takes off her glasses.

JULIANNA: Well, I don't know how much of a healing vacation this is going to
be. The only good thing so far is that Carl isn't here. Carl would have had
a fit at the airport, once he found out about the suitcase, he would have
raged, *raged* at that tiny middle eastern baggage claim person, made him
cry, shattered him with his voice, I see you've picked your bed already. You
want to be by the balcony, the light, the beach, that's fine, I'll be by the
wall.
(Wilson gets up and lies down on the bed by the wall, face buried in the pillow,
as Julianna notices the painting over that bed.)
JULIANNA: I think we should take down that painting, don't you? Why be prey
to *that* for ten days, who chooses decor for hotel rooms and what are their
qualifications? Nothing in this room tells us we're in Florida, why not palm
trees, sunny splashes, bougainvillea?
(Julianna goes to the painting and tries to remove it.)
JULIANNA: I'll call mother and tell her about the suitcase she's going to be so

upset. I don't mind this bed, Wilson, you have the other one, oh glory be. It's nailed to the wall, it is the wall, it's raised distressed plasterboard, they're afraid people will want to *steal* this? Wilson, can you breathe?

(She looks at the other bed, the sliding glass door to the balcony.)

JULIANNA: Do you think anyone can get to our balcony?

(She walks to the sliding glass door, unlocks it, opens it up.)

JULIANNA: This lock is made of a very cheap metal, not even a real metal I don't think, some soft alloy, Carl would know. *(She steps outside.)* There's the beach. Wilson. *(Chipperly.)* There's the ocean. Ocean front room.

(She stares briefly out to sea.)

JULIANNA: Morgan would be out there by now, before we'd even made it to our room, she'd be out there jumping in the waves. The surf. *(She closes the door and locks it. Wilson doesn't move.)* Of course, if someone were to break in, in the pitch black darkness of the night, the first person they'd encounter would be whoever's sleeping in *that* bed. The bed you're on seems a little protected. And it's closer to the bathroom. That'll be convenient for you.

(Wilson gets up and lies down on the other bed, her face revealed, eyes open to show she is depressed, not sleepy. Julianna is going for her purse.)

JULIANNA: I packed you some sunscreen and mace. SPF 30. I know the state of your skin is the last thing on your mind, but melanoma cases are on the rise exponentially and it wouldn't hurt for you to experience a gesture of caring for yourself. Your mace is on your bedside table.

(She closes the drawer. Goes to the phone and dials.)

JULIANNA: That painting reminds me of Carl, I don't know. Shouting, all those loud colors. You're sure you put that tag on the suitcase? Wilson?

WILSON: *(Detached.)* Yes.

JULIANNA: The one I mailed you? It was properly attached?

WILSON: Yes.

JULIANNA: There's a double thing there on the buckle, you have to guide the leather strap back through you did?

(Pause.)

JULIANNA: Or else it doesn't work, it comes undone, just hangs there, limp, Wilson, can we just clarify, the ashes are in your missing suitcase, yes or no? Mother, it's Julianna, we're here, something terrible has happened, how are your knees, have you been to Dr. Saddler yet? Mother, you should be examined immediately, take pictures of the bruises. You *have* to sue them, those courier cyclists must be stopped they can't be permitted to mow the population down. Oh, nice. Not really sunny but not exactly cloudy. She's lying down. *(Studying Wilson.)* Not really. Mother, the suitcase with Morgan's ashes in it is lost, it missed the connection in Atlanta. They don't know. It could be, it could be on its way anywhere, Wilson says she put a tag on it, so. It should, you're right, it should show up somewhere sometime. We will, in the meantime we'll just be on vacation. We'll have a wonderful vacation in Florida, Wilson, you have anything to say to Mother?

(Julianna looks at Wilson who doesn't move. Back into the phone.)

JULIANNA: She sends her love. So, we'll call as soon as we hear anything. Mother, please do go to the doctor, and call that lawyer. We will. Bye.

(Julianna hangs up and heads toward the dimmer switch.)

JULIANNA: Wilson, you really shouldn't install these without turning the electricity off, everybody says it's very dangerous. One day you're going to get zapped and we'll all be flying somewhere to scatter *your* ashes. So.

(Having turned the light up all the way, she picks up a pile of brochures and sits on the bed.)

JULIANNA: I picked up these brochures at the front desk there are so many things to do in this area, so many fun interesting things to do. And so much history, history galore, did you know St. Augustine is the oldest settlement in the country? I don't know whether we should go ahead and charter a boat or wait and see if the suitcase shows up. The Spanish, Ponce de Leon, we can visit his Fountain of Youth, "Here Ponce de Leon came ashore to landmark and record for all time the first moment of our nation's history." My.

(Wilson gets up, opens her suitcase and starts to unpack. She lifts up ten identical men's polo shirts neatly stacked which she carries over to hang up methodically on hangers.)

JULIANNA: One thing no one realizes is just how young this country is, how very adolescent, it's no wonder no one has any sense of who they are. You're unpacking? *(Going through brochures.)* Fountain of Youth, Our Lady of La Leche Shrine, the Lightner Museum, St. Augustine by sightseeing train, Whetstone Chocolate Factory tour, simply gesture if any of these appeals to you, Zoroyda Castle has "a sacred cat rug made from the hair of prehistoric cats that roamed the Nile," mn—I wouldn't like that, to get out of the tub and stand barefoot on a cat hair rug, little stubby, muddy, prehistoric hairs, like a bristle brush—Cafe Alcazar, Spanish Military Hospital, go ahead, use all the hangers we'll get some more, Museum of Weapons and Early American History, the Oldest Wooden Schoolhouse, Potter's Wax Museum, Alligator Farm. Now that's what Carl would make a bee-line for, the alligator farm, "Don't miss Gomek, giant crocodile from New Guinea," Carl would fixate on that. He always gravitates toward the perverse, the very unnatural. Carl and Gomek. You have ten of those shirts? One for each day? Wilson?

WILSON: Huh?

JULIANNA: You have ten of the same identical shirt?

WILSON: I like this shirt.

JULIANNA: You must like it. You must like it very much.

(Wilson finishes hanging the last one.)

JULIANNA: Did you buy them in the men's department?

(Wilson crosses back to her bed.)

WILSON: Eddie Bauer.

JULIANNA: Eddie Bauer? They look like Eddie Bauer.

(Wilson takes the rest of her things out of the suitcase—underwear, socks, hooded sweatshirt, and stuffs them in a dresser drawer.)

JULIANNA: You brought ten Eddie Bauer shirts and one pair of shorts? You have other shorts in your other suitcase? Wilson?

(Wilson glances over at her.)

JULIANNA: Did you pack more shorts in the suitcase that's lost? With the ashes?

WILSON: *(Matter of factly.)* No.

(Julianna picks up the brochures again.)

JULIANNA: So. Which of these places do you want to go to first? Or do you want to go to the beach first?

WILSON: No.

(Wilson lies down again. She is not angry or emotionally engaged at all with Julianna. She is depressed, emotionally miles away. Silence.)

JULIANNA: Wilson. There are a lot of other ways I could have chosen to spend my vacation, a lot of other places I could have gone, a world of places, a lot of other people I could have gone with, myriad, but I thought it was important for us to spend some time together. We haven't spent any time together since the funeral and that was two years ago. Morgan wanted this. This was Morgan's plan for us all to come down here.

(After a few moments, Julianna gets up to unpack, puts a suitcase on the bed and opens it. Takes out two books on top, puts them on her bedside table.)

JULIANNA: Mother sent me these to get you to talk. Talking aids.

(She takes out several dresses and hangs them all up as she talks. Puts away other clothes in drawers. Her wardrobe is that of a woman with great style and flair, adept at attracting men. Julianna is trying relentlessly to be upbeat and positive.)

JULIANNA: I don't know if you noticed I registered under my maiden name. I haven't used my maiden name in twenty years. I surprised myself, I didn't plan on using it, when I got to the blank I just wrote...Julianna Finley.

Julianna Finley. I feel braces on my teeth when I think that name. I feel myself waiting at the bus stop for the bus to school, standing there on the curb, so small, clutching my book bag, the air warm, my bangs feathered away from my face. It's very strange, you can't imagine. Having a name that's half as old as you are. Julianna Finley. Mrs. Carl Randolph.

(There is a knock on the door. Julianna rushes to the mirror and puts on some lipstick. Another knock.)

JULIANNA: *(Liltingly.)* Coming! Let's hope it's Morgan.

(She straightens her dress, flounces her hair, and opens the door. No one is there. She looks down and sees a folded up map.)

JULIANNA: Oh. *(She picks it up, closes the door.)* It's a sightseeing map of St. Augustine and its beaches. I asked for one at the front desk but they were out of them. *(She sits on the bed and looks at it.)* You know one thing about Carl, for all his grimacing, he would have made that suitcase appear. If Carl were here, and I am thrilled he is not, but if he were here, if Carl were here, the suitcase would be here. He would have dragged it out of that middle eastern baggage claim man. Wrestled it from that tiny pathetic person's most superhuman efforts. Of course, Carl wouldn't have put his sister's ashes in a suitcase and checked it onto a plane in the first place, a plane where luggage is often misplaced. He would have carried the ashes with him, on his person, something that valuable. *(Pause.)* You know, it's just like Morgan to arrange for us all to be somewhere, and then go galavanting off somewhere else.

(Wilson doesn't move. Julianna stares off, hands folded in her lap.)

(Lights fade.)

Scene Two

Wilson is lying, lifeless, on the bed. During the scene change, many more of Julianna's outfits have been hung. Julianna enters carrying a few bags from Woolworth's and a box of salt water taffy.

JULIANNA: I've *got* to get out of this dress.

(She puts down the taffy, the bags. Starts to undress.)

JULIANNA: Well, the Lightner Museum was fascinating, I did feel a *little* awkward wandering around on my own, the *only* person there by herself. I bought some salt water taffy, you're welcome to. Wilson, you're in the same position you were in when I left six hours ago, you're like some still life, some twisted contemporary still life, *never* have I ever been so desperate to get out of a dress…

(She pulls the dress off over her head and throws it on the floor.)

JULIANNA: Unhh. What a relief. I saw myself in a full length mirror in Woolworth's, I said *who* is that person, that Sears Roebuck catalogue woman from Akron, Ohio, some luncheon hostess at an Olive Garden chain restaurant, did the airline call? *God*, that dress.

(She goes to the phone, dressed in a slip, and dials.)

JULIANNA: I bought some postcards. Pelicans, sunsets, a recipe for key lime pie, you might want to check out the postcards at the front desk, Wilson, of this Holiday Inn, the rooms, you might want to send those to your friends if this room is all you plan to see of Florida…American Airlines, may I have lost baggage, please? Of course I'm starving, I'm not about to go into a restaurant by myself. Hello, this is Mrs. Carl Randolph, yes, I was wondering if my lost suitcase has been found. I did fill out a description form, this is the third time I have called today. Maroon, yes. Maroon, a Samsonite hard quite old suitcase with an identifying tag attached, correctly, *(Glancing at Wilson.)* it is thought. Well, that's most regrettable. I'll call again the morning and then again until it's recovered. The value of the suitcase? Wilson, what's the value of the suitcase? The value of the suitcase, sir, is, at the very least, inestimable. I hope so. Good bye.

(Julianna hangs up, goes to the closet.)

JULIANNA: Yellow, mustard yellow, that's the color I need to wear which actually brings up an interesting topic I will share with you, feel free to speak.

(Julianna reaches for a yellow dress and puts it on.)

JULIANNA: I haven't mentioned this to mother but I've been receiving some acupuncture lately from a beginner acupuncturist, at a discount because he's in need of accumulating hours. For a minor medical condition, minor, don't be too concerned. I can't explain it all now but the basic theory is that the cause of illness has to do with an imbalance of the five elements that make up chi: wood, fire, earth, metal, water, and one way to diagnose which element is out of balance is by color, what color do you feel very strongly about, love or detest. First he thought I had a fire imbalance, someone who is cold physically and emotionally, as in one's fire is out, feeling parched and arid in mind, body, spirit. The color that corresponds to fire is red. Well, I didn't think that was right, I wasn't feeling passionate about red either way. I'm not going to wear this dress, I look like I should be offering people cheese samples on a large Corningware plate in a supermarket.

(After studying herself in a full length mirror, she pulls off that dress and starts assembling another outfit, perhaps a blouse and a print skirt.)

JULIANNA: Then he thought maybe I had an earth imbalance which has to do with the intake of nourishment and getting nourished, or not, lacking the ability to create roots for oneself, easily pushed over, that seemed more like it. I certainly have not been feeling particularly nourished lately, but then there was all this implication about having difficulty with sterility I told him it was my husband who had that problem not me. Anyway, the color for an earth imbalance is yellow.

(Not satisfied, she unbuttons the blouse and hangs it up. Reaches for another one.)

JULIANNA: Then I read about water and I was sure I had a water imbalance, meanwhile all along he's taking my pulses sticking needles in me as though it's earth. The organs associated with water are the kidneys and the bladder and you know I have the bladder of a grasshopper. The flavor that corresponds to water is salty, me, Mrs. Ruffles potato chip, the sense organ governed by the water element is the ears, my hearing is painfully acute, the color blue. Well, my car is blue. Is this me? I think not.

(Studies herself in the mirror, takes off the blouse and the skirt. Stares at the closet. During the following puts on another outfit and takes it off.)

JULIANNA: It was disconcerting. Not to be sure which element was out of balance and having him treating me perhaps making it all worse. Well, the emotion corresponding to metal is grief, and I've suffered my share of that recently. The sound corresponding to metal is weeping, God knows I have wept these past two years and dreams associated with metal are of cruel killing of people, I've had those. The color is white. Well? Any thoughts? You know one thing, Wilson, about living alone now, ever since Carl moved out, I find myself speaking out loud. I'll find myself in the kitchen talking with no one there. I feel like a loon. I'm thinking about getting a cat or a goldfish, just to have a target to aim my voice at. At least now, here, *you're* listening. I'm not just ranting and raving to myself. Wilson?

(She looks at Wilson who hasn't moved, puts on a robe and picks up one of the books she referred to in the first scene. It's a Mensa genius quiz-a-day book. She opens and reads aloud.)

JULIANNA: "Which is more, seconds in 100 hours or inches in 100 yards?"

(Wilson doesn't move or look at her, but responds, without emotion, from another world.)

WILSON: Seconds in a hundred hours.

JULIANNA: "What are three single digits whose sum is the same as that of the digits multiplied?"

WILSON: One, two and three.

JULIANNA: "People afraid of the number 13 are said to have triskaidekaphobia. What are the names for each of the following phobias? Fear of cats."

WILSON: Ailurophobia.

JULIANNA: "Fear of foreigners."

WILSON: Xenophobia.

JULIANNA: "Fear of open places."

(Julianna gets more comfortable.)

WILSON: Agoraphobia.

JULIANNA: "Divide 110 into two parts so that one will be 150 percent of the other. What are the two numbers?" Do you remember, Wilson, that time we all went on vacation together at Old Orchard Beach in Maine…

WILSON: *(Still not moving.)* Sixty-six and forty-four.

JULIANNA: "If three salesmen can sell three stoves in seven minutes, how many stoves can six salesmen sell in seventy minutes?" Daddy was still alive, you and Morgan were only maybe five, Morgan was wild, *wild*…

WILSON: Sixty stoves.

JULIANNA: "If six puzzle makers can compose nine puzzles in a day and a half, how many puzzle makers does it take to compose 270 puzzles in thirty days?" She disappeared and we finally saw her at the top of the ferris wheel, they'd stopped it, delirious with joy, kicking her feet in the air, she'd snuck on and was sitting with the actor Fred MacMurray and his wife, not his TV wife, daddy recognized him…

WILSON: Nine.

JULIANNA: Nine what?

WILSON: Puzzle makers.

JULIANNA: Correct. Of course Morgan didn't know who Fred MacMurray was, she just lived in the star realm without even knowing it. "What is the highest four-digit number, with no zeroes, in which the first digit is one-quarter of the third digit, the second digit is three times the first digit, and the third and last digits are the same?" I can still hear her, shrieking with glee, way up there, the rest of us on the ground, staring up…

WILSON: Two thousand, six hundred and eighty-eight.

(For once, Julianna is silent, lost in thought. Wilson lifts herself up slightly and looks at her; repeats the answer, nudging for another question.)

WILSON: Two thousand, six hundred and eighty-eight.

JULIANNA: What other word can be made from the letters "insatiable"?

(Wilson lies back down. Julianna sits up and puts the book down.)

JULIANNA: I know. I'm going to wear a white dress. I'm going to put on a white dress and go walk along the beach and look for shells. I'll be a woman in a white dress looking for shells.

WILSON: Banalities.

(Julianna reaches for a summery white dress and holds it up against herself.)

JULIANNA: That's who I'll be. It's been nice finally having a conversation with you, Wilson.

(She looks in the mirror. Lights fade.)

Scene Three

It is three days later. The room should reflect that. Wilson is lying down, wearing a different Eddie Bauer shirt. Julianna enters in an outfit we haven't seen yet, one she can slip on quickly. She carries shopping bags with souvenirs in them.

JULIANNA: *(Elated.)* There's an historical enactment tonight, in the center of town, Sir Francis Drake's raid on St. Augustine, 1586, Wilson, it's bad for your heart to be lying down so much. I stumbled upon them in the Fountain of Youth Park, the actors. The military camps are all set up, old white tents, I was the only person there not in costume, the only one. *(Setting her souvenirs up around the room.)* I happened to be wandering around after hours, after the last exhibit at the planetarium, they show you the night sky when Ponce de Leon landed in Florida, after I'd drunk a little paper cupful of the fountain of youth. It was so bizarre, Wilson, because I drank the Fountain of Youth and an hour later I was in the sixteenth century! They were cooking corn over open fires, polishing their armor, children playing, the British and the Spanish. I met a conquistador, Juan de Santa de Mingo, he was so…conquistadorial, dashing, he had these big…hands. He showed me with such graceful respect how he'd made his own chain mail shirt out of half a mile of galvanized electric fence it weighed 25 pounds. A conquistador, Wilson, imagine.

(There is a knock on the door. Julianna primps, moves towards it.)

JULIANNA: He offered me a mug of mead with such distinguished Spanish flair and told me, so politely, he wanted to take me out to dinner. I thought to myself, that would be wonderful and novel as the only meals I've had in Florida for the past three days have been in my Holiday Inn hotel room. Of course, I wasn't that bold with him.

(She opens the door and a waiter, Bobby, enters with room service for three. He has a deep southern accent, several tattoos; rough but appealing. Julianna pours her charm on for him.)

JULIANNA: And how are you this evening?

(*Bobby smiles politely, wheels in the cart and begins setting up the table.*)

JULIANNA: I hope you haven't eaten.

(*Bobby smiles again, wanly, sets out the silverware, etc., three dinners.*)

JULIANNA: Do you mind if I inquire what your name is?

BOBBY: Bobby.

JULIANNA: Bobby. I'm Julianna Finley and that woman lying on the bed for three days choosing not to accompany me anywhere is my sister, Wilson Finley. She's somewhat of an anomaly, don't take it personally. So, we just need one more chair...

JULIANNA: Won't you join us? I've ordered for you.

BOBBY: Pardon?

JULIANNA: We'd be so grateful if you'd dine with us tonight.

BOBBY: Ma'am, I need to get back to the kitchen.

JULIANNA: Oh please, we'd so enjoy your company, we could use another adept conversationalist at the table. Just join us for five minutes, won't you? Would you prefer the red snapper or the turkey club? I'd offer you the plate of mashed potatoes but that's Wilson's. She appears intent on gaining weight.

(*Julianna sits down and smiles at him. After much hesitation he sits down.*)

JULIANNA: Which will it be, fish or turkey?

BOBBY: I cain't eat fish, ma'am.

JULIANNA: (*With curiosity.*) Oh no?

BOBBY: (*Reluctantly.*) My wrists swell up.

JULIANNA: Then turkey it is.

(*Julianna passes Bobby the turkey club and starts eating the red snapper. Wilson stays in bed.*)

JULIANNA: So, Bobby. Where are you from?

BOBBY: Jacksonville.

JULIANNA: Jacksonville. In which state is that?

BOBBY: Florida.

JULIANNA: Ah, this state.

(*Bobby shakes his head slightly, agitated by something in his ear. Then he takes a frilled toothpick out of a sandwich quarter and starts to eat.*)

JULIANNA: Would you like to know where we're from?

BOBBY: Uh-huh.

JULIANNA: Isn't this an interesting dynamic, Wilson? One person says something and the other person responds. We're from up north in Massachusetts. Originally, we're from Lexington, but now my sister lives in Cleveland and I dwell in Ipswich on the north shore. We haven't seen each other in two years and now that we're reunited in this sunny cultural heritage, umpteen things to do, my sister, my one and only sister, chooses to stay in bed. Don't you find that disquieting? Excuse me.

(She takes a napkin and discreetly wipes some food from her mouth.)

JULIANNA: My sister is a chemical engineer, much sought after by head hunters. You'd never know it to look at her, but she scored a perfect 1600 on her combined S.A.T.'s. I myself am in between careers. Will you have a roll?

(Pause.)

BOBBY: When?

JULIANNA: Now.

BOBBY: No. Thank you. Ma'am.

JULIANNA: Julianna, call me Julianna. After all, we're on vacation. Can I just ask you…what career would you have thought I had?

BOBBY: Beg your pardon?

JULIANNA: By looking at me. Who do I look like to you? A professional woman? Interior decorator? What?

BOBBY: I don't know, ma'am.

JULIANNA: Take a guess. I'm curious. Don't you ever wonder, how you appear to others?

BOBBY: Well, down here we get a lot of divorcees.

JULIANNA: *(Not thrilled.)* I look like a divorcee?

BOBBY: Just down here. *(Realizing it was the wrong answer.)* Maybe.

JULIANNA: Mm. Wilson, your mashed potatoes are getting cold.

(Pause.)

BOBBY: School teacher?

JULIANNA: Ah, our mother is a school teacher. She was to have joined us here in St. Augustine but unfortunately she was hit by a bicycle courier messenger person in New York City. She was laid out flat. Would anyone care for my broccoli?

(Bobby gestures no.)

JULIANNA: It's curious, none of your vegetables here at the Holiday Inn retains any color. Wilson had a twin sister, and it's because of her that we're here, to scatter her ashes from the prow of a boat into the sea. Her name was Morgan and she was exceptionally charismatic. Morgan/Wilson, that's what we called them, Morgan/Wilson, sounds like a shipping company, doesn't it? I can't tell if this fish's flesh is red or if it's the paprika. They were fraternal twins and they couldn't have been more different but they were inseparable. Morgan/Wilson. Wilson was the brains, Morgan was the *(Suddenly tearing up, her voice breaks.)* heart.

(She takes a sip of water. Recovers.)

JULIANNA: Do you have a sister, Bobby?

BOBBY: Yes, ma'am.

JULIANNA: And what does she do?

BOBBY: *(Subdued.)* She works in a titty bar.

JULIANNA: A what kind of bar?

BOBBY: Titty bar.

JULIANNA: *(Doesn't get it.)* Oh. Identity is such an interesting thing, don't you think? I've been thinking about it lately. Sometimes I wonder what the difference between personality and identity is. If perhaps they're the same thing, the one perceived from without the other from within?

(Bobby hits the side of his head a couple of times. Resumes eating. Julianna eyes him but politely pretends not to have noticed.)

JULIANNA: What is it about me that made you think school teacher?

(Bobby has picked up the toothpick and is turning the frilled end around in his ear.)

JULIANNA: Is there something wrong with your ear?

BOBBY: Damn barnacle. Pardon me.

(He puts down the toothpick. Keeps eating.)

JULIANNA: Barnacle?

BOBBY: Got a barnacle, growing in my ear.

(Julianna is horrified. Puts down her fork.)

JULIANNA: A *barnacle*? In your *ear*?

BOBBY: I clean boats, underwater. Up the Seafarer's marina. You gotta rinse your ears out real good cause those barnacles, they'll squirt out *(He makes a squirting motion with his hand.)* well…not…sperm, pardon me, but something like. Little tiny barnacle eggs, I guess. Microscopic. They'll settle in your ear next thing you know you got a barnacle. Settin' up house.

JULIANNA: How *awful*.

(Wilson gets up and comes and joins them. Eats her mashed potatoes, head down. Bobby tries to assuage Julianna's horror; she's covering her ears with her hands.)

BOBBY: I've had it before. I just need to get to a doctor, get me some special chemical is all.

(They continue eating in silence.)

BOBBY: How're your potatoes?

WILSON: *(Barely looking at him.)* Good.

BOBBY: I peeled them.

WILSON: You peeled them very well.

BOBBY: Thanks. *(Pause.)* Mind if I try a bite?

WILSON: Help yourself.

(*Wilson holds her plate out to him and he takes a bite.*)

BOBBY: Good. No peel.

WILSON: Sometimes less is better.

BOBBY: You got that right.

(*Pause.*)

WILSON: Sometimes less is zilch.

BOBBY: (*Inanely.*) Been there, too.

(*Julianna is staring into his ear. He becomes aware of it, turning back toward her, and they simultaneously back away.*)

JULIANNA: Forgive me. I can't stop thinking about your barnacle. I may have an earth imbalance one result of which is it makes me too empathetic, I feel excessively what others feel.

BOBBY: That's all right, ma'am. The reason your broccoli's so pale?

JULIANNA: Yes?

BOBBY: Is on account it's a cauliflower.

JULIANNA: Oh.

(*Bobby and Wilson continue eating. Julianna has stopped.*)

BOBBY: (*Leaning in.*) How'd your twin die?

WILSON: She had childhood diabetes. She had all kinds of health complications all her life. Finally, her heart just quit.

BOBBY: You didn't have it, being a twin?

WILSON: No.

BOBBY: You were the lucky one, huh?

(*Wilson looks at him. Goes back to eating. Bobby leans back, taps the side of his chair with enthusiasm.*)

BOBBY: So. How long you girls in town?

(*Lights fade.*)

Scene Four

> *That night. Dinner has not been cleared away. Wilson is lying on the floor, her legs up on her bed, listening to a baseball game. She has put a blue lightbulb in the lamp on her bedside table. It's the only light now on. The phone rings. After about eight rings she finally answers.*

WILSON: Hello? Really? All right.

(*She hangs up. Keeps listening to the ball game. There is a knock on the door. She goes and answers it. Steps into the hall and then back into the room with an old Samsonite maroon suitcase. She puts it down. Stares at it. Puts it up on the bed. Runs her hands over the suitcase, studying it.)*

WILSON: Morgan?

(Cautiously, she opens the suitcase which is full of clothes. She slowly picks up a Pittsburgh Pirates baseball cap which she examines carefully. She puts it on her head, looks in the mirror and studies herself. Reaches over and turns on Julianna's bedside lamp. Stares at herself some more. Turns off the game. She closes the suitcase, picks it up and stands it on the floor. Sits back down on the floor, wearing the hat, staring at the suitcase. Julianna enters.)

JULIANNA: Well, I wish you'd come with me, Wilson, I really do. It's a little awkward going to these events by oneself, one is so clearly a single woman. It gives people the wrong idea, men, especially in such a setting, people behaving wildly, running up and down the streets, firing muskets, cannons blasting, looters on horseback, the horses are frightened. It stops feeling like a reenactment and more like an actment, is it really so very much to ask of you to go somewhere with me? What *is* it, Wilson? *(This last question not in response to an action from Wilson.)*

WILSON: *(With a new intensity.)* I need the car tomorrow.

JULIANNA: What?

WILSON: I need the car. Tomorrow.

JULIANNA: What for?

WILSON: I'm going to Bradenton.

JULIANNA: Bradenton? Where is Bradenton?

WILSON: I don't know. I'm going there.

JULIANNA: You're going there? And what do you plan to do in Bradenton?

WILSON: I need to go there.

JULIANNA: Well. I don't know what to say. You finally want to go somewhere. You finally want to go somewhere the very day the one day I might…be…busy. I might see this conquistador, Juan, I didn't see him tonight—I hope he wasn't hurt, the British were so wound up, in a marauding frenzy—but he did intimate, well, more than that, he did say that tomorrow he'd pick me up and take me out to dinner. I would go with you, Wilson, but how often does one get asked to dinner by a dashing conquistador? Do you think maybe you'll be back by dinner?

WILSON: *(Very focused.)* No.

JULIANNA: Oh.

WILSON: I'm leaving early. I'll be gone when you get up.

(Wilson goes into the bathroom to brush her teeth.)

JULIANNA: Oh. You're sure you can find your way out of this room? *(She notices the suitcase.)* Oh my God. They found it. I don't believe it.

WILSON: Don't believe it. That's not it.

JULIANNA: That's not what?

WILSON: My suitcase.

JULIANNA: It's not?

(Standing in the bathroom doorway, brushing her teeth.)

WILSON: No.

JULIANNA: It looks like it's part of the set.

WILSON: It's not.

JULIANNA: Are you sure?

WILSON: I'm sure.

(She goes back into the bathroom and Julianna inspects the suitcase.)

JULIANNA: What a pity. Remember when Morgan won the set in a national sweepstakes five pieces. Maybe this one is part of a set someone else won in the same national sweepstakes. *(She cracks it and peeks inside.)* And where is that person now? *(She takes out a large slipper.)* Missing his slippers. Mm. Size thirteen. That seems unnaturally large, I didn't know men's feet went up that high. Carl has trouble finding shoes that are *wide* enough for him, I'm always on the look-out for double B width. Flip-flops. That's what he'd be wearing now, if he were here, flip-flops. Never happier than in his flip flops. His feet unrestrained—free. *(She suddenly puts the slipper back in and closes the case.)* Well, we'll have to call the airport, what a shame. *(She carries the suitcase to the door.)* I hate to think of Morgan, out there, just drifting. *(Julianna starts clearing up the dishes, piling them onto the table or tray and eventually wheeling it out into the hall.)*

JULIANNA: I can't get that boy's barnacle out of my mind. I feel like it's growing in my mind, this hard white sharp jagged thought. Just imagine it in your ear, *listening* to it growing, getting bigger and bigger. Carl would have loved that story. He would have embraced Bobby when he told it, it would have lifted his spirits, made his vacation. He would have been inspired to actually buy postcards so he could write all his friends about the barnacle. I almost feel like calling him and telling him.

(She wheels the cart out into the hall. Comes back in. She takes off her dress.)

JULIANNA: You know, Wilson, the only thing you've missed out on by not getting married, the only thing, is not getting to experience the pleasure of divorce. You'll never know the joy of divorcing a horrific abusive person.

(Wilson is in bed, wearing her cap.)

JULIANNA: You're wearing that hat to bed? What does the P stand for?

WILSON: The Pittsburgh Pirates.

JULIANNA: *(Julianna, wearing her slip, goes into the bathroom for a glass of water.)* Pirates. Pirates and conquistadors. History everywhere. None of it in the present tense. Whatever happened to the present tense?

WILSON: They were Morgan's favorite team.

JULIANNA: *(Heading for bed.)* Who were?

WILSON: The Pittsburgh Pirates.

JULIANNA: Really? I didn't know that. Where are my sleeping pills? I can't sleep without them.

(She finds and takes two pills and gets into bed in her slip.)

JULIANNA: Right now, he's listening to that barnacle. Bobby is lying in bed in the dark listening to that white crustacean, oozing more calcium deposits, building up, encroaching on his eardrum. Is a barnacle a crustacean? Wilson?

WILSON: It's a shellfish.

JULIANNA: *(An attempt at humor.)* It's selfish?

WILSON: Shellfish.

JULIANNA: I know. But is it a crustacean?

WILSON: It falls in a sub-class of Crustacean called cirripedia.

JULIANNA: Oh.

WILSON: The majority of cirripedia are hermaphrodites.

JULIANNA: Oh. Well.

(Pause.)

JULIANNA: Hermaphrodites never have to get divorced. You know, it's the oddest thing, Wilson. Maybe it's the pills I'm taking that give me these bizarrely lurid dreams but I have dreamt more than once that it's Morgan I'm divorcing and Carl is the one who died. Everything happened too fast.

(Lights fade.)

Scene Five

The next night. Julianna is in a nightgown, on the phone. The suitcase is gone and so is Wilson.

JULIANNA: Mother, I hope you're all right, it's almost midnight, I don't know why you're out so late. Your machine is making a funny noise. The suitcase still hasn't shown up, now Wilson is missing. She's gone to Bradenton— Bradenton, Florida don't ask me why, it must be five hours from here. That's a ten hour drive for someone adept at driving which Wilson is not.

It's so different without Morgan, being with her; I can't tell if she's still grieving or just being herself. I bought a new dress this morning, unfortunately the person I was supposed to go out to dinner with tonight never showed up. *(Disappointed.)* It's a print, greens, pinks, yellows. I bought some shells, they're superior to the ones on the beach, a key chain with a shell, a shell night light with a pelican artfully painted I could have gone with Wilson, to Bradenton, but…so. I mailed you some oranges and grapefruits, half and half, a surprise but now I've told you. So…call us tomorrow, mother. I wish you were here, with us. I wish so much you were here. Sweet dreams.

(She hangs up. Looks around the room, appears lonely, disappointed. Takes two of her sleeping pills. Goes to the sliding glass door and opens it. Steps outside onto the balcony. Comes back in and closes the door. Goes to the table where she's been writing postcards. Picks up pen and starts another postcard. Wilson enters, changed: charged, tired, focused.)

JULIANNA: Well…you're back.

WILSON: Hi.

(Wilson aims for the bathroom, closes the door.)

JULIANNA: I'll be with you in a minute. I'm busy writing a card here to a dear friend I've been meaning to write for a long time, I'll be through shortly. Victoria Trent. Victoria worked with me in the Country Kitchen, she gave excellent demonstrations with the bread machines; whole wheat breads were her strength, the heavier doughs. We used to have lunch together, she had separated from her husband just like I had so we had a lot to share, but then she and her husband got back together again.

(Wilson comes out of the bathroom ready for bed.)

JULIANNA: It's been such a busy, full day, I've hardly had time to think.

(Wilson gets into bed.)

JULIANNA: So. How was Bradenton?

WILSON: Good.

JULIANNA: Good.

(Julianna neatly stacks her postcards on the table and goes and gets into bed. The only light on is on her bedside table.)

JULIANNA: What did you do in Bradenton?

WILSON: Bradenton is where the Pittsburgh Pirates go for spring training, Julianna. I went to their field. I lay down in the outfield.

JULIANNA: You lay down in the outfield? That's why you went to Bradenton? To lie down in the outfield? *(A little aghast.)* Was there anybody there to see you?

WILSON: No.

JULIANNA: Thank goodness. Then what did you do?

WILSON: Then I got up, and I lay down in the infield.

JULIANNA: Was it different?

WILSON: It was very different.

(Pause.)

JULIANNA: How?

WILSON: *(Emotionally full.)* There was more action.

(Pause.)

(Julianna gets up and goes into the bathroom. Wilson suddenly sits up in bed, bursts into tears. She sobs intensely, quietly. A huge release. She uses the sheet to wipe away her tears. Eventually, she lies back down on her back, exhausted, arms outstretched. Julianna comes out of the bathroom, goes to her bedside table, takes out her sleeping pill bottle again.)

JULIANNA: I can't remember if I took these already or not.

(She swallows two more and gets into bed, sitting up, leaning back against the pillows.)

JULIANNA: I've been thinking. I told you, at the Fountain of Youth, there was a Planetarium, a very old Navigator's Planetarium. They had an hour long demonstration with a huge old globe with lit up blinking arrows sweeping around, showing the exploratory routes of the Spanish: sextants, navigational tools. The young man turned out the light and showed the night sky above us, all around us, what the night sky was like exactly when Ponce de Leon landed in Florida, exactly where the stars were, and he pointed out this one star, the Pole star, and explained that it remains in exactly the same point and all the other stars and planets rotate around it, so when navigators were lost they could always find their bearings from this one special fixed star. And I was thinking how Morgan was our pole star, even though she was the one who was always moving, orbiting. She was our point of reference, her illness, and now that she's gone, we've all lost our bearings.

(Julianna curls up with her back to Wilson. Wilson sits up, surges of energy jolting through her.)

(Lights fade.)

Scene Six

Later that night. They're both asleep. It is dark in the room but the light from the balcony casts some light into it. There is a sound of metal clanging on the balcony as a climbing tool with a piece of rope on it is pitched up onto it from below. Wilson picks her head up, puts it back down. A figure appears on the balcony, climbing up the rope. It's the conquistador, in full regalia. He carries with him a branch with large white magnolia blossoms on it. He opens the sliding glass door which is unlocked and enters. The conquistador tiptoes. tripping slightly [a tad drunk] to Wilson's bed, the closer bed, and lays the branch alongside her. Pause. She sits up. He bows with great flourish. Pause. She raises up her hand, offering it to him. He takes it, kisses it, gracefully slips alongside her, on top of her, as all lights fade.

END OF ACT ONE

ACT TWO
Scene One

In the blackout, the ethereal sound of wind-chimes is heard. After the sound has dissipated, lights are brought up in the form of sunlight streaming through the balcony door. The drapes are open. The beds are made. Julianna enters carrying bags from a shopping spree, wearing shorts, a top over a halter top, sandals. Turns on the lights.

JULIANNA: Wilson? Wilson?

(She looks around, puts the bags down and sits on the bed. Gets up and gets a piece of salt water taffy. Opens it up, puts it in her mouth, puts the wrapper in the waste paper basket, sits down on the bed and sucks the candy. Puts her finger in her mouth to loosen a wad stuck to her teeth. Lies back, legs dangling over the bed in a posture that echoes Wilson's. There is the sound of keys in the lock. Wilson enters, intense, carrying a few shopping bags. Julianna sits up and looks at her.)

JULIANNA: You've been shopping?

(Wilson looks at her, appears distracted.)

JULIANNA: Wilson? Shopping? I'm stunned. Why didn't you wake me, I would have gone with you.

(Wilson goes over to her bedside table and takes out her wallet. Gets some cash which she rams into her pocket. Throws her cap on the bed.)

JULIANNA: What time did you get up?

WILSON: Early.

JULIANNA: Early, I'll say, I didn't even hear you.

(Wilson changes polo shirts. Smells her armpits.)

JULIANNA: I see you have some new sneakers. What's the occasion? *(Pause.)* There's a special at the Ripley's Believe It or Not Museum this afternoon. Two for the price of one. Does that appeal to you?

WILSON: Do you have any deodorant?

JULIANNA: Deodorant? Yes, I do. In the bathroom.

(Wilson goes into the bathroom. There is the sound of running water as she washes.)

JULIANNA: Do you remember when we all went to the Ripley's Believe It or Not Museum in New Orleans the summer we went camping cross-country? Morgan told a couple from Iowa that you were her deaf and dumb daughter, that Ripley had found you in Iceland living with a tribe that ate only starfish. I remember her describing the nougat-like centers of the starfish. She made you stand in the corner with her, posing like an exhibit. You were probably, well…

(She lies back down.)

JULIANNA: I was going into seventh grade that summer, so you must have been eight. Morgan got hysterical when we tried to leave. She said that the museum was her home and if she and her daughter were forced outside they would turn to dust in the cruel night air and scatter in the wind. Then of course you got scared and refused to leave. You grabbed the banister and daddy and I had to pry your fingers loose and carry you out of there, screaming. *(Pause.)* Morgan, meanwhile, was skipping happily to the camper.

(She lies there, lost in the memory. Wilson comes out of the bathroom. With her left hand she moves her right shoulder around a couple of times.)

WILSON: Julianna, I might not be around much for the next few days.

JULIANNA: Oh no? What are you doing? Moving to Bradenton?

WILSON: I won't be back for dinner tonight. Are you okay with that? *(Pause.)* Julianna?

JULIANNA: *(Hurt.)* Okay? Okay.

(Wilson reaches into her pocket for a fireball.)

WILSON: Are you sure? You have plans?

JULIANNA: Plans? I can make. Plans.

WILSON: You want a fireball?

JULIANNA: A fireball? No, thank you.

(Wilson pops it in her mouth. Heads for the door.)

WILSON: Bye.

(Wilson starts to exit with two bags as Julianna waves, awkwardly.)

JULIANNA: You know, Wilson. We only have four more days left to our vacation.

WILSON: Four?

(Wilson looks toward the hangers where only four of her shirts remain hanging.)

JULIANNA: That's all. We should do *something* for Morgan.

WILSON: Oops.

(Wilson goes back to her bed for her cap. Looks in the mirror again, curious, as if studying some odd new species. Exits. Julianna stands there, staring at the closed door. She looks around, at loose ends. Tries to get focused. She grabs a beach towel, a beach bag, her sunglasses, a hat, a book. Exits.)

(Lights fade.)

Scene Two

Same day, late in the evening. The room is dark. There is a knock on the door.

PHIL: Yoo hoo!

(Another knock; louder, more insistent.)

PHIL: Yoody hoody hoo! Julie. Julie!

(More knocking. Julianna answers very feebly.)

JULIANNA: Who is it?

PHIL: It's me. Phil.

JULIANNA: Phil...I'm afraid I'm not going to be able to see you tonight.

PHIL: What?

JULIANNA: Something's come up.

PHIL: Julie...

JULIANNA: My name is Julianna.

PHIL: I got the tickets.

JULIANNA: I'm so sorry.

PHIL: Don't be sorry. You wanted them. They're the tickets *you* wanted, babe.

JULIANNA: Perhaps there's someone else.

PHIL: Julie. Sweetheart. Don't do this to me.

JULIANNA: Please. Don't take it personally.

PHIL: Forty-five dollars a pop. Ninety bucks I spent. Open the door.

JULIANNA: I can't open the door.

PHIL: Open the door.

JULIANNA: Phil. I can't stand up. I'm very, very badly sunburned.

PHIL: You're sunburned?

JULIANNA: Yes.

(Pause.)

PHIL: Open the door.

JULIANNA: I went to sleep by the pool. I can't even undress.

PHIL: Open the door.

JULIANNA: You're repeating yourself to no avail.

PHIL: I don't believe this.

JULIANNA: I'm sorry but would you kindly depart? I don't feel well.

PHIL: You're the one who wanted to see Kate and Anna McGarrigle. I never even heard of Kate and Anna McGarrigle. You're the one who shook change out of her shorts, jumping up and down.

JULIANNA: You'll like them.

PHIL: What are they, pop? Rock?

JULIANNA: I'm not sure. I think they're Canadian.

PHIL: Canadian?

JULIANNA: They were my sister's favorite band.

PHIL: Where's your sister? Call her up.

JULIANNA: I can't call her up.

PHIL: Call her up.

JULIANNA: She's dead.

PHIL: What?

JULIANNA: She's dead!

> (Pause.)

PHIL: You're dicking with me. Open the door.

JULIANNA: If you don't go away, I'm going to call the hotel manager.

PHIL: *Shit!!* Oh fuck great. This is great. Great. Fucking great.

JULIANNA: I'm sorry.

PHIL: *(Hitting the door through this.)* Just my luck. Just my…fucking Canadians. Fucking Florida. The worst goddamned vacation of my life. I get ripped off…My last night. I rent a BMW, get a fucking perm, I get fucking stood up.

JULIANNA: Phil, if I'd known how filthy your mouth was I'd never have deigned to play shuffleboard with you.

PHIL: Fuck.

JULIANNA: How can you work in a court of law with a mouth like that?

> (Silence.)

JULIANNA: If it's any comfort, I know how you feel. I was stood up last night by a conquistador with a far more sterling character than yours. *(Pause.)* Phil? Phillip?

> (There's no answer. Julianna turns on the light, wincing at it. She is lying on her stomach partially covered by a sheet. Has been there a few hours. Her back and shoulders are bright red. Stiffly and painfully, she reaches over to the phone and dials.)

JULIANNA: Hello, room service, I'd like to request…if I ordered some food would you have Bobby bring it to me, please? His day off? *And* tomorrow? He needs two days off? *(Pause.)* No, no, I don't want anything. Thank you. *(She hangs up. She slowly and painfully sits up wearing a halter top that she can't undo from the back. Stares at the phone. Picks it up and dials. Holds the receiver apprehensively. When a voice answers, she seems surprised. She looks at the receiver, puzzled, and hangs up. Dials again.)*

JULIANNA: *Who* is this? *(Sharply.)* This is an acquaintance, a close acquaintance of Mr. Randolph, who is this? Victoria? Victoria who? Hello? Hello? *(She hangs up. Stares at the phone.)*

JULIANNA: Victoria? *(Realizing.)* Oh my god! Victoria Trent! Oh my god! Oh my god! It's Victoria Trent! Oh my god!

(Very slowly, she lies back down on her stomach.)

JULIANNA: Oh my god. Oh my god. Victoria Trent. Oh my god.

(Lights fade.)

Scene Three

Later that night. Julianna and Wilson are in bed.

WILSON: Julianna. Are you awake?

JULIANNA: Yes.

(Pause.)

WILSON: Your silence has a very specific sound.

(Pause.)

WILSON: I can't go to sleep.

(Pause.)

WILSON: I just see balls coming at me. White hard balls. Speeding towards me. Ninety miles an hour. One after another. Like broken lines of a highway. Each time one comes, my mind pulls back, to the right. Comes up. Pulls back, into the pillow. Into that waiting room over my right foot where everything collects. Muscle, anticipation, weight. Ready to be harnessed, launched, exploited in my swing. Each time, trying to pack more in less. Gain economy. Finesse the wood, my stance. Streamlining for the perfect hit. Adjusting time, stalking the ball at ninety miles an hour. Meeting it halfway. Slamming into its speed with my gaze. Slowing its flight and directing it, folding it into the grain of the oncoming wood, slaughtering it, the crack resonating in my skull. Aiming for that sound as much as anything else. The follow through. The wind up. Again, again. They keep coming.

(Pause.)

JULIANNA: Perhaps you'd like one of my sleeping pills?

WILSON: I wish I could describe it to you, Julianna, really describe what happened tonight. In the batting cage.

JULIANNA: I have no idea what you're talking about.

WILSON: It's just up the road. I saw it on my way back from Bradenton. It's a fenced in area with machines that pitch balls at different speeds. Twelve for a quarter. Some throw softballs. Some throw hard balls. You hit them with a bat and the balls fly up into restraining nets.

JULIANNA: I assume this is for children.

WILSON: First I batted against Slow Sam, fifty miles an hour, and every one, every one, I sent sailing. It was so *easy.* You never came to our games,

Morgan and mine, you never knew how bad she was in right field, she couldn't keep a glove on her hand, couldn't get under a ball, couldn't hit one, but everybody wanted her on the team because she was so… great. And I always…always held back, because of her, it didn't seem fair; she couldn't do it. So I didn't. I kept her company on the bench. It was the first time, tonight, I really let loose at the plate. To have a moving target coming at you, outside of you, that's not your own demon, your own twisted thought, to be able to meet it dead on, attack it, pummel it, drive it soaring, sailing away..I can't tell you…Next, Medium Mike. Seventy miles an hour. I was sweating when I started. Twelve in a row, I called them. "Low line drive up the center! To left! To right! Home run! Home run! Through the hole!" Twelve more. *Twelve more.* A crowd started to form. The boys back behind the machines were all straining to look at me as they dropped balls down the chutes until all the other batters quit to watch me. The owner came out, they cheered me on to Rapid Robert, Julianna, ninety miles an hour. Picture a car driving at you ninety miles an hour in the form of a small hard ball. Sometimes they're wild pitches, they can hit you, you have to duck, swing wide. The tokens were flowing from the crowd. Some little Italian guy in raspberry bell-bottoms was putting them in for me, pressing the button. Twenty-four in a row, I called them all. "High line drive to left! To right! Through the hole!" The crowd went ballistic, people were *running* over from miniature golf. *(Pause.)* I stepped back. I could sense Rapid Robert breathing in the dark blur beyond that spinning arm. *(Kicking off her bed covers.)* I wanted to *annihilate* him, *murder* him, take everything he was throwing at me and throw it back at him ten-fold. The crowd was chanting thirty-six, go for thirty-six. I adjusted my gloves, my helmet. Went for a slightly heavier bat. Stepped up to the plate.

(Wilson is standing on the bed now, swinging an imaginary bat.)

WILSON: One! Two! Three! "Right field! Left field!" Six! "Center! Through the hole! Shortstop!" Sometimes I'd point, sometimes I'd call them. *Bam,* twelve, the crowd was counting for me, *bam, bam,* twenty-four, at around thirty, I got wildly dizzy but it passed, and then I noticed his persona was changing, Rapid Robert. He was no longer evil, an adversary, he'd become…familiar, an ally, we were joining forces, jumping tracks, stepping out, our synchronicity whirring like mad cicadas, you know cicadas at the height of summer. Bam! Bam! Bam! Little League kids were gasping, fathers were spitting. "Home run! Low line drive to right!" I was sweating hard, my arms ached, my thigh muscles burned, I nailed those balls again, again, again, again, leaning back, following through, leaning back, following through, and then I actually came, around ball forty, an orgasm, it overtook me like some wild animal jumping on our backs, on me and Rapid Robert, caught up in this gorgeous huge slick machine, my legs were shaking, I thought I must be lit up, I must be this wild flurry of flashing neon lights, twisting through the night air, the bat, swinging, my hips, rotating, describing circles of light, bam, I kept going, I kept coming, up to forty-five, "Right field! Through the hole!" cameras were flashing, forty-seven, I was crying but it was all right, crying, letting go, some part of my brain fixed on Morgan…remembering how scared she was when she went in for her kidney transplant three years ago, not wanting us to know, buying *us* all presents, bam, bam, remembering her under the anesthesia in the hospital so small in that big white hospital bed, no muscle to speak of, her skin yellow, "Line drive to left!" remembering wondering why it wasn't me instead of her who'd had to suffer all that pain, that trouble with her eyes, her feet, all those injections, at summer camp sometimes I'd give myself injections with her, just to keep her company, *bam, bam,* crying, but it was all right. We'd come through, Rapid Robert and I, our great dark tangle of force. All right. And then they stopped. Coming. The balls. The boy, had stopped, he'd had enough, couldn't take it anymore. Maybe it was my expression, maybe he saw me crying, but he stopped loading the machine. He just grabbed hold of the fence and stared at me. Sixty consecutive hits. A record. *(Kneeling down on the bed.)* I sat down, and remembered through the cheers of the crowd, lying in that infield, in Bradenton. Hearing Morgan talk to me, actually *hearing* her voice, Julianna, telling me what she'd told me all of our lives. Her diabetes was a gift. It gave her special powers. *(Pause.)* I shouldn't feel guilty. I should get up off the bench.

JULIANNA: One question. Do you…have any idea…what it is like to be so lonely, so *lonely* that you actually look forward to going to the dentist just for the pleasure of feeling a man's hands, anyone's hands, pressed against your face?

WILSON: Julianna…

(During the following Julianna sits up very slowly, painstakingly.)

JULIANNA: So lonely that even a visit to a novice acupuncturist is something to be looked forward to. To be pleasantly anticipated, the chance to spend time with a person who is so inept at sticking needles into your body that he misses the points he is aiming for and has to stick them in again and again, hurting you over and over? Do you know how *lonely* it is to go on vacation with a sister who won't talk to you or be seen in public with you? To go off on your own to inane tourist attractions where you have to listen to the sound of lethargic disgusting fat alligators crunching on the bones of large species of muskrat at feeding time? In the name of entertainment? To sit on a tour bus by yourself while everyone else is sharing, talking, pointing out historic landmarks, laughing? To lie sunburnt, alone in bed, burnt to a crisp, and then hear your sister talking for the first time in a week describe to you in panoramic epic detail how she had an orgasm in a giant cage in front of a cheering crowd. Wilson? I'm speechless.

WILSON: I doubt it.

JULIANNA: I can't believe you would share that perverse experience with me on this, of all trips, when we're supposed to be mourning Morgan.

WILSON: I wanted to tell you that I heard Morgan talk to me.

JULIANNA: And I wanted to tell you that no one talks to me.

WILSON: I'm talking to you.

JULIANNA: You've never talked to me.

WILSON: I'm talking to you now.

JULIANNA: This is not my idea of talk.

WILSON: Your idea of talk, Julianna, is listening to the sound of your own airy voice babbling on inanely, relentlessly, ad nauseum, on and on and on filling the room like some environmentally toxic, *ineffective* insulation foam.

JULIANNA: *(Standing up on her bed.)* Oh good. Now you've said it. You've finally said it, Wilson. What you've always wanted to say.

WILSON: *(Standing up on the bed.)* No! What I've always wanted to say to you, Julianna, was that I have never appreciated your frequent use of that catchy little phrase you're so fond of, "Wilson has the brains; Morgan has the heart. Oh, Wilson has the brains; Morgan has the heart." I have a heart!

JULIANNA: Well, you've never shown it to me!

WILSON: You've never wanted to see it!

JULIANNA: Tell me, Wilson. Just how much heart were you showing when you lost Morgan's ashes?

WILSON: *(Jumps down and starts making her bed.)* I didn't lose her ashes. I know exactly where they are.

JULIANNA: *(Aghast.)* Where are they?

WILSON: Home!

JULIANNA: Home?

WILSON: I left them there.

JULIANNA: You left them at home, intentionally?

WILSON: You think I'm gonna dump her ashes into the ocean? Are you insane?

JULIANNA: You…! I can't believe…! Wilson! You knew how upset I was! You lied to me! You told me you attached that tag I sent you!

WILSON: I put the ashes in my suitcase, I put that moron-proof tag on and I left the suitcase in my closet!

(Wilson goes into the bathroom.)

JULIANNA: When I think of that poor middle eastern baggage claim man. How I berated him, and you just stood by. I'm going to write him a letter of apology. How dare you make that decision by yourself, to leave her at home! She's my sister, too!

WILSON: *(Opens the bathroom door.)* Oh spare me!

JULIANNA: Spare yourself!

(Wilson slams the door shut.)

(Lights fade.)

Scene Four

Lights come up. It's early the next morning. Julianna is still lying on her stomach. She picks her head up and looks over at Wilson's bed which is empty and unmade. The phone rings.

JULIANNA: Hello? *(Long pause.)* What? *(Long pause.)* I'll call them, I'll call them, but I don't understand, you were doing pull-ups on the shower rod? *(Perplexed.)* A pull-up…? As in a *chin*-up? *(Pause. She sighs.)* Wilson. I'll call maintenance and tell them to come repair the shower rod, but I have to tell you, I've reached rock bottom.

(She hangs up. Presses number 7 on the phone.)

JULIANNA: Hello, this is Mrs. Carl Randolph in room 544. *Mrs. Carl Randolph.* Oh, excuse me, I mean Julianna Finley, I'm sorry, Mrs. Carl Randolph died during the night. There's been some kind of athletic misfortune accident in our shower stall and our shower rod has been dislocated from its socket. No, no one is hurt, just the rod. I can not tell you, I've only heard reports, I've not inspected the site. Whenever, we're in no hurry. Mrs. Randolph? Oh no, not a sudden death, no. More of a prolonged lingering twenty year kind of tortured agony, she's better off out of her misery. A blessing really, yes. You're too kind. Thank you.

(She hangs up. Stares over at a Gomek the alligator souvenir she bought; maybe a foot and a half long. Gets up, slowly and painfully walks over to it. Grabs it by the tail, walks over to the sliding glass door and opens it. Tries to bring her arm back to throw it, but it is too painful; throws it underhanded over the balcony. Goes back to bed. Puts her head back down on the pillow.)

(Long slow rich play with lights, signifying the passing of the day; from early morning to high noon to afternoon. With each new light cue, Julianna shifts to a new position, which she holds for at least a slow count of ten. She still wears the halter top she can't take off because of her sunburn.)

(There is a knock at the door.)

JULIANNA: *(Sitting up.)* Oh god help me. Maintenance.

(Another knock.)

DELIVERY MAN: Ms. Julianna Finley?

JULIANNA: Just a minute.

(Slowly and painfully, she gets up and walks to the door.)

JULIANNA: Ow.

(She opens the door, is handed a large bouquet of red roses in a vase lavishly decorated with a bow. The delivery man stays in the hall.)

JULIANNA: What are these?

DELIVERY MAN: Roses, ma'am.

JULIANNA: Roses?

DELIVERY MAN: Have a good day.

JULIANNA: *(He starts to leave and she grabs his arm.)* Wait, wait. Please don't go. Please. It's just, I'm all alone.

(She holds the flowers, holds him. The delivery man stands quietly by for a few seconds.)

JULIANNA: Okay. Okay, thank you so much.

(The delivery man leaves and Julianna turns the vase around looking for a card; there is none. She walks into the middle of the room awkwardly. Stands there, numb, too overcome to react. She sits on the edge of her bed, holding the vase on her lap, and stares at the roses. Bursts into tears. Cries into the roses. Eventually, lies down curled up with her back to the audience, holding the vase upright against her, still crying. Lights fade.

Lights come up. It is early evening. She is sitting at the table, just staring at the roses which are now on the table. She gets up and goes outside onto the balcony. Sounds of waves, birds, life. She stares up at the sky, breathes deep. Lights fade.)

Scene Five

The next day, mid-morning. Julianna is sitting cross-legged on the covers, on her bed, now wearing one of Wilson's Eddie Bauer shirts. She seems peaceful, almost sedated. Bobby is comfortably settled in somewhere, leaning back, drinking a milkshake. On the table is a tray with a covered dinner plate on it. The roses have been moved to a dresser.

JULIANNA: She had her tongue pierced with a diamond stud?

BOBBY: I begged her not to.

JULIANNA: Doesn't it make it difficult to eat?

BOBBY: Makes it difficult for *me* to eat. You can see it glitter in her food. And it clacks. On her teeth.

JULIANNA: You know, last week that story would have upset me, would have really upset me. The thought of someone getting their tongue pierced. Having a needle go through the middle, the thickest part, perhaps half an inch of tongue, and then having a hard metal stud stuck there. But today, today I just think…mmn.

BOBBY: Easy for you to say, you don't have to kiss her.

JULIANNA: No, I don't. I don't have to kiss her. That's true.

BOBBY: She's got more holes and metal and hardware stuck in her body…I'm afraid I'm gonna *rip* myself on her. You want your mashed potatoes now?

JULIANNA: Not yet, thank you.

(He slurps his milkshake.)

BOBBY: Now she's talking about getting another tattoo. *(He shakes his head.)* Mutilation queen.

JULIANNA: Maybe she's trying to find herself.

BOBBY: She should go through a metal detector, she'll find herself real quick. Yeah, I picked up your order, saw the mashed potatoes, said now that's not the sister likes potatoes that's up there. *That* sister's at the batting cage.

JULIANNA: How do you know?

BOBBY: I seen her from the road coming in. Seen her there yesterday. Big crowd. She's the main attraction on the strip.

JULIANNA: *(Concealing her horror.)* She's visible from the road?

BOBBY: Brennan wants to hire her full-time, be a batting coach. I heard she's looking for a condo.

(Pause. Julianna gets up and walks over to sliding glass door. Looks out.)

BOBBY: Yup. Her picture's in today's paper.

JULIANNA: *(Smiling slightly.)* Really?

BOBBY: Sports page. And I know her. Personally.

(Julianna looks back out.)

JULIANNA: It's curious, how those big black birds sit so still, with their wings outstretched.

BOBBY: Cormorants.

JULIANNA: Cormorants. They're beautiful. They look like they're flying—standing still.

BOBBY: They're drying out their wings; that's why they spread 'em like that. Their feathers aren't waterproof. An ocean bird that's not waterproof... go figure.

JULIANNA: Bobby, did you ever not know who you were?

BOBBY: When?

JULIANNA: Ever.

BOBBY: *(Confused.)* Who I *was*? You mean, before?

JULIANNA: Before what?

BOBBY: Now?

JULIANNA: *(Equally confused.)* Okay.

BOBBY: No. I mean, uh... *(Thinks deeply; changes the subject.)* You want your potatoes now?

JULIANNA: Yes, I do, please. Thank you.

(Bobby uncovers the plate and she goes and sits down at the table. Takes the fork out of the napkin and starts to eat.)

JULIANNA: Mashed potatoes are very soothing, aren't they?

BOBBY: *(Smiling.)* Yes ma'am.

JULIANNA: That's one thing we can be sure of. Mashed potatoes are soothing. And you know what, a year from now, they'll still be soothing. We can count on it. At the very least, Bobby, we know this: we are people who like and can always count on the soothing quality of mashed potatoes. *(Smiling.)* It's a start.

BOBBY: *(Smiling.)* Now you got my appetite up. I gotta go. I'll get in trouble again. *(He heads toward the door.)*

JULIANNA: Do you think you could get me today's paper?

BOBBY: Sure thing.

JULIANNA: Thanks.

BOBBY: Pretty flowers.

JULIANNA: Thank you. *(Having fun with the fantasy.)* They were sent to me by a conquistador...from the sixteenth century.

BOBBY: Pretty. You have a good one, Julianna.

JULIANNA: You have a good one, too, Bobby.

(He exits. Julianna calmly eats the potatoes. Her hair hasn't been brushed. She has no make-up on at all. Lights fade.)

Scene Six

It is two days later. Julianna, wearing Wilson's shirt with a skirt, is finishing packing a suitcase on her bed. One packed suitcase is on the floor. Wilson enters. She looks pretty great, athletic and more feminine (without pushing it), dressed in athletic gear—spandex leggings, an Adidas warm-up jacket, headband, hair back in a pony tail. She sits at the table and watches Julianna. Silence. There is still much tension between them as they haven't really spoken since their fight.

WILSON: How are you getting to the airport?

JULIANNA: Taxi.

(Pause.)

WILSON: Nice shirt.

JULIANNA: I was wondering if I could purchase this shirt from you. It's comfortable and you have nine others exactly like it.

WILSON: You can have it.

JULIANNA: No, I'll buy it. I'll mail you a check, I'm low on cash at the moment.

WILSON: You can have it.

JULIANNA: Actually, I could just order one from Eddie Bauer, couldn't I? Do you want this Mensa book?

WILSON: No.

(Julianna throws it away. Keeps packing.)

JULIANNA: Geena Davis the actress is in Mensa. It can't be that hard to get in.

(Keeps packing.)

WILSON: Are you taking your roses with you?

JULIANNA: I am taking my roses with me, yes.

WILSON: The vase comes with them.

(Julianna looks at her.)

WILSON: *(Awkwardly.)* I mean, I assume the vase would come with them.

JULIANNA: You know your ticket is nonrefundable. After today it can't be used.

(Wilson looks away. Julianna starts to lock up her suitcase. There is a knock on the door.)

JULIANNA: My taxi.

(Wilson goes to the door, picking up one of Julianna's suitcases on the way. She opens the door and their mother, Peg, smiles at her. She is a plain, rather small woman, a New Englander, in her early sixties, unpretentious, great depth of character, dressed in a plain A-line skirt, cardigan sweater, blouse with rounded collar, scarf that doesn't quite work, practical walking shoes. Also, wearing a knapsack, carrying a pastry box and a small maroon Samsonite suitcase. She kisses Wilson who is stunned to see her.)

WILSON: Mom.

PEG: Wilson, you've lost weight.

JULIANNA: Mother!

PEG: *(To Wilson.)* Funny, you look more like Morgan. What is it? Your eyes, they're all lit up. You've had a good vacation.

(They hug.)

JULIANNA: You made the trip.

(Peg enters the room and walks over to Julianna and kisses her.)

PEG: Hello, sweetheart. How are you?

JULIANNA: *(Pleased.)* I can't believe you're here.

PEG: You look more like Morgan, too. In a different way, how strange.

JULIANNA: How did you get here?

PEG: Train.

JULIANNA: Why did you take a train?

PEG: *(Beaming.)* I wanted to.

JULIANNA: I thought you were too sore to travel.

PEG: I'm fine, I know I should have called. I wanted to surprise you.

JULIANNA: Mother, our vacation ends today. I'm leaving now.

PEG: Well, you can't. You have to stay another night. There's so much to do. We should get started.

JULIANNA: My plane…

PEG: Never mind, love. I'll get you another ticket. This is a key lime pie.

(She puts it down on the table. Wilson, hungry, gets very focused on it.)

PEG: Per Morgan's instructions. She has a list of events, in great detail, we'll be up all night.

(Peg puts the maroon suitcase up on a bed.)

WILSON: Morgan's instructions?

PEG: I read them on the train. I had no idea, the extent of it all. She told me long ago to put the suitcase away and bring it when we all came down here. Cassettes, novels, poems, letters, she wants us to read them all out loud. Nothing about the ashes. *(To Wilson.)* She must have known you'd want to keep them. You did, didn't you, love? Bonfire on the beach, we'll just make a *little* fire, don't you think that'll suffice, sunrise walk on the beach…

JULIANNA: Oh…

PEG: Do you have a knife to cut the pie? I'm famished.

JULIANNA: Mother.

PEG: Yes?

JULIANNA: I'm just…so stunned you're here. I thought you were incapable of coming.

PEG: *(Meaning emotionally.)* I thought I was, too. Oh, I have Morgan's swiss army knife.

(She reaches for the knife in her bag. Also takes out paper plates and forks which she puts on the table near the pie.)

JULIANNA: The way you described it, the bicycle slamming into you, the police, the ambulance…you look perfectly fine.

PEG: *(Beaming.)* Isn't it…extraordinary?

WILSON: You look different.

(Peg looks at Wilson, as if discovered.)

PEG: So. *(She slices the pie.)* Tell me about your week. What have you two been up to?

(Both Julianna and Wilson turn away. Peg takes note.)

PEG: I see there's a Ripley's Believe It or Not Museum in town. Do you remember the one in New Orleans, Morgan and Wilson were a believe it or not mother and daughter exhibit. Julianna was caught shoplifting in the gift shop.

JULIANNA: Mother…

PEG: It's all right, dear, you just needed some attention. And your father got in a row with a guard for stepping over the rail. He always did that in museums, had to get right up close. He was pitched out of the Met more than once.

(Peg goes over to Julianna and guides her to the table, serving her a piece.)

WILSON: Tell us about the accident.

PEG: Oh…it sounds so foolish, when I try to talk about it. I tried telling Addie and she got very concerned. Mm, this looks so good. A taste of Florida.

(Wilson pulls up a chair and Peg serves her a piece. Studies both her daughters.)

PEG: It was really quite remarkable. Definitely worth experiencing.

JULIANNA: How could that be?

(Peg takes a third seat at the table. Throughout the following, both daughters eat with relish; Wilson consumes a second piece she cuts for herself.)

PEG: My first minute in New York, a block from Grand Central, Madison and 43rd, I was crossing at the crosswalk, the light said walk, so I proceeded to walk. A pedestrian coming towards me glanced to his right so I glanced to my left and there was this young man on a bicycle, one of those courier messengers, aiming right for me. I stopped and turned toward him, letting *him* decide how not to hit me, thinking, well not having time to think but *knowing* it would be in both our best interests if he didn't hit me so…I made eye contact with him. I remember looking at him as if to say, "Well, what are you going to do, *hit me?*" bringing my arms up in a friendly *humorous* gesture of surrender. The next thing I was in the air doing a back flip then bam down on the pavement and he and the bike were on top of me, pounding me, this tangle of metal and bodies traveling halfway up the block, it went on forever. And through it all, there was this voice inside me, observing, calmly, that said, "Just relax, go with it, *this is how you do it.*" And it was. In all my life I have never had such a sense of myself.

(Both daughters empathize with her. Peg looks at the pie. Picks up a fork and takes a bite.)

PEG: Mm. This is disappearing fast. Peculiar, isn't it? To find oneself, at age sixty-two, in a brawl with a bicycle. This pie is scrumptious.

JULIANNA: It's divine.

WILSON: I want to hear Morgan's instructions.

PEG: Mm, we'll get cracking.

(Peg gets up and goes over to the suitcase.)

JULIANNA: We don't have to start immediately, mother. Sit down and relax for a while.

PEG: Oh, but we do. The reading list is daunting. Here. The program's on top.

(She takes out three stacks of books, novels, poetry collections, letters, papers, each tied with a ribbon. Hands a stack to each daughter. Wilson's has a starfish on the top.)

PEG: For you, love. And you. Could you close the drapes, sweetheart?

JULIANNA: Mother.

(Peg looks at her.)

JULIANNA: I'm just so glad you're here.

PEG: So am I.

(Julianna closes the drapes. The lighting shifts, altering the mood. It should warmly embrace the three of them. Wilson sits off on her own away from the table, staring down at the pile in her lap.)

PEG: Of course she wants us down on the floor around a candle but I'd really rather not. I am still, well, a *little* sore.

(Peg takes out a cassette player, cassettes, puts them on the table. Sits and looks through them. Julianna sits next to her.)

PEG: All right. Cassette number one. *(Chuckling.)* Mm, she's got a picture of the three of us, sitting in the wheelbarrow. Everybody ready?

(She looks at both her daughters, sits in a chair by the table. The third empty chair is pulled away slightly from the table. A dim white spotlight shines on it.)

JULIANNA: She knew. We had to wait two years. We couldn't have done this last year.

PEG: Always thinking of the family.

(Peg starts the cassette and a piece of music plays, preferably from Kate and Anna McGarrigle. Peg starts to sniffle and takes out a Kleenex to wipe her nose.

Julianna reaches over and rests her hand on her mother's arm, comforting her. Wilson is still staring down at the program. The spotlight on the empty chair grows stronger. Julianna reaches over and puts the music on pause.)

JULIANNA: Wilson. Thank you for the roses.

(Wilson looks up at her. The three of them freeze in these positions. The lighting on them dims gradually as the spotlight on the empty chair grows. Soon the only light is the spotlight which stays bright for at least twenty seconds, then dims. All lights fade.)

END OF PLAY

Going, Going, Gone
An Article by Anne Bogart

BIOGRAPHY

Anne Bogart is the co-artistic director of the Saratoga International Theater Institute (SITI), the recipient of two Obie Awards and a Bessie Award and is an associate professor at Columbia University. Her work was the subject of the Brown-Forman Classics in Context Festival—Modern Masters—in January, 1995, which included a revival of Elmer Rice's *The Adding Machine* and the SITI productions of *The Medium and Small Lives/Big Dreams*. Also at Actor's Theatre of Louisville, she directed *Picnic and In the Eye of the Hurricane* (15th Humana Festival of New American Plays). Ms. Bogart's other recent productions include: *Hot 'n' Throbbing* (American Repertory Theater), *Marathon Dancing* (En Garde Arts), *Escape From Paradise* (Circle Rep), *The Women* (Hartford Stage) and *Baltimore Waltz* (Circle Rep).

HUMANA FESTIVAL PRODUCTION

Going, Going, Gone was performed at the 1996 Humana Festival of New American Plays, March, 1996. It was conceived and directed by Anne Bogart and created by The Saratoga International Theater Institute with the following cast:

Woman	Ellen Lauren
Man	Tom Nelis
Guest	Karenjune Sánchez
Guest	Stephen Webber

and the following production staff:

Assistant Director	Devorah Herbert
Scenic Designer	Paul Owen
Costume Designer	Kevin R. McLeod
Lighting Designer	T.J. Gerckens
Soundscape	Darron L. West
Properties Master	Mark J. Bissonette
Stage Manager	Megan Wanlass
Dramaturg	Liz Engelman

GOING, GOING, GONE

About ten years ago I read an article in *The New York Times Sunday Magazine* featuring Stephen Hawking on the cover. It stated that recent discoveries in quantum and astral physics are so significant and powerful that they must necessarily have consequences in our daily lives. The article suggested that an understanding of the basic notions of quantum physics is an important part of living in our modern world. I was fascinated and inspired to learn more. In high school I was a flop in math and science and in college I avoided anything resembling physics. But now, inspired by *The New York Times* article, I was intrigued and willing to try.

I started with books on physics written for nonprofessionals. At first, my attempts were unsuccessful. Invariably, I would reach a mathematical equation or a disturbing or disorienting notion and quit—close the book. I felt inadequate because I couldn't get past the most fundamental notions in quantum physics. After several tries, I all but gave up.

A few years later I discovered books-on-tape. At the time, I was making many long distance car trips. To pass the time, I bought some tapes about the new physics and tried them out as I was driving. What happened in the car became a great lesson to me. I listened intently to the tapes until the inevitable mathematical equation or difficult hypothesis would show up. Rather than switching off the tape, as I had closed the book while reading, I let it continue and allowed myself to stop paying close attention. As I drove, and the tape kept on, I gazed at the landscape and let my mind wander. And then came the unexpected jolts. "Oh, my God!" I shouted involuntarily, "I just understood special relativity!" or "*That's* Heisenberg's Uncertainty Principle!" or "I just got Bell's Theorem!"

Physicists agree that you cannot focus with too much effort on the notions in the new physics because the act of looking changes them. You must use an indirect approach. You must use fuzzy logic. You must think intuitively, allowing rather than forcing necessary leaps in logic and in the patterns of your own perception.

As I began to absorb the new physics, my notions about life, mortality, relationships and art began to change dramatically. *The New York Times* article was right and the attention to ideas in physics paid off. My success in grasping the rudimentary notions in physics made me want to study and learn more.

I decided to create a theater piece with my company, The Saratoga International Theater Institute (SITI), in which the audience would experience something similar to what happened to me as I drove my car watching the scenery and listening to the tapes. I wanted to create a diversion so that the audience would give up *trying* to understand the text and, instead, get involved in the "scenery" or story, and then, finally, receive surprising jolts of insights into the way the world functions. And this would be achieved by the audience hearing the text alongside of, but not necessarily illustrating, the action of the play, and making unexpected personal connections and associations with these ideas.

I knew that the spoken dialogue in the new play should, like the tapes, introduce the theories in science that were so astonishing to me. And I knew that the scenario should be accessible; a story that the audience could get involved in. A play like this would demand that the actors say one thing physically and something quite different, i.e., the physics text, verbally.

For the scenario I chose Edward Albee's play *Who's Afraid of Virginia Woolf?*, which is by now a cultural icon. The play elicits certain impressions and associations through its familiarity to film- and theater-goers. The story takes place during a late evening in which an older couple hosts a younger couple in their home. When the unsuspecting guests arrive, the games begin. As the evening unravels, so does the thin veneer of their everyday realities. Sexual overtures are attempted and complicated intrigues are carried out. This scenario would provide a map for the action of the piece.

To develop the dialogue I started collecting fragments from hundreds of sources that in various ways addressed the process and effect of the new physics. And so the play I set out to create with the SITI company, i.e., the text—beginning with my interest in physics, followed by an idea or notion for a framework and finally a collection of writings—became *Going, Going, Gone*.

To publish the text of *Going, Going, Gone* would be to publish samples of many many writers, many notions, many words, ranging from the scientific theories of Richard Feynmen, Stephen Hawking, Michio Kaku, Nick Herbert, Lawrence M. Krauss, Murray Gell-Mann to literary sources including the Bible, T.S. Eliot, Goethe, Lewis Carroll, Aristotle, Fredrich Nietzsche, Oscar Wilde, Walt Whitman, Bertrand Russell, William Blake and others. In addition to samples from published sources, the dialogues includes downloaded conversations between cutting edge physicists found on the Internet. These writings would provide the "text" of the piece. *[See sample of text at end of article.]* But were they, alone, the play itself?

What is a play? Is it the words on a page? Is it action performed in relation to sounds made in patterns that are discernable? Is it the product of one person's imagination or the product of many?

I know that a play is not just ONE thing. I know that a play in performance is a complex juxtaposition of the many languages of the stage. Combined with the audience's imagination, the experience is often created by the difference between what is seen and what is heard. It can be the tension between the visual and the aural languages that creates the poetic dialectic of the stage. Sometimes the less that the visual and the aural agree, the more poignant the theatrical truth. For example, imagine the words "I love you" uttered by a man while directly facing a woman. Now imagine "I love you" uttered as the man turns his body away from the woman, eyes on his watch. The tension of the turn away is more dynamic and disturbing and hence richer in associative information than the collapse of tension in the first example. The tension of the aural "yes" and the visual "no" can energize an audience's interest and participation in the story.

Separated from the actual performance, the words of *Going, Going, Gone* cannot achieve the play's intended effect. The performance has all to do with the interplay of the words and the action together; somewhere in the tension between those two elements, in their shifting collisions and sudden harmonies, is where the actual meaning of the play resides. For this reason, rather than offering you the actual script, I decided to describe the inception of the work and the intentions behind the production and how it was put together. I hope that this essay will engender further thought and discussion on the notions of what a play might possibly be.

Going, Going, Gone was created collectively by four actors—Ellen Lauren, Tom Nelis, Karen June Sanchez and Steven Webber—sound designer Darron West and myself as well as dramaturgs Devorah Herbert and Liz Engelman. There are no clear lines about who did what, who came up with which idea. Rather, we followed a scent, asked a question, tried stuff out.

In our play, the stage is a living room that is also the entire universe. The four characters find their lives slipping from a Newtonian to a quantum logic with every drink poured and every game played. They go about the action of the play as we know it but instead of speaking lines from *Who's Afraid of Virginia Woolf?*, the characters discuss and argue about cutting-edge ideas in physics: notions of parallel universes, observer-created reality, uncertainty, complementarity, probability, relativity, and the role of the imagination.

Of particular interest in the rehearsal and in the performance of *Going, Going, Gone* was that the actors had to consistently play the subtext of *Who's Afraid of Virginia Woolf?* while speaking dialogue which was quite removed from the desired ends of the characters at any given moment. The characters engage in intense social and personal battles all the while talking about complex notions of physics. This tightrope walk brought up fascinating issues about acting.

Words are, in the theater, a physical event. We decided that what might make the complete text accessible would be the relationship of the words to the actor's physicality and intentions. The actors tried to find the moment-to-moment reality by focusing on playing the *intentions* of *Who's Afraid of Virginia Woolf?* while speaking the physics text. This was made more difficult because the intentions rarely illustrated the text. The trick was that the language had to come out with both the clarity of the character's persona *and* the sense of the science.

Playing out the unbridled circumstances of *Who's Afraid of Virginia Woolf?* produced powerful emotions in the four actors. They had to keep the physics text bright and understandable and at the same time allow for the necessary emotional impact. As dense as it is, the dialogue still had to sound cognitive, clear, emotional and full of intention. Ultimately the actors were responsible for getting the audience interested in what was being done *and* what was being said. This task demanded from our company an extreme and specific kind of acting work. The overall effect for the audience was at first disorienting and then surprisingly lucid and fun.

We hoped, that through a sort of sleight of hand, the audience would respond to the odd chemistry of the ingredients and get involved in the overall drama of the stage event. In that way they might give up understanding the text and the ideas, give over to the drama played out, and ultimately, unexpectedly, receive insight into the complex yet exhilarating notions of science.

As the great physicists suggested, we had to go through the back door to get to the front. The whole process may appear like an overly complex and elaborate stratagem, but *Going, Going, Gone* was finally, in production, quite straightforward. Like *Alice Through the Looking Glass*, everyone involved—actors and audience alike—went through the process of giving up understanding in order to come out on the other side.

• • •

[The following is an excerpt of the script Going, Going, Gone. These lines have been sampled from various sources, and the authors include: Arthur Schopenhauer, Isaac Newton, Michio Kaku, Albert Einstein.]

PLUCK: The world is my idea.
TOP: How did the universe begin?
PLUCK: Force equals mass times acceleration. Newton's second law?
TOP: The boundary condition of the universe is that it has no boundary?
    (Doorbell.)
PLUCK: No edge of space time. Neither created nor destroyed; it would just be. Wag, wag, wag...
    (Doorbell.)
TOP: With doubt and uncertainty!
PLUCK: Ha HA! *(Sings.)* Almost as soon as the electron was born, it began causing problems.
TOP: GOD DOES NOT PLAY DICE!
PLUCK: It seems that god does play dice.
TOP: God.

• • •

Contract With Jackie
by Jimmy Breslin

BIOGRAPHY

Jimmy Breslin, a Pulitzer Prize-winning New York newspaper columnist, had his full-length play, *The Queen of the Leaky Roof Circuit*, produced at ATL in 1988 (12th Humana Festival). He started in New York as a copyboy, a term now banned from newspaper cityrooms, and went on to write a daily column. He also wrote the best-selling novels *The Gang That Couldn't Shoot Straight, Table Money, and World Without End, Amen*. His non-fiction subjects include baseball, *Can't Anybody Here Play This Game?*, and Washington politics, *How the Good Guys Finally Won*. Mr. Breslin lives in Manhattan with his wife, Ronnie M. Eldridge. They have nine children, three daughters-in-law, two sons-in-law, seven grandchildren, and Ms. Eldridge has a 92-year-old mother.

ORIGINAL PRODUCTION

Contract With Jackie was first performed at the 1996 Humana Festival of New American Plays, March, 1996. It was directed by Frazier W. Marsh with the following cast:

Jackie	Divina Marsh
Newt	William McNulty

and the following production staff:

Scenic Designer	Paul Owen
Costume Designer	Kevin R. McLeod
Lighting Designer	T.J. Gerckens
Sound Designer	Martin R. Desjardins
Properties Manager	Ron Riall
Stage Manager	Lori M. Doyle
Dramaturg	Michael Bigelow Dixon
New York Casting Arrangements	Laura Richin Casting

CHARACTERS

JACKIE
NEWT

PLACE

A hospital room in Atlanta, 1980.

CONTRACT WITH JACKIE

Hospital room, Emory University Hospital, Atlanta, 1980. Woman in bed with post-op IV's. Husband enters.

NEWT: I'm here—1980's most promising freshman congressman and the groundswell that's gonna produce the third wave information age post-industrial society. How are you, Jackie?

JACKIE: I didn't think you felt anything about me anymore. You never even call.

NEWT: I'd have to lose the sight of God not to come here.

JACKIE: *(Pleased sound.)* Mmmmmm.

NEWT: You have no idea of the trouble I had getting here from Washington. They actually bumped Newt Gingrich off a Delta flight. How can they do that to me? They said they were overbooked. They can't make room for a United States Congressman flying home to his own district in 1980. I noticed two flight attendants getting on. I said what about them, why can't they wait for the next flight. The ticket counter person said, "Oh, they're needed in Atlanta." I was never so insulted in my life. I am going to have the FAA close the Delta Airline rest rooms.

JACKIE: *(She sounds pain.)*

NEWT: Do the doctors know if they got it all this time?

JACKIE: They seem to think so. But that's what they thought when they operated on me the first time.

(Pause.)

NEWT: *(Smiling as he looks into briefcase and brings out a yellow legal pad. He draws a line right down the middle. From here on, he makes notes as he talks.)* How's the house? You know I haven't really looked at it for a whole year.

JACKIE: The bookshelves in the den look like they're going to just fall down. The washing machine makes a noise like a truck. The garage door won't go up. I sure could use you. I guess I let things go too long.

NEWT: With all due respect, that's why I really think it's a spectacularly good idea for us to spend some time together right now. We have a lot to talk about, Jackie. I have a general vision of where I want this marriage to go. *(Makes a note on the pad.)*

JACKIE: We're going on a good seven months with this separation.

NEWT: The girls call and tell me about you, but sometimes I'm going so fast in Washington that I'm not able to listen carefully. *(Closes eyes and smiles.)* NEWT! NEWT! NEWT! It's a weird experience. I don't like it at all. What with being alone, separated from the daughters, too. But we have to have the…moral courage to change or perish. I want to come out of here today with some very positive changes.

JACKIE: You've done pretty well. You got through colleges and to Congress. Who knows better than me? I paid for all your degrees. The one graduate school loan, I paid most of that off, too.

NEWT: *(Writing furiously.)* Jackie, when I get power someday, that's the first thing I'm going to go after. That loan could have made me a pauper. That loan represents a sick, helpless society. These limp-wristed yellow draft dodgers who get a Ph.D. so they don't have to hear a gun fire. Higher education is out of control. The anti-Vietnam radicals dominate the faculties. They teach destruction of our culture. We're subsidizing cowardice and petty barbarism.

JACKIE: You didn't go to Vietnam, either.

NEWT: I had two daughters. It would have made no sense to go into the army just because there was a war. Besides, colleges should give people the commitment to solve real problems. If you're homeless, then just get a home and then you're not homeless. If you're unemployed, get a job and now you're employed. If you need food, go to the store. If you're a weak yellow coward liberal, then get some backbone and you won't be a cheap draft dodger. You can be a war hero.

JACKIE: Newt.

NEWT: What?

JACKIE: I'm glad you're here. I missed you. Do you think we might have a chance?

NEWT: Of course we have a chance. We can change our lives and change society, too. Not to be egotistical, but I'm the same honorable, moral man I was when you married me. But I can see more now. I can see things in the context of the whole society. Listen. Learn. Help. Lead. NEWT! NEWT! NEWT! NEWT! I also know what compassion truly is.

JACKIE: I could use some of it this time.

NEWT: But the more important thing, I'll tell you the great example, I made a positive speech on the floor that affects you and this entire country. Jackie, in the third wave information age post-industrial society, you are going to sit in your diagnostic chair at home, sensors will take your blood pressure, analyze a blood sample, do throat cultures. You only go to a hospital when something is seriously wrong. If you have some life-threatening disease, information systems will allow you to study the most advanced work all over the world. Jackie, this hold by this medical guild has been broken. It's just an opening to a new beginning in medicine. And I thought of you when I spoke about it.

JACKIE: Newt, these computers don't work in cars. How do I sit in a chair and find a tumor?

NEWT: Jackie, that's the sheer brilliance of the idea. If anyone in this country needs a specialist, a databank at your fingertips gives you a range of choices, based on cost, reputation and outcome patterns.

JACKIE: In other words, you don't find the tumor.

NEWT: Yes, but the doctors who specialize in tumors are in the databank at your fingertips.

JACKIE: By the time the databank gets the doctor's name, he's either retired or dead. So am I, by the way.

NEWT: But remember that we're only at the new beginning.

JACKIE: A man with an aneurysm was in one of the operating rooms yesterday. They said he had the worst headache of his life, and that was the only symptom. The symptom after that is known as bingo.

NEWT: In the third wave information age post-industrial society, we're going to find out about these things simply by tapping the right key.

JACKIE: *(Grunts.)* If you have an aneurysm, do you just put your head back in the chair and wait for it to explode?

NEWT: That's just a detail. I know there will be advances that will help you. Just let me say one thing. You mention cars. You still have the Volkswagon, right? *(She nods and he makes note.)* And I have the Thunderbird.

JACKIE: You got it at cost when they told the assembly plant manager that you were going to win the elec—What are you writing down all the time?

NEWT: Show it all to you in a minute. First, I want this one thing straight. There is nothing illegal if the assembly plant at Hapeville sells me one of its cars at cost right off the assembly line.

(Jackie has a pain spasm.)

NEWT: All right?

JACKIE: Uh huh. Look at me. I thought I'd be in New York this week looking at Impressionists.

NEWT: New York! What do you want to go there for?

JACKIE: I went to all that trouble saving my money every week for a trip to New York and look where I wind up. I wanted to see the Impressionists at the Metropolitan Museum.

NEWT: How could you even consider going there with your money? You can't bring anything to New York. The federal government sends billions to New York and the Mafia steals it all. You have the Mafia there because of these cheap liberal wimps.

JACKIE: Does the Mafia have that much of a hold on New York?

NEWT: Second only to Israel. All the fault of the liberals. Just like the French. The Germans came through Caen on the Belgian border in 1871, then in 1914. These limp liberal French disarmed. In 1940, the Germans poured through Caen again. It's precisely the same thing in New York.

(She shows pain or discomfort.)

NEWT: I understand this kind of pain and suffering and anguish. We've been through this once before. Cancer is a test of the soul, of our resolve to triumph over a deadly foe and go on to a better, more prosperous, rewarding, enriching life.

JACKIE: Newt, that's a campaign speech.

NEWT: With all due respect, I really mean what I'm saying.

JACKIE: Newt, I was standing right next to you while you made this same speech in Monticello. At the Farmers Market. About my first operation.

NEWT: I only introduced you that night.

JACKIE: You told them right out loud, "The cancer my wife has just been through. Please vote for us."

NEWT: I may have mentioned you were ill.

JACKIE: Deathly ill was your phrase.

NEWT: If I did bring it up, it was only to appeal to the sense of faith and religion of the audience. Certainly, I wasn't using it for votes. Only somebody shallow and despicable would use his wife's cancer to get ahead. Besides we were right in the furnace of a political campaign.

JACKIE: Sometimes it was fun to be in a campaign.

NEWT: You always told me you hated them.

JACKIE: I didn't like it when you told people they had to be nasty.

NEWT: You can't fight fair against these liberal traitors and you've got to be nasty when you fight the lying liberal media. But I didn't think you liked any of the campaigns at all.

JACKIE: Newt, how could I enjoy most of them? I had my teaching job. I had two little girls at home. And I had cancer. But you know what I was thinking of? Making all those peanut butter and jelly sandwiches.

NEWT: When that Shapard has a Democrat barbecue, fifty dollars a head, I just knew what we had to do. Get up a mountain of peanut butter and jelly sandwiches and give 'em away free.

JACKIE: I started making them the night before and never stopped.

NEWT: They charged fifty dollars for listening to nothing. That's the Democrats for you. But we gave the people free peanut butter and jelly to show I was one of the common folks. And then they listened to my new, great ideas. We have to teach more about Benjamin Franklin. Make drug users pay up to a third of their gross assets. Let's see some cocaine snorting shortstop pay a million dollar fine. And I was the first to point out that there are literally hundreds of babies left in dumpsters in Washington, D.C. You can't fit a newspaper in because of all the dead babies stuffed in the dumpster. That's the fault of our liberal national elite and their insane welfare policies. I told the people my stunning, unique and totally brilliant idea on how to end welfare. We will take all the women and children off welfare and there will be no more welfare. *(He claps hands together.)* Lord, isn't it wonderful to be able to see ahead! Remember when I told them that, Jackie? How there wasn't a sound in the crowd when I talked?

JACKIE: They had their mouths stuck together with peanut butter.

NEWT: That peanut butter and jelly was the best idea I had. It was forward thinking. The best.

JACKIE: I thought I was the one thought of the peanut butter and jelly.

NEWT: Then that Democrat woman Shapard handed it to us when she said that if she got elected she wouldn't make her family move to Washington. *(He smiles broadly.)*

JACKIE: Yeah, you made me write a letter to all of the garden clubs saying that she was going to break up a family unit, and that we were going to go to Washington together. Remember I wrote, "Let our family represent your family in Congress." I wasn't so proud of that.

NEWT: I was. I said her family values were the same that cause these welfare people to be out killing, murdering, and slaughtering people in the cities. And I let good decent people know how we lived as a family in Carrolton, Georgia.

JACKIE: And they all had a pool going on election night as to how long we'd last together in Washington.

NEWT: That was all those Democrats. They're all sick, vicious enemies of mine. Limp liberals.

JACKIE: Newt, your own press secretary won the pool. Dave Worley. He bet on a breakup inside of eleven months. He sure was right.

NEWT: No, that old fat liberal, Shapard, was at the bottom of that.

JACKIE: I wish you wouldn't call her that. I'm slightly overweight myself.

NEWT: Ole fat liberal.

JACKIE: *(After pause.)* Was that what happened with me in Washington? I got too heavy?

NEWT: Uh, naw, well, so much went on.

JACKIE: Was it my age? Newt, I'm the same seven years older that I always was. When you started coming onto me in the back of my geometry classroom. I could hardly believe it. I was the teacher and I got a high school kid looking at me. And me liking it! What did I do, suddenly seem older in Washington? With all those young wives? Do you think that you can't be the Speaker or get to the White House with a wife looks like me?

NEWT: *(Looks up from writing on pad.)* Jackie, with all due respect, I didn't come here to hurt you. Believe me, I'm the same compassionate man I always was.

JACKIE: And you know I wouldn't do anything to turn the girls against you.

NEWT: Oh, I know that. If there is one thing I know about you it's that you're loyal. Loyalty. I want to thank you for having it, Jack —

JACKIE: — I don't know so much if it's loyalty. That sounds like a political word. It's just I was raised in Columbus, Georgia, to be a lady and never diminish the reputation of the father. Even if he isn't worth the effort.

NEWT: *(Jumps up impulsively.)* And you're still a lady from Columbus.

JACKIE: *(Struggles to sit up and smiles faintly.)* Come here.

NEWT: *(Energetically going to bedside and instead of kissing her, thrusts pad in front of her.)* Here.

JACKIE: What is this?

NEWT: Why don't you just sign it. That'll give us an agreement.

JACKIE: What kind of agreement?

NEWT: A divorce.

JACKIE: A wha…? What are you talking about?

NEWT: A sensible settlement. And speedy. You'll never see me in a negotiation that breaks down.

JACKIE: Newt, I can't sign anything without a lawyer.

NEWT: A lawyer! We've allowed lawyers to run our affairs. Who are they? Scurrilous people who get rapists and child molesters off. We ought to remember that. Every time you hire a lawyer, you help a rapist.

JACKIE: I didn't expect this from you.

NEWT: Jackie, do you realize how sick that is? Have you lost all your family values? Do you realize how truly sick you are?

JACKIE: That's what the doctors say.

NEWT: I can't stand here and see you like this…If it's too much for you to read, here: "Newt. Clothing allowance, four hundred a month. Jackie, alimony, nothing." Let me explain the alimony. If I get three suits and you have no new clothes, then just by me having three new suits, you will have a new outfit. That's the American dynamic. But if I pay alimony to you...in other words if you go on welfare...you'll be weak and dependent on handouts. You can cure people on welfare. Every time they moan, tell them to go out and open a business. They have to learn a hard lesson in self reliance. Just like you, Jackie.

(With this, she puts her head back on the pillows and falls asleep.)

NEWT: If it's too much for you to sign, just initial it.

(Lights fade to black.)

END OF PLAY

Flesh and Blood
by Elizabeth Dewberry

BIOGRAPHY

Elizabeth Dewberry made her playwriting debut at the 1995 Humana Festival with *Head On*. She is the author of three novels—*Many Things Have Happened Since He Died* (published by Doubleday, 1990 and Vintage Contemporaries, 1992), *Break the Heart of Me* (Nan A. Talese/Doubleday, 1994), and *How to Get to the Magic Kingdom* (forthcoming). Ms. Dewberry holds a Ph.D. in 20th-century American literarture from Emory University and a B.S. in English from Vanderbilt. She has taught creative writing and American literature at Emory, The University of the South, Ohio State, the University of Southern California and at the Bread Loaf and Sewanee Writers' conferences. She lives in Lake Charles, Louisiana, with her husband, author Robert Olen Butler.

ORIGINAL PRODUCTION

Flesh and Blood was first performed at the 1996 Humana Festival of New American Plays, March, 1996. It was directed by Mark Brokaw with the following cast:

Charlotte . . . . Karen Grassle
Dorris . . . . Adale O'Brien
Judd . . . . .V Craig Heidenreich
Crystal . . . . Liann Pattison

and the following production staff:

Scenic Designer . . . . Paul Owen
Costume Designer . . . . Nanzi Adzima
Lighting Designer . . . . Mimi Jordan Sherin
Sound Designer . . . . .Martin R. Desjardins
Properties Master . . . . Ron Riall
Stage Manager . . . . Paul Mills Holmes
Assistant Stage Manager . . . . Cind Senensieb
Dramaturg . . . . Liz Engelman
New York Casting Arrangements . . . . Laura Richin Casting

CHARACTERS

CHARLOTTE: Age 40. A little overweight and not particularly attractive. She is dressed nicely, for her sister's wedding, but also frumpily, out of habit.

DORRIS: Charlotte's mother. Early sixties. Dressed at first for the wedding, she later wears a house dress or other casual clothes.

JUDD: Charlotte's husband. Early forties. He can't wait to get out of his sports coat and tie. He is wearing a starched shirt, and he's uncomfortable in it.

CRYSTAL: Charlotte's sister, Dorris' daughter. She is thirty-seven, thin, and pretty. She is dressed for her second wedding—no train, but something that obviously registers as a wedding dress, and her hair is twisted up with tiny flowers on top and tendrils framing her face and neck.

PLACE

Summer, late afternoon. Dorris' backyard, kitchen and den, somewhere in the present-day suburban South. The backyard has a weathered picnic table. It leads to Dorris' small kitchen, which is separated from her cozy den only by a counter. The den has a sofa and an easy chair, and the house is clean and well cared for but a little shabby.

FLESH AND BLOOD

As the lights come up, Charlotte, Dorris, Judd, and Crystal enter the kitchen through the yard, single file, in that order. Charlotte and Dorris busy themselves in the kitchen, Charlotte in a state of agitation, opening and closing cabinets and drawers, Dorris in a state of forced cheerfulness, sponging off the already-clean counter tops. Judd takes off his coat and tie as he makes his way to the den and sits in a chair. Crystal goes straight to the sofa. She tries to turn on the lamp next to her, but it won't turn on.

CHARLOTTE: *(To Dorris.)* Mama, what do you have to eat?

DORRIS: There's M&M's in the freezer. Crystal, you want some frozen M&M's?

CHARLOTTE: Mama, it's dinner time.

JUDD: *(Gently, to Crystal.)* You want a beer?
   (He touches her.)

CRYSTAL: Don't.

DORRIS: *(To Charlotte.)* Put them in a bowl for her.
   (Charlotte, who notices the exchange between Judd and Crystal, doesn't move, so Dorris quickly wipes out a bowl with a dish towel. She will dump the candy into the bowl and set it in front of Crystal.)

CHARLOTTE: Don't you have anything healthy?

DORRIS: *(To Crystal, setting down the candy.)* Here, hon.

CHARLOTTE: What were you going to give the girls tomorrow?
   (Judd gets a light bulb from the kitchen and begins to change the bulb in the lamp. Crystal watches him. When he finishes, he will turn on the lamp.)

DORRIS: There's turkey hot dogs and orange jello and for dessert I made a little—

CHARLOTTE: They don't eat jello.

DORRIS: They do when they eat here.

CHARLOTTE: It's nothing but empty calories.

DORRIS: I put fruit cocktail in it. There's grapes, maraschino cherries, and…squares.

CHARLOTTE: But the vitamin content of jello—

DORRIS: I know, you obviously turned out malnourished. It's a thankless job, Crystal. Maybe you made the right choice, not having them.

CRYSTAL: I haven't made that choice yet, Mother.

DORRIS: You made your choice this afternoon.

(*Tense pause.*)

CHARLOTTE: Why don't I make up some egg salad sandwiches?

(*She opens the refrigerator.*)

CHARLOTTE: Mama, do you have any eggs?

DORRIS: I don't know.

CRYSTAL: Everybody hates egg salad.

(*Charlotte takes a carton of eggs out of the refrigerator, then closes it.*)

CHARLOTTE: What do you want, Crystal?

CRYSTAL: Nothing.

CHARLOTTE: Then why do you care if I make egg salad?

(*Charlotte goes to fill a pan with water.*)

DORRIS: Don't use tap water.

CHARLOTTE: For boiling eggs?

DORRIS: It has human *waste* in it. It'll kill you.

CHARLOTTE: Since when?

DORRIS: I saw a TV show about it last week. I'm not making this up. Use that.

(*She indicates a spring water cooler.*)

CHARLOTTE: Mama, you're wasting your money.

DORRIS: They've done studies. If you give your family tap water, you have no room to complain about jello. They won't live long enough to need the extra vitamins.

CHARLOTTE: Fine, it's your money.

DORRIS: Crystal, you should eat something. I always feel better after I eat.

CRYSTAL: Mother, this is not a blood sugar problem. Eating won't help.

(*Charlotte fills the pan with water. Then she will gather things for egg salad: a bowl, mayonnaise, spices, etc. Dorris picks up an M&M.*)

DORRIS: One M&M. Nothing's ever quite as bleak when you've got an M&M in your stomach. Open your mouth.

(*She offers to feed it to Crystal.*)

CRYSTAL: Stop it.

DORRIS: Just one. Come on. It'll help, I promise.

(*Crystal eats a handful of M&M's.*)

CRYSTAL: I don't feel any better, Mother. Are you satisfied?

(*Charlotte tries to open the mayonnaise jar, but she can't.*)

DORRIS: Well. No.

(*Dorris eats the M&M.*)

JUDD: I'll go get fried chicken.

DORRIS: That's a good idea. Crystal loves fried chicken. Crystal, you love fried chicken.

(As Charlotte speaks, she hands Judd the mayonnaise jar. He will open it and give it back to her.)

CHARLOTTE: I'm perfectly capable of making egg salad.

DORRIS: Crystal doesn't want egg salad.

CHARLOTTE: Fine, then I'll make deviled eggs.

CRYSTAL: Everybody hates deviled eggs.

CHARLOTTE: I don't. Do I count? No.

CRYSTAL: Egg salad scooped onto boiled chicken placentas.

JUDD: *(To Crystal.)* You want baked beans or potato salad?

CHARLOTTE: No, Judd, I said I'm making deviled eggs. Mama, do you have any drinks?

(Charlotte looks in the refrigerator.)

JUDD: I'll get drinks.

DORRIS: I'll make iced tea.

JUDD: Want to come, Crystal?

CRYSTAL: No.

(Charlotte takes money out of her purse and offers it to Judd.)

CHARLOTTE: Leave Crystal alone and don't get drinks. And only extra crispy white meat. Even if you have to pay more.

JUDD: I'll pay for it.

DORRIS: Let me pay. You spend that money on yourself.

CHARLOTTE: No, Mama, I got it.

(Charlotte makes Judd take her money. Dorris starts fishing in her purse.)

JUDD: *(To Crystal.)* You sure you don't want to come?

CRYSTAL: Judd, look at me. I can't wait in line for a bucket of chicken dressed like this.

JUDD: Sorry.

CHARLOTTE: *(To Judd.)* Go on. And don't stop by the auto parts store.

DORRIS: *(To Judd, still fishing in her purse.)* Wait a minute.

CHARLOTTE: *(To Judd.)* Did you hear me?

JUDD: Why would I go to the parts store right now?

CHARLOTTE: Because you always—

JUDD: Don't, Charlotte.

CHARLOTTE: Don't what?

(Dorris takes Charlotte's money out of Judd's hand and puts it on the counter. Then she puts her own money in Judd's hand.)

DORRIS: Here.

CHARLOTTE: Mama, I'm paying.

(Charlotte switches the money again.)

CHARLOTTE : Just go, Judd.

DORRIS: *(Overlapping.)* No, let me get this.

(She gives Judd her money.)

CRYSTAL: It's not going to be more than fifteen dollars. Would y'all not start World War Three over fifteen dollars?

JUDD: *(Putting all the money on the counter as he leaves.)* I'll pay for it.

DORRIS: I was just trying to help.

(Pause.)

DORRIS : So. Here we are. Chicken's on its way.

CHARLOTTE: Crystal, you want to…talk?

(Charlotte and Dorris come in the living room and sit with Crystal.)

DORRIS: That's a good idea. We could talk.

CRYSTAL: Okay.

(Long pause.)

DORRIS: Well then say something.

CRYSTAL: What?

CHARLOTTE: Calm down, Mama. Crystal, how do you feel?

CRYSTAL: Depressed.

CHARLOTTE: Oh, right. Okay. What else?

CRYSTAL: Empty. I'm all out of words.

(Beat.)

CHARLOTTE: It'll be okay.

CRYSTAL: How do you know?

(The phone rings. Charlotte and Dorris move to answer it.)

CRYSTAL: Don't answer that.

DORRIS: But it might be…something, an emergency.

(The phone rings again.)

CHARLOTTE: It might be the girls.

CRYSTAL: It might be Mac and I don't want to talk to him.

DORRIS: But if—

(It rings again, but stops mid-ring. Pause while they wait to see if it will ring again.)

CHARLOTTE: What if that was the girls? What if they need me?

CRYSTAL: Call them up and find out.

(Charlotte makes a phone call.)

DORRIS: What am I going to tell people when they do call? They're going to be calling to congratulate me.

(Crystal gets a dishrag and wraps it around some ice cubes.)

CRYSTAL: Tell them the truth.

DORRIS: I don't know the truth.

(Crystal goes back to the sofa, lies down, and puts the ice pack over her eyes.)

CRYSTAL: The wedding was called off. That's the truth.

DORRIS: But Crystal.

CRYSTAL: What?

DORRIS: Don't do that. You'll mess up your makeup.

CRYSTAL: *(Ice pack off.)* Mother!

DORRIS: Fine. Sorry.

   (Beat. Crystal puts the ice pack back on.)

DORRIS: Crystal?

CRYSTAL: What?

DORRIS: Why?

   (Crystal sits up, takes the ice pack off.)

CRYSTAL: Because, Mama…*(She looks at Charlotte.)* I don't know.

DORRIS: You don't know? How could…? Why would a person call off their own wedding without even knowing why?

CRYSTAL: I don't know.

DORRIS: *(To Charlotte.)* Are they all right?

CHARLOTTE: *(Her hand over the receiver.)* They're watching MTV, but other than that—

DORRIS: *(Grabbing the phone, speaking into it pseudo-sweetly.)* Sweetheart, this is Grandma. Mama's gonna call you back later, okay? Bye bye.

   (Dorris hangs up, then hands Crystal the phone.)

DORRIS: Here. Call him.

CRYSTAL: No.

DORRIS: Say, "I don't know why I did it."

CRYSTAL: No, Mother.

DORRIS: Tell him you made a mistake.

CRYSTAL: No!

DORRIS: He'll understand. Everybody makes mistakes. I've made them.

CRYSTAL: I know that.

DORRIS: Charlotte's made them.

CRYSTAL: Mother.

DORRIS: Crystal, let's not beat around the bush here.

CRYSTAL: I'm being as direct as I know how to be.

DORRIS: You're thirty-seven years old.

   (Crystal lies back down, covers her eyes again.)

CRYSTAL: I realize that.

DORRIS: You don't have a career. No matter what you say, retail sales will never—

CRYSTAL: I'm very much aware of the limitations of my job.

DORRIS: You've already ruined one marriage—

CRYSTAL: I'm aware of that as well.

DORRIS: And while you have kept yourself up, this might be your last shot. Men don't just grow on trees.

(Crystal sits up and takes off the ice pack.)

CRYSTAL: Mother, put down the phone.

DORRIS: Children don't grow on trees either.

CRYSTAL: Mother!

DORRIS: I mean, they don't—

CRYSTAL: I know what you mean.

DORRIS: Because by the time I was thirty-seven you girls were...Well, look at Charlotte.

CRYSTAL: I don't want to look at Charlotte.

DORRIS: Charlotte's girls are already—

CRYSTAL: I know what Charlotte's kids are.

DORRIS: I mean, the joy of...motherhood. You want me to call him?

CRYSTAL: Stop it, Mother.

DORRIS: I just don't want you to miss out. Don't you have a biological clock?

CRYSTAL: Something inside me is ticking, but I don't know if it's a clock or a bomb.

DORRIS: It's probably a clock. I've never heard of a biological bomb.

(Crystal goes outside, taking the ice pack with her. She sits at the picnic table, dumps the melting ice onto the table, and washes her neck and behind her ears with the rag, messing up some of the tendrils in her hair. Dorris and Charlotte lower their voices.)

DORRIS: You talk to her. I'm going to take a shower.

CHARLOTTE: In tap water? You realize you're bathing in human waste?

DORRIS: *(Upset.)* We all are, but what choice do we have? We have no choice.

CHARLOTTE: Calm down, Mama.

DORRIS: Believe you me, if I could change it I would.

CHARLOTTE: I didn't mean it. It was just a joke.

DORRIS: Oh. Well why did you...It's hard enough to feel clean. You didn't have to point that out.

CHARLOTTE: I'm sorry.

DORRIS: Don't talk that way to Crystal.

CHARLOTTE: I won't. I'm not going to talk to her at all.

DORRIS: Yes you are.

CHARLOTTE: She won't listen to me. She won't even talk to me.

DORRIS: She looks up to you.

CHARLOTTE: She does not. She thinks my life is banal.

DORRIS: You're her sister. Doesn't that mean anything?

CHARLOTTE: You're her mother.

DORRIS: I just tried. That's why she's out there. You do it. Tell her you and Judd have had problems, but you've worked through them. Tell her everybody has—

CHARLOTTE: Mama, Crystal and I have never had one real conversation.

DORRIS: Yes you have. You two used to scream bloody murder at each other half the time.

CHARLOTTE: That's not conversation.

DORRIS: It is so. It's just loud conversation. But you used to talk, regular, too.

CHARLOTTE: When?

(Beat.)

DORRIS: Oh. Well, why didn't you talk?

CHARLOTTE: I don't know.

DORRIS: Remember when we bought that aquarium, all those beautiful fish, and we put it on top of the TV?

CHARLOTTE: *(Touchy.)* What happened to my fish is not relevant here.

DORRIS: You two were so close. You were going to open a tropical fish store together.

CHARLOTTE: Mama, that idea lasted for two weeks, about as long as the fish.

DORRIS: I didn't handle that whole thing very well.

CHARLOTTE: No, you didn't.

(Crystal goes to the kitchen door.)

DORRIS: I don't think Crystal believed me when I told her that by flushing them down the toilet we were setting them free.

(Crystal goes in the kitchen and gets an ashtray. Dorris and Charlotte ignore her until she speaks.)

CHARLOTTE: She believed anything you told her. I was the one who knew you were lying. I always knew when you lied.

CRYSTAL: I knew they were dead. I figured if y'all were too stupid not to know it already, there wasn't any point in telling you.

(Crystal goes back out to the picnic table and starts smoking a cigarette.)

DORRIS: *(To Crystal.)* Well, I'm sorry! I did the best I could and that obviously wasn't good enough. You're letting the air conditioning out.

(She closes the kitchen door.)

DORRIS: *(To Charlotte.)* Okay, the fish were a bad example. My point is…I don't know what my point is. If you won't go talk to her I will.

CHARLOTTE: Good luck.

(Dorris goes outside. Charlotte stays in the kitchen, finds a sack of potatoes, and starts peeling them into the kitchen sink.)

DORRIS: Oh, honey, you shouldn't be sitting there in that dress.

(She runs back inside and grabs a clean dishtowel, then runs back outside, holding it out to Crystal.)

DORRIS: Here, sit on this.

CRYSTAL: What difference does it make?

DORRIS: The chair, it's filthy.

CRYSTAL: It's all right.

DORRIS: I mean, not dirt, but tree sap, bird poop.

CRYSTAL: I'm not going to wear this again.

DORRIS: But you look so beautiful in it. You never know what tomorrow will—

CRYSTAL: I'm not. I know that much.

DORRIS: *(Still holding out the dishtowel.)* But Crystal...What if somebody comes over...or...something?

CRYSTAL: Who's going to come over? Everybody you know thinks you're at my wedding. The only person who would possibly come over now is a robber and he won't care if my dress is dirty. If anything, he'll make me lie down at gunpoint on the ground and it'll just get dirtier. If he shoots me it'll have a hole in it, not to mention blood all over it, and it's ruined forever. Either way, bird shit on my ass is not going to make a goddamn bit of difference.

(Dorris carefully lays the towel on the chair opposite Crystal and sits on it herself.)

DORRIS: You don't have to get hysterical. I was just trying to help.

CRYSTAL: I'm sorry, Mother. I'm under a little bit of stress.

(Beat.)

DORRIS: What can I do?

CRYSTAL: Nothing.

DORRIS: I'll take your dress to the cleaners for you next week.

CRYSTAL: Fine.

DORRIS: Do you want me to call the restaurant where we were going to have dinner and cancel the reservations?

CRYSTAL: No.

DORRIS: Because I'll do it for you. I'll be happy—

CRYSTAL: Mac will take care of it.

DORRIS: Honey, did you put a wedding announcement in tomorrow's paper?

CRYSTAL: Mother, please.

DORRIS: I'm just asking because I need—

CRYSTAL: No, there's not going to be an announcement in the paper.

DORRIS: Well, that's a relief. No sense in airing your dirty laundry.

(Dorris gets a potted plant and puts it on the table.)

CRYSTAL: I'm just going to let that one pass.

(Crystal puts out her cigarette in the plant.)

DORRIS: Crystal, what happened? You're supposed to be married right now, and I don't even know what happened. What am I going to tell people?

CRYSTAL: I don't know.

(Crystal takes a flower out of her hair and puts it in the plant. As she unpins the flowers, her hair gets messed up.)

DORRIS: Did you find out about another woman so you left him at the altar?

CRYSTAL: No.

DORRIS: Nobody would criticize you for that. They'll think you went easy on the bastard. Which if that's what happened, believe me, you did.

CRYSTAL: It's not another woman.

(Another flower in the plant.)

DORRIS: Another man?

CRYSTAL: Oh Mama, how did you guess?

DORRIS: *(Overlapping.)* I knew it. I knew it the first time I met him. I wasn't going to say anything, but he was just a little too interested in my African violets.

CRYSTAL: What?

DORRIS: Don't you worry about a thing, Crystal. It's not your fault. Everybody'll feel sorry for you.

CRYSTAL: No, Mama.

(She puts the last flower in the plant.)

DORRIS: Yes they will. Except for the ones who say you can't keep your men. But those people are going to say that regardless. My shamrock is not a garbage can.

(Dorris picks up the cigarette butt and the flowers and throws them away.)

CRYSTAL: He's not gay.

DORRIS: Oh.

CRYSTAL: Where does this come from?

DORRIS: This pot? I have no idea. Probably a wedding present. You're going to have to return all your wedding presents, you know. But you still have to write thank-you notes.

CRYSTAL: It's a canceled wedding, not dirty laundry. Please, Mother.

DORRIS: Honey, I'm being supportive. I'm saying I think you made the right decision. About the announcement. Even if you had gone through with the wedding. I think it's generally good advice not to have your picture in the paper for any reason if you can avoid it. It makes you a target, you know.

Burglars, kidnappers, stalkers, murderers. They read the paper like every-body else.

CRYSTAL: Are you ashamed of me?

DORRIS: No. I'm...I just care about you, Crystal. I just want you to be happy. I'm sorry I said dirty laundry.

CRYSTAL: It's okay.

(Beat.)

DORRIS: I'm sorry about the fish.

CRYSTAL: It wasn't your fault.

DORRIS: I'm sorry about the jello.

CRYSTAL: Charlotte's more upset about that than I am.

DORRIS: I've made some mistakes, but I'm sorry. That should count for something.

CRYSTAL: You're right. It should.

DORRIS: So what can I do? Tell me anything.

CRYSTAL: Okay. I need a place to stay, just for a little while.

DORRIS: Of course. I'm happy as a clam to have you, Roomie.

(She touches Crystal, who withdraws from her touch.)

CRYSTAL: Not your roommate, your guest.

DORRIS: You can't be a guest in your own home. This is your home. If this is not your home, what is?

(Crystal shakes her head.)

CRYSTAL: I don't know.

DORRIS: It won't even be like mother-daughter. We'll be like sisters!

CRYSTAL: (Horrified.) No.

DORRIS: Friends, we'll be like friends. I mean, we are friends, aren't we?

CRYSTAL: Yes. Of course we're friends.

DORRIS: Good. Friends. Hey, why don't we paint your room?

CRYSTAL: Because I don't want to.

DORRIS: I haven't changed the colors in this house since, well, not since your father died. My goodness. That's too long. I need to paint the house.

(Charlotte takes the kitchen garbage outside and puts it in a trash container. The container might be just off-stage, as long as Charlotte gets out of the kitchen to overhear this segment of the conversation between Crystal and Dorris.)

DORRIS: Talk about a bastard.

CRYSTAL: Mother, don't, please.

DORRIS: Don't call him a bastard? It's the truth. There are things about him you don't know.

CHARLOTTE: Mother, can you help me inside?

CRYSTAL: I'm sure there are, but do we have to talk about this today of all days?

DORRIS: No. Of course not. That just slipped out, from the stress. I'm under some stress today myself, you know. Let's forget I said it. Forget I said it? (*She waits for Crystal to say her line. This is a ritual they've observed before, and Crystal is tired of it, but she goes through the motion of saying it anyway.*)

CRYSTAL: Said what.

(*Dorris goes back to same excited tone of voice and manner she used before she mentioned the father. Charlotte goes back in the kitchen.*)

DORRIS: And I can do one or two other things around the house just because I need to, I've been meaning to, can't I?

CRYSTAL: You could do something about the curtain in there.

DORRIS: You know I made those old curtains, it must be, you were fourteen, thirty-seven minus fourteen, twenty-three years ago. Out of sheets. I don't guess I've looked at them since. Let's get new curtains. And new sheets!

CRYSTAL: Fine. Something heavy, though. You can't sleep in that room in the morning. The light falls on your face and wakes you up.

DORRIS: It does? Why didn't you tell me before?

CRYSTAL: I told you the sun woke me up in the mornings and you said that was what it was there for.

DORRIS: I did?

CRYSTAL: Yes.

DORRIS: What did you say to that?

CRYSTAL: I said okay.

DORRIS: What if you spent your whole childhood sleep-deprived? It might have stunted your growth. Why didn't you say, "Mama, I need a different curtain"?

CRYSTAL: Because I didn't know it could be different. I didn't know anything could be different from how it was.

DORRIS: Oh, honey, I'm sorry.

CRYSTAL: It's a little thing, and it's not your fault. It's just how I was. Stupid.

DORRIS: That's not stupid. In a way, it's lucky, not to know things could be different. I always, for as long as I can remember, I've always wanted everything to be different.

CRYSTAL: Well, I just got this way.

DORRIS: I hope you didn't get it from me. It makes everything harder.

(*Charlotte brings out a tablecloth, sets it on the table, and goes back inside.*)

CHARLOTTE: There's another potato peeler in there, if anybody's looking.

DORRIS: That's a good idea. Cover up this old ugly table. Brighten things up.

(*Dorris sets the plant on the bench, unfolds the cloth, spreads it over the table, and puts the plant back. Charlotte speaks from the kitchen doorway.*)

CHARLOTTE: Mama, are you going to make the tea, or do you want me to do everything?

DORRIS: I said I'd make it. I'll make it.

(Charlotte goes back into the kitchen and moves to the sink to fill a tea pot with water as Dorris comes into the kitchen. Crystal stays at the picnic table and lights a cigarette. She has a great sadness on her.)

DORRIS: Don't use that water.

CHARLOTTE: Mama, I need to talk with you.

DORRIS: It's filthy.

(Charlotte takes Dorris' hand and leads her into the den, where they sit.)

CHARLOTTE: Come here, Mama. What did you say to Crystal about Daddy?

DORRIS: I told her he was a bastard. But she already knew that.

CHARLOTTE: What else?

DORRIS: Nothing.

CHARLOTTE: Let's just don't talk about Daddy today, okay?

DORRIS: Fine. I've said all I have to say.

CHARLOTTE: We're all under some stress.

DORRIS: I'm under a lot of stress.

CHARLOTTE: I know you are, and we all tend to say things we shouldn't when we're under stress.

DORRIS: You're saying we but you mean me, don't you?

CHARLOTTE: Well, Mama…

DORRIS: You worry too much. I'm not going to say anything, but even if something slipped out, it was a long time ago.

CHARLOTTE: So?

DORRIS: And I didn't mean any harm.

CHARLOTTE: Yes you did.

DORRIS: Not any *real* harm.

CHARLOTTE: I don't blame you, but you did.

DORRIS: I just wanted him to have a stomach ache.

CHARLOTTE: You wanted more than that.

DORRIS: Okay, a little vomiting. Maybe a little diarrhea. But the rest was a mistake. It could have happened to anybody.

CHARLOTTE: What part of it could have happened to anybody?

DORRIS: Lots of people have potato salad go bad on them. Especially back then.

CHARLOTTE: True. But most of those people don't make that potato salad with bits of raw pork in it—

DORRIS: That was flavoring.

CHARLOTTE: —and they don't leave it in the trunk of a hot car for two days.

DORRIS: Probably not.

CHARLOTTE: No.

DORRIS: But I think Crystal would understand. She's made mistakes too.

(Crystal takes off her earrings and necklace.)

CHARLOTTE: I don't think she would. Most people don't.

DORRIS: Crystal's not most people.

CHARLOTTE: No, but she's not us, either.

DORRIS: She's family. Surely that means something. I raised you two exactly alike.

CHARLOTTE: Not exactly.

DORRIS: Well, close.

CHARLOTTE: No, Mama. You told *me* the truth.

DORRIS: You caught me getting the potato salad out of the trunk. What else could I do?

CHARLOTTE: You could have lied.

DORRIS: I thought you were old enough to understand.

CHARLOTTE: I was nine.

DORRIS: But you did. You did understand.

CHARLOTTE: Right. And Crystal will never understand, no matter how old she gets. That's why you still lie to her.

DORRIS: What are you saying?

CHARLOTTE: Just, if you need to talk to somebody, talk to me, okay?

DORRIS: Okay. But look at Crystal. Who's going to talk to her?

CHARLOTTE: Judd talks to her.

DORRIS: Maybe she's in the same boat I was in, maybe Mac's got a woman on the side and she has no idea what to do about it.

CHARLOTTE: She doesn't even see *that*, how we do.

DORRIS: What?

CHARLOTTE: She doesn't hold on to the things she loves.

DORRIS: Yes she does.

CHARLOTTE: But not the way we do. You and me, we never got divorced or called off a wedding. When we love a man, we don't let him go.

DORRIS: No, we don't. I'm so tired.

CHARLOTTE: Why don't you go lie down?

DORRIS: It's not that kind of tired. Crystal's tired too. I can see that. She's all alone and she's looking at the idea of spending the rest of her life alone and I know how she feels. You don't. Thank God you don't, but you don't.

CHARLOTTE: Maybe I do.

DORRIS: I don't know how much longer I've got on this planet.

CHARLOTTE: Mama, don't be silly. You're not old and you're in good health.

DORRIS: But you never know what could happen. Car accidents, strokes, heart attacks, ptomaine poisoning. They happen every day, you know.

CHARLOTTE: I know.

DORRIS: Okay. I'm just going to take that shower now.

CHARLOTTE: I love you, Mama.

DORRIS: I love you too, Sweetie. Charlotte?

CHARLOTTE: What, Mama?

DORRIS: I have to ask you a question. I want you to tell me the truth.

CHARLOTTE: Okay.

DORRIS: Do you really think I did it on purpose?

CHARLOTTE: Yes.

DORRIS: It's not like I shot him.

CHARLOTTE: Yes it is.

DORRIS: You really think so?

CHARLOTTE: Yes. Mama, think. Remember. Don't you?

DORRIS: Yeah.

CHARLOTTE: Mama?

DORRIS: Yeah?

CHARLOTTE: You can't feel bad.

DORRIS: I don't know. Sometimes I do.

CHARLOTTE: He was yours, your husband, the father of your children, and he betrayed you.

DORRIS: (Tentatively.) That's true.

CHARLOTTE: Mama, listen to me.

DORRIS: What?

CHARLOTTE: He deserved everything he got.

DORRIS: You're right. You're a good daughter.

CHARLOTTE: When I brought up you telling me the truth?

DORRIS: Yes?

CHARLOTTE: I wasn't saying I regret that.

DORRIS: Good. You can't feel bad either.

CHARLOTTE: I don't.

DORRIS: Not even for the lies you told the police?

CHARLOTTE: Not for the lies I told everybody. I love you, Mama. I'd do anything for you. And I know you'd do the same for me.

DORRIS: I love you too.

(They hug.)

DORRIS: You know what's kind of funny?

CHARLOTTE: What?

DORRIS: I tasted that potato salad.

CHARLOTTE: Was it good?

DORRIS: Best I ever made. He liked it pungent.

CHARLOTTE: That's probably why he ate so much of it.

(They giggle, then stop abruptly.)

DORRIS: I'm going to take that shower now. You want to borrow some clothes?

CHARLOTTE: No, I'll just wear this.

(Dorris walks to the kitchen door, calls out to Crystal.)

DORRIS: Charlotte, you want to borrow some clothes? Change into something more comfortable?

CRYSTAL: No.

DORRIS: You sure?

CRYSTAL: I don't want to wear your clothes today, Mother.

DORRIS: Okay.

CHARLOTTE: Mama, you called her Charlotte.

DORRIS: I did?

CHARLOTTE: I'm Charlotte. She's Crystal.

DORRIS: I know that. I'm sorry. I just need a shower.

CHARLOTTE: Mama?

DORRIS: I'm very tired.

(Dorris exits through the den toward the rest of the house. Pause while Charlotte gets out a knife and starts cutting up vegetables. She's disturbed—angry, but something else too. Crystal comes inside, puts her jewelry on the counter, and gets herself a glass of water from the cooler.)

CRYSTAL: Hi.

CHARLOTTE: Hi.

CRYSTAL: Is Mama okay?

CHARLOTTE: She's fine.

CRYSTAL: What's going on?

CHARLOTTE: Nothing. I'm making potato salad and then I'm going to make deviled eggs and if Mama hasn't made the tea by then, I'll make the tea. I don't understand people who can sit around waiting for their food like it's going to fall from heaven. Somebody has to make it.

CRYSTAL: I didn't think it was going to fall from heaven.

CHARLOTTE: Well, I know you didn't think that.

CRYSTAL: I thought Judd was going to bring it.

CHARLOTTE: I'm just…trying to help.

(Beat. Charlotte puts down her knife.)

CHARLOTTE: I don't know how to help you.

CRYSTAL: I know you don't.

CHARLOTTE: Tell me.

(Beat.)

CRYSTAL: *(Sadly.)* I guess I just don't want your help, Charlotte.

(Charlotte starts the food preparations back up—puts the eggs on to boil, gets out mustard, relish, etc.)

CHARLOTTE: *(Offended.)* Well. I'm here if you need me. How do you think making the deviled eggs with spicy mustard…

CRYSTAL: You are not.

(Beat.)

CHARLOTTE: I am! I always—

CRYSTAL: After the way you—

CHARLOTTE: I have never once turned down a request for help from you. Have I ever turned you down?

CRYSTAL: After the way you reacted to my divorce, I would have to be way past desperate to ask for your help now.

CHARLOTTE: The way I reacted? Crystal, I called you up, practically in tears, as soon as Mama told me. I offered to come over. I'm your sister.

CRYSTAL: You did not.

CHARLOTTE: Well, Katie had the chicken pox, but I told you I wanted to come over. I told you I would if I could. Do you not remember me saying that?

CRYSTAL: I remember it.

CHARLOTTE: I said I wished I could do something for you and you said there wasn't anything. You said that.

CRYSTAL: And you believed me?

CHARLOTTE: Are you saying I should have assumed you were lying?

CRYSTAL: Charlotte, how long did the chicken pox last?

CHARLOTTE: Not very. And by the time Katy got well, you were already bringing your new boyfriend home with you for Sunday lunch.

(Crystal gets four cloth napkins out of a drawer and begins folding them elaborately, as if for a formal dinner party.)

CRYSTAL: I was afraid!

(Charlotte picks up a knife and sharpens it.)

CHARLOTTE: Afraid!

CRYSTAL: I was terrified of sitting here, alone, and you and Mother and Judd all…looking at me…like I was a failure.

(Charlotte chops a green pepper for the potato salad.)

CHARLOTTE: We're your family.

CRYSTAL: Exactly.

CHARLOTTE: What are you doing?

CRYSTAL: Other than folding napkins? Is this a trick question?

(Charlotte stops chopping vegetables to get out the paper napkins and set them in front of Crystal.)

CHARLOTTE: Those are Mama's good cloth napkins. This is a picnic.

CRYSTAL: I'm trying to make things…better.

(Crystal puts the paper napkins away.)

CHARLOTTE: Don't you know what a picnic is supposed to look like?

CRYSTAL: What do you care?

CHARLOTTE: I care!

(Very angry, Charlotte resumes chopping her green pepper, then green onions for the potato salad.)

CHARLOTTE: Look, if you want to use cloth napkins I'm not going to stop you, but when you…*(She stops chopping.)* Don't you value family?

CRYSTAL: Yes, as a general principle.

(Charlotte gets plates, utensils, glasses, etc. out of the cabinets and puts them on the counter to go outside.)

CHARLOTTE: No you don't. Crystal, family is about sticking together through the hard times, no matter what. And when you bring your boyfriend over here, move right out of Richard's house into Mac's, you make a mockery of everything I—

CRYSTAL: What you have with Judd and what I had with Richard are two entirely different things. You have no idea what being married to Richard was like.

CHARLOTTE: What makes you think you're some kind of expert on being married to Judd?

(Charlotte gets the paper napkins out again and puts them with the plates.)

CRYSTAL: Fine. Paper napkins. Are you happy?

(Crystal puts the cloth napkins away.)

CHARLOTTE: It's not about being happy.

CRYSTAL: What is it about, then?

CHARLOTTE: What is what about?

CRYSTAL: Family. *(Beat.)* Charlotte, when I was married to Richard, did you ever see bruises on my arms? Did you ever ask yourself—

CHARLOTTE: No. What are you saying?

CRYSTAL: Never?

CHARLOTTE: I mean sometimes I saw bruises, but Crystal, there's a lot of ways to get bruised.

CRYSTAL: So why didn't you ask me?

CHARLOTTE: I don't know. I just…I didn't want to embarrass you.

CRYSTAL: It's not any less embarrassing now. It's just pointless.

CHARLOTTE: Well, why didn't you come to me? You could have come to me. You could have asked for my help if you needed it.

CRYSTAL: No I couldn't. You're just like Mother. Every time I tried to tell you anything other than—

CHARLOTTE: I am not just like Mama!

CRYSTAL: You didn't want to hear it.

CHARLOTTE: I am not!

CRYSTAL: The only person in this family who would listen to me is Judd.

CHARLOTTE: Leave Judd out of this. You take it all back about Mama right now.

CRYSTAL: All right, fine. I take it back. Now we'll just pretend I never said it, any of it, okay?

CHARLOTTE: Okay.

(Beat. Charlotte returns to dinner preparations.)

CRYSTAL: See? Just like her.

CHARLOTTE: I am not! If I were like Mama, the jello chef, I'd be back there showering in my own shit instead of trying to get dinner on the table, but I'm not. I'm out here doing what needs to be done.

CRYSTAL: Right.

CHARLOTTE: Crystal, I deal with things. I'm the one who's not trying to pretend you were never married to Richard. Mama, she's acting like you're eighteen years old and Richard never existed.

CRYSTAL: She's just trying to—

CHARLOTTE: She took down every picture of him in the house. Went through the scrapbooks. Every picture that had Richard in it, she tore up. I was in some of those pictures. Judd and my children were. That was our history too, and she—

CRYSTAL: I'm sorry, Charlotte, but what should she have done? I don't want to look at pictures of Richard when I come over here. For me that's like decorating with roaches.

CHARLOTTE: Very funny.

CRYSTAL: All right. Let's just make dinner. What do you want me to do?

CHARLOTTE: See if you can find some sweet relish in there.

(Crystal goes to the refrigerator. Charlotte puts several eggs in the pot of water on the stove.)

CRYSTAL: I hate relish. Hate the smell of it. It reminds me of sex.

CHARLOTTE: It's not for you. It's for the deviled eggs.

CRYSTAL: (Handing Charlotte the relish.) Here.

CHARLOTTE: Thanks.

(She smells the relish.)

CHARLOTTE: It reminds me of Easter eggs.

(She puts a spoonful of relish in a bowl.)

CHARLOTTE: I hope I don't regret asking you this, but I'm getting a mental image of your body covered with relish that I don't want to have, so would you mind telling me what it is about relish that reminds you of sex?

CRYSTAL: Certain men, when they sweat, it's how they smell…there.

CHARLOTTE: Oh. I see. Thank you.

(Beat. Charlotte closes the relish jar and hands it to Crystal.)

CHARLOTTE: Judd just smells like a car engine, all over.

(Crystal opens the refrigerator to put the relish away.)

CRYSTAL: That's better than relish. Look at this.

(Crystal takes a cake out of the refrigerator.)

CRYSTAL: What is it?

CHARLOTTE: It's a cake.

CRYSTAL: But look what she drew in icing on the top.

(They look at it together. They have no idea what the picture is.)

CHARLOTTE: Is it a battle scene?

CRYSTAL: It could be an orgy.

CHARLOTTE: Crystal!

CRYSTAL: I'm not saying I think it is.

CHARLOTTE: I'm not eating it.

CRYSTAL: Neither am I.

(She sets the cake aside as Dorris enters. Her hair is wet, and she's wearing casual clothes.)

DORRIS: I feel better. There's nothing like washing your hair to put everything in perspective, is there?

CRYSTAL: Nope.

(Dorris sees the cake on the counter.)

DORRIS: Who took that cake out?

CHARLOTTE: Crystal.

CRYSTAL: Charlotte!

DORRIS: Well, put it back. That's cream cheese icing. It needs to stay in the refrigerator or it'll go bad.

(Crystal picks up the cake.)

CRYSTAL: What's the picture on top?

DORRIS: It's a bride and groom, for the girls. I made it last night.

CRYSTAL: That's me and that's Mac?

DORRIS: *(Indicating the opposite.)* No, that's you and that's Mac.

CRYSTAL: I'm not even going to ask what the raisins are.

DORRIS: Want a little piece? Just a bite?

CHARLOTTE: Dinner is almost ready.

(Crystal picks up a knife and considers cutting a slice of cake. She reconsiders, then stabs the cake with the knife and lets go. She is calm.)

DORRIS: Crystal!

CRYSTAL: Now I feel better too.

(Dorris slices a piece of cake and puts it on a plate for Crystal. She does not put the cake back into the refrigerator.)

DORRIS: Here, eat this.

CRYSTAL: I can't eat, Mother. My stomach is upset.

(Crystal goes back to the sofa and sits. Charlotte continues the food preparations as quietly as possible but the sounds seem to be slightly magnified. Dorris pours a glass of water and brings some pills to Crystal.)

DORRIS: We're all upset, and what we all need is food. Here.

CRYSTAL: If that's valium, I'm not going to take it. Last time—

DORRIS: I'm off valium. It's just ibuprofen.

CRYSTAL: Thanks.

(Crystal takes the pills, then leans forward and puts her face in her hands. Dorris starts rubbing her back. Charlotte stops working, comes in the den, and sits in the chair.)

CHARLOTTE: (Sincerely.) Crystal, I'm sorry if you think I wasn't there for you.

CRYSTAL: I know you weren't there for me.

CHARLOTTE: (Curtly.) Okay. I'm sorry for that.

CRYSTAL: (Also curtly.) Okay. I accept your apology.

CHARLOTTE: Okay.

CRYSTAL: Okay.

CHARLOTTE: (Softening.) I meant that.

CRYSTAL: (Also softening.) So did I.

(Beat.)

CHARLOTTE: You want to…hug?

DORRIS: Let's all hug.

CRYSTAL: Let's not push it.

CHARLOTTE: Right.

(The phone rings. Charlotte moves to answer it.)

CRYSTAL: Don't get that.

(Charlotte restrains herself, but she can't stand not answering a ringing phone.)

CHARLOTTE: I want to be here for you now.

(The phone rings again. Charlotte looks at it, then back at Crystal.)

CHARLOTTE: I do.

DORRIS: We are. We're all in this together.

    (Beat. The phone rings.)

CHARLOTTE: It could be Judd. He could have had car trouble.

    (Beat.)

CHARLOTTE: The car's been making a funny sound.

    (Beat. It rings again.)

CHARLOTTE: Sort of going WAAAA.

DORRIS: That sounds serious.

CRYSTAL: He's a mechanic. If he has a problem with the car, he'll fix it.

    (The phone rings again and Charlotte moves toward it.)

CHARLOTTE: Not without his tools. I'm sorry, Crystal, but your misery doesn't run the world.

    (Crystal grabs the knife.)

CRYSTAL: If you pick up that phone I'll cut the line.

    (Charlotte picks it up and holds it out to show her; it's a portable phone, with no line, obviously.)

CRYSTAL: I'll unplug the base unit. I'll cut that line.

    (It rings.)

CRYSTAL: Don't answer it, Charlotte.

    (Charlotte punches the talk button. Crystal waits.)

CHARLOTTE: *(Into the receiver.)* Hello?…Oh. Crystal's not taking any calls today. Sorry.

    (Charlotte hangs up the phone. Crystal puts down the knife and stares at the phone. Awkward pause.)

CRYSTAL: Who was it?

CHARLOTTE: How should I know?

DORRIS: It could have been Mac. *(To Crystal.)* You want me to call him back?

CRYSTAL: No.

DORRIS: Charlotte, what's wrong with you? Why didn't you ask who it was, talk to him, keep him on the line?

CHARLOTTE: It's not a kidnapping, Mama.

DORRIS: Who said it was a kidnapping?

CHARLOTTE: Mama, you really ought to get an answering machine. That's what we should have done, is let a machine answer it. I don't understand people who won't get answering machines. I think it's a sign you're getting old.

DORRIS: I've never had an answering machine.

CRYSTAL: Who was it?

CHARLOTTE: Exactly. It's harder and harder for you to adapt to change.

DORRIS: No it isn't. I got this new haircut for the wedding and nobody even noticed.

CRYSTAL: It looks good, Mama. I'm sorry I didn't say anything.

DORRIS: It's okay. Nobody looks at the mother of the bride. I have to go blow dry it.

(She exits.)

CRYSTAL: Was it Mac?

CHARLOTTE: He didn't say.

(Crystal lets out a sigh of exasperation. Charlotte, who has stopped fixing dinner, goes back to the food preparations.)

CHARLOTTE: You didn't even want me to answer it. How was I supposed to know you wanted me to ask who it was? That's not reasonable. Was I wrong to assume you were going to be reasonable?

CRYSTAL: In assuming that matters of the heart are ever reasonable, yes, you were wrong.

CHARLOTTE: Don't go getting philosophical on me. I don't need that. I was trying to help and you're expecting me to read minds. If you'd wanted me to ask all you had to do was tell me to ask.

CRYSTAL: Fine.

CHARLOTTE: It's not like I mind asking who's calling. I don't. But I didn't know what you wanted.

CRYSTAL: All right, Charlotte, it was my fault.

CHARLOTTE: It's okay.

(Beat.)

CRYSTAL: You know, Charlotte, sometimes I really wish we could have what you and Mama have, where we could sit down on the sofa together and just...talk. I have some things I need to tell you.

(Pause. Crystal goes back to her original place on the sofa. She takes off her shoes and starts brushing the curls out of her hair. Then she will put it in a ponytail. Charlotte keeps fixing dinner, making more noise than she needs to, watching Crystal, who doesn't look up.)

CHARLOTTE: It was probably Mac. It was a man. Who else would it be? There's not anybody else, is there?

(Beat.)

CHARLOTTE: I'm sorry. Of course there's not. I didn't mean that. It was a joke, actually. A bad joke. Not a joke, but...

(Beat. She sets down the knife.)

CHARLOTTE: I really do want to help you. I just don't have any idea how. Tell me what you need.

CRYSTAL: I don't know how to tell you.

> (Beat.)

CRYSTAL: Do you ever wish we could be like those sisters who hug?

CHARLOTTE: Which sisters?

CRYSTAL: Not any specific ones. Forget it.

CHARLOTTE: We could hug.

CRYSTAL: We don't have to.

CHARLOTTE: I know. But let's do.

CRYSTAL: No, I was just…okay.

> (They hug briefly, awkwardly.)

CRYSTAL: Thanks.

> (Beat.)

CHARLOTTE: I don't know why. Our family just never was much for hugs.

CRYSTAL: We were all…busy.

CHARLOTTE: You feel any better?

CRYSTAL: I guess I don't hug other women very often. I could feel your breasts.

CHARLOTTE: Crystal!

CRYSTAL: Well, I could. I'm not saying I liked it. Didn't you feel mine?

CHARLOTTE: Yeah, but I wasn't going to mention it.

CRYSTAL: Sorry. I shouldn't have said it.

> (Beat.)

CHARLOTTE: You're about the only one, lately.

CRYSTAL: Only one of what?

CHARLOTTE: I was trying to…talk to you.

CRYSTAL: Oh. I'm sorry. Are you okay?

CHARLOTTE: I'm okay. I just don't know how long it's been since Judd touched my breasts.

CRYSTAL: Oh. Sorry.

> (Beat. Then they both start peeling eggs at top speed. Crystal peels one, then stops. Charlotte will keep going.)

CRYSTAL: Why did this happen? Why did everything start falling apart?

CHARLOTTE: What?

CRYSTAL: Our family. My life. Your life.

CHARLOTTE: My life isn't—

CRYSTAL: Why can't we do anything right in this family? Why did you put salt in the aquarium? You knew it would kill my fish.

CHARLOTTE: I did not.

CRYSTAL: Why'd you tear the heads off my puppets?

CHARLOTTE: I never tore anything off your puppets.

CRYSTAL: Well, somehow they all lost their heads. We didn't have a dog.

CHARLOTTE: I don't like being accused.

CRYSTAL: That's not my point. Why didn't Mother ever—

CHARLOTTE: Crystal, if you want to go back to our childhood and accuse somebody of making things fall apart, start with Daddy.

CRYSTAL: I would like to, but I can't. I don't even remember Daddy. When I try to picture him, it's black, nothing. The first memory I have is what I wore to his funeral. My dress was pink and black plaid with a little white monogrammed collar and I didn't like it because I thought it made me look fat. *(Crystal starts taking off her makeup, mostly her foundation and blush at this point, with the dishrag. She can use soap from the kitchen sink if she needs it. She should do this slowly.)*

CHARLOTTE: That was my dress.

CRYSTAL: I can think about that all day, but it doesn't begin to explain to me why at thirty-seven years old I'm sitting here in Mama's living room in my wedding dress with no husband, no kids, no home, no career, and no real future to look forward to. Oh God.

CHARLOTTE: You want me to tell you what Daddy was like? You think knowing about Daddy would explain you to yourself and help you solve all your problems?

CRYSTAL: It might be a start.

(Beat.)

CHARLOTTE: Well, you're wrong.

(Charlotte gathers the plates and utensils and takes them outside to the picnic table. Crystal follows her.)

CRYSTAL: I'm the same age Daddy was when he died and I've got less to show for my life than he did.

(Charlotte sets the table. Crystal starts taking off her eye makeup.)

CHARLOTTE: Crystal, it's not true.

CRYSTAL: He didn't do much, but he had a family. He left behind two people who wouldn't be alive today if he hadn't existed. That's more than I can say.

CHARLOTTE: So he's two fucks ahead of you.

CRYSTAL: That's not how I meant it. God, Charlotte.

CHARLOTTE: That's how he saw us, though.

(Beat.)

CRYSTAL: Are you still trying to help?

CHARLOTTE: Yes. I'm trying to help you see things the way they are.

CRYSTAL: No wonder Judd—

CHARLOTTE: No wonder Judd what?

CRYSTAL: What happened to you? Why can't you—

CHARLOTTE: Nothing.

CRYSTAL: Do you feel things?

CHARLOTTE: Yes.

CRYSTAL: Have you ever felt any real and deep connection to another human being?

CHARLOTTE: Yes.

CRYSTAL: Have you ever felt passion?

(Beat.)

CHARLOTTE: No wonder Judd what?

CRYSTAL: Your own daughters barely speak to you. Your husband doesn't touch you. I'm trying to tell you something, on the day my wedding was canceled, to explain to you what I'm going through, and what do I get—who's ahead of who in the great fuck count of life. I give up.

CHARLOTTE: I'm sorry, Crystal.

CRYSTAL: So am I.

CHARLOTTE: No, I'm really sorry.

CRYSTAL: I'm just tired of hearing it, okay? Let's finish making dinner. I need some food.

CHARLOTTE: I can't explain what happened, how we got this way. I put one foot on Mama's property and something—

CRYSTAL: It's not Mama's property. You're like this everywhere, to everybody.

CHARLOTTE: Not everybody, just family.

CRYSTAL: Lucky us.

CHARLOTTE: When I'm around the family, I feel these, it's like a hand, a fist, inside me. I don't know how to explain. Do you understand what I'm saying?

CRYSTAL: I'm trying to.

CHARLOTTE: Remember when I had my hysterectomy?

CRYSTAL: Of course.

CHARLOTTE: There was about a week, before we found out it was a tumor, when I thought I was pregnant.

CRYSTAL: Charlotte.

CHARLOTTE: Because it felt just like my other two pregnancies, like a rock inside me that was making me vomit. But I was so happy, and I loved that little growth inside me. I would have given my life for it.

(Beat.)

CHARLOTTE: Of course after I found out what it was, that it could have killed me, destroyed my family...what do you do with that love?

CRYSTAL: I don't know.

CHARLOTTE: I don't know either. But when I come over here I feel like I felt when they told me I was carrying a tumor instead of a baby.

(Beat.)

CHARLOTTE: Does that makes any sense?

CRYSTAL: Some. We just...Wait. So in that analogy, I'm the tumor?

CHARLOTTE: Yeah.

CRYSTAL: I'm malignant? You need to have me cut out?

CHARLOTTE: No, you're benign.

CRYSTAL: You think of me as a tumor?

CHARLOTTE: You're not the tumor. Nobody's the tumor. I don't know how to say this.

CRYSTAL: I'm sorry. About the tumor.

CHARLOTTE: I didn't bring it up for that.

CRYSTAL: I mean about the baby. I know how much you can come to love what you think is going to be your baby.

CHARLOTTE: They're easy to love in that state.

(Beat.)

CRYSTAL: I was pregnant, once. I had a miscarriage.

CHARLOTTE: *(Astonished.)* When?

CRYSTAL: About a year ago.

CHARLOTTE: Crystal, I can't believe this. What happened? Why didn't you tell me?

CRYSTAL: He pushed me down the stairs.

CHARLOTTE: I would have brought you food.

CRYSTAL: The impact of the fall...

(Beat.)

CHARLOTTE: What stairs? You don't have stairs.

CRYSTAL: Who cares what stairs?

CHARLOTTE: I'm not saying I *liked* Richard—

CRYSTAL: You hated Richard.

CHARLOTTE: But maybe you lost your balance and it *seemed* like he was pushing you but he was really trying to help.

CRYSTAL: I don't need that kind of help.

CHARLOTTE: Why would he do a thing like that? What did you do?

CRYSTAL: Nothing! What do you mean, what did I do? My God, Charlotte, I got pregnant.

CHARLOTTE: Well if he pushed you—

CRYSTAL: He *did* push me! And he did it on purpose.

CHARLOTTE: But why?

CRYSTAL: We were fighting. He didn't want to have the baby. I did. He won.

CHARLOTTE: Oh, Crystal, I'm sorry. I really am. That baby was yours. You should have killed Richard.

CRYSTAL: Oh come on, Charlotte.

CHARLOTTE: That would have been my niece or nephew. I could kill him right now. With my bare hands.

CRYSTAL: This is not helping.

CHARLOTTE: But I didn't know. Why didn't you stop me and say, "Charlotte, I need you"?

CRYSTAL: Because, what if I'd told you and you didn't believe me?

CHARLOTTE: But I—

CRYSTAL: What if I'd come right out and asked for it, "Will you help me," and you'd said, *(Shaking her head.)* "I would if I could."

CHARLOTTE: But I wouldn't have.

CRYSTAL: You did. You just did.

(A tense silence. The tea kettle starts to whistle. Crystal goes inside and takes it off the burner. Charlotte follows her in and gets out tea bags, and Dorris, now with dry hair, also comes back in the kitchen.)

DORRIS: *(To Charlotte, referring to the tea bags.)* I told you I'd do that.

CHARLOTTE: Well, you didn't do it.

DORRIS: Crystal, have you been crying?

CRYSTAL: No.

DORRIS: Well, your makeup—

CRYSTAL: I'm going to have another cigarette.

DORRIS: Another nail in your coffin.

CRYSTAL: Mother.

DORRIS: Fine, get cancer. That's fine with me.

(Crystal goes outside and gets out a cigarette but doesn't light it.)

CHARLOTTE: I need your help, Mama.

DORRIS: She looks terrible. I don't see the point in looking terrible. I'm worried about her.

(Charlotte keeps making dinner. Dorris watches Crystal. A tense, palpable silence hovers over them. Then Judd enters, carrying bags of fast-food chicken and side dishes.)

JUDD: I got the food.

(He takes it out of the bags and sets it on the table. Crystal helps. Then, as Charlotte watches, he lights both their cigarettes and Crystal cups her hand over the lighter in his hand when he lights hers. Charlotte goes back to work and they sit there together and smoke, and their smoke mingles above them and there is something connecting them.)

CHARLOTTE: *(To Dorris.)* Mama, I need your help.

DORRIS: I said I'll help. I'll help.

> *(Dorris takes over the tea preparations. Charlotte continues watching Crystal and Judd as she and Dorris work in the kitchen. After a few moments, Charlotte steps outside. She is angry.)*

CHARLOTTE: How long have you been back? I didn't hear you drive up.

JUDD: Just now.

CHARLOTTE: Just this second?

> *(Judd indicates the table, where he and Crystal have unpacked everything.)*

JUDD: No.

CHARLOTTE: What's all this shit?

JUDD: *(Pointing out different containers.)* Baked beans, coleslaw, potato salad.

CHARLOTTE: Shit.

JUDD: What, Charlotte?

CHARLOTTE: *(Very angrily.)* Nothing!

JUDD: Charlotte…

> *(Crystal opens the potato salad and starts eating it with a plastic fork Judd has set on the table.)*

CHARLOTTE: Crystal, don't eat that. Judd, I didn't tell you to get all this. Didn't you hear me? Do you ever hear a word I say?

CRYSTAL: *(Mouth full.)* This is delicious, Judd.

CHARLOTTE: Don't eat that, Crystal.

JUDD: All day you've been telling me to eat.

CHARLOTTE: I have not. That was Mama. Don't confuse us again.

JUDD: What happened?

CHARLOTTE: Tell Crystal I feel passion, Judd.

JUDD: *(To Crystal.)* What did you say?

CRYSTAL: Not what you think.

CHARLOTTE: Crystal's decided we don't *feel* enough so she's dragging the most painful thing in everybody's private life out into the open so we can all *talk* about it. Well I've had enough for one day. I am up to here.

> *(Dorris comes outside.)*

JUDD: Dammit, Crystal.

DORRIS: Charlotte, you're outside.

JUDD: You told her?

CRYSTAL: *(To Judd.)* No, wait.

JUDD: Goddammit, Crystal.

DORRIS: *(Fanning herself.)* Will y'all lower your voices?

CRYSTAL: *(To Judd.)* Stop.

JUDD: You could have talked to me about this first.

CRYSTAL: *(Trying to stop him.)* No, I didn't—

JUDD: I gave you an opportunity. Couldn't you think of anybody but yourself?

CRYSTAL: Shut up.

JUDD: *(To Charlotte, talking fast.)* I'm sorry, Sweetheart. I love you. I don't know. Shit. I'm really sorry. I don't even know how to talk about a thing like this because I'm not going to try to justify...

(Pause. He looks at their shocked faces.)

JUDD: Oh shit.

CHARLOTTE: *(In a furious calm.)* What are you not going to try to justify?

JUDD: Nothing. It's nothing. I just—

DORRIS: Nobody needs to justify anything. We're all family here. Let's just go inside—

CHARLOTTE: Crystal, tell me what Judd is not going to try to justify.

DORRIS: This is entirely too stressful.

CRYSTAL: I don't know.

DORRIS: We're all going to get cancer.

CHARLOTTE: Don't take me for an idiot.

DORRIS: You can get it from stress. I think I'm getting hives. *(Holding out her arm.)* Look, hives.

CRYSTAL: Those are mosquito bites.

DORRIS: No they're not. There's a different quality to the itching. It's like my body's making little visual sirens.

(She points out three hives on her arm, making a siren sound for each one.)

CHARLOTTE: Stop it!

CRYSTAL: Charlotte, let her calm down.

CHARLOTTE: Nobody ever died of hives.

DORRIS: *(Holding Charlotte's arm.)* This is not the place for this. Please, come inside.

(Charlotte doesn't budge.)

CHARLOTTE: You're sleeping together.

CRYSTAL: Charlotte, please believe me. We're not.

DORRIS: They're not.

JUDD: We're not.

(Dorris and Crystal begin gathering the tableware to take it inside.)

DORRIS: Of course not. Let's all go inside and calm down and have some tea. I'll bring dinner inside. It's too hot to eat outside today. Somehow my blood sugar seems worse in the heat. And the stress.

CHARLOTTE: *(To Crystal.)* You hypocrite. Ten minutes ago, you're asking me why did everything fall apart, and do you know what? I actually felt sorry for you. Poor little lost Crystal, searching for the answers. Well, I'll tell you why everything fell apart. Because you started fucking my husband.

(Beat. Crystal puts her handful of knives and forks on the table and sits down.)

DORRIS: I'm going inside.

(Dorris goes inside, scratching her arms, and closes the door behind her. She goes in the den, turns off the light, and sits in the dark. She puts the bowl of M&M's in her lap and starts eating them.)

CHARLOTTE: Oh. Jesus.

CRYSTAL: It was a long time ago.

JUDD: Charlotte...

CHARLOTTE: You stay out of this. I can't even look at you.

JUDD: Charlotte, please, let me —

CHARLOTTE: *(To Judd, without looking at him.)* Get out of my sight, Judd.

JUDD: Charlotte.

CHARLOTTE: I mean it. Go away.

JUDD: I'm not going to leave you. Crystal knows that.

CHARLOTTE: I'm not going to argue with you. If you won't leave, at least go in the house, because I cannot be in your presence right now. I can't.

JUDD: Okay. I'll be here, whenever you need me.

(He goes inside. Dorris exits through the den, carrying the bowl of M&Ms. Charlotte waits until she hears the kitchen door close.)

CHARLOTTE: When?

CRYSTAL: I don't know exactly because it's—

CHARLOTTE: When did you fuck my husband?

CRYSTAL: What difference does it make when, Charlotte?

CHARLOTTE: I have to know. I have to be able to figure out what I was doing, where the girls were, at the exact moment.

CRYSTAL: I'm sorry, but that's really not your business. It's between me and Judd.

CHARLOTTE: You are my sister. He is my husband. This is my business.

(Beat.)

CRYSTAL: Three weeks ago today.

CHARLOTTE: You said it was a long time ago.

CRYSTAL: It seems like a long time ago now.

CHARLOTTE: Three weeks before your wedding. Crystal! You liar, on top of every-thing else. What were you thinking? Where was I? What was I doing?

CRYSTAL: You were taking the girls shopping—

CHARLOTTE: For dresses to wear to your wedding.

CRYSTAL: You and Judd had an argument that morning, and so did Mac and I and we ran into each other at the liquor store—

CHARLOTTE: You seduced my husband at the liquor store?

CRYSTAL: Not seduced.

CHARLOTTE: He told me he went to the garage to rebuild an engine.

CHARLOTTE: Maybe he went there too, after. It was sort of quick.

CHARLOTTE: Where?

CRYSTAL: Charlotte, really, I don't think—

CHARLOTTE: My house? Did you do it in my house?

CRYSTAL: Look, we don't have to—

CHARLOTTE: If you don't tell me, I'm going to imagine you in three hundred different places. Was it here? At the garage? A car? Because if it was in a car in the middle of the day, if it was in our car...

CRYSTAL: It was at my house. *(She corrects herself.)* Mac's house.

CHARLOTTE: Mac's sofa?

CRYSTAL: The bed.

(Beat.)

CHARLOTTE: The bed.

CRYSTAL: Yeah.

CHARLOTTE: You fucked my husband on your boyfriend's, your fiancé's bed. Three weeks before your wedding. I see. Give me a minute here. I'm just trying to take all this in. You know, a bed is different from a sofa.

CRYSTAL: I know that.

CHARLOTTE: I would have preferred a sofa, I think. Want to know why?

CRYSTAL: Not really.

CHARLOTTE: Because a sofa, it all could have happened without there ever having been a moment where you stood up and he took your hand and you walked to the bed, knowing exactly what you were going to do and deciding to do it anyway. I could have made myself believe that. What do they call it, a crime of passion. Something you think I know nothing about. But a bed—

CRYSTAL: It wasn't like that.

CHARLOTTE: No? He carried you to the bed? You were resisting? You rolled?

(Beat.)

CHARLOTTE: How did you get to the goddamn bed?

CRYSTAL: We walked.

CHARLOTTE: Were you drunk?

CRYSTAL: No.

CHARLOTTE: Had you had anything to drink?

CRYSTAL: Lemonade.

CHARLOTTE: I think I would have preferred it if you were drunk. Then I could...Judd doesn't even like lemonade!

CRYSTAL: He didn't drink it. He had a beer. We were hot.

CHARLOTTE: *We* were hot.

CRYSTAL: I was hot. Judd was hot.

CHARLOTTE: Did you take off your clothes?

CRYSTAL: Charlotte.

CHARLOTTE: Did you take your clothes off?

CRYSTAL: Charlotte, you sort of, have to.

CHARLOTTE: Did you take off your bra?

CRYSTAL: No.

CHARLOTTE: Judd took it off.

CRYSTAL: Nobody took it off. I wasn't wearing one.

(Pause.)

CRYSTAL: It was a mistake.

CHARLOTTE: A mistake? You slept with my husband by mistake? You had a mental lapse and you thought he was Mac? That's what you're asking me to believe?

CRYSTAL: You know what I mean.

CHARLOTTE: A mistake is when you put too much detergent in the washing machine and the clothes come out with dried soap on them. A mistake is when you burn the biscuits and they're black on the bottom and they taste like soot. A mistake—

CRYSTAL: You know what I mean.

CHARLOTTE: No. I have no idea what it means to sleep with your sister's husband by mistake.

CRYSTAL: I'm telling you it shouldn't have happened.

CHARLOTTE: I could have told you that.

CRYSTAL: Judd and I both realize that.

CHARLOTTE: Then all three of us realize it. Big deal. Does that excuse it? Does it fix anything? Does it make any goddamn difference whatsoever? No.

(Charlotte goes in the house. Crystal follows her.)

CHARLOTTE : *(To Judd.)* How many times have you made love to me wishing it was her?

JUDD: Charlotte, listen to me.

CHARLOTTE: How many times?

JUDD: Never, I swear.

CHARLOTTE: *(To Crystal.)* We have a picture of you on the dresser in our bedroom. *(To Judd.)* You look at that picture while—

JUDD: No I don't.

CHARLOTTE: Oh my God. How could I have been so stupid?

JUDD: Charlotte, honey.

CHARLOTTE: Don't call me honey.

JUDD: Charlotte.

CHARLOTTE: Don't call me Charlotte.

JUDD: What do you want me to call you?

CHARLOTTE: Nothing. I don't know what to say to you. I'm redoing every Christmas, every Thanksgiving, every birthday, Sunday lunch, every time the family was together the last twenty years. Twenty goddamned years of foreplay. When I can't get five minutes out of you. And Crystal was headed toward it before you even came in the picture. *(To Crystal.)* You always...When you were a baby you ate off my plate, when we were kids you named my fish, when we were teenagers you flirted with my dates on the rare occasions when somebody would ask me out instead of you, and now, this. And all my life I've been so busy making dinner, I never even guessed it was coming. But I'm trying. I'm trying to see what's happening right under my...And I'm looking at my future, and it's pitch black. *(To Judd.)* I don't know if five minutes from now I'm going to fall into your arms and beg you not to leave me and the girls or go get Daddy's gun and blow your fucking head off. I'm fully capable of doing both of those things. I know that. What I don't know is whether I'm capable of doing something reasonable. Because at this moment I can't even think what a reasonable response to all this is. Cannot even imagine it.

(Beat.)

CHARLOTTE: *(To Crystal.)* You want my girls, too, don't you?

CRYSTAL: No.

JUDD: She doesn't want the girls, Charlotte.

CHARLOTTE: Stop defending her. *(To Crystal.)* What else? What else do I have that you want?

CRYSTAL: Nothing. I don't even—

CHARLOTTE: That's because I have nothing else.

CRYSTAL: I don't want your life, Charlotte. I want my own life.

CHARLOTTE: You could have had your own life, first with Richard and then with Mac but no, you called it off, Crystal. Well, it's not that hard to figure out why.

CRYSTAL: I didn't call off the wedding. Mac did.

(Beat.)

CHARLOTTE: But at the courthouse you said—

CRYSTAL: I said I'm not going to get married, and mother said don't be crazy, yes you are, and I said the decision is final.

CHARLOTTE: But you looked so calm. We just assumed it was your decision.

CRYSTAL: Well, things aren't always how they look.

CHARLOTTE: Obviously not.

(Charlotte gets out the phone book, looks up a number, and dials it.)

CRYSTAL: What are you doing? Charlotte, please, let's just stop and calm down and have something to eat and pull ourselves together, get a little perspective, because we're both, we're all tired and confused and hungry and please, Charlotte, wait…

(Dorris enters, carrying an old curtain made out of a sheet.)

CHARLOTTE: *(Into the phone.)* Hi, Mac, this is Charlotte. We're all over here at Mother's, and I don't know if you've been trying to call…somebody has…but if you want to talk to Crystal, you should come over here and do it in person.

(She hangs up.)

DORRIS: That was a good idea. I may not need to replace this curtain after all. I think all they need—

CRYSTAL: You knew I didn't want—

CHARLOTTE: Didn't want me to? Let me ask you something. When you were fucking my husband, did you think I wanted you to?

DORRIS: Oh dear.

(Dorris exits.)

CRYSTAL: Is he coming?

CHARLOTTE: I don't know. That was his machine.

(Beat.)

CRYSTAL: Mother needs to eat. People with low blood sugar can't just wait around all day. Mother…*(Realizing she's gone, then calling toward the back of the house.)* Mother! Dinner's ready. *(To Charlotte.)* If he comes, I want to be eating dinner when he gets here.

CHARLOTTE: I'm not finished. And I'm not going to stop when Mama comes back. *(To Judd.)* I want details. I want to know everything. I want to know why.

JUDD: Look, it's not going to happen again, I promise you that, so what does it matter?

CHARLOTTE: It matters to me. If I'm going to go on from here, I need to make sense of all this.

JUDD: By poisoning yourself with information that doesn't do anybody any good? What do you want? What is it you really want here?

CHARLOTTE: I don't know. I want my daughters not to grow up without a father.

JUDD: They're not going to grow up without their father. That's not a question.

CHARLOTTE: It would be if I killed you.

CRYSTAL: Charlotte, don't talk like that.

CHARLOTTE: *(To Crystal.)* I'm not going to kill him. *(To Judd.)* Because I want them to have what I always wanted. To be able to wake up in the middle of the night and know their father is right down the hall and he loves them. Or if not that, at least I want them to know you exist. If they wanted to, they could call you, come visit you, write you letters. Oh my God, when you had your miscarriage, whose baby was it?

CRYSTAL: It was mine!

CHARLOTTE: It was Judd's, wasn't it.

(The phone rings.)

CRYSTAL: No.

(Crystal goes in the kitchen, pulls the base unit out of the wall, brings it to the chopping block, and chops the plug off with the knife. Another phone can be heard, still ringing, offstage, and Crystal exits to the rest of the house, carrying the knife with her.)

JUDD: I swear to you, Charlotte…

CHARLOTTE: Shut up.

(Charlotte is in something of a state of shock, and as she speaks, she will go in the kitchen, throw away the phone, the base unit and the cut cord, wipe off the chopping block, and start rather mechanically preparing dinner. Then the offstage phone will stop, mid-ring.)

CHARLOTTE : I want you to get out of town. You can have all the money that's in my purse, but take the car and go far away and go now. Don't stop by home first because I want to talk to the girls before you do. In a few days call me and we'll see what's happened then. For now, just leave. Please.

JUDD: I need to tell you—

CHARLOTTE: Too late. You got what you needed three weeks ago. I'm telling you what I need now. If you give one tiny damn about what I need.

JUDD: Okay.

(Crystal returns, outwardly calm now, still carrying the knife. Judd picks up his coat and tie and looks for his keys.)

CHARLOTTE: What's Mama doing?

CRYSTAL: She'll be right out.

(Silently, they work on dinner. Then Dorris appears in the doorway, looking a little ashen.)

CHARLOTTE: *(To Crystal.)* That's why he pushed you, isn't it?

JUDD: Where are my keys?

CRYSTAL: No.

DORRIS: Who pushed you?

CRYSTAL: Mama! You hungry?

DORRIS: I'm a little confused. My blood sugar. Could you get me a glass of orange juice?

(Crystal gets the juice.)

CRYSTAL: Are you okay?

(Dorris drinks the juice.)

DORRIS: I think I waited too long to eat. Did Mac push you?

CRYSTAL: No.

DORRIS: Crystal, did you cut all the phone lines? What if there's an emergency?

CRYSTAL: I'm hungry. I'm starving. You want to eat inside? Is it too hot to eat outside?

CHARLOTTE: *(To Judd.)* What now?

DORRIS: No, we can eat outside.

JUDD: I can't find the goddamn keys.

DORRIS: You can't leave, Judd, we're about to eat.

CHARLOTTE: I'm not finished, Crystal.

(As Crystal speaks, she will get out her lipstick. As soon as she finishes speaking, she will put it on.)

CRYSTAL: Then you'll finish later. Right now we're going to eat. All four of us. When Mac gets here we're going to be sitting around the table eating dinner like everything is perfectly normal.

DORRIS: Mac's coming?

CRYSTAL: Mama needs to eat. And she doesn't need to be upset.

(Crystal ushers Dorris outside.)

CHARLOTTE: *(To Judd.)* Okay, but right after we eat, you go.

DORRIS: If Mac's coming there's not enough food. Somebody get the jello.

CRYSTAL: No, Mama, you sit down and start eating. Everything's about to be ruined.

DORRIS: Just let me get the jello.

CRYSTAL: I will get it, Mother. Sit down. Everybody sit down and eat before all the food's ice cold.

(Dorris sits.)

CRYSTAL: Now eat! I'll be right there.

(She gets the jello. Charlotte and Judd sit down, and Crystal scurries around, trying to get dinner on the table.)

CHARLOTTE: *(To Judd.)* Don't sit across from Crystal, don't look at her, and don't imagine her breasts.

JUDD: I won't.

(Dorris and Judd trade places. Crystal joins them and they pause to see if Dorris is going to want to say a blessing.)

DORRIS: *(Holding out her hands.)* Let's have a blessing.

(After a moment's hesitation they all hold hands, bow their heads, and close their eyes. During the blessing, Crystal and Judd will open their eyes, look at each other briefly, then close their eyes again.)

DORRIS: Dear God, we thank you for this food and the loving hands that prepared it. We thank you for bringing us here, blessing our bodies with health and our souls with each other. And we ask you to keep us together always. Amen.

CRYSTAL, CHARLOTTE, AND JUDD: *(Mumbling.)* Amen.

(Beat. They quickly let go of each other's hands. Then nobody moves.)

DORRIS: So. Should we pass to the right or the left?

CRYSTAL: We always pass to the right.

DORRIS: Right. Everybody pass to the right. Judd, make sure you get the biggest piece of chicken.

(They start passing the food, reaching across the table, serving their plates.)

JUDD: Okay.

DORRIS: Two different kinds of potato salad, that's a treat. Like one of those great big hotel buffets.

(Charlotte picks up the fast-food potato salad, takes it in the kitchen, and throws it away.)

DORRIS : Of course homemade is always best. Nothing beats homemade.

(Beat.)

DORRIS: Everybody got everything they need?

(Pause. They eat quietly, tensely. Crystal picks at her food.)

DORRIS: This potato salad sure is good.

CHARLOTTE: It's warm and the potatoes are too hard.

DORRIS: But it's good. I've seen recipes for warm potato salad. It's gourmet.

(Beat.)

DORRIS: It's delicious. That's how they're cooking vegetables now. Crispy. It leaves more of the nutrients in. So it's better for you.

(Beat.)

DORRIS: Mm-mmm. Crystal, have you tried it? Crystal, you're not eating.

CRYSTAL: I'm eating. I'm just eating slowly.

DORRIS: You don't have any chicken. You love chicken. Judd went and got the chicken just for you.

CRYSTAL: I'm going to have chicken in a minute.

DORRIS: Hand Crystal that chicken.

(Charlotte hands Crystal the chicken.)

CRYSTAL: Thanks.

(They all eat in tense silence.)

DORRIS: Judd, that's a nice shirt. You hardly ever wear starched shirts. I love the smell of a man in a starched shirt. Don't you, Charlotte? Smells so clean.

CHARLOTTE: Not if you wash it in human waste.

(Beat.)

DORRIS: *(To Judd.)* Well, so much for starch. Not really all that interesting a subject, is it? No. So. How are things at the garage?

JUDD: Fine. Three wrecks came in yesterday. The strangest thing, one of them, the carburetor was—

(Charlotte clears her throat. She doesn't want to hear it.)

DORRIS: You can always count on people having wrecks, can't you?

JUDD: Yep.

DORRIS: Somebody's always in a hurry, or being careless. Not thinking. Right?

JUDD: Yep.

DORRIS: So is there a particular time of year when people wreck more often than others?

JUDD: Holidays. Or if there's ice, you know, but otherwise it's pretty steady.

DORRIS: Day in, day out, huh?

JUDD: Yep.

DORRIS: It must be nice to look at a wreck and know you can fix it.

JUDD: Unless it's totaled.

DORRIS: Oh. Of course. *(To Charlotte and Crystal.)* Isn't that good, girls, being able to fix wrecks?

(Beat.)

DORRIS: Charlotte, how are things at the hospital?

CHARLOTTE: Two people on my floor died last week.

DORRIS: What a shame. What did they die of?

CHARLOTTE: Mother, I work in the cancer ward. They died of cancer.

DORRIS: It's not like if you have cancer you're immune to everything else.

(Beat.)

DORRIS: They could have choked. They could have had internal hemorrhaging and bled to death. They could have had strokes, heart attacks. *(She notices the potato salad on her fork.)* Ptomaine poisoning! They could have been murdered by some relative who just couldn't wait for their inheritance. Take that plug and...

(She pulls an imaginary plug out of an imaginary wall.)

CHARLOTTE: Well, they both died of cancer.

DORRIS: That's probably best. I mean. I don't know what I mean.

(Beat.)

DORRIS: Crystal? How's your work?

CRYSTAL: We're having a sale.

DORRIS: A sale!

CRYSTAL: End-of-summer crap.

DORRIS: Charlotte, maybe you should take the girls to get some school clothes.

CHARLOTTE: End-of-summer crap?

DORRIS: Well, I'm sure if Crystal helped you, showed you where to look, they could find some pretty—

CHARLOTTE: I don't want to take the girls shopping, Mother. From now on, Judd will take them. Or they'll go by themselves.

DORRIS: You're a good father. *(To Charlotte.)* He's a good father.

(Beat.)

CHARLOTTE: *(To Crystal.)* I've never even seen your breasts!

(Pause.)

CHARLOTTE: I can't even imagine.

(Pause.)

CRYSTAL: They look just like yours.

CHARLOTTE: My God.

(Pause.)

DORRIS: *(Talking quickly, trying desperately to ease the tension.)* I'm afraid you girls both got my breasts. All the women in my family have small breasts, we all do, every last one of us. It's like a curse. Charlotte, I hate to say it, but it looks like your girls will have them too. Of course now people get implants and you'll have to talk them out of that because it's not safe, no matter what anybody says, they'll die of cancer before they're forty. And they got those wonder bras, even wonder bathing suits that are supposed to—

CRYSTAL: Can we please change the subject? If Mac comes, I don't want to be discussing the inadequacies of my breasts.

DORRIS: Of course.

(Beat.)

DORRIS: But they're not inadequate. I mean, at least we don't sag. No riding around in wheelchairs with nipples down to our belly buttons in our old age. Nope. But you're right. Enough of that. *(To Judd.)* Excuse me. You know I don't usually discuss intimate bodily parts at the table. Or anywhere else, for that matter. I'm just…

(Beat. Dorris scratches.)

DORRIS : Y'all could help me out here. This is a little stressful for me. I've still got hives. They *are* hives. Have you ever seen a mosquito bite that big? I haven't.

(Long pause while Dorris scratches.)

DORRIS: Well, I've had enough. Has everybody had enough? I have.

(Dorris takes her plate into the kitchen and exits to the rest of the house. Then Crystal takes her plate in. She is about to come back outside when she realizes what Charlotte and Judd are discussing. She listens from the door.)

CHARLOTTE: *(To Judd.)* Where did Crystal get the idea that her breasts look just like mine?

JUDD: I don't know. You're sisters?

CHARLOTTE: You said it. You told her her breasts looked just like mine, didn't you?

JUDD: If I did, I can't tell you how much I regret it now. The whole thing I…Crystal means nothing to me. It was just a fuck.

CHARLOTTE: You bastard.

(Crystal comes back out to the yard.)

CRYSTAL: Stop it, both of you. Please. Please, just stop. We all need to calm down and talk this out. I think if we could just get it all out on the table, see everything for what it really is…

(Charlotte picks up the bowl of homemade potato salad.)

CHARLOTTE: This is inedible.

(She goes in the kitchen and throws it away. She stands by the garbage can trying to collect herself. For the first time in the play, she is still.)

JUDD: I didn't mean that. About you. I'm sorry. I was just…

(He motions toward Charlotte.)

CRYSTAL: Why don't you go fuck yourself?

JUDD: I didn't mean to hurt you. All I was trying to do in the first place is to stop you from hurting.

CRYSTAL: It was a pity fuck?

JUDD: You know that's not what it was. I needed all the same things you did. But Katie and Andrea need me more. The way Charlotte is, they need me there in the house, and I guess I feel like fixing cars isn't very important in the big picture, but being there for your family, letting your kids know you love them, that is. So it's going to be harder now, but that's what I'm going to try to do. I just hope it's not all shot to hell.

CRYSTAL: But I'm not asking—

JUDD: I know you're not. I just wanted you to know. It's why I can't do what you did today, just walk away. And why, to be honest, I wish you hadn't.

CRYSTAL: I spent the entire morning trying to talk myself out of it. I kept thinking, as soon as I've had my coffee, as soon as my hair's done, as soon as I'm in my wedding dress, once we're at the courthouse, once I see Charlotte. Only this feeling that I was making a mistake didn't go away. So I told him.

JUDD: *(Softly.)* Shit.

CRYSTAL: Because I thought maybe if what happened between you and me wasn't a secret, if it was just one thing that happened one day that I could put behind me instead of always keeping it here *(Her chest.)*. So I could keep it hidden, then it wouldn't feel quite so big inside me, and I'd have more room for Mac.

JUDD: But you knew that marriage wasn't going to work, for reasons that had nothing to do with me.

CRYSTAL: I know that.

JUDD: You knew it three weeks ago. That's why you slept with me.

CRYSTAL: One of the reasons.

JUDD: So why didn't you just leave me out of it and call it off yourself?

CRYSTAL: I don't know. The same reason cancer patients don't kill themselves. The same reason we all don't put bullets through our brains the day we realize we're not immortal.

JUDD: What?

CRYSTAL: I was hoping. And I was afraid. I didn't want to be alone.

JUDD: Then you should have kept your mouth shut.

CRYSTAL: I needed not to have to spend the rest of my life covering up the truth. I thought I needed that. I don't know what I need.

(Charlotte walks outside and hands Judd the keys.)

CHARLOTTE: *(To Judd.)* It's time for you to go. Crystal and I need to talk in private.

JUDD: You want me to go home?

CHARLOTTE: You don't have a home. Just get on the highway and don't stop driving until you can't keep your eyes open any longer and then get up tomorrow and do the same thing.

JUDD: Fuck. Fuck you both.

(Judd exits.)

CHARLOTTE: *(To Crystal.)* I want to know the truth.

CRYSTAL: I want to tell you the truth. I do. This is good. What happened between me and—

CHARLOTTE: I want to see your breasts.

CRYSTAL: What?

CHARLOTTE: Show me.

CRYSTAL: Charlotte, we're outside. Be reasonable.

CHARLOTTE: Fine. That's a reasonable request. Go inside.

(Crystal goes inside and stops in the kitchen. Charlotte follows her.)

CRYSTAL: Now Charlotte…

CHARLOTTE: Did that, walking inside, did that feel anything like walking to the bed?

CRYSTAL: No.

CHARLOTTE: Full of anticipation? Anxiety? Vulnerability?

CRYSTAL: No.

CHARLOTTE: That's because you were wearing clothes. Take off your clothes.

CRYSTAL: God, Charlotte, I'm not minimizing what I did…

CHARLOTTE: I know how Judd is about breasts.

CRYSTAL: But these things happen…

CHARLOTTE: I want to see what he saw.

CRYSTAL: …and people get over it.

CHARLOTTE: I want to see what he sucked on. Did he suck on your breasts?

CRYSTAL: They go on with their lives like everything was normal.

CHARLOTTE: Did my husband suck on your breasts?

CRYSTAL: Just barely.

CHARLOTTE: Take off your dress.

CRYSTAL: They stay married, even. They raise children together.

CHARLOTTE: Shut up. I'm trying to concentrate. Take it off.

CRYSTAL: They put it behind them.

CHARLOTTE: Take it off, Crystal, before I rip it off.

CRYSTAL: They get it out in the open and then they forgive each other and just pretend it never happened. We could do that. We could. Please.

(As she speaks, she unzips her dress and lets it fall to the floor. She is wearing a strapless bra and a half slip, and her body is very beautiful.)

CHARLOTTE: They lie to the police.

CRYSTAL: Right! Anything!

CHARLOTTE: They cover for each other, even when there's murder involved.

CRYSTAL: Of course they do. That's what families…It's how they keep…

(Beat.)

CHARLOTTE: Take off your bra.

CRYSTAL: Or else they fall apart.

(Silence. Crystal hesitates, then unclasps it and lets it fall. Charlotte looks at her for several moments.)

CHARLOTTE: You're not like me at all. Not at all.

(Pause. Then Crystal rushes to Charlotte, sobbing, and throws her arms around her. Charlotte leaves her own arms at her side.)

CRYSTAL: Yes I am. Charlotte, I'm your sister. I'm your flesh and blood, your family. Please.

(With one hand, Charlotte touches Crystal's back, an attempt at a hug. Crystal is still sobbing. Then, with her other hand, Charlotte picks up the knife off the kitchen counter and stabs Crystal in the back, puncturing her heart. Crystal slumps to the floor. They look at each other. Crystal loses consciousness. Long pause.)

CHARLOTTE: Mama.

(Pause. Dorris appears in the doorway. When she sees Crystal, she covers her mouth with one hand.)

CHARLOTTE: I need your help.

(Dorris brings her other hand to her mouth.)

(The lights fade to black.)

END OF PLAY

Trying To Find Chinatown
by David Henry Hwang

BIOGRAPHY

David Henry Hwang won the 1988 Tony, Drama Desk, Outer Critics Circle and John Gassner awards and the 1991 L.A. Drama Critics Circle Award for his Broadway debut, *M. Butterfly*, which has since been produced in some three dozen countries around the world. His one-act play, *Bondage*, premiered in Actor's Theatre of Louisville's 1992 Humana Festival. He is the author of *F.O.B., The Dance and the Railroad, Family Devotions, The House of Sleeping Beauties* and *The Sound of a Voice*, all of which were produced at the New York Shakespeare Festival. His *Rich Relations* premiered in 1986 at Second Stage. He wrote the libretto for Philip Glass's opera *The Voyage* (1992 Metropolitan Opera House premiere). He previously collaborated with Glass and designer Jerome Sirlin on *1,000 Airplanes on the Roof*. Born in Los Angeles in 1957, Mr. Hwang attended Stanford and the Yale School of Drama.

ORIGINAL PRODUCTION

Trying To Find Chinatown was first performed at the 1996 Humana Festival of New American Plays, March, 1996. It was directed by Paul McCrane with the following cast:

Benjamin . . . . Richard Thompson
Ronnie . . . . Zar Acayan

and the following production staff:

Scenic Designer . . . . Paul Owen
Costume Designer . . . . Kevin R. McLeod
Lighting Designer . . . . T.J. Gerckens
Sound Designer . . . . Martin R. Desjardins
Properties Manager . . . . Ron Riall
Stage Manager . . . . Julie A. Richardson
Dramaturg . . . . .Michael Bigelow Dixon
New York Casting Arrangements . . . . Laura Richin Casting
Original Violin Music . . . . Derek Reeves

CHARACTERS

BENJAMIN: A Caucasian male, early-20s.
RONNIE: An Asian American male, mid-20s, a musician.

PLACE

A street corner on the Lower East Side, New York City. The present.

NOTE ON MUSIC

Obviously, it would be foolish to require that the actor portraying "Ronnie" perform the specified violin music live. The score of this play can be played on tape over the house speakers, and the actor can feign playing the violin using a bow treated with soap. However, in order to effect a convincing illusion, it is desirable that the actor possess some familiarity with the violin, or at least another stringed instrument.

TRYING TO FIND
CHINATOWN

Darkness. Over the house speakers, fade in Hendrix-like virtuoso rock 'n' roll riffs—heavy feedback, distortion, phase shifting, wah-wah—amplified over a tiny Fender pug-nose.

Lights fade up to reveal that the music's being played over a solid-body electric violin by Ronnie, a Chinese American male in his mid-20s, dressed in retro-60s clothing, with a few requisite 90s body mutilations. He's playing on a sidewalk for money, his violin case open before him, change and a few stray bills having been left by previous passers-by.

Enter Benjamin, early-20s, blonde, blue-eyed, looking like a Midwestern tourist in the big city. He holds a scrap of paper in his hands, scanning street signs for an address. He pauses before Ronnie, listens for awhile. With a truly bravura run, Ronnie concludes the number, falls to his knees, gasping. Benjamin applauds.

BENJAMIN: Good. That was really great. *(Pause.)* I didn't...I mean, a fiddle...I mean, I'd heard them at square dances, on country stations and all, but I never...wow, this must really be New York City!
(He applauds, starts to walk on. Still on his knees, Ronnie clears his throat loudly.)
BENJAMIN: Oh, I...you're not just doing this for your health, right?
(He reaches in his pocket, pulls out a couple of coins. Ronnie clears his throat again.)
BENJAMIN: Look, I'm not a millionaire, I'm just...
(Benjamin pulls out his wallet, removes a dollar bill. Ronnie nods his head, gestures towards the violin case, as he sits on the sidewalk, takes out a pack of cigarettes, lights one.)
RONNIE: And don't call it a "fiddle," OK?
BENJAMIN: Oh. Well, I didn't mean to—
RONNIE: You sound like a wuss. A hick. A dipshit.

BENJAMIN: It just slipped out. I didn't really—

RONNIE: If this was a fiddle, I'd be sitting here with a cob pipe, stomping my cowboy boots and kicking up hay. Then I'd go home and fuck my cousin.

BENJAMIN: Oh! Well, I don't really think—

RONNIE: Do you see a cob pipe? Am I fucking my cousin?

BENJAMIN: Well, no, not at the moment, but—

RONNIE: All right. Then this is a violin, you hand over the money, and I ignore the insult, herein endeth the lesson.

(Pause.)

BENJAMIN: Look, a dollar's more than I've ever given to a…to someone asking for money.

RONNIE: Yeah, well, this is New York. Welcome to the cost of living.

BENJAMIN: What I mean is, maybe in exchange, you could help me—?

RONNIE: Jesus Christ! Do you see a sign around my neck reading, "Big Apple Fucking Tourist Bureau?"

BENJAMIN: I'm just looking for an address, I don't think it's far from here, maybe you could…?

(Ronnie snatches the scrap of paper from Benjamin.)

RONNIE: You're lucky I'm such a goddamn softie. *(He looks at the paper.)* Oh, fuck you. Just suck my dick, you and the cousin you rode in on.

BENJAMIN: I don't get it! What are you—?

RONNIE: Eat me. You know exactly what I—

BENJAMIN: I'm just asking for a little—

RONNIE: "13 Doyers St.?" Like you don't know where that is?

BENJAMIN: Of course I don't know! That's why I'm asking—

RONNIE: C'mon, you trailer-park refugee. You don't know that's Chinatown?

BENJAMIN: Sure I know that's Chinatown.

RONNIE: I know you know that's Chinatown.

BENJAMIN: So? That doesn't mean I know where Chinatown—

RONNIE: So why is it that you picked *me*, of all the street musicians in the City—to point you in the direction of Chinatown? Lemme guess—is it the earring? No, I don't think so. The Hendrix riffs? Guess again, you fucking moron.

BENJAMIN: Now, wait a minute. I see what you're—

RONNIE: What are you gonna ask me next? Where you can find the best dim sum in the City? Whether I can direct you to a genuine opium den? Or do I happen to know how you can meet Miss Saigon for a night of nookie-nookie followed by a good old-fashioned ritual suicide? *(He picks up his violin.)* Now, get your white ass off my sidewalk. One dollar doesn't even begin to make up for all this aggravation. Why don't you go back home and race bullfrogs, or whatever it is you do for—?

BENJAMIN: Brother, I can absolutely relate to your anger. Righteous rage, I suppose would be a more appropriate term. To be marginalized, as we are, by a white racist patriarchy, to the point where the accomplishments of our people are obliterated from the history books, this is cultural genocide of the first order, leading to the fact that you must do battle with all of Euro-America's emasculating and brutal stereotypes of Asians—the opium den, the sexual objectification of the Asian female, the exoticized image of a tourist's Chinatown which ignores the exploitation of workers, the failure to unionize, the high rate of mental illness and tuberculosis—against these, each day, you rage, no, not as a victim, but as a survivor, yes, brother, a glorious warrior survivor!

(Silence.)

RONNIE: Say what?

BENJAMIN: So, I hope you can see that my request is not—

RONNIE: Wait, wait.

BENJAMIN: —motivated by the sorts of racist assumptions—

RONNIE: But, but where...how did you learn all that?

BENJAMIN: All what?

RONNIE: All that—you know—oppression stuff—tuberculosis...

BENJAMIN: It's statistically irrefutable. TB occurs in the community at a rate—

RONNIE: Where did *you* learn it?

BENJAMIN: Well...I took Asian American studies. In college.

RONNIE: Where did you go to college?

BENJAMIN: University of Wisconsin. Madison.

RONNIE: Madison, Wisconsin?

BENJAMIN: That's not where the bridges are, by the way.

RONNIE: Huh? Oh, right...

BENJAMIN: You wouldn't believe the number of people who—

RONNIE: They have Asian American studies in Madison, Wisconsin? Since when?

BENJAMIN: Since the last Third World Unity sit-in and hunger strike. *(Pause.)* Why do you look so surprised? We're down.

RONNIE: I dunno. It just never occurred to me, the idea of Asian students in the Midwest going on a hunger strike.

BENJAMIN: Well, a lot of them had midterms that week, so they fasted in shifts. *(Pause.)* The Administration never figured it out. The Asian students put that "They all look alike" stereotype to good use.

RONNIE: OK, so they got Asian American studies. That still doesn't explain—

BENJAMIN: What?

RONNIE: What *you* were doing taking it?

BENJAMIN: Just like everyone else. I wanted to explore my roots. After a lifetime of assimilation, I wanted to find out who I really am.

(Pause.)

RONNIE: And did you?

BENJAMIN: Sure. I learned to take pride in my ancestors who built the railroads, my Popo who would make me a hot bowl of jok with thousand day-old eggs when the white kids chased me home yelling, "Gook! Chink! Slant-eyes!"

RONNIE: OK, OK, that's enough!

BENJAMIN: Painful to listen to, isn't it?

RONNIE: I don't know what kind of bullshit ethnic studies program they're running over in Wisconsin, but did they bother to teach you that in order to find your Asian "roots," it's a good idea first to be Asian?

(Pause.)

BENJAMIN: Are you speaking metaphorically?

RONNIE: No! Literally! Look at your skin!

(Ronnie grabs Benjamin's hands, holds them up before his face.)

BENJAMIN: You know, it's very stereotypical to think that all Asian skin tones conform to a single hue.

RONNIE: You're white! Is this some kind of redneck joke or something? Am I the first person in the world to tell you this?

BENJAMIN: Oh! Oh! Oh!

RONNIE: I know real Asians are scarce in the Midwest, but…Jesus!

BENJAMIN: No, of course, I…I see where your misunderstanding arises.

RONNIE: Yeah. It's called, "You white."

BENJAMIN: It's just that—in my hometown of Tribune, Kansas, and then at school—see, everyone knows me—so this sort of thing never comes up. *(He offers his hand.)* Benjamin Wong. I forget that a society wedded to racial constructs constantly forces me to explain my very existence.

RONNIE: Ronnie Chang. Otherwise known as, "The BowMan."

BENJAMIN: You see, I was adopted by Chinese American parents at birth. So clearly, I'm an Asian American—

RONNIE: Even though they could put a picture of you in the dictionary next to the definition of "WASP."

BENJAMIN: Well, you can't judge my race by my genetic heritage.

RONNIE: If genes don't determine race, what does?

BENJAMIN: Maybe you'd prefer that I continue in denial, masquerading as a white man?

RONNIE: Listen, you can't just wake up and say, "Gee, I *feel* Black today."

BENJAMIN: Brother, I'm just trying to find what you've already got.

RONNIE: What do I got?

BENJAMIN: A home. With your people. Picketing with the laundry workers. Taking refuge from the daily slights against your masculinity in the noble image of Gwan Gung.

RONNIE: Gwan *who*?

BENJAMIN: C'mon—the Chinese God of warriors and—what do you take me for? There're altars to him up all over the community.

RONNIE: I dunno what community you're talking about, but it's sure as hell not mine.

(Pause.)

BENJAMIN: What do you mean?

RONNIE: I mean, if you wanna call Chinatown *your* community, OK, knock yourself out, learn to use chopsticks. Go ahead, try and find your "roots" in some dim sum parlor with headless ducks hanging in the window. Those places don't tell you a thing about who *I* am.

BENJAMIN: Oh, I get it.

RONNIE: You get what?

BENJAMIN: You're one of those self-hating, *assimilated* Chinese Americans, aren't you?

RONNIE: Oh, Jesus.

BENJAMIN: You probably call yourself, "Oriental," right? Look, maybe I can help you. I have some books I can—

RONNIE: Hey, I read all those Asian identity books when you were still slathering on industrial-strength sunblock. *(Pause.)* Sure, I'm Chinese. But folks like you act like that means something. Like all of a sudden, you know who I am. You think identity's that simple? That you can wrap it all up in a neat package and say, I have ethnicity, therefore I am? All you fucking ethnic fundamentalists. Always looking for easy answers. You say you're looking for identity, but you can't begin to face the real mysteries of the search. So instead, you go skin-deep, and call it a day.

(Pause. Ronnie turns away from Benjamin, starts to play his violin—slow and bluesy.)

BENJAMIN: So what are you? "Just a human being?" That's like saying you *have* no identity. If you asked me to describe my dog, I'd say more than, "He's just a dog."

RONNIE: There're worlds out there, worlds you haven't even begun to understand. Open your eyes. Hear with your ears.

(He holds his violin at chest level, does not attempt to play during the following monologue. As he speaks, a montage of rock and jazz violin tracks fades in and out over the house speakers, bringing to life the styles of music he describes.)

RONNIE: I concede—it was called a fiddle long ago—but that was even before the birth of jazz. When the hollering in the fields, the rank injustice of human bondage, the struggle of God's children against the plagues of the devil's white man, when all these boiled up into that bittersweet brew, called by later generations, the blues. That's when fiddlers like Son Sims held their chin rests at their chests, and sawed away like the hillbillies still do today. And with the coming of ragtime appeared the pioneer Stuff Smith, who sang as he stroked the catgut, with his raspy, Louis Armstrong-voice—gruff and sweet like the timbre of horsehair riding south below the fingerboard, and who finally sailed for Europe to find ears that would hear. Europe—where Stephane Grapelli initiated a magical French violin, to be passed from generation to generation—first he, to Jean-Luc Ponty, then Ponty to Dedier Lockwood. Listening to Grapelli play "A Nightingale Sang in Berkeley Square" is to understand not only the song of birds, but also how they learn to fly, fall in love on the wing, and finally falter one day, to wait for darkness beneath a London street lamp. And Ponty, he showed us how the modern violin man can accompany the shadow of his own lead lines, which cascade, one over another, into some netherworld beyond the range of human hearing. Joe Venutti, Noel Pointer, Sven Asmussen. Even the Kronos Quartet with their arrangement of "Purple Haze." Now, tell me, could any legacy be more rich, more crowded with mythology and heroes to inspire pride? What can I say if the banging of a gong or the clinking of a pickax on the Transcontinental Railroad fails to move me even as much as one note, played through the violin MIDI controller of Michael Urbaniak?

(Ronnie puts his violin to his chin, begins to play a jazz composition of his own invention.)

RONNIE: Does it have to sound like Chinese opera before people like you decide that I know who I am?

(Benjamin stands for a long moment, listening to Ronnie play. Then, he drops his dollar into the case, turns and exits.)

(Ronnie continues to play a long moment. Then Benjamin enters, illuminated in his own special. He sits on the floor of the stage, his feet dangling off the lip. As he speaks, Ronnie continues playing his tune, which becomes underscoring

for Benjamin's monologue. As the music continues, does it slowly begin to reflect the influence of Chinese music?)

BENJAMIN: When I finally found Doyers St., I scanned the buildings for Number 13. Walking down an alley where the scent of freshly-steamed char siu bao lingered in the air, I felt immediately that I had entered a world where all things were finally familiar. *(Pause.)* An old woman bumped me with her shopping bag—screaming to her friend in Cantonese, though they walked no more than a few inches apart. Another man—shouting to a vendor in Sze-Yup. A youth, in a white undershirt, perhaps a recent newcomer, bargaining with a grocer in Hokkien. I walked through this ocean of dialects, breathing in the richness with deep gulps, exhilarated by the energy this symphony brought to my step. And when I finally saw the number 13, I nearly wept at my good fortune. An old tenement, paint peeling, inside walls no doubt thick with a century of grease and broken dreams—and yet, to me, a temple—the house where my father was born. I suddenly saw it all: Gung Gung, coming home from his 16-hour days pressing shirts he could never afford to own, bringing with him candies for my father, each sweet wrapped in the hope of a better life. When my father left the ghetto, he swore he would never return. But he had, this day, in the thoughts and memories of his son, just six months after his death. And as I sat on the stoop, I pulled a hua-moi from my pocket, sucked on it, and felt his spirit returning. To the place where his ghost, and the dutiful hearts of all his descendants, would always call home.

(He listens for a long moment.)

And I felt an ache in my heart for all those lost souls, denied this most important of revelations: to know who they truly are.

(Benjamin sits on the stage, sucking his salted plum, and listening to the sounds around him. Ronnie continues to play. The two remain oblivious of one another.)
(Lights fade slowly to black.)

END OF PLAY

Reverse Transcription

Six Playwrights Bury a Seventh
A Ten-Minute Play That's Nearly Twenty Minutes Long

by Tony Kushner

BIOGRAPHY

Tony Kushner is the author of *A Bright Room Called Day*, *The Illusion* (freely adapted from Corneille), *Angels in America, A Gay Fantasia on National Themes, Part One: Millennium Approaches and Part Two: Perestroika,* and adaptations of Goethe's *Stella,* Brecht's *The Good Person of Setzuan* and Ansky's *The Dybbuk.* He was last at Actors Theatre of Louisville in 1994 for the premiere of *Slavs! (Thinking About The Longstanding Problems of Virtue and Happiness),* which has now been performed in theatres around the United States, in London, Berlin, Vienna and Paris; and which won a 1995 Obie award. A collection of recent writings, titled *Thinking About The Longstanding Problems of Virtue and Happiness,* was published by Theatre Communications Group. Mr. Kushner was born in Manhattan and grew up in Lake Charles, Louisiana. He has a BA from Columbia University and an MFA in directing from New York University.

ORIGINAL PRODUCTION

Reverse Transcription was first performed at the 1996 Humana Festival of New American Plays, March, 1996. It was directed by Tony Kushner with the following cast:

Hautflote	John Leonard Thompson
Aspera	Jennifer Hubbard
Biff	Daniel Oreskes
Happy	Christopher Evan Welch
Ottoline	Fanni Green
Flatty	Fred Major
Ding	

and the following production staff:

Scenic Designer	Paul Owen
Costume Designer	Kevin R. McLeod
Lighting Designer	T.J. Gerckens
Sound Designer	Martin R. Desjardins
Properties Manager	Ron Riall
Stage Manager	Cind Senensieb
Dramaturg	Liz Engelman
New York Casting Arrangements	Laura Richin Casting

CHARACTERS

HAUTFLOTE: A playwright in his late thirties. He writes beautiful plays everyone admires; he has a following and little financial success. He was Ding's best friend, the executor of his will and his wishes.

ASPERA: A playwright in her early thirties. She writes fierce splendidly intelligent challenging plays, frequently with lesbian characters, and cannot get an American theater to produce her for love or money. So she lives in London where she is acclaimed. She is cool and is beginning to sound British.

BIFF: A playwright in his late thirties. Scruffy, bisexual, one success, several subsequent failures, cannot stay away from political themes though his analysis is not rigorous. He is overdue; he should be home, writing; he should not be here.

HAPPY: A playwright in his late thirties. His early plays were widely admired, then one big success and he's become a Hollywood writer, TV mostly, rich now, a little bored, but very happy. He plans to go back to writing for the theater someday.

OTTOLINE: A playwright in her fifties. African-American, genuinely great hugely influential experimentalist whom everyone adores but who is now languishing in relative obscurity and neglect, though she continues to write prolifically. She is the best writer of the bunch and the least well remunerated. Hers is a deep bitterness; the surface is immensely gracious. She teaches playwrights and has a zoological fascination, watching them. Ding was her protégé, sort of. She is an old friend of Flatty's.

FLATTY: A playwright in his late forties. Colossally rich. An easy target for negativity of all kinds though he is in fact a good writer, hugely prolific, very hard-working and generous to his fellow 'wrights.

DING: A dead playwright wrapped in a winding sheet. A very talented writer, whom everyone admired for wildly different reasons.

PLACE

A cemetary on Abel's Hill, Martha's Vineyard, in December near midnight.

NOTE

Abel's Hill is a real place, a spectacularly beautiful mostly 19th Century Yankee graveyard; it's way too expensive for any mortal to get a plot in it now. Lillian Hellman and Dashiell Hammett are buried there. So is John Belushi, whose tombstone kept getting stolen by fans till Dan Ackroyd put a gigantic boulder on Belushi's grave, too huge for anyone to lift. From the crest of the hill you can see the ocean.

Everyone has shovels, and several have bottles of various liquors.

The night is beautiful and very cold.

They are writers so they love words. Their speech is precise, easy, articulate; they are showing off a little. They are at that stage of drunk, right before sloppy, where you are eloquent, impressing yourself. They are making pronouncements, aware of their wit; this mustn't be pinched, crabbed, dour, effortful. They are having fun on this mad adventure; they relish its drama. Underneath is a very deep grief.

They all really loved Ding.

REVERSE TRANSCRIPTION

High atop Abel's Hill, a cemetery on Martha's Vineyard. Just athwart the crest. Tombstones all around. As the voice of the playwright is heard on tape, with an accompanying obligato of a typewriter's clattering, Biff, Happy, Aspera, Ottoline and Flatty gather, facing downhill. HAUTFLOTE appears, carrying the body of Ding, wrapped in a winding sheet. HAUTFLOTE places the body before them, then runs off, then returns with six shovels. The other playwrights look about uneasily, and then sit. They have come to bury him illegally. It's nearly midnight.

THE VOICE OF THE PLAYWRIGHT

DRAMATIS PERSONAE: Seven characters, all playwrights. BIFF, scruffy, bisexual, one success, several subsequent failures, cannot stay away from political themes though his analysis is not rigorous. He is overdue; he should be home, writing; he should not be here. HAPPY, his early plays were widely admired, then one big success an he's become a Hollywood writer, TV mostly, rich now, a little bored, but very...um, well, happy. He plans to go back to writing for the theater someday. ASPERA writes fierce splendidly intelligent challenging plays, frequently with lesbian characters, and she cannot get an American theater to produce her for love or money. So she lives in London where she is acclaimed. OTTOLINE, African-American, genuinely great hugely influential experimentalist whom everyone adores but who is now languishing in relative obscurity and neglect, the best writer of the bunch and the least well remunerated. She is an old friend of FLATTY, colossally successful. colossally rich. An easy target for negativity of all kinds though he is in fact a good writer, hugely prolific. HAUTFLOTE writes beautiful experimental plays, has a small loyal following and little financial success; the best friend and the executor of the estate of DING, a dead playwright wrapped in a winding sheet, very talented, whom everyone admired for wildly different reasons. Seven characters are too many for a ten-minute play. It'll be twenty minutes long! Fuck it. One of them is dead and the others can all talk fast. The play takes place in Abel's Hill cemetery, a spectacularly beautiful, mostly 19th Century Yankee graveyard, way too expensive for any mortal to get a plot in it now. On Abel's Hill, Martha's Vineyard, in December near midnight.

(When the voice is finished, Hautflote goes to a nearby headstone, on the side of which is a light switch. He flicks it on; a full moon appears in the sky.)

HAUTFLOTE: Ah!

(The play begins.)

HAUTFLOTE: Here. We should start digging.

ASPERA: Athwart the crest. Facing the sea. As Ding demanded.

OTTOLINE: Isn't this massively illegal?

FLATTY: Trespass, destruction of private property, destruction of a historical landmark I shouldn't wonder, conveyance of tissue, i.e. poor Ding, in an advanced state of morbidity, on public transportation...

HAUTFLOTE: He's been *preserved*. He's hazardous to no one's health.

(Small pause.)

He traveled here in a steamer trunk. The porters helped.

BIFF: *(Apostrophizing.)* O please come to me short sweet simple perfect *idea*. A seed, a plot.

HAUTFLOTE: He's under a deadline.

BIFF: I'm doomed.

HAUTFLOTE: Now shoulder your shovels...

BIFF: There's no dignity, have you noticed? In being *this*. An American playwright. What is that?

OTTOLINE: Well, we drink.

HAPPY: No one really drinks now. None of us, at least not publicly.

FLATTY: I can't remember something.

HAPPY: We're...*(Looking for the word.)*

FLATTY: A name.

HAPPY: Healthier!

HAUTFLOTE: What name?

FLATTY: The name of the country that makes me despair.

HAPPY: But tonight we are drunk.

BIFF: In honor of Ding.

HAUTFLOTE: What letter does it begin with?

BIFF: Poor Ding.

(They all look at Ding. Little pause.)

ASPERA: "And Poor Ding Who Is Dead."

(Little pause.)

FLATTY: R.

HAUTFLOTE: Rwanda.

FLATTY: *That's* it.

OTTOLINE: How could you *forget*, Flatty? Rwanda?

FLATTY: I've never had a head for names. Not in the news much, anymore, Rwanda.

OTTOLINE: We are afraid to stick the shovel in.

HAUTFLOTE: Yes.

OTTOLINE: Believing it to be a desecration.

HAUTFLOTE: Of this holy earth.

OTTOLINE: Not *holy*: Pure. Authentic.

HAPPY: Yankee.

OTTOLINE: Pilgrim.

HAPPY: Puritan.

OTTOLINE: Originary. Forefatherly.

ASPERA: Oh fuck me, "forefatherly"; John Belushi's buried here!

FLATTY: And he had enough drugs in him when he died to poison all the waters from here to Nantucket.

OTTOLINE: And the people steal his tombstone.

FLATTY: No!

OTTOLINE: Or the hill keeps swallowing it up. It doesn't rest in peace. A pretender, you see.

ASPERA: Lillian Hellman's buried here. She's a playwright.

HAUTFLOTE: Appropriate or no it's what Ding wanted.

OTTOLINE: And that's another thing. It cost two hundred thirty seven dollars and fifty cents for a round trip ticket. From New York. This is an *island*. Martha's Vineyard is an *island!* Did Ding *realize* that? One has to *ferry* across. Fucking Ding. Maybe *you all* have money. For ferry passage. I don't have money. I've got no money.

FLATTY: I told you I'd pay for you.

OTTOLINE: Well we all know *you've* got money.

BIFF: O come to me short sweet simple idea!

FLATTY: I want something magical to happen.

BIFF: A plot. The Horseleech hath two daughters. It's a start. And these daughters...Do...What?

HAPPY: They cry!

OTTOLINE: Give, give!

BIFF: Brecht in exile circumnavigated the globe. Berlin. Skovbostrand.

Stockholm. Helsinki. Leningrad. Moscow. Vladivostock. Manila. L.A.. Quick stop in D.C. to visit the HUAC. New York. Paris. Zurich. Salzburg. Prague. Berlin. An American playwright, what is that? Never in exile, always in extremis. The list of cities: AIDS, loss, fear of infection, unsafe sex he says gazing upon the corpse of a fallen comrade, I fuck men and women. I dream my favorite actor has been shot by the police, I dream I shoot Jesse Helms in the head and it doesn't kill him...

FLATTY: Eeewww, *politics.*

BIFF: I dream we are intervening in Bosnia merely to give Germany hegemony over Eastern Europe. Why, I dream myself in my dream asking myself, do you dream that? You do not dream a play, you *write* a play. And this play is due, and there's *(Pointing to Ding's corpse.)* the deadline. I write in my notebook that I am glad we are sending troops to former Yugoslavia but I *(He makes the "in quotes" gesture with his fingers.)* "inadvertently" spell troops "T-R-O-U-P-E-S" as in troupes as in theatrical troupes, traveling players, we are sending *troupes* to former Yugoslavia.

HAUTFLOTE: I don't think we can avoid it any longer. The digging.

FLATTY: I imagine it's worth serious jail time for us all.

HAPPY: Incarcerated playwrights. Now *that* has dignity. Until it's learned what for.

BIFF: I repulse myself, I am not of this earth, if I were more serious I would be an essayist if I were more observant a novelist more articulate more intelligent a poet more...succinct more *ballsy* a screenwriter and then I could buy an apartment.

HAUTFLOTE: Fuck the public. It's all Ding asked for. He never got his own, alive.

ASPERA: Poor poor Ding.

HAUTFLOTE: He grew obsessed with his cemetery, in his final months. We visited it years ago. On a day trip, we could never afford...to *stay* here. Or anywhere. Or anything. Health Insurance. "Bury me on Abel's Hill." His final words. I think he thought this place would give him a retroactive pedigree.

OTTOLINE: That's it, *pedigree*, not *holiness.* Blood, genes. Of which we playwrights are envious. We're mutts. Amphibians.

ASPERA: Not of the land not of the sea. Not of the page nor of the moment.

HAPPY: Perdurable page. Fleeting moment.

FLATTY: Something magical should happen now.

HAUTFLOTE: Ding wanted to belong. Or rather, he never wanted not to. Or rather he never didn't want to, he *wanted* to not want to, but did. In his final months he grew finical.

ASPERA: When I saw him he wasn't finical, he was horrible. He looked horrible and he screamed at everyone all day and all night and there was no way he could get warm, ever. It was quite a change. I hadn't seen him in months, I was visiting from London WHERE I LIVE, *IN EXILE*, PRODUCED, APPLAUDED, *LAUDED* EVEN and NO ONE IN AMERICA WILL *TOUCH* MY WORK, but anyway he was somehow very very angry but not bitter. One felt envied, but not blamed. At Ding's deathbed.

HAUTFLOTE: Ding Bat. Der Dingle. Ding-An-Sich.

HAPPY: I remember being impressed when I learned that the HIV virus, which has robbed us of our Ding, reads and writes its genetic alphabets backwards, RNA transcribing DNA transcribing RNA, hence *retro*virus, reverse transcription. I'm not gay but I am a Jew and so of course I, too, "read backwards, write backwards"; I think of Hebrew.

FLATTY: You're not gay?

HAPPY: No.

FLATTY: You're *not*?

HAPPY: No.

FLATTY: Everyone thinks you are. Everyone wants to sleep with you. Everyone *Everyone*. Oops. You were saying?

HAPPY: I was saying that in my grief I thought…Well here I attempt a metaphor doomed to fail…I mean here we are, playwrights in a graveyard, here to dig, right? So, digging, I think: HIV, reverse transcribing, dust to dust, writing backwards, Hebrew and the Great and Terrible magic of that backwards alphabet, which runs against the grain, counter to the current of European tradition, heritage, thought: a language of fiery, consuming revelation, of refusal, the proper way, so I was taught, to address oneself to God…*(He puts his hands on Ding's body.)* Perhaps, maybe, this backwards-writing viral nightmare is keeping some secret, subterraneanly affianced to a principle of…Reversals: good reversals and also very bad, where good meets bad, perhaps, the place of mystery where back meets forth, where our sorrow's not the point, where the forward flow of life brutally throws itself into reverse, to reveal…*(He lies alongside the body, curls up to it, head on Ding's shoulder, listening.)* What? Hebrew always looked to me like zipper teeth unzipped. What awesome thing is it we're zipping open? To what do we return when we write in reverse? What's relinquished, what's released? What does it sound like I'm doing here?

ASPERA: It sounds like you're equating Hebrew and AIDS.

HAPPY: I'm…

ASPERA: I'm not Jewish but I am a dyke and I think either way, AIDS equals Hebrew or the reverse, you're in BIG trouble. I'm going to beat you up.

HAPPY: Not *equals*, I…I'm lonely. I'm among playwrights. Back East for the first time in months. So I get to talk. And none of you listen anyway. In Culver City everyone listens, they listen listen listen. They take notes. They take you at your word. You are playwrights. So be inattentive. If you paid attention you'd be novelists.

FLATTY: Aspera has spent five years in London. She's acquired the listening disease.

OTTOLINE: Soon, unless she watches herself, she will be an American playwright no longer but British, her plays will be all nuance, inference.

FLATTY: Yes, nuance, unless she's careful, or a socialist feminist.

BIFF: Everyone hates you Flatty.

OTTOLINE: Oops.

FLATTY: *(Unfazed, not missing a beat.)* And then there will be no nuance at all.

ASPERA: *Does* everyone hate you?

FLATTY: No, they don't.

ASPERA: I live in London now, I'm out of the loop.

FLATTY: They don't hate me, they envy me my money.

ASPERA: *(To Happy.)* I wouldn't *really* beat you up.

FLATTY: I could buy and sell the lot of you. Even *you*, Happy and *you write sitcoms*. There. I've said it. I am wealthy. My plays have made me wealthy. I am richer than essayists, novelists, at least the respectable ones, and all poets ever. Envy is rather *like* hatred but as it's more debilitating to its votaries and votaresses (because it's so inherently undignified) it's of less danger ultimately to its targets.

BIFF: I don't envy your money. I envy your reviews.

HAUTFLOTE: I think we should dig now and bury Ding. This ground is patrolled. The night doesn't last forever. Ding's waiting.

OTTOLINE: *(Softly, firmly.)* Ding's dead. I love this place. It was worth two hundred and thirty seven dollars and fifty cents to get here. Yes Flatty you can pay my way. Send me a check. Biff's got a point. It's the reviews, isn't it. I've worked tirelessly for decades. Three at least. What I have done no one has ever done and no one does it nearly so well. But what I do is break the vessels because they never fit me right and I despise their elegance and I like the sound the breaking makes, it's a new music. What I do is make mess apparent or make apparent messes, I cannot tell which myself I signal disenfranchisement, dysfunction, disinheritance well I *am* a black woman what do they expect it's hard stuff but it's life but I am *perverse* I do not want my stories straight up the narrative the narrative the miserable fucking narrative the universe is post-Cartesian post-Einsteinian it's not at any rate what it's post-to-be let's throw some curve balls already who cares if they never cross the plate it's hard too hard for folks to apprehend easy so I get no big money reviews and no box office and I'm broke, I'm fifty or sixty or maybe I've turned eighty, I collected the box at the Cafe Cinno yes I am THAT old, and poor but no matter, I have a great talent for poverty. Oblivion, on the other hand, scares me. Death. And this may shock you but *(To Flatty.)* I ENVY you…your RENOWN. *(Roaring.) I DON'T WANT ANOTHER OBIE! I want a hit! I want to hit a home run! I WANT A MARQUEE!* I'm too old to be ashamed of my hunger.

BIFF: O come to me short sweet *(He blows a raspberry.)*. There's just no dignity. I am oppressed by theatre critics.

FLATTY: I gave up on dignity *years* ago. I am prolific. That's my revenge. If you want dignity you should marry a lighting designer.

OTTOLINE: Perhaps now we have worn out our terror, or at least winded it.

HAUTFLOTE: At darkest midnight December in the bleak midwinter athwart the crest of Abel's Hill on Martha's Vineyard six moderately inebriated playwrights stood shovels poised to inter…

FLATTY: Illegally.

HAUTFLOTE: …the earthly remains of a seventh.

HAPPY: Who might at least have agreed to the convenience of a cremation.

HAUTFLOTE: Being a creature of paper as well as of the fleeting moment Ding naturally had a horror of fire. *I knew him best.* For a long time now. I loved him.

OTTOLINE: We all did.

HAUTFLOTE: Yet not one of us dares break ground.

HAPPY: Wind perhaps, but never ground.

ASPERA: Wind for sure but not the Law. But is it the law or what's underground which immobilizes us? Incarceration or an excess of freedom? Enchainment or liberation? For who knows what dreams may come? Who knows what's underneath? Who knows if anything is, if the shovel will strike stone, or pay dirt, or nothing whatsoever?

BIFF: It's the Nothing stopping me. I can speak only for myself.

FLATTY: Bad thing in a playwright.

BIFF: The horseleech hath two daughters. There's a play in there, somewhere, of course. I used to say: it won't come out. Fecal or something, expulsive metaphor. I was stuffed, full and withholding. In more generous times. Before the fear…of the Deficit, before the Balanced Budget became the final face of the Angel of the Apocalypse. Now instead I say: I'm not going to go there. A geographical metaphor. Why? *I'm nearly forty* is one explanation. *"There"* meaning…That bleachy bone land. Into that pit. That plot. To meet that deadline.

OTTOLINE: When is the play actually due?

BIFF: Day after yesterday.

HAPPY: Rehearsals starting...?

BIFF: Start*ed*.

ASPERA: What, without a script?

BIFF: They're *improvising*.
(*Everyone shudders.*)

FLATTY: You shouldn't be here! You should be home writing!

BIFF: Did I mention how much I hate you, Flatty.

FLATTY: Marry a lighting designer. It worked for me. Sobered me right up.

HAPPY: I never meant...This reverse transcription thing. I'll work on it.

ASPERA: You do that.

HAPPY: I never meant to equate Hebrew and...It's just the words: reverse transcription. *Thinking* about it. Something I can't help doing. Writing began with the effort to record speech. All writing is an attempt to fix intangibles—thought, speech, what the eye observes—fixed on clay tablets, in stone, on paper. Writers *capture*. We playwrights on the other hand write or rather "wright" to set these free again. Not inscribing, not *de*-scribing but...*ex*-scribing (?)..."W-R-I-G-H-T," that archaism, because it's something earlier we do, cruder, something one does with one's mitts, one's paws. To claw words up...!
(*Happy falls to his knees beside Ding, and starts to dig with his hands.*)

HAPPY: To startle words back into the air again, to...evanesce. It is...unwriting, to do it is to die, yes, but. A lively form of doom.

ASPERA: Ah, so now you are equating...

HAPPY: It's not about *equation*. It's about the transmutation of horror into meaning.

ASPERA: And doomed to fail.

HAPPY: Dirty work...(*He shows his hands.*)

ASPERA: A mongrel business. This Un-earthing.

HAUTFLOTE: For which we Un-earthly are singularly fit. Now or never.

BIFF: I'm nearly forty. My back hurts.

FLATTY: Whose doesn't? No dignity but in our labors.
(*They hoist their shovels.*)

ASPERA: Good night old Ding. Rest easy baby. And flights of self-dramatizing hypochondriacal hypersensitive self-pitying paroxysmical angels saddlebag you off to sleep.

BIFF: (*Apostrophizing Ding's corpse.*) Oh Dog Weary.

HAUTFLOTE: Many of these graves are cenotaphs, you know. Empty tombs, honorifics. Sailors lost on whalers, lost at sea, no body ever found, air and memory interred instead. All other headstones in the graveyard peristalith-ic to these few empty tombs, whose ghostly drama utterly overwhelms The Real.

OTTOLINE: Dig. Shovel tips to earth.

(*They are.*)

OTTOLINE: The smell of earth will rise to meet us. Our nostrils fill with dark brown, roots ends, decomposing warmth and manufactory, earthworm action. The loam.

FLATTY: I don't want to go to jail. Doesn't David Mamet live around here some-where?

OTTOLINE: Push in.

(*They do.*)

END OF PLAY

What I Meant Was
by Craig Lucas

For Connie Weinstock

"...but he would have us remember most of all
to be enthusiastic over the night,
not only for the sense of wonder
it alone has to offer, but also

because it needs our love."

— W.H. Auden, "In Memory of Sigmund Freud"

BIOGRAPHY

Craig Lucas is the author of *Missing Persons* (1995 Drama Desk nominee for best play), *Reckless, Blue Window, Three Postcards* (Burns Mantle Theatre Yearbook, best musical 1986-87), *Prelude To A Kiss* (Tony nomination for best play, 1990), *God's Heart* and *The Dying Gaul*. With director Norman René, he conceived *Marry Me A Little* (fashioned from 17 previously unpublished Sondheim songs) and they worked on four films — *Blue Window, Longtime Companion* (Audience Award, 1990 Sundance Film Festival), *Prelude To A Kiss* and *Reckless*. Mr. Lucas has written two opera texts with composer Gerald Busby, *Breedlove* and *Orpheus in Love*. A graduate of Boston University, where he studied with poets Anne Sexton and George Starbuck, he is the recipient of numerous awards including an Outer Critics Circle Award, the L.A. Drama Critics Award, an Obie Award and Rockefeller and Guggenheim Fellowships.

HUMANA FESTIVAL PRODUCTION

What I Meant Was was first performed at the 1996 Humana Festival of New American Plays, March, 1996. It was directed by Jon Jory with the following cast:

Fritzie	Allen Jeffrey Rein
J. Fred	Bob Burrus
Helen	Peggy Cowles
Nana	Adale O'Brien

and the following production staff:

Scenic Designer	Paul Owen
Costume Designer	Kevin R. McLeod
Lighting Designer	T.J. Gerckens
Sound Designer	Martin R. Desjardins
Properties Manager	Ron Riall
Stage Manager	Carey Upton
Dramaturg	Liz Engelman
New York Casting Arrangements	Laura Richin Casting

CHARACTERS

HELEN, 49
J. FRED, her husband, 47
FRITZIE, their son, 17
NANA, Helen's mother, 77

PLACE

A dinner table in Columbia, Maryland, 1968.

WHAT I MEANT WAS

Helen, J. Fred, Nana and Fritzie are at the dinner table in their suburban kitchen. All but Fritzie are frozen, reaching for plates, mid-conversation. Fritzie looks front; he wears jeans and a flannel shirt, untucked.

FRITZIE: It's 1968 and we're at the dinner table in Columbia, Maryland — about 18 miles southwest of downtown Baltimore. Upstairs on my parents' dresser is a photograph inscribed to me from J. Edgar Hoover the year I was born. My mother has gone over the faded ink with a ballpoint pen so you can be sure to still read it. On this wall in another eight years will hang a letter to my mother from Gerald Ford thanking her for her letter of support. Right now we're in the middle of discussing the length of my hair and the clothes I have taken to wearing. The year before this I painted my entire bedroom black. Here then is everything we meant to say.
(The others unfreeze; they calmly eat their food and affectionately address one another throughout.)

J. FRED: What I think is probably at the root of our discomfort with your favoring long hair and denim is that for your mother and me and also for Nana, because we all survived the Great Depression and in some way feel we triumphed over that — coming from the working class and from immigrant stock, and because so much effort went into that struggle...

FRITZIE: Yes.

J. FRED: ...and we know in a way that you probably never will know what it means to go hungry and to have to work with your hands...

FRITZIE: Probably not.

HELEN: Let's hope not.

J. FRED: ...it seems an affront to our values to see you purposely dressing like a hobo. For that's what denim is, the costume of laborers, the unemployed. When we have seen so many people forced into that position very much against their will.

FRITZIE: I can understand that.

HELEN: And for dad's generation and mine, the idea of protesting a war which our own government has deemed to be necessary, much less desecrating our flag or burning your draft card, again flies in the face of so much we consider essential to our being.

FRITZIE: Yes.

HELEN: I know that a time will come when we will all look back and we'll say, "Perhaps this war was ill-advised," and, "Wasn't that quaint that we were so upset about the way Fritzie dressed," and we will recognize that we were probably as upset about the fact that you were growing up and we were going to have to let you go as we were about your hair which, in the final analysis, is absurdly superficial.

J. FRED: Yes, and your mother and I were also trying to grapple, in admittedly inchoate fashion, with the subterranean knowledge that you were, and are, homosexual.

FRITZIE: I know.

HELEN: And we didn't want you to live a lonely, persecuted existence which, after all, is all we were ever told about the lives of gay people.

FRITZIE: And I know, Dad, that I most likely made you feel in some way personally culpable, as if my sexual orientation were some cruel whim of fate, implicitly criticizing you for having been a special agent for the F.B.I. which did so much to help contribute to our national perception of gays as threats to society.

J. FRED: Of course, I can see now with the benefit of hindsight, and the education which you have so patiently provided, that my activities in the bureau, though they may have added further burdens to the lives of many gays already freighted with discriminatory laws and at least one whole millennium worth of religious persecution, didn't actually make you gay.

FRITZIE: No.

NANA: But you know, what I notice in all of this: Fritzie is struggling with the normal tensions and fears any adolescent would be having, regardless of his sexual orientation.

FRITZIE: Thank you, Nana.

NANA: And he is also trying, since he knows he was adopted, and now also knows that he was an abandoned baby — *(To Helen.)* And though you didn't tell him that until you felt he could assimilate the knowledge in a way that wouldn't be destructive to his sense of self-worth.

FRITZIE: And I appreciate that.

NANA: Still Fritzie is searching for an identity, and that can't be a simple matter in a family which in many ways has hidden its own identity, and even fled from its roots.

HELEN: *(To Nana.)* Yes, by converting from Judaism to Christianity, you were effectively deracinating all your offspring and their progeny as well.

FRITZIE: But I can understand why Nana wanted to do that. Growing up Jewish in the deep South at the beginning of this century can't have been easy for her; and then the subsequent scorn heaped upon her by her sisters for what they considered to be her cowardice.

HELEN: And you know Nana's brother was homosexual.

NANA: Well, we didn't call it that; we didn't call it anything back then.

HELEN: When I married your father, Uncle Julian told me he thought your dad was "gorgeous." I was terribly embarrassed, and I wish to this day I could take it back and hug him and tell him that we loved him, no matter how he made love.

NANA: But I think we've made it difficult and confusing for Fritzie at times — and at this very table — by referring to some of my relatives as "kikes."

FRITZIE: I guess it was hard for me to understand where all this animosity towards the Jews was coming from, especially from you, Dad, because you weren't hiding anything; none of your relatives are Jewish, are they?

J. FRED: No, but you know how illiterate and ignorant my mother was. Well, you didn't really.

HELEN: No, I made your father ashamed of her, because I was; she was so uneducated, uncultured. Perhaps dad thought he could distance himself from the Jew he knew I was by —

J. FRED: My mother didn't want me to marry your mom.

NANA: I had called her up and told her we were Jewish. *(To Helen.)* Because I didn't want to lose you. I didn't think I should be alone.

FRITZIE: *(To J. Fred.)* Mom's having ovarian cancer and the burden of keeping that secret from her and from me when I was eleven must have fueled some of your anger as well. You must have wondered how you were going to manage if she died, and been looking for someplace to vent that rage and fear.

J. FRED: Yes, I think I was.

FRITZIE: I can't even imagine what that was like for you.

HELEN: You know, I think in a sense I must have known it was true. That I was sick. Because the doctor wouldn't give me any hormones, and sex was so incredibly painful. I begged him. *(To J. Fred.)* I thought if I didn't give you sex, you might leave me.

FRITZIE: Maybe that's another reason why you and daddy drank so much.

HELEN: Well, Nana drank. And my father.

NANA: *(To Fritzie.)* Everyone. And you will, too. And take LSD and snort cocaine. And risk your life by having sex with hundreds of strangers in the dark on the broken-down and abandoned piers of New York, even after the AIDS epidemic begins. You watched us losing ourselves over cocktails and cigarettes and thought, "That's what adults do." You wanted to justify our actions, make us good somehow, by emulating us.

FRITZIE: I think all that's true. And Mom, I want you to know I understand that the only reason you wanted to sleep with me and would crawl into my bed until the day I left for B.U. and snuggle up against me and kiss me and breathe your liquory breath so close to my face was that you yourself were molested by your dad.

HELEN: I was.

J. FRED: We've all seen and survived terrible things.

FRITZIE: In some ways I feel, because so many of my friends have died now —

J. FRED: Well, your first lover.

HELEN: And your second.

NANA: And Tom is sick now, too.

FRITZIE: Well…I'm more prepared to face my own death than you'll be, Mom.

J. FRED: Well, we have thirty years before she gets lung cancer.

FRITZIE: But Nana already is senile.

(Nana nods.)

FRITZIE: And all of us are alcoholics.

HELEN AND J. FRED: Yes.

HELEN: Well, not Nana.

NANA: I'm not really. I wasn't.

(Fritzie kisses Nana on the cheek.)

FRITZIE: You were the first person I really knew who died.

J. FRED: No. My mother was the first.

FRITZIE: Oh, that's right.

J. FRED: I think you didn't say you were sorry the night we told you she was dead because I never held you or told you I loved you, and you had no idea how to relate to me emotionally.

FRITZIE: I really didn't. I didn't know what I was supposed to say. When I saw you cry at her funeral, I couldn't imagine what was wrong with you. I thought you had a foot cramp. Literally. It was so shocking — that contortion seizing your face in the middle of your walk back from the casket.

J. FRED: I do love you.

FRITZIE: I love you.

J. FRED: And I forgive you for saying it to me so often when you know how uncomfortable it makes me feel.

HELEN: *(To J. Fred.)* And I forgive you for never saying it in fifty years of marriage. For saying "Phew!" which, if you recorded it and slowed it down,
might sound like "I love you." "Phew!" "I love you!" but to ordinary human
ears sounds like "Phew, I didn't have to say I love you!"

J. FRED: And I forgive you for not having children, for being afraid.

HELEN: And I forgive you for not magically knowing the doctors were wrong
about my kidneys being too weak, and for not being able to take that fear
away, or any of my fears, because you were in some ways more afraid than I.

NANA: I forgive you all for screaming at me when I couldn't remember anything.
(To Helen.) When I picked up the knife and tried to stab you.

HELEN: I understood.

NANA: And for putting me in a home.

FRITZIE: Mom, I'm sorry I threw the plate of pasta at you and called you a
"Cunt."

HELEN: I'm sorry I said your therapy wasn't working.

FRITZIE: *(To J. Fred.)* I'm sorry I embarrassed you by doing the cha-cha in the
outfield and being so disinterested in and poor at sports.

HELEN: *(To Fritzie.)* I'm sorry we didn't let you know it would be okay if you
turned out to be gay.

NANA: And an atheist.

J. FRED: And a Communist.

HELEN: And I'm sorry I told you your father hated homosexuals when it was me,
and it was only fear and ignorance.

FRITZIE: *(To J. Fred.)* I'm sorry I asked if I could touch your penis the only time
we ever took a shower together, when I was four. I know that freaked you
out.

J. FRED: *(To Helen.)* And I forgive you for getting lung cancer.

FRITZIE: I do, too.

NANA: I'll be dead by then. *(To Fritzie.)* I forgive you for calling me a racist pig
when I said Martin Luther King was an uppity nigger.

FRITZIE: It's the way you were raised. *(To Helen.)* I forgive you for telling me that
my career was more important than going to the hospital in Denver with
Tom when he had AIDS-related TB and that was the only place he could
get treatment, and for suggesting that I should let him go by himself.

HELEN: *(To Fritzie.)* I forgive you for lighting the woods on fire. And for making me feel like such a failure as a mother up until and even including this
very instant.

J. FRED: *(To Fritzie.)* And I forgive you for what you and I both know you did
once and I can't say, or you'll probably be sued.

FRITZIE: Thank you.

HELEN: *(To Fritzie.)* And I forgive you for trying to kill yourself and leaving that awful, long note saying your father and I were "NOT TO BLAME" over and over. I forgive you for pretending you didn't know me when I walked into the wall of plate glass at your grade school and broke my nose.

FRITZIE: I forgive you for not being the parents I wanted — articulate and literate and calm.

HELEN: People who knew how to use words like "deracinate."

J. FRED: "Inchoate."

NANA: "Emulate."

J. FRED: I forgive you for being ashamed of us, for telling us that you were going to look for your natural parents; I forgive you for not finding them and being so horrified at whatever you found you had to come begging our forgiveness.

HELEN: I do, too. And for telling everyone that I pushed you onto the stage and saying to Deborah Norville and Bryant Gumbol that you were gay when I asked you not to. When I said I would lose all my friends if you did.

J. FRED: Well…it was important.

FRITZIE: And you didn't. Did you? Is that why you seem so alone now?

J. FRED: No.

FRITZIE: Did I do that?

(Helen looks at him for a moment. She gently shakes her head.)

J. FRED: Love is the hardest thing in the universe. Isn't it?

(Pause.)

NANA: No.

(They stare, lost in contemplation. Fritzie gently kisses each of his parents on the cheek.)

END OF PLAY

Jack And Jill

— a romance —

by Jane Martin

BIOGRAPHY

Jane Martin, a Kentuckian, first came to national attention for *Talking With*, a collection of monologues that premiered at Actors Theatre of Lousiville in 1981. Since its New York premiere at the Manhattan Theatre Club in 1982, *Talking With* has been performed around the world, winning the Best Foreign Play of the Year award in Germany from *Theater Heute* magazine. Her other work includes *Cementville* (1991 Humana Festival), *Summer* (1984 Shorts Festival) and *Vital Signs* (1990 Humana Festival). Ms. Martin's *Keely and Du*, which premiered in the 1993 Humana Festival, was nominated for the Pulitzer Prize in drama and won the American Theatre Critics Association Award for Best New Play. Her play *Middle-Aged White Guys* premiered in the 19th Humana Festival.

ORIGINAL PRODUCTION

Jack and Jill was first performed at the 1996 Humana Festival of New American Plays, March, 1996. It was directed by Jon Jory with the following cast:

Jack . . . . John Leonard Thompson
Jill . . . . Pamela Stewart
Dressers . . . . David A. Baecker, Elizabeth Dwyer,
Heather LaFace, Sean McNall

and the following production staff:

Scenic Designer . . . . Paul Owen
Costume Designer . . . . Jeanette deJong
Lighting Designer . . . . T.J. Gerckens
Sound Designer . . . . Michael Rasbury
Properties Master . . . . Mark J. Bissonnette
Movement Director . . . . Gail Benedict
Stage Manager . . . . Lori M. Doyle
Assistant Stage Manager . . . . Susan M. McCarthy
Dramaturg . . . . .Michael Bigelow Dixon
New York Casting Arrangements . . . . Laura Richin Casting

CHARACTERS

JACK
JILL
DRESSERS

PLACE

Present, in various locations.

DIRECTOR'S NOTE

The stage never goes to black except at the ends of acts. The music is classical, played by small ensembles; perhaps Beethoven in Act I, and Mozart in Act II. To give some sense of pace, Act I runs 48 minutes, Act II runs 52 minutes. The final scene is more painful than romantic. They are old warriors meeting on the road.

GROUNDPLAN

The setting is utterly simple. The floor is a deep, shiny maroon. At various times we see four black chairs. There is a mustard colored table. We see a deep green bed with white sheets and pillows with similarly covered bedside tables. On the tables are maroon lamps with white shades. The chairs also arrange as other pieces of furniture during the action. The play is performed by one man and one woman in their mid-thirties. There are four stagehand/dressers who assist on- and offstage costume changes, move furniture pieces and deliver props. They are not characters but regard the actors with grave interest as they go about their duties. They wear clothes in a brown tone that are in the same world as Jack and Jill. The time is now.

JACK AND JILL

— a romance —

ACT ONE

A woman sits in a single chair reading a book by Sylvia Plath. A man, sitting and holding several books, stands and crosses toward her. He stops and looks at her for a time. Finally, he speaks.

JACK: Hi.

JILL: Hi.

JACK: Listen, I've been…one minute of your time…sitting over there, and I…no place is safe, right? I'm sorry. By the way, you're reading a poet I admire…in the face of that tragic life, she…wait, wait, I'm backing up here…I was, from over there in the stacks, struck, struck by you…viscerally struck…as if you cared, right? Why, why am I…look, I'm Jack, unpronounceable second name…we could…well, this is fairly mortifying. Let me try to do this without artifice…I'm going to erase this desperate preamble and, uh, say this: I, Jack, would like to meet you, a female person, for…ummm, non-threatening relating. Why? Because awhile ago I lost some serious relating, and I really miss the feeling. So, severe and transcendent beauty, how about a cup of coffee with me, Jack Stojadinovac? *(Pause)* I have this…intuition…that I am dog meat.

JILL: Jack.

JACK: Yes.

JILL: Jack Stojadinovac.

JACK: That was unbelievably perfect.

JILL: I'm having some problems with men, Jack. On a…yes…lot of levels. I am finding my relating to them is…not to mention the problems implicit here in my name being Jill…relating to men…so to speak, recently is…is like dropping my finite reserves of energy and, umm, insight and empathy down a mine shaft. Doubtless my problem, but…all right, umm, I will seriously relate to you in this way…I will tell you that doing this makes me infinitely lonelier than being alone.

JACK: But…

JILL: Wait, Jack...I'm...listen...I want to say to you...to you...I'm not beautiful, Jack, so...no...well, actually I resent...disdain...no, resent...I don't
know, but...your calling me that makes me...very wary...I could think
you were a hustler...no-good guy, and I'm...I'm not in the market for the
wrong compliment, Jack. What a world, huh? I know. Believe me. How is
it possible for a man to approach a woman? I know. Tough. Because I am,
I think, unapproachable, I mean now, and for some time before this. So,
please, and I mean this, don't take leaving me alone personally...
(He takes a step forward.) ...but leave me alone. Bye, Jack.
(He takes a step back indecisively. She speaks gently. Lights change.)
JACK: *(While he speaks to the audience, the dressers re-set the chairs and take books
from him and carry them offstage.)* Man. Woman. My mother and father
were married for 40 years, and they couldn't stand each other. I met a Greek
woman on the ferry from Skiros to San Torini; she didn't speak English, I
didn't speak Greek. We stood by the rail, shoulders touching, in perfect har-
mony for nine hours. Naturally I never saw her again. Somebody understands this. I just wondered if by any chance they were here tonight?

*(New Scene. The stage is re-set, abstractly, as Jill's apartment. Her living room.
He looks out a window. She stands, trying to look comfortable.)*

JACK: View, huh? Nice. Nice view. Nice apartment. Ummm...are you nervous?
I'm very nervous. Nice apartment though.
JILL: I have scotch and, uh, what? Cheap vodka. This much scotch, actually.
JACK: I don't...
JILL: You don't? I don't either really, that's why...
JACK: Use scotch, drink it.
JILL: Oh, I...
JACK: You know...I...
JILL: Not since...I am nervous.
JACK: Well, this is...
JILL: I guess, if I think about it...I've never been...
JACK: Picked up. Listen...
JILL: Actually I was going to say...
JACK: Not that that's...
JILL: Sounds a little retro...
JACK: This?
JILL: You know...
JACK: Not this.

JILL: How about, "Swept me off my feet."

JACK: Pardon?

JILL: Let's say you "swept me off my feet."

JACK: Me?

JILL: What my mother used to say.

JACK: Well, I'd say...

JILL: About my dad. Though I was sitting.

JACK: What?

JILL: When you swept me off my feet. Joke.

JACK: Right. *(Pause.)* Vodka.

JILL: Oh vodka...

JACK: Tonic, straight, whatever.

JILL: I thought you didn't...

JACK: Well, you know...

JILL: Unless you'd like to smoke?

JACK: Actually...

JILL: A joint, but...

JACK: Ummm.

JILL: You don't...?

JACK: What?

JILL: Ganja, weed...

JACK: Oh, hey...

JILL: Reefer, Mary Jane...

JACK: No, really, erase the vodka, I...

JILL: Hang on.

   (Exits.)

JACK: I was married, was married and...

JILL: Can't hear you...

JACK: *(Louder.)* She did no stimulants...with a vengeance.

JILL: Just rolling in here.

JACK: No Coca-Cola, no caffeine...she had her adrenal glands surgically removed.

JILL: Stuff's a little old.

JACK: She was, actually, a person who would have benefited from stimulants.

JILL: Coming.

JACK: Post-divorce, I stayed like...massively whacked out...you know, reacting.

JILL: *(Reappearing with ashtray and joint.)* Have you been married?

JACK: Well, I...

JILL: What's an imagist?

JACK: Well, images...

JILL: I was married.

JACK: Ah.

JILL: Let's not get into that.

JACK: Images are a vocabulary.

JILL: Wait…I'm sorry…one thing…

JACK: What?

JILL: Wait.

JACK: No problem.

JILL: Okay. Wait. If we smoke this, we're going to get involved.

JACK: Involved?

JILL: Historically I'm…susceptible.

JACK: To?

JILL: Physically.

JACK: Am I…

JILL: When I…

JACK: You mean…

JILL: We, Jack. We will get involved physically.

JACK: Us?

JILL: Yes.

JACK: Well…really?

JILL: Really.

JACK: Well…

JILL: Wait…I mean, I didn't mean to interrupt you.

JACK: So you mean…

JILL: But I know myself.

JACK: Sure…well, I mean you would.

JILL: So what are your feelings?

JACK: My feelings?

JILL: About smoking?

JACK: Smoking…ummm…fine.

JILL: Given my susceptibility.

JACK: Susceptibility. Yes.

JILL: But…

JACK: I am…*(Meaning yes.)*

JILL: You mean…

JACK: Sure.

JILL: Okay. Okay, there are some things…

JACK: Absolutely.

JILL: I am completely clean. Vaginally.

JACK: Right…I'm, uh…

JILL: Condoms.

JACK: *(Reaches for wallet.)* I…I…

JILL: I have condoms.

JACK: I…

JILL: You?

JACK: Me?

JILL: You know.

JACK: Oh!

JILL: You know.

JACK: Clean.

JILL: Good. *(They smile.)* Of course, you can't trust anybody.

JACK: I…

JILL: No penetration.

JACK: Me.

JILL: Jack, who ordinarily penetrates?

JACK: Right, I just…

JILL: Agreed?

JACK: Look, we don't have to…

 (Dresser enters with condoms.)

JILL: I want to. I didn't expect to want to, but…I want to.

 (Jill takes condoms from dresser. Dresser exits.)

JACK: Well, I…

JILL: You don't want to? You came on very strong.

JACK: I do…no, I do…only…

JILL: Talk to me.

JACK: Jill, I really do, but…

JILL: You called me Jill.

JACK: Jesus, you're not Jill?

JILL: I am.

JACK: Thank God.

JILL: I liked it. I'm Jill.

JACK: Can I admit to being nervous? Because…

JILL: Would you kiss me.

JACK: Because historically…

 (She kisses him.)

JILL: There.

JACK: Right.

JILL: Contact. One thing…

JACK: There have been times…

JILL: And then, you know, whatever happens…

JACK: Okay.

JILL: Condoms, right? *(He nods.)* Sorry, but…condom, no penetration, then afterwards…

JACK: Then why the condom?

JILL: Not everybody pays attention.

JACK: I promise you…

JILL: And not paying attention is…

JACK: Absolutely…hey…

JILL: Good. Ummm. Listen, do you…can we talk a little bit about oral sex?

JACK: Jill, please…

JILL: Which is to say that, I know, stupid but…

JACK: Too much structure, and I…

JILL: Otherwise…

JACK: My turn, my turn…

JILL: Nothing bad, nothing bad, I just thought…

JACK: Jill…

JILL: Yes?

JACK: Jill…

JILL: What?

JACK: Close your eyes.

JILL: Why?

JACK: Because I can't say this to open eyes.

JILL: My eyes are closed.

JACK: Oh, God. I have, you know, sometimes in the past, had uh, okay, some-thing I'm…still working on, not even, not even a pattern…

JILL: Problems with functioning.

JACK: Well, umm, you know…yes. Maybe stress or…

JILL: Jack…

JACK: Sometimes months at a time, whoosh, smooth sailing, but uh…but uh…

JILL: Jack?

JACK: What?

JILL: It's perfect. It fits right in with no penetration. It's good.

JACK: Yeah, but later…

JILL: We're not anywhere near later, we're trying to do now.

JACK: Thanks.

JILL: Can I light this joint?

(Jack removes jacket and hangs over chair back.)

JACK: You were married?

JILL: A disaster.

JACK: Long?

JILL: Long.

JACK: *(Points to himself.)* Of moderate length.

JILL: Here. *(Hands him joint.)*

JACK: Every mistake...I made that mistake. One time...I don't know if you...should I go into this?

JILL: Unbutton my blouse.

JACK: *(Pause.)* You're sure?

JILL: Sure of what?

JACK: This is all right?

JILL: Please. *(He reaches out.)* One thing...

JACK: Okay, but only one...

JILL: You can't stay over.

JACK: Could we please not...

JILL: Sorry, that's the deal.

> *(While he responds, she unbuttons and takes off her blouse.)*

JACK: But see...I, uh...this staying over thing...see, I have this, reaction...you know, to...this is, um, embarrassing...I can never go back to sleep, my God, you're beautiful! *(Last line said as one sentence.)*

JILL: And don't ever call me beautiful.

> *(She kisses him. Lights change. Jack and Jill walk into separate spots while the chairs are shifted and a table is added. Each speaks while putting on a sweater given to them by separate dressers.)*

JACK: Feeling. I don't know...overloaded.

JILL: Feelings.

JACK: To feel. Oh boy. Why?

JILL: Unlooked for.

JACK: Pretty dismaying.

> *(Lights change. New Scene. Dresser hands Jill roses. She moves to Jack.)*

JILL: *(She hands him a dozen roses.)* For you.

JACK: You're kidding.

JILL: *(She shakes her head.)* You look like someone who never got flowers, Jack.

JACK: No, I never got flowers. I never expected to get flowers.

JILL: Well, you should have.

> *(Jack stands looking at the flowers, then hands them to a dresser.)*

(Lights change. New Scene. His place. They move to the table and sit.)

JACK: Okay, okay, if this was a negotiation…

JILL: It's not a negotiation…

JACK: If it was…

JILL: I said…

JACK: Jill, Jill, don't go off on me…if it was…

JILL: I'm not moving to California…

JACK: I didn't tell you…

JILL: "N" …"O."

JACK: Wait…

JILL: No, negative…it's not…

JACK: Five minutes of logic, okay?

> *(A beat.)*

JILL: Are you patronizing me?

JACK: Umm, no…I hope not…I'm saying…

JILL: Like you represent cool, lucid…

JACK: Oh boy…

JILL: Objective process…

JACK: No…

JILL: And I…

JACK: Back up…

JILL: Untamed, misty…

JACK: Hold it…

JILL: Intuition mixed with P.M.S.?

JACK: Your job can move…you're laughing?

JILL: Well…move my job…I am laughing…don't you…my job to accommodate your career opportunity…

JACK: No…

JILL: And you don't see…

JACK: You have topped out, Jill, that's what I'm saying…

JILL: No…

JACK: You already manage…wait…a nine-person office for an orthopedic surgeon…

JILL: Like, "Throw her on the wagon, boys, we're movin' west!"

JACK: Okay, point, good point, but…

JILL: I know you don't…

JACK: Unless you go to medical school…

JILL: You're saying I couldn't?

JACK: …but unless you do…

JILL: But are you saying I couldn't?

JACK: Jill, objectively aside…listen, let's not react for a second…

JILL: But are you saying I couldn't?

JACK: Jill, stop reacting and listen…

JILL: Don't give me your "I'm dealing with a barely rational creature" voice. It's demeaning.

JACK: As a woman?

JILL: As a woman, yes.

JACK: Great.

JILL: What?

JACK: Is every waking conversation a male/female issue?

JILL: Is this a good-natured question?

JACK: Do we have any aspirin?

JILL: Male/female issue? Do you know what culture you're living in?

JACK: Jill.

JILL: How could you…

JACK: Jill, do you love me?

JILL: I…bathroom.

JACK: What?

JILL: Aspirin. *(Jack exits.)* Listen, don't confuse love with leverage.

JACK: Bullshit.

JILL: Sure, right, you say that to me from, see, another room. I would like to have one companion…

JACK: This is Advil…

JILL: Who would stay in the room while we…you're all wusses.

JACK: Oh boy…

(Jack enters with a bottle of Advil and a glass of water.)

JILL: You got me to move in with that hustle about you…you did…having two bedrooms.

JACK: I stay in the room.

JILL: You just went…

JACK: I have a splitting…

JILL: And you have two bedrooms…

JACK: Don't start…

JILL: …because of basic inequalities in the…

JACK AND JILL: Pay scale.

JACK: But it makes sense, given our…

JILL: Yes, it made sense, and the sense it made…

JACK: More work space, we agreed…

　　(Jack exits with Advil and glass.)

JILL: Because males, from infancy, get more space…

JACK: What? I had a split-level crib?

JILL: And if I want more space…

　　(Jack enters empty-handed.)

JACK: You got more space…you're in more space…

JILL: At the price of giving up my space and…

JACK: Practicality, puh-leeze, isn't a feminist issue…

JILL: Cook for you.

JACK: I said I would cook.

JILL: You eat out of cans, Jack. You know how to grill three kinds of horrible
　　meat…good, you're laughing.

JACK: California.

JILL: So?

JACK: Think about it, I do images for a living. Where is image everything?

JILL: I understand why it is advantageous for…

JACK: And they will snap you up. You will be able to walk to the beach over the
　　supplicant backs of orthopedic surgeons.

JILL: Jack…

JACK: What?

JILL: I must not do this again.

JACK: It's not…

JILL: I really must not. Build a life around somebody else…

JACK: With.

JILL: It's bad for me, it's bad for you…

JACK: With, not "around."

JILL: It's identity, Jack.

JACK: Marry me.

　　(A pause.)

JILL: That's kind of blockheaded, given the moment.

JACK: I mean it.

JILL: You mean to be blockheaded?

JACK: You say that to me when I'm asking you to be my wife?

JILL: You just heard me say it was a question of identity.

JACK: It's a question of commitment…

JILL: I have to get some stuff straight…

JACK: Don't start…

JILL: Because until then…

JACK: Jill…

JILL: What do I bring?

JACK: Don't start!

JILL: Don't yell at me!

JACK: I love you.

JILL: There's no such thing.

JACK: I love you!

JILL: There's no such thing!

JACK: What, then?

JILL: Companions.

JACK: Yes.

JILL: Meaning…

JACK: Yes?

JILL: Equal voice.

JACK: My God, you make 90%…

JILL: Of the completely peripheral…

JACK: Of the…not peripheral…all the decisions…

JILL: I'm not talking about movies or restaurants…

JACK: I am talking about every…

JILL: Forget it.

JACK: No, I won't forget it, I…

(Jill gets coin from purse.)

JILL: I'll flip you for it.

JACK: Will you stick to the…

JILL: Heads it's California, tails it's here.

JACK: You're kidding?

JILL: Huh-uh.

JACK: We can't make this decision based on…

JILL: Why not?

(Beat.)

JACK: Did you hear me propose to you?

JILL: No.

JACK: No?

JILL: I'm proposing to you. *(He breaks into frustrated laughter.)* I'm serious.

JACK: I just…

JILL: But first, the prenuptial agreement.

JACK: This is your idea of romance?

JILL: Don't beat me up with "romance."

JACK: I love you!!

JILL: There's no such thing. Now, heads we go, tails we stay.

JACK: I can't get the work here.

JILL: And Dr. Lake can't get me into medical school there.

(A pause.)

JACK: Medical school?

JILL: Yes.

JACK: That's seven years or something.

JILL: Yes. Will you marry me, yes or no?

JACK: I asked you!!

JILL: You dismissed the prenuptial agreement!

JACK: You are...really...flip the goddamn coin.

JILL: That would be premature.

JACK: All right, I'll marry you!

JILL: Was that so hard?

(She flips.)

JACK: What is it?

JILL: Let's not look yet.

JACK: Jill...

JILL: Tell me 10 reasons you love me. Good reasons. If I think they're good, I'll show you the prenuptial agreement.

JACK: If they're good.

JILL: Yeah. Then we go to dinner...you pick the restaurant, then we go to bed.

JACK: Does this include penetration?

JILL: It demands it. Then you get up and grill me some meat, and we look at the coin, which is binding.

JACK: What if there are problems with the agreement?

JILL: We only look at the coin when we're clear.

JACK: That could take...

JILL: Coins wait. Now what's the first reason?

JACK: Reason for what?

JILL: That you love me, remember?

JACK: You are an implacable hard-ass.

JILL: That is very, very good. What's number two?

(Lights change. Jill exits to do fast change into traditional wedding dress over swimsuit. During his monologue, Jack first removes his sweater, hands it to a dresser. He later removes his shirt, hands it to a dresser. He is wearing a long-sleeved T-shirt and looks disheveled. During monologue, dressers also strike the table and chairs.)

JACK: You get, you know, married. . .time passes. . .you get, you know, divorced. "A" leads to "B." Yin/Yang. Why is this? Let's see. Well, up to that point… getting married…the only, you know, long-term relationship most, um, people have had is with their parents. And, of course, you blew that. Plus, naturally, in most cases, different sexes are involved, mainly, sort of like mating antelopes and tigers. Plus, some sexes are smarter than other sexes… and some sexes earn more money. How could this ever work out? And, of course, it doesn't.

(A dresser hands him a beer bottle, and he takes a swig.)

So, why would you get married in the first place…why?…why would you do that? My God, why would you do that!?

(Lights change. New Scene. He knocks on the air; we hear the knock.)

JILL'S VOICE: Who is it?

JACK: Me, Jack.

JILL'S VOICE: You can't come in.

JACK: I have to come in.

JILL'S VOICE: It would be bad luck.

JACK: I have a problem.

JILL'S VOICE: What, Jack?

JACK: I can't get married.

(Jill appears in a traditional white wedding dress. She is radiantly beautiful.)

JILL: Don't fuck with me, Jack.

JACK: You're wearing white…

JILL: Yes…

JACK: But…

JILL: Jack, the first time, I didn't wear white as a protest against, who knows… traditional values. This time I'm wearing white, okay?

JACK: Sure.

JILL: What, Jack?

JACK: I can't marry you, I'm a bad person.

JILL: I see.

JACK: I have a very bad track record, Jill. While involved with one person, I have had, you know, sexual congress with others. More than once. I am…secretive by nature. Hell, I don't really know myself. I pretend to be nice, but I'm not nice. I'm very self-centered. I feel…I do…women should take care of me. I should be their, you know, priority. I will share the housework, yes, but secretly I will hate the housework and whoever made me do it. I think

I think, when I really examine it, that men are better. And, believing that, the long and the short of it is, I believe I'm a shit.

JILL: I see.

JACK: So I wanted to tell you, you know, while we could...still turn back.

JILL: First of all, Jack, you look very handsome.

JACK: Thank you, but I'm a shit.

JILL: Doubt's okay. Thanks for coming to tell me. Nobody likes housework. It is not only men who have affairs. I think women are better, but I don't want to marry one. I know I drive you crazy, Jack, with all my doubts and regrets and sexual politics and questionable karma and tragedies of the past and unresolved this's and half understood that's, but you're the only one...the only one who has ever seemed to love me, doubts, luggage, ferocity and all, and that is incredibly meaningful to me, Jack, and...uh...I'm a bride, Jack, see...all dressed in white, and I am...full of feeling, and umm...full of hope...and...

JACK: Shhhh.

JILL:...and I would like to marry you and cherish and be cherished, I really would. I really, really would. So please marry me. I would like to try.

JACK: *(A pause, then simply.)* Okay.

JILL: I love you...or something.

(Lights change. Jack goes offstage where he changes into swim trunks. Jill stays and, as she speaks, the dressers remove her shoes, veil and wedding dress, revealing her swimsuit. Both add wedding rings.)

JILL: I have always felt, ummm, alone. Sort of like I was, well, alone. Not...look, I responded, related...sure, I kept up my end...absolutely...even mistaken for outgoing, but...okay, okay, the watchamacallit...water sport...on TV, c'mon head...synchronized swimming. In sync. Two people...effortless, frictionless...completely...as if grace descended and what's outside the "sync," outside the two of you, seems...infinitely clumsier...alienated, divided...*(Two dressers spread towels on the stage.)* I mean we all experience that...for...for brief periods...you have..."in sync." That's probably the paradise they speak of.

(Lights change. New Scene. They lie down on towels. They are bathed in sunset.)

JILL: Incredible. God, can you...it's, oh...

JACK: *(The sky.)* Overwhelming.

JILL: Like we're inside the sunset.

JACK: Amazing…

JILL: Amazing grace. *(A pause.)* Why doesn't everybody live here?

JACK: Fear of perfection.

JILL: Yeah. *(A moment.)* Right. Tell me I don't have to go back.

JACK: You don't have to go back.

JILL: *(A moment.)* Jack?

JACK: What?

JILL: Tickle me.

JACK: Really?

JILL: Yeah.

JACK: You want me to tickle you?

JILL: I do. Gimme, gimme, gimme.

> *(He leaps on her and tickles her unmercifully. Cries of "Wait," "Jack!," "Not there," "Not so hard," "You bastard," "No more, no more, no more!" etc. After complete wrestling hysteria, he just as suddenly leaps off. She regards him gravely.)*

JILL: Thank you.

JACK: *(Just as gravely.)* Please, think nothing of it.

> *(A moment. He begins kissing her chin and kisses slowly to her toes.)*

JILL: *(Somewhere in the process.)* Sometimes, Jack, I think…

JACK: Shhhhhh.

JILL: I think we are like…

JACK: *(Still involved.)* Skin. *(He kisses.)* What?

JILL: More kissing. *(He does.)* Incredible weather…a complex conjunction of…

JACK: Not weather…

JILL: Unprecedented, but it could pass through and…

JACK: An amalgam…

JILL: No, really…

JACK: You make aluminum…

JILL: Change is the precondition, so…

JACK: It stays aluminum.

JILL: This could change.

JACK: No. *(Jack finishes kissing.)* That's looking for trouble…

JILL: I want, God, I want to be in sync, deeply…with you, but I don't…look at me…don't want to lose myself in you, Jack, and you shouldn't either.

JACK: I am lost in you.

JILL: I don't think that works, Jack, when I've done that before…

JACK: This isn't before…

JILL: No, but…

JACK: Hold me.

JILL: Jack…

JACK: C'mon.

(*They hug.*)

JILL: (*Not unkindly.*) I can't reassure you every…

JACK: This isn't…

JILL: Just saying…

JACK: Okay…

(*They break embrace. He stands.*)

JILL: We need to keep some resources outside…

JACK: (*More seriously.*) Stop.

JILL: Outside this. That's all I'm saying.

(*A moment.*)

JACK: I understand that.

(*They take hands and lie down. She withdraws. A moment.*)

JILL: (*Wiping her eyes.*) Faith. Got to keep the faith. Help me keep the faith, Jack. Maybe I'm just petrified of my good fortune. (*She sits up.*) Oh, my God…

JACK: What?

JILL: Look at that big dead fish.

(*Lights change. He exits and changes to khakis, boat shoes, T-shirt, design shirt and sports coat. During Jill's monologue, dressers enter and assist her as she puts on slacks and matching jacket, long-sleeved shirt and low-heeled pumps. Other dressers set two chairs and strike the towels.*)

JILL: So weird, the feelings…who's in here feeling this? To be clear, so hard to be clear…if you had a child and…would you…at this point…what would you teach this child? Would you…for instance, teach her…obedience, respect, diligence, propriety, cotillion, S.A.T. skills…I mean, given the way things are…you know, the way they're going…in the paper…or…given how those…virtues…what they've made…what we…maybe you should teach her disobedience, disrespect, impropriety, pagan rituals, carpentry, and see if that works out…better.

(*Lights change. New Scene. Jack enters. They are dressed. Jill sits in a chair. Jack sits across from her.*)

JACK: Whew. Damn. Long day. Whew. How about you?

(She doesn't answer. During the following exchange, the dressers set the stage for a future scene, a table piled with dishes in another area of the stage. We're talking at least 18 plates and two stacks of three bowls each.)

JILL: I started taking the pill again.

JACK: What?

JILL: The pill, I'm on it.

JACK: *(Pause.)* Well...Jesus, Jill.

JILL: I don't...I don't want a baby now.

JACK: What about what I want?

JILL: Ummm...okay, you have a baby.

JACK: Don't...we, hey, talked about this, I...

JILL: Since we talked about it...

JACK: Said that...

JILL: You hardly come near me.

JACK: Last night...

JILL: You pulled out before you came, how...

JACK: That wasn't...

JILL: Wasn't what?

JACK: Okay, all right, mixed feelings for a second...

JILL: Should we have a baby with mixed feelings?

JACK: That was...we're not so young, Jill, you...

JILL: Hey, I have mixed feelings, so...

JACK: Yes. Okay. You could have asked.

JILL: I did. You didn't tell me, don't...okay so I'm asking. I need you to tell me, Jack. *(A pause. He exhales.)* No baby, Jack. Not right now, right? Don't you think? Talk to me. *(Pause.)* So, how was your day?

(Lights change. New Scene. They rise. She removes her jacket and exchanges it for a dustbuster with a dresser. The dustbuster is on, and she vacuums invisible drapes. Another dresser hands Jack a slip of paper. Other dressers remove the chairs.)

JACK: What is this?

JILL: It's a phone message.

JACK: It's a guy's name and you...did you draw these hearts?

JILL: What!? Yes.

JACK: So who is he?

JILL: I was doodling, Jack.

JACK: Who is he?!

(Jill turns dustbuster off.)
JILL: Are you kidding?
JACK: No, I'm not kidding, I...I'm sick of this, do you understand me, I go to these, yes, hospital parties these guys...
JILL: If you...
JACK: Are all over you, they...
JILL: These are...
JACK: You leave me standing there...
JILL: Are my colleagues, they...
JACK: I don't like it, do you hear me?
(Jill hands dustbuster to dresser.)
JILL: I hear you, but...
JACK: I am...last week, you go bowling with, wait...a bunch of these...on the one night...
JILL: They are my friends, you said...
JACK: What am I supposed to say?
JILL: We needed to blow off some...
JACK: Who is this guy, Marty indecipherable, with hearts?
JILL: I can't believe this.
JACK: Who, goddamnit, is he?!
JILL: *(Pause.)* He has been assigned to me. I am his secret Valentine. I'm supposed to send him jelly beans and a card at a total cost of less than two dollars.
JACK: Yeah?
JILL: Yeah. Anonymously.
JACK: *(A moment.)* Well, I don't like it. I don't like this stuff. Do you hear me clearly?
JILL: *(A pause. Levelly.)* Will you stop?

(A moment. Lights change. New Scene. She goes to the dishes and begins breaking three of them. Jack exits and puts on sports coat. Then he enters when she's broken three dishes.)

JACK: Hi.
JILL: *(Smash.)* Hi.
JACK: You uh...I guess you aren't...
JILL: Don't say anything stupid, Jack.
      (Smash.)
JACK: Bad day at work.
JILL: Bad day at work.

(Smash.)

JACK: Listen, I understand…

JILL: You don't understand. Just…just…

JACK: The amount of stress…

JILL: Do not explain this to me!

JACK: I am on your side!

JILL: Great.

    (Smash.)

JACK: I know what you're feeling.

JILL: Goddamnit! Does everything I feel have to…to pass through you to exist? Why? Why, Jack? What is your…I don't know…compulsion…as if…compulsion to translate for me as if I didn't…

JACK: I'm not…

JILL: Like I have no feelings unless you define them.

    (Smash.)

JACK: You tell me all the time to relate, damn it, I'm relating.

JILL: Well, I don't want to relate, I want to break the dishes.

    (Crash.)

JACK: I understand it's…valuable to…to get the feelings…

JILL: And don't patronize me.

    (Crash.)

JACK: You're patronizing me.

JILL: Jack, aren't you…something else…aren't you cataloguing images or something?

JACK: While you…

JILL: Don't you have something else to do, Jack?

    (Crash.)

JACK: Oh, I should alphabetize slides…

JILL: Good…

    (Crash.)

JACK: While you destroy the house?

JILL: I don't want…

JACK: Or what, what?

JILL: I'm saying I don't want to be…

JACK: Be what?

JILL: Interpreted.

    (Crash.)

JACK: This is a marriage, what you do…

JILL: You want to fix it, right?

JACK: Don't start with that, Jill…

JILL: It's like having a plumber for my feelings.

JACK: And I...

JILL: You can't fix me, do you understand?

   (Crash.)

JACK: This is stress because of your residency.

JILL: My God, I can't shut you out, you're like the ocean, you're all-enveloping.

JACK: I am your companion, I love you, this is our house.

JILL: I am your companion. This has nothing to do with you. I'm not mad at you. I don't mean to hurt your feelings. I don't need to be placated. I just want to break these dishes.

JACK: Let's go out and grab a beer.

JILL: I don't want a beer.

JACK: Coffee, tea, cheesecake, a movie...

JILL: I was enjoying breaking the dishes...

JACK: I doesn't make any sense...

JILL: I'm not making sense, Jack, I'm breaking the dishes.

   (She shoves a stack of bowls onto the floor.)

JACK: Goddamnit, stop that!

JILL: Don't worry, I'll pay you for them.

JACK: That is really cheap, Jill.

JILL: Oh, it wasn't in your mind?

JACK: It was in my mind that it's wasteful.

JILL: Well, you can make a big point of replacing them.

   (Crash.)

JACK: You mean I'm financially brutalizing you?

JILL: Tell me you don't trade on my dependence?

JACK: I don't even think about it.

JILL: Bullshit.

JACK: Don't tell me what I think.

JILL: You know you like it.

JACK: It is incredibly temporary...

JILL: But it's a hold.

JACK: As a physician, you'll make...

JILL: So it's not merely supportive?

JACK: I'm not supportive?

JILL: Financially, yes.

JACK: That's the only way you find me supportive?

JILL: Don't give me the martyred look.

JACK: If that's your perception, I can fix it.

JILL: Fix it?

JACK: What is it that's wanted here, anger?

JILL: Will you…Jack…listen to yourself, "What is it that's wanted here." Jesus!

JACK: Yes?

JILL: That's not an emotion, that's a preface.

JACK: The question, damnit, precedes the answer.

JILL: Jack, you start with a question and then, worse, worse, you immediately try…

JACK: Fix it. I try to fix it. Yes, right, I know my sins. God forbid we should try to do anything about anything…*(Smash.)*…we should, we should experience it…or something, imbibe it, embody it, swim in it or some goddamn…

JILL: I want you to leave the room.

JACK: What?

JILL: You asked what I want, I want you to leave the room.

JACK: This room…

JILL: Is your room…

JACK: I never said…

JILL: Your room, your apartment…

JACK: Goddamnit!

JILL: …your life, your agenda, your wife.
     (Smash.)

JACK: You are my wife, yes. And I…

JILL: Jesus, I wish I was out of here…

JACK: You are in the middle of a residency…

JILL: Why did I ever think…

JACK: The hours are horrendous, the sleep deprivation is brutal, you have no time to yourself…

JILL: Because every second I have, you're there.

JACK: We have no time…

JILL: I don't need "we" time, I need…

JACK: I need "we" time.

JILL: I don't.

JACK: How can you say…

JILL: I want to be alone, Jack. I know…believe me…it's a terrible failing… I'm…anti-social or something…there are times…yesterday, all day, I thought about you, but you never tell me I irritate you…don't I irritate you? You irritate me. For one thing, you can't do anything, Jack…don't get martyred…it's just the way you were raised, but it's…it's oppressive, so…what, what are you doing?

(Jack begins pushing fragments into piles with feet.)

JACK: It is very indulgent.

JILL: What?

JACK: Breaking things. Being anti-social. Showing off your emotions. Pretending who has what money or whatever is the point here. It is very, very, very indulgent. Now, let's stick with one problem and fix it.

JILL: Jack, you can't fix a toilet, you can't cope with…

JACK: Here we go…

JILL: Okay, it's not easy…the insurance…

JACK: I can cope with…

JILL: Canceled.

JACK: One time.

JILL: They turned off the phone.

JACK: One time.

JILL: The car registration.

JACK: All right, Jesus, I get the point.

JILL: And I'm not saying…

JACK: And they didn't turn off the phone.

JILL: That you're not generous, because you are, you are so generous it's like water torture.

JACK: Jill, I love you. My heart…this life, it's richer, more…more various, just better.

JILL: Wait…

JACK: No. You give value…you change me.

JILL: It's sweet, it's…vague. I don't recognize…I wish, I really do…recognize me, Jill, as that person, Jack…that value-adding person…you are making up, and that's generous, too, this person who…I am selfish, I am ambitious, I am…oh, yes…unpleasant, angry, I-don't-know-what person…it's a burden…really…I'm sorry it's this way…but, Jesus, feeling like a shit all the time because I'm not…that! That stuff you make up to sustain this. Honestly say to me that you don't see…

JACK: I want connection, and you…

JILL: I want…

JACK: To be, see…one with you and…

JILL: Baloney.

JACK: To be one…

JILL: This is nice, Jack.

JACK: Nice?

JILL: Nice, yes, this is something somebody would want to hear...

JACK: But I mean it.

JILL: Which is nice, which is your specialty.

JACK: Nice is?

JILL: Yes.

JACK: I want this central, but...

JILL: But disingenuous.

JACK: I am not...

JILL: Disingenuous. You obsess on my stimulus...

JACK: I wouldn't...wait...

JILL: Stir things up...keep you...

JACK: No, I want to share...

JILL: But you don't share. I don't know what you're feeling...

JACK: What?

JILL: Right now, now I don't...you just...Jack, you say a bunch of stuff just to...to restore order...to reduce people to calm...you don't care what you say...you'd say anything.

JACK: Right now?

JILL: Yes.

JACK: I am pissed off.

JILL: At what?

JACK: At what?

JILL: At what?

JACK: This, this conversation. The...the dishes, you know, to mention one...the tone...all of it.

JILL: And your feelings?

JACK: My feelings?

JILL: Yes, Jack, your feelings.

JACK: My feelings are...damn, Jill...what are these endless...endless feelings... c'mon Jill, these goddamn whatevers...right?...that you say I'm not having?

JILL: You want me to tell you about your feelings?

JACK: No, as a matter of fact, I know my feelings, actually, I'm having them.

JILL: And?

JACK: And what?

JILL: They are?

JACK: This is ridiculous, you know my feelings!

JILL: Say them!

JACK: I'm upset, this is upsetting.

JILL: What is?

JACK: You say you're leaving.

JILL: When in this conversation did I…

JACK: About being alone…treating you…wanting to be alone.

JILL: I only want to be alone because I'm already alone with you.

JACK: How can you say that? How dare you say that?

JILL: What-are-you-feeling-Jack?!

JACK: I don't give a shit what I'm feeling!

JILL: And that's why I'm alone!

> *(She starts out.)*

JACK: Don't walk out on this!

JILL: *(Simply.)* What are you feeling, Jack?

> *(She waits. He is at a complete impasse. She goes and adds a vest and uses scarf to tie ponytail.)*

JACK: *(Another moment.)* Goddamnit! Goddamnit!!

> *(He shoves the rest of the dishes and bowls to the floor. Lights change. During monologue, Jack removes sports coat and tosses it offstage. Later, he removes shirt and tosses it offstage. Also during monologue, two dressers sweep broken dishes into a large circle, inside which the last scene is played. Other dressers strike the table and spread books and empty boxes on the floor within the circle.)*

JACK: Nice, right? Nice. Okay. One second. One second. This nice we are talking about here…"don't be nice, Jack." This "nice" has a bad name…to say the goddamn least. Women, to generalize, hate nice…no, no, they like it in clerks, they like it in auto mechanics…but…nice guys finish last, right? Why? Because "nice" is essentially thought to lack complexity, mystery. "Nice" just…has no sex appeal…it just doesn't understand the situation. Women distrust "nice" because, given the cultural context, they themselves can't possibly be nice. How can the powerless be "nice." What good is nice to the "exploited?" So women loathe nice because they see, they know what a phony mask it is in their own lives, so when they perceive it in a man it just pisses them off. What they prefer are abusive qualities moderated by charm, because they are already abused personalities, given the culture. I'm not kidding. Hey, I don't buy it because there is another "nice," a hard-won, complex, covered-with-blood-and-gore "nice." An existential, steel willed, utterly crucial and necessary "nice" that says to the skags in the motorcycle gang, "Fuck you and the hogs you rode in on. I exemplify hope and reason and concern." See, I raise the fallen banner high, Jill, so satirize me, shoot me, stab me, dismiss me, go screw the Four Horsemen of the Apocalypse if that's what turns you on, I'm nice!! *(He slowly turns back into himself. Jill enters and sits by stack of books.)* Sorry, I didn't, uh…don't know how I got into that…just "nice," you know…well, anyway, sorry.

(Lights change. New Scene. He turns back and is now involved in dividing books with Jill.)

JILL: Are all the Joyce Carol Oates…

JACK: All yours.

JILL: Not all.

JACK: Just take them!

JILL: We can't divide them if you won't divide.

JACK: Goddamnit, you divide them!

JILL: So you can criticize how I do it?

JACK: *(Looking away.)* Bitch.

JILL: God, Jack…

JACK: Let's just do the books.

JILL: You called me a "bitch."

JACK: I did, yes.

JILL: You don't think that's sad?

JACK: Get off it!

JILL: *(Calm, not sarcastic.)* Do you mean "bitch" in the sense that I told you something you didn't want to hear? Or that I'm "uppity" and don't do what I'm told…

JACK: Just shut up, okay?

JILL:…or remind you of Bette Davis or have assumed the male role…

JACK: I'm warning you…

JILL: Warning me?

JACK: Do the books, Jill.

JILL: Or is it just a lot simpler, and you mean "bitch" as a kind of catch-all general category for a woman who is truly, really sick of trying to laugh off your endlessly passive-aggressive behavior?

JACK: I want you out of here! Out of this space. Out of my life. Out of my nervous system. Out of here!

JILL: Why can't we…

JACK: Because we can't.

JILL: Close this out with some sense we were right to try.

JACK: *(Packing.)* Because we obviously weren't.

JILL: Since it's a failure, why can't it be a useful failure?

JACK: Dostoevski, mine. Dr. Doolittle, mine. Toni Morrison, yours.

JILL: This is just another version of you walking out of the room.

JACK: Don't start with me. Goddamnit! What I would like is to finish this up and walk out of here without punching you out!

JILL: Whoa??

JACK: You want to know what I think? I think you can't feel anything but an extreme. I think the middle ground is without sensation for you. You drive too fast, you love the unknown, you love extremes. I think I was your last experiment in the ordinary, and it didn't have enough tingle, so you blew it off.

JILL: You don't think punching me out would be an extreme?

JACK: I think punching people out is the final, frustrated expression of the ordinary mind. I think you would like me to hit you so this would be all my fault. It is the only stupid, vulgar, debasing male idiocy you haven't been able to pry out of me, but you uh...you'll never know how...do you have any sense how close...this close...to nailing you...yes, there...happy now?

JILL: I'm supposed to feel sorry for you because you wanted to hit me?

JACK: I was making...

JILL: Well, I do. I am sorry.

JACK: You are, huh?

JILL: Really sorry.

JACK: Have I ever hit you?

JILL: Not the point.

JACK: Then why are we talking about this?

JILL: Jack...

JACK: No.

JILL: Jack. *(A moment.)* I think marriage is like the cockpit of a commercial airliner...you know...all those switches...and they all...all 200...have to be in...the right positions, only in aviation they know what those are, and in marriage you never do, so the odds...the odds are astronomical you won't...stay in the air. So I don't think we're bad people, Jack, I think we are disgruntled victims...of the odds.

JACK: But you always thought...

JILL: I thought they were long...the odds, yes, I did.

JACK: So we're a self-fulfilling prophecy.

(They look at each other.)

JILL: We don't have the switches in the right places...so...it won't stay...up. "The Age of Reason?"

JACK: Mine.

JILL: "Anna Karenina."

JACK: Yours.

JILL: "Co-Dependence in Contemporary Marriage?"

JACK: Mine.

JILL: "The Hardy Boys."

JACK: Very funny.

(A pause.)

JILL: Hey, Jack?

JACK: What?!

JILL: Come kiss me goodbye. *(He stops packing but doesn't look at her.)* Come on, Jack, be my pal. *(He looks at her but doesn't move.)* Okay, I'll come over there.

(She goes and wraps her arms around him. Finally, he raises his arms and puts them around her.)

JACK: Bye, Jill.

JILL: Bye, Jack.

(They sit holding each other. The lights go out.)

END OF ACT ONE

ACT TWO

The scene begins in the dark. Jack and Jill are in bed.

JILL: *(A dream.)* No!

JACK: Ow. What?…Ow!

JILL: Wait…what?…wait.

JACK: Right in the…

JILL: Oh no…

JACK: It's okay. Ow.

JILL: Jack?

JACK: Your elbow…

JILL: Jack.

JACK: Jack, yes. I don't think it's broken.

JILL: I had no…

JACK: That hurt…

JILL:…idea, not a clue.

JACK: What idea?

JILL: Who you were…
  (Switches light on.)

JACK: No!
  (She switches light off.)

JILL: You're bleeding.

JACK: Nothing…it's just a…

JILL: Get you a Kleenex.

JACK: Forget it.

JILL: Really sorry…here. *(Switches light on. Hands him Kleenex.)* It's been years…

JACK: Thanks. Please…
  (She switches light off.)

JILL: I'm so used to being…

JACK: Time thing…
  (Referring to a glowing clock face.)

JILL:…alone. So you touching me…

JACK: Clock?

JILL: It just startled…
  (He turns on the light on his side.)

JACK: Three A.M.

JILL: God…

JACK: You've been alone?

JILL: Look, we're on different sides.

JACK: Where?

JILL: Of the bed.

JACK: Who changed?

JILL: I did. Oh, my God…

JACK: What?

JILL: Three A.M. Once I'm up…

JACK: Me neither. You look great, Doctor.

JILL: Your poor nose…

JACK: About this alone.

JILL: I'd really rather…

JACK: Are you?

JILL: Jack…

JACK: What?

JILL: Knock it off.

JACK: I'd call this…

JILL: Please…

JACK: Chemistry.

JILL: Nostalgia.

JACK: We pass on two moving stairways in an airport…

JILL: Dopey.

JACK: Cinematic.

JILL: So…

JACK: So…

JILL: Maybe you should go back to the hotel.

JACK: Huh-uh.

JILL: We should leave it at this.

JACK: That's just anxiety.

JILL: Just?

JACK: Normal two-years-divorced, pass-in-the-airport, cancel-a-plane, take-a-taxi, rip-off-our-clothes anxiety.

JILL: This was fine, but…

JACK: Really?

JILL: All right, good then…

JACK: Objectively.

JILL: I don't mean I didn't like it.

JACK: You liked it.

JILL: Don't tell me what I liked.

JACK: Sorry.

JILL: You blew it.

JACK: I meant I liked it.

JILL: Okay, but…*(He turns out the light.)* I don't want…

JACK: One minute.

JILL: No, Jack…

JACK: Thirty seconds.

JILL: When I say no…

JACK: Please. Please. Just…please. *(Silence in the dark.)* Oh, God…

JILL: Jack?

JACK: This is…better. Much, much…better.

JILL: This wasn't…

JACK: Shhhhhhhhhh.

    (A silence.)

JILL: What are we doing?

JACK: We're restoring.

JILL: That feels good.

JACK: Sometimes things fall into disrepair and then if you care about them, you restore them.

JILL: Not what is restoring, restoring what?

JACK: Us.

JILL: *(Turns on his light.)* You really need to go back to your hotel.

JACK: *(Turns off light.)* I'm serious, Jill.

JILL: Turn on the light.

JACK: Listen…

JILL: Turn it on.

JACK: No.

JILL: No?

JACK: Just…

JILL: You say "no" in my bed? No in my house? You have no authority in my universe.

    (She hits him.)

JACK: Ow.

JILL: You cannot restore me to someone you can say no to.

    (She hits him again.)

JACK: Ow.

JILL: Do you get it?

JACK: What would you call this if I was hitting you?

JILL: I would call this not being listened to.

JACK: So don't do it again.

JILL: I am turning on the light.

　　(She does. A dresser helps her into a robe.)

JACK: I want this.

JILL: If people, once, you know, were what we were...

JACK: Don't put on the robe.

JILL: At the center, central...no Jack...then realistically there's a residue...

JACK: Beautiful.

JILL: Stop it. A residue...

JACK: And don't tell me...

JILL: That can be played on...

JACK: That isn't...

JILL: In certain situations...

JACK: Going on here.

JILL: What?

JACK: We are.

JILL: Residue can flare up briefly...stop looking at me.

JACK: You like it.

JILL: I am turning out the light.

　　(She does.)

JACK: Fine.

　　(Jill turns light back on.)

JILL: Which doesn't mean...

JACK: Fine.

　　(She turns it out.)

JILL: Because I want to say this undistracted...

JACK: Where are you?

JILL: I loved you, and...

JACK: And I...

JILL: Shhhh. But it malfunctioned...

JACK: Take my hand.

JILL: Jack, I was...ill defined...I...you defined me...

JACK: But...

JILL: Shhh.

JACK: My hand...

JILL: Okay. And you were, without, um, question, perfect to be ill defined with, really...because nobody, no-body beats you for reassurance, Jack...you were nicer to be nobody with than anybody, hands down, but when I...and you supported...sustained, sympathized...all the S's, and I got...really, you were wonderful...when I started defining...separating from your...reassurance…well, you…you were still back there with the S's…you…redoubled your efforts because…why not? You were way, way better suited to support me than to acknowledge me, and you were, meaning no harm, plain fucking oppressive, Jack. Sorry, but…so I'm, well, whatever I am now, but it's alone, I'm afraid, barring a little…screwing around…and that's just…my old friend…*(Turns on her light.)* Just the way I like it. Amen.

JACK: My turn…

JILL: Look, Jack…

JACK: My turn. My turn. *(He turns on his light.)* To really support…really support someone is acknowledgment, okay? Plus, plus…when you…okay…were busy defining, separating…look, no offense, self-realizing, would there were another word, Jill, that's important, no doubt about it, but I give it a six on degree of difficulty, keeping something going between two humans, that's what you, I know you're going to hate this, you grow up for. That's a grown-up's job. *(A pause.)* Okay, okay, I had to say it.

JILL: Jack…

JACK: What?

JILL: Hotel.

JACK: Let me…

JILL: The end. With empathy.

JACK: What are you feeling?

JILL: You asked me what I'm feeling.

JACK: Yes.

JILL: You said the word, "feeling."

JACK: Yes.

JILL: Wow. Well, freed up…or…

JACK: For what?

JILL: Unpatterned, maybe.

JACK: Because free to do what?

JILL: In the sense of not…

JACK: Because free…

JILL: Banging up against somebody's borders.

JACK: Because freedom's just another word for nothing left to lose.

JILL: I know.

JACK: Which is why I got off the moving stairway…

JILL: The freedom doesn't oppress me, Jack.

JACK: Look, I'll fit in around the edges.

JILL: Oh, Jack…

JACK: I'm a little confused.

JILL: Who wouldn't be?

JACK: I don't want to go back to the hotel.

JILL: I don't want somebody around the edges...

JACK: It would feel truly terrible...

JILL: It would.

JACK: At the hotel.

JILL: Oh.

JACK: I'm sincerely feeling...

JILL: What's happened to you?

JACK: You, at the airport.

    (Pause)

JILL: Okay, Jack, but no more...only sleeping.

JACK: Only sleeping.

    (He turns off his light.)

JILL: For auld lang syne.

JACK: For auld lang syne.

JILL: *(Pointing at him.)* Don't mess with me. *(She turns off her light.)* No touching. *(A pause.)* No touching. *(A pause.)* Oh, to hell with it.

(Silence. An alarm rings; it's morning. Lights change. New Scene. Jack dresses in the clothes he has left on the floor: dress slacks, button-down shirt, shoes and socks. Jill exits and dresses in her business suit for the hospital: matching skirt and blazer, silk blouse and pumps.)

JACK: *(Dressing. To Jill, who is offstage, rather than to the audience.)* So I...California...very uh...image collages for, uh, big-time screenwriters...weighty paychecks but, you know, uh...uh...severe loss of anything resembling meaning and...dates, I would date...

JILL: *(From offstage.)* No???!!

JACK:...that didn't...I don't know...go too well because...absence of you...like a hole in my chest...this size...and nothing I could stuff in there, things, people, sex, drugs, travel, Stephen King books, cappuccino...nothing filled it up...*(Jill enters, putting up her hair.)*...massage therapy...nothing...that's the God's truth, cross my heart...and I don't...there is, still is such a thing as love...call me stupid...no co-dependency, not paternal-uh-Jill-ism... not the self-help library...c'mon, there has to be...the fit...the fit...don't you think there has to be the fit? Heloise and Abelard, you know. Love which is...love between, you know, man and woman...or, of course, other combinations, but anyway...

(They are dressed. A dresser brings on Jack's suit coat. By now, the dressers have cleared away the bed and side tables.)

JILL: I have to go, Jack…wait, your collar…

JACK: Could we…

JILL: I don't think so.

JACK: Just…

JILL: Cat hair, oh God, look…

JACK: Brunch.

JILL: I'm at the hospital till…

JACK: Lunch.

JILL: Jack, don't get me confused…

JACK: Goddamn you…

JILL: Hey…

JACK: This isn't…this won't come again, don't you understand that?

(A dresser hands Jill a lint brush, which she uses on Jack's coat.)

JILL: Jack, the Industrial Revolution is over. It doesn't take two people to live a life. We don't till the soil. One person is plenty…that's what Lean Cuisine is for. You are sweet and…fulsome…I don't want to step on those feelings…your idea is beautiful…really…*(Jill returns lint brush to dresser.)*…in 50 years maybe, on some new basis, umm, romantic love, God bless it, will make a comeback. Try me again in the nursing home. *(Kisses him lightly.)* I have to go.

JACK: Lunch.

JILL: Lunch I run, you know, running.

JACK: Okay.

JILL: Yi, yi, yi. Five miles.

JACK: Okay.

JILL: You don't have any…

JACK: I'll get some.

JILL: Couldn't we just be…

JACK: I can run five miles.

JILL: You can?

JACK: Yeah.

JILL: *(A moment.)* You know what?

JACK: What?

JILL: Never mind.

JACK: Okay.

JILL: This is confusing, Jack.

JACK: What "this?"

JILL: You…here…so pleasurably, densely…familiar. It is…it is comfortable. You are a complex damn comfort, Jack. Boy. I am still often scared, Jack, and you are masterfully…familiar.

JACK: Somebody asked once what I saw in you…and I said you never, never told me anything I already know, which quality excels agreement.

JILL: You are…a serious person. No kidding. And they are…in short supply.

JACK: And?

JILL: Is that a dare, Jack?

JACK: What?

(She studies him.)

JILL: I'm wavering. Yes, I am.

JACK: Great.

JILL: I'm a sucker for a dare, Jack. *(A moment.)* Okay, let's go to the airport.

JACK: Jill?

JILL: Get a flight. Prague. Sao Paulo. Go out the door, go down the steps and do that. We could do it. Get a cab. Right now. Right now. *(A moment.)* But we would have to do it in the next 15 seconds, because…*(A moment.)* We could.

JACK: *(A slight nervous laugh.)* Jill, you…I have a camera crew over on…hey, really, come on…you won't do lunch, but you'll do Prague? We need time now…absolutely…yes…I'm clear in March…I can clear March…are you…

JILL: Never mind, just…just kidding, I…what time is it?

JACK: Hey, it's just I have a crew…

JILL: *(Dresser enters and hands Jill her watch.)* Oh, boy. Hey, I'm a hospital administrator, Jack. Did I tell you that? No more hands-on. I live by the clock. I have five meetings, two committees. Anyway, listen, this was good, I never…I told a date last week that if I had to choose between great sex and a good executive secretary, I would…

JACK: I can be a secretary…

JILL: *(Laughing.)* Jack…

JACK: Plus…

JILL: Okay.

JACK: I now cook like an angel, I even took a pastry class…I can do tarts. I know wines, I can fold origami napkins, I can do flower arrangements.

JILL: You win. You win. Lunch.

JACK: Lunch. Good. What about March?

JILL: Lunch.

JACK: Okay. *(She starts to go.)* Maybe we could make that three miles.

(Lights change. The dressers now begin to dress both people into running gear; Jill onstage, Jack off. Dresser enters with a chair and her clothes. Jill removes shoes, skirt and coat and pulls on jogging sweatpants. She then removes blouse and puts on sleeveless T-shirt. Then she sits and puts on shoes and socks—all during monologue.)

JILL: What is this battlefield upon which we are engaged? Who has done what to whom? You know as I get the power, men...the money and the power men used to...well that they essentially had as their own province...now I don't like admitting this...I feel less. Yeah, diminished...bound in...where I existed in a universe of feelings, intuitions...now, they're receding. They don't get the same workout in money and power land...oh-oh...I wake up halfway through a day in the...well, great American market place and I say, "Hey, Jill," literally, "I know what you're doing, but what the hell are you feeling?" Because, and this scares the shit out of me, if my feelings are not functional, if they atrophy in the marketplace, then just who and what is being sold here? *(She stands and ties sweat jacket around her waist. A dresser enters and strikes clothing and chair.)* I want...

(Lights change. New Scene. Jack enters and begins running with her. For stage purposes, they run in place throughout most of the scene. He is wearing a bright orange jogging outfit and very white sneakers and socks that he bought that morning.)

JILL: *(Referring to his outfit.)* You are very orange.
JACK: Yeah. They had sold all the blue and dark green ones.
JILL: Well, the hunters won't get you.
JACK: Whew. Wow. You do this every day?
JILL: Every day. Jack?
JACK: Yeah, what?
JILL: Breathe.
JACK: Right.
JILL: Find a rhythm.
JACK: What rhythm?
JILL: Your rhythm.
JACK: A perspective.
JILL: Yes.
JACK: Other men?
JILL: Yes.

JACK: Are they like me?

JILL: No, they have giant dicks and wild untamed emotions.

JACK: I thought so.

JILL: And blue running suits.

JACK: Ah. Are they such, these men, that you could love them?

JILL: No.

JACK: Why?

JILL: Because I don't want to.

JACK: Stop.

JILL: Jack…

JACK: Stop.

JILL: Damnit.

(They do.)

JACK: Tell me what you want.

JILL: What I want? Look out! (They jump to one side.) We are standing…Look out! (They jump the other way.) Jack…

JACK: You want?

JILL: I want a control in my life that is still full of feeling. I want to be…I don't know…powerful and amazed. This is ridiculous…

JACK: Are you okay?

JILL: Run.

(They run in place.)

JACK: But you're sad.

JILL: No.

JACK: But you are.

JILL: Will you shut up?

JACK: I am.

JILL: Well, you're a melancholy baby, Jack.

JACK: Are you?

JILL: (She points.) See the guy with the sores, urinating on the street?(They run.) In the morning paper was a picture of a six-month-old baby who got hit with shrapnel and had her leg amputated. And here we are, I don't know, getting aerobic on a lunch date. (They stop running.) Okay, you want the straight dope, Jack? I can't possibly be sad because I am too goddamn privileged. Now, let's run.

(They do, taking one full lap around the stage.)

JACK: The problem isn't…

JILL: You can't fix it, Jack.

JACK: The problem is…

JILL: Breathe.

JACK: Satisfaction.

JILL: Pick it up.

JACK: And how we, whew, how we get it?

JILL: We don't. I can't…unbelievable…*(They stop running.)* I can't believe you are doing this to my run.

JACK: Seriously.

JILL: Okay, seriously. We won't get satisfaction because the culture isn't based on satisfaction. They only fabricate the idea of satisfaction so we'll keep buying things. The bad news, Jack, is there is no satisfaction.

JACK: Except this.

JILL: What?

JACK: This.

JILL: Come on, Jack…

JACK: Being sad in your company. That is elegantly satisfying. And I am really very sad.

JILL: *(She looks at him.)* Oh, boy. *(She wipes his brow with her hand.)* You're an okay guy, Jack. You want a Kleenex?

JACK: Where would you keep a Kleenex?

JILL: Viola. *(She hands him one.)*

JACK: Thanks. *(Wipes eyes.)* What are you doing tonight?

JILL: You give no quarter.

JACK: I find I can't.

JILL: I am attending, God help me, a charity ball.

JACK: Should I wear a tux?

JILL: I have a date.

JACK: Ah.

(A long pause. They look at each other.)

JILL: But I will call and tell him I have Legionnaire's Disease.

JACK: Thank you…very, very much.

JILL: But then, oh avid one, I go on with my life.

JACK: Sure.

JILL: Hotel Gaulitier.

(She jogs to the other side of the stage.)

JACK: Right.

JILL: Nine o'clock. *(He nods and starts off.)* Jack?

JACK: What?

JILL: You don't dance.

JACK: I dance like the wind. My feet are like thistledown.

JILL: Really.

JACK: Lessons every Wednesday from Fred Astaire.

(He exits. She runs two more laps. Lights change. A dresser enters with a chair. Jill sits and removes sneakers and socks. Two dressers enter with evening gown, shawl, slip and heels.)

JILL: *(As she's changing.)* It should...I think so...be mandated...three years alone...this is as an adult...no companion, no significant other...both sexes. And uh, after that, barring children...two hours a day. A room, a chair and...you. See without that, and who gets it, you? Me? Him? No. You never, absolutely never...cannot process this life. Cannot take it in. What are you making of it, you know, what? You can...can do this living and...incredibly...never be introduced to...to yourself, actually...you can live 80 years...whatever...and your consciousness, your sense of the event... well, there's damn little difference, none really, between you and a lab rat. *(Jill has finished change, and dressers strike chair and jogging clothes.)* The unexamined life, followed by cancer and the life-support system. Of course, not you, not me, I speak, naturally, of the others.

(The dance band plays. Lights change. New Scene. Jack, in a truly tacky tux moves directly into Jill's arms, and they dance.)

JACK: Only one they had.

JILL: Elvis, you came.

JACK: I did.

JILL: He cooks, he dances...

JACK: He plumbs, as in plumbing.

JILL: No.

JACK: Yeah, adult education.

JILL: What possessed you, Jack?

JACK: I wanted to be able to fix something. To fix the toilet, this is power.

JILL: Dead on.

JACK: Napoleon could feel no more.

JILL: Jack?

JACK: Yes.

JILL: Who is all this for?

JACK: Ah, a trick question.

JILL: Well...

JACK: You thought I'd say, "for you."

JILL: I did.

JACK: And then you'd say…

JILL: Wrong answer…

JACK AND JILL: It should have been for yourself.

JILL: A little obvious, but…

JACK: Relevant. Listen…

JILL: Yes?

JACK: Where can we meet?

JILL: You mean…

JACK: In this life?

JILL: Ah.

JACK:…on level ground.

JILL: Let's just be here, okay?

JACK: And?

JILL: Let's just be here, Jack.

   (The music ends.)

JACK: Dumb orchestra.

JILL: It is not desirable they should overshadow the gowns.

JACK: I will go where you go. I will be your friend, your…more important-
   ly…plumber.

JILL: You turned down Prague, Jack.

JACK: That was a fantasy.

JILL: Because you say so?

JACK: We have jobs, we have responsibilities, we have mortgages that are no fantasy. We couldn't do that. We could do this.

   (New music begins. Mirror ball goes on.)

JILL: What "this?"

JACK: This!

   (They dance again.)

JILL: (Pause.) You know what I don't want to be?

JACK: Pursued.

JILL: You don't really want to catch me, Jack.

JACK: What the hell are you…

JILL: You don't want me, you want…

JACK: How can I…

JILL: An "object of desire."

JACK:…make clear to you…

JILL: Hey, Jack. I think you have changed in some ways. I think you have worked hard at it. But I don't know that we change essentially, Jack. You know, after a certain age. You always touch me because you are…of good will. You are a good person in a bad tux, Jack. I should love you, there's no doubt about that. I should. You deserve that. But something in me is in revolt. Something warns me about you. It whispers to me, you are making me up.

JACK: I love you.

JILL: What don't you like?

JACK: Excuse me.

JILL: About me, Jack?

JACK: We're dancing.

JILL: You never tell me.

JACK: I don't?

JILL: Never.

JACK: Ummm…

JILL: Let's assume I have a downside.

JACK: *(Laughing.)* Not now.

JILL: *(Dead serious.)* It's hard to love somebody who's afraid of you, Jack.

JACK: Okay.

JILL: Good.

JACK: Judged for accuracy?

JILL: Judged for insight.
    (They stop dancing.)

JACK: You're a bully.

JILL: A hit.

JACK: You isolate yourself to maintain control and then make other people responsible for your isolation.

JILL: A palpable hit.
    (Music and mirror ball end.)

JACK: You're a snob. You mask a lot of self-loathing. You need to win, and you'll raise the stakes until you do. You're judgmental, you're manipulative, you sweat the small stuff, you tease with an edge, you hate holidays, you have no empathy for insecurity, and you make no leap of faith.

JILL: But am I pretty?

JACK: You're a real babe. *(A moment.)* Why did you make me say all that stuff?

JILL: Because you don't.

JACK: But how was my analysis?

JILL: Rudimentary…but painful. And with an interesting hint of malice.

JACK: And me?
    (New music begins.)

JILL: My criticism of you? You're a nice man, Jack. It's how you control every-
  body...usually.
  (A pause.)
JACK: One more dance.
JILL: One more.
JACK: But you lead.
JILL: I can do that.

*(They whirl away. Lights change. New Scene. They turn to face each other; they
are at her place, in the middle of a conversation.)*

JACK: No, really...
JILL: Jack, come on...
JACK: Really, seriously.
JILL: No...
JACK: Jack and Jill went up the hill to fetch a pail of water; Jack fell down and...
  (Dresser enters with two beers and hands them to Jill.)
JILL: How did I know we would get to this?
JACK: "Went up the hill?" The search, the need for intimacy...fetch water...they
  sought meaning together...
JILL: I have to get up early.
JACK: Listen, listen. He didn't have the tools, he fell down...
JILL: So did she, Jack...
JACK: Yes, yes. Their destinies are entwined.
JILL: Where is it written?
JACK: It's implied. They both climbed...
JILL: They both fell...
JACK: Then what happened?
JILL: No second verse, Jack. Kiss me and go home.
  (He pulls her into a serious kiss. She responds. She pulls back.)
JACK: I think because...
JILL: I didn't...I mean...to let you come home with me...last night, fine...two
  nights...
JACK:...does not live by bread alone.
JILL: Man. Man doesn't. A woman with any sense...
JACK: Why do the first climb over? Why do that?
JILL: *(She sits in chair and removes her heels and shawl.)* What time is it, Jack?
JACK: Three A.M.
JILL: It is always three A.M. between us. Why is that? What does that say to you?

JACK: It says it's too late to do over. We've carved each other like glaciers, for God's sake. *(Jill takes Jack's beer from him and hands it to dresser.)* What the hell is different about you? Something's gone. Something's...I don't know, I'm scared for you...*(She moves to him and removes his jacket.)* What?

JILL: I'm taking off your jacket.

JACK: I feel it's...Jesus, Jill, it was so...

JILL: Painful.

JACK: Really painful...but...we could, you know, skip a grade...move on...not take the same...

JILL: *(She points at his waist.)* Pray you, undo this button.

JACK: *(He does and unzips his fly.)*...the same fall, you know, because history...*(She begins removing his pants.)* God, let's believe...

JILL: Sit down.

(He does.)

JACK: History, between people...*(She kneels and removes his shoes.)* Goddamnit, it has to be worth something...it has to be the basis...some way to...what are you doing?

JILL: *(She pulls his pants off, pulling them by the cuffs.)* I'm paying you a compliment.

JACK: Because one way or another...you know this...you'll hook up...make connection...so why not...why pick some...some guy when...why not...

JILL: *(Her dress.)* Unzip this.

JACK: *(He does.)*...because the pain was for something...give the pain some respect, it was for something.

JILL: *(She is in a slip. He is in a tux shirt, vest, tie, underwear and socks.)* Be quiet. *(She kisses him. They get involved.)* Jack. *(He's busy with her neck.)* Jack.

JACK: Sorry.

JILL: We're going to...obviously...I want you here tonight...and I...you know I do, appreciate the...the history.

JACK: Missing the point...

JILL: I am ever so glad you came, Jack. Truly. Deeply. Truly. I want you to eat me alive. And tomorrow...

JACK: Right...

JILL: I have to be alone and do stuff.

JACK: In the morning?

JILL: Forever. Now if that's understood...

JACK: It's not understood...

JILL: Well, it has to be. Because that's the way it is. New ways with new people. I want...I'm sorry, I want, for now, no history. *(He looks at her.)* I'm just all out of romance, Jack. Not in a bad way. I'm good. I think you're, you're good. See, we can go on.

JACK: What a waste.

JILL: We were never a waste, God, Jack…whatever you…you can't have, you want to wipe off the map. Whoa. No. Listen, we'll…we'll talk, Jack, but…but all that is tomorrow. Some other universe, but…in this moment…surely I don't have to explain this moment to you?

JACK: Fuck you.

(He picks up his clothes and exits. Lights change.)

JILL:…he said, and he left. Well, you know, stuff…stuff has to end some way. I mean the end wasn't what it was. What it was, was…*(She shakes her head, at a loss.)*…'Bye, Jack.

(A moment. A dresser enters and helps Jill into a silk robe. Dresser strikes chair and exits. Another dresser enters and strikes ballgown, her beer and her heels.)

JILL: My dog died. I was little, seven, I don't know, six…my dog died and I, well, I was hysterical, hysterical for days because I couldn't feel sad, wasn't devastated…cried, wept, rocked myself in my room because I couldn't cry for my dog. I grieved I couldn't grieve. I mourned I couldn't mourn…it was that way with Jack. I missed Jack, but…hey, I was a mess for two weeks because I wasn't a mess…and then…then I realized…the decks are clear…really, really clear. I could…I was mine. At the wheel of my own ship…or something. Time passes, my time passes, and I'm…you know…medically empowered…have some authority…no one dictates…very few at this level, gender issues…well, some, but…I have stocks, I have bonds, my car turns heads, I have a vacation…cabin. You know, doctor stuff. I feel good. I feel calm. Have some control. So the deal now is…the deal…in most situations…well I could, at the very least, negotiate. Very least. The question being…with whom?

(Lights change. New Scene. A dresser hands Jill a cell phone. A phone rings. Jack enters on opposite side of stage, carrying a phone. He picks it up. He's wearing a robe over clothes for the next scene: dark khakis, button-down shirt, pullover sweater and socks.)

JILL: Hi.

JACK: Hello. *(A pause.)* Jack Stojadinovac.

JILL: Happy birthday.

JACK: Who is this? Hello? Who is this?

JILL: I'm not bad, how are you?

JACK: Jill? Is this Jill?

JILL: Am I interrupting?

JACK: No…no.

(A pause.)

JILL: Well, this seems like a bad idea.

(A pause.)

JACK: Listen…ummm…where are you? Are you okay?

JILL: I'm well, Jack.

JACK: Great. Really. Really great.

JILL: Happy birthday, Jack.

JACK: Thanks. It's, uh, it's tomorrow actually.

JILL: It is tomorrow.

JACK: God, what time is it?

JILL: Three A.M. *(A pause.)* Hey, Jack, remember you asked me what was gone? I didn't…couldn't say, but…I'm not angry anymore, Jack. Not you, it's not specific, I…I must have left the window open, the door, and it just let go. I didn't know it. It was always just…right there…below…underneath every other feeling…but I don't have it anymore, isn't that weird, I just sloughed it off or…just wore it out…and it had always been there, but…I just realized and I didn't have…nobody to celebrate with…no one who knew what it was…so I…happy birthday, Jack. *(He can't answer.)* Jack? *(He doesn't answer.)* Talk to me. *(A moment.)* Jack, damnit.

(No answer. He clicks off. Lights change. Jill exits and changes offstage. A moment. He hands off the phone to a dresser. Then he removes his robe and hands same to dresser.)

JACK: Okay. That's it. Done. I can…handle that. I can tear out that root system because if you can't…take mortality, you know, for example…if you can't handle loss…the idea…the ideal is self-reliance, and you better…I better…any instant could leave you alone…a cancer cell…a brake lining…the wrong time in the wrong place, and in a finger snap, man…so protect some part of yourself…don't give yourself away…*(A dresser enters with Jack's loafers. He steps into them.)*…build up some callus on your heart, some deep remove, because…we know this…you and I…because any dependence is an affront to chaos…and when…when riled, that chaos will eat your lunch. The temptation to leave someone who really…powerfully…profoundly wants your company is just too delicious…and a person who wants to know herself…themselves…well, my conclusion is she couldn't resist it. *(A dresser enters and helps him on with raincoat and hands him an umbrella.)* It was a cosmic dare. Well, I have had that need arterioscopically removed. I'm the ice man. There is some part of me you couldn't touch with all your need and skill. No way. *(He opens umbrella.)* I'm there.

(Lights change. Thunder and lightning. New Scene. Jill enters, dressed in dress, lace-up boots, long raincoat and carrying open umbrella. Jack and Jill walk by each other.)

JILL: Jack?

JACK: What? Oh.

JILL: My God…

JACK: Geez.

JILL: I'm just…I can't believe this.

JACK: In town?

JILL: In town.

JACK: Wow.

JILL: So…um…speechless

JACK: Fine.

JILL: Fine?

JACK: What? You didn't ask how I was?

JILL: Did I?

JACK: Sorry I'm…

JILL: Listen…

JACK: Gosh, I have to…

JILL: Now?

JACK: Yeah…one o'clock.

JILL: *(Checking watch.)* Yeah.

JACK: Sorry…

JILL: No, I just…

JACK: On business?

JILL: My sister…

JACK: She's…?

JILL: Fine…she just…complicated…she's fine.

JACK: Right…look…it's, uh…how's, uh…?

JILL: Sure. You know…nice to…

JACK: Absolutely…you look…

JILL: Don't ask.

JACK: Ummm.

JILL: Damn.

JACK: Well...oh, this was funny...

JILL: Yeah?

JACK: Last, uh, Wednesday...no, Thursday...last week I was...the movies, um-mm...on this, uh, date...no big deal, but we, uh, my date, we sit down... terrible film with, uh, what's her name? The blond...married to the writer.

JILL: Oh, the writer.

(During the next speech, they notice the rain has stopped and close their umbrellas.)

JACK: Never mind...and she...we sit down and...get this...umm, incredible... next to her, Laura, the date, where we sat...crowded completely...was, uh, her ex-husband...unbelievable...

JILL: ...ex-husband...

JACK: And he is with this, umm, woman she, Laura, roomed with in, uh, college, really...I mean the odds...

JILL: Right.

JACK: So everybody talks, you know...the guy's Wilson...little confusing but later, post-film, the four of us, Laura, Wilson, the ex-husband, Laura and Wilson, yattata, yattata, yattata...they leave together...can you...you know, great...together and I'm there, you know, the other one, hair out to here...the college friend...so, hey, what could I do...I offer, you know...anyway we go outside, maybe a drink later...on the street, Laura and Wilson, locked in combat, screaming and slapping...so it ends up... wait, before that...Laura, earlier...oh, oh, I met this guy...the one...where am I, I am completely...

JILL: Coincidence. Big one.

JACK: Exactly. Unbelievable.

(Pause.)

JILL: So is this sad or what?

JACK: *(Looks at his watch.)* Actually...

JILL: Ten of...

JACK: Downtown. 20th.

JILL: 20th.

JACK: Gotta go. *(Jack starts to go, then returns.)* Oh, Jessica Lange.

JILL: Right.

(He exits. Lights change. Jill stands. Finally, she takes in the audience and speaks to them.)

JILL: I have a friend with a three-year-old, and I had borrowed…five-year-old, too…anyway, I brought it back about eight at night, and she opened the door and involuntarily, I kind of blanched, and she said, "I look like Night of the Living Dead, right?" And I said, "God, you look exhausted." And she said, "The five-year-old has chicken pox, the three-year-old is in my closet peeing on my shoes, plus I haven't cleaned up the legos or the Play-Doh or the crayons and the Barbie parts, not to mention, God help me, the orange marker all over the sofa." So I asked, "What's the good part?" And she said, "How can you ask me that?" *(A pause. A dresser enters, and Jill removes raincoat and hands coat and umbrella to dresser, who exits.)* When I come home, my house is neat. The lights automatically turn on. I eat what I want. I stay up late. I see who I please. I'm in charge of my environment. My book is book-marked. My TV guide is underlined. My bed is hard but with slight surface give. My pre-cooked meals are ready. I'm not too tired. My mind is clear. I have no desire to go out. I think I'm in deep shit.

(Lights change. New Scene. Two dressers enter and set chairs. Same library as ACT I, Scene 1. Jack enters and sits, reading Mother Goose.)

JILL: Hi. *(He looks at her. He is amazed.)* Listen, I've been…been over in the stacks watching you…you care for a, uh…no place is safe, huh? That, by the way, is a poet I admire…so…look…I am…I'm Jill, medical dominatrix, who would…would like to meet you, Jack Stojadinovac, because… well…some years ago I lost…mislaid…mislaid is better…some serious relating…umm…serious relating, and I find now…in my heart…I would like to meet you, severe and conflicted beauty…for…at a time you found conducive, ummm, such as now or…well, shortly after now. *(Pause.)* Or if you…I have the feeling…well, what the hell, never hurts to roll the dice. Jill, by the way. *(Pause.)* Your turn.

JACK: Fuck.

JILL: Yeah, who knows, maybe after coffee…but, you know, right here in the reading room…?

JACK: To what, Jill, do I owe this honor?

JILL: I miss you.

JACK: You miss me?

JILL: I miss you, Jack.

JACK: *(Pounding his forehead.)* How…is…this…possible?

JILL: First I was alone. Then you came, and I wasn't. Then I needed to know I could be. Now I can, and I don't need to. And to a person who doesn't need to be alone, you were the first person who came to mind. So, anyway, I thought I'd check in.

JACK: I just…can't you see what it feels like to…I just got you…out…off…but to do that…to do that…as if, really, I plunged my hand into my chest, tore out my heart, ripped you off it, put it back in, closed it up…came in out of the goddamn rain…now I turn around…what in hell are you doing here!

JILL: I needed…

JACK: You needed!? Well, it's a little late for what you needed, wouldn't you say? People whose needs don't get met over and over again are bloody likely not to meet the needs of the people they needed when those people show up with their needs! I practically begged you, in case you don't remember, saying I would, I don't know, fit in around the edges, turn into a plumber and pastry chef, turn myself inside out, only to be told to give you a try in the nursing home! *(Jack rises, rounding on someone in the library.)* Don't tell me to be quiet so you can read *Cosmopolitan!* *(Back to Jill.)* I may not have known how to love you but I loved you unendurably, whether or not love exists, and if you had invested in what I felt, we could have shaped it any way that would have worked for both of us, but you were in such a narcissistic fit of self-realization you wouldn't have known if a perfect union walked up and bit you in the ass.

JILL: Thank you.

JACK: Thank me?

JILL: For saying what you feel, Jack.

JACK: Forget it…

JILL: Don't cut me off!

JACK: What I'm feeling? I am feeling that there is the possible and the impossible, and this is impossible!

JILL: *(Topping him.)* Just because it isn't possible doesn't mean it isn't necessary! *(Aware of the other people in the library.)* Sorry.

JACK: Really sorry.

JILL: Sorry. *(They focus back on each other.)* Oh, Jack. I alone have…escaped…to bring you…stuff. Being fully and capable alone, Jack, maybe in the end that is…that is the one thing you have to fix.

JACK: Why me?

JILL: You know why.

JACK: I swear to God I don't.

JILL: Because I don't know if there is anything called love, Jack, but there is "being known," which I've done without and done without, and I see now the time is getting short, and I plain old can't afford to do without, and I see now, given the lovers I'm meeting and the lovers I knew, that you were the one who wanted to know me...really, really wanted to know.

JACK: I wanted to know you.

JILL: Well, I want to be known.

JACK: I think the time came and went, Jill.

JILL: Are you sure?

JACK: How the hell would I be sure?

JILL: Well, because some of us are not what we used to be, we could take what we are feeling now and put it in a room, and we could talk.

JACK: *(Looking down. To himself.)* Bloody hell. *(To Jill.)* No.

JILL: Jack...

JACK: No...huh-uh...no. Listen, I am really...we just shouldn't, you know what I mean?

JILL: I don't. No.

JACK: I need...somebody...somebody softer.

JILL: There's nobody softer than me, Jack. Not when you come right down to it. I will support every good thing in you. I will kill anybody who messes with you. We'll have a kid. We will work. I will take no shit. I will be your mate. How about it? *(A pause.)* Jack?

JACK: No.

JILL: Okay. *(A pause.)* Really no?

JACK: Yes.

JILL: Oh, Jack...

JACK: I can't.

JILL: *(A pause.)* Okay. I took the Red Eye. I hate the Red Eye. Could I possibly have a hug?

JACK: *(Looking directly at her.)* No.

JILL: Because I'm a bitch? Because this is payback? Because timing is everything? I do have bad timing. I do.

JACK: You were wrong about change.

JILL: What did I say?

JACK: It doesn't matter.

JILL: Tell me. *(He doesn't answer.)* Anything? *(He doesn't answer.)* So, anyway... *(They stand in silence. Finally, she turns and starts to go.)*

JACK: Maybe.

(She turns.)

JILL: *(Wary.)* Did you say "maybe?"

JACK: *(A pause.)* Maybe.

JILL: As opposed to "no?" *(He doesn't answer.)* Okay then. *(Accepting it doesn't have to be clear.)* Okay, Jack.

(They stand looking at each other, not moving.)

END OF PLAY

Chilean Holiday
by Guillermo Reyes

BIOGRAPHY

Guillermo Reyes is a native of Santiago, Chile, who has lived in the U.S. since 1971. He studied playwriting at the University of California, San Diego, and received his master's degree in theatre in 1990. He currently works as Assistant Professor of Theatre at Arizona State University in Tempe, AZ. His *The Seductions of Johnny Diego* was produced in the Mark Taper Forum's New Plays Festival and *The Silence of a Kiss* was produced at Los Angeles' Celebration Theater. Also at Celebration Theater, his monologue play, *Men on the Verge of a His-Panic Breakdown*, was nominated for four Ovation Awards and it won the Best Play in a Smaller Theater and the Best Writing of a World Premiere Play awards. It has been produced at San Francisco's Theater Rhinoceros and at City Lights Theater in San Jose. His latest work includes *Allende by Pinochet* and *Deporting the Divas*, which made its world premiere at the Celebration Theater in 1996, and was subsequently produced at Borderlands Theater in Tucson, AZ and Theatre Rhinoceros in San Francisco.

ORIGINAL PRODUCTION

Chilean Holiday was first performed at the 1996 Humana Festival of New American Plays, March, 1996. It was directed by Lillian Garrett-Groag with the following cast:

Digna . . . . Isabel Keating
Cecilia . . . . Rose Portillo
Don Pablo . . . . Bob Burrus
Lautaro . . . . Bobby Cannavale
Dona Conchita . . . . Divina Cook
Dona Irma . . . . Suzan Mikiel

and the following production staff:

Scenic Designer . . . . Paul Owen
Costume Designer . . . . Nanzi Adzima
Lighting Designer . . . . Mimi Jordan Sherin
Sound Designer . . . . Martin R. Desjardins
Properties Master . . . . Ron Riall
Stage Manager . . . . Carey Upton
Assistant Stage Manager . . . . Juliet Horn
Dramaturg . . . . Michael Bigelow Dixon
Los Angeles Casting Arrangements . . . . Patrick Baca Casting, Ltd.
New York Casting Arrangements . . . . .Laura Richin Casting

CHARACTERS

DIGNA: Age 30. Woman in post-youth crisis.

CECILIA: Age 33. Married to Digna's father.

DON PABLO: Age 65. Digna's father and Cecilia's older husband.

LAUTARO: Age 25. Officer in the Chilean National Police (the Carabineros).

TITO: Age 16. Cecilia's son. Outspoken, bright.

DONA CONCHITA: In her fifties. Lautaro's mother.

DONA IRMA'S VOICE: In her seventies. Elderly renter upstairs.

PLACE

The patio of a small house in the working-class district of Conchali in Santiago, Chile. Prologue: September 11, 1973. The rest of the play, two years later.

NOTE

The "Carabineros" are the Chilean National Police who are part of the Armed Forces, comprised of four branches: Army, Navy, Air Force and the National Police.

CHILEAN HOLIDAY

PROLOGUE

September 11, 1973. Noon in the patio of Don Pablo's house in the Conchali district of Santiago, a working-class district with some middle-class and lower-middle-class areas. This home is somewhere in that shadowy in-between area. The place has a rundown, shoddy look. The tiles have cracked through the years, repaired by concrete which holds them together but looks sloppy. The tablecloth on the tea table is plastic and has a few hole marks of cigarette burns on it. In the background, a white sparkling color emanates from the Andes Mountains. This might look appealingly majestic were it not for the smoggy air obscuring the view.

First, we hear the sounds of a spirited Mambo. Digna is dancing by herself. It's a drunken, comic, somewhat pathetic sight, but she's quite committed to it. She has a tiny birthday cake on the coffee table with one candle on it. An open champagne bottle, half empty, stands right next to it. Clearly, no one else is coming to this birthday party. Planes suddenly fly low, enough to startle anyone on the ground. She feels the weight of her solitude even more now.

DIGNA: Dad!….Helena!….I know the country's in crisis, but we still have priorities, don't we?
(She sets up a sign, HAPPY BIRTHDAY TO ME. It's as if she's resigned herself to celebrating on her own. But she can't ignore what's going on outside. Planes fly by again, and this time, drop bombs at a distance, startling her. This event, however, puts her in a gung-ho celebratory spirit. It's a happy day of "liberation," for some.)

She grabs the champagne bottle and drinks directly from it as the foam spews out of it. She clenches her fist, shouting "Yeah, yeah!" The sounds intensify: sounds of planes flying by and dropping bombs in the downtown area are heard enough to shake up buildings far from it.

Her face lights up with an odd patriotic idea. She runs inside undoing her blouse. When she comes back, she's got the Chilean flag wrapped around her chest. Then, she exits upstage. We see her shadow as she faces the street. A platoon of soldiers is heard marching outside. She shouts.)

DIGNA: Viva Chile!

(She exposes her breasts at them. The soldiers applaud. Lights down)

ACT ONE
Scene One

Two years later in the same setting. By all appearances, nothing has changed. Tiles are still cracked, air still smoggy, but there's a stillness in the air. Silence of tentative peace and death.

It's mid-morning, around 9:45, the air is cool. Cecilia, a woman in her early 30s, stands by a laundry facility, a cement trough, where she's been scrubbing white linen. Don Pablo, her husband, 65, has finished reading the daily, "El Mercurio," and is drinking his morning tea as he sits by the patio table. He's been eyeing the letter with U.S. Air Mail postage on it at the edge of the table, tempting him, making him curious.

Tito, 16, Cecilia's son, is drinking his own tea, dressed in pajamas, and sits apart to be independent, almost detached and uninvolved. But then he sees Don Pablo eyeing the letter. Don Pablo reaches for it.

TITO: Ma, he's doing it again.

CECILIA: Don't you dare, old man!

DON PABLO: If she's not going to open it—

CECILIA: It's still her letter.

DON PABLO: It's my house.

CECILIA: Yeah, but who's really in charge? Down! Now! *(He relents, frustrated.)* Attaboy!

TITO: Besides, they write to each other in English now so we won't peek.

DON PABLO: I can figure out English.

TITO: No, you can't.

DON PABLO: I saw John Wayne in *Stagecoach*, *The Green Berets* and *True Grit* ten times: no need to read subtitles now, I say.

TITO: John Wayne is reactionary manure.

DON PABLO: *(To Cecilia.)* Teach that boy some manners.

CECILIA: John Wayne is your stepfather's hero, Tito.

TITO: I prefer Ghandi personally. Or Mick Jagger. *(Shakes his head like rocker.)*

DON PABLO: Look, I don't care what you fools say, I'm gonna open this—
(He grabs the letter back.)

CECILIA: No! You don't.

TITO: Get him, ma.
(Don Pablo tries to open it. He and Cecilia go through a playful struggle. He ends up grabbing her but she ends up with the letter anyway.)

CECILIA: That's enough, Don Pablo, don't you come near it ever again!…Look at you, doesn't take much to get you out of breath!

DON PABLO: I'm still going strong for a man my age!

CECILIA: I want you to last, dear, till I conceive.

DON PABLO: I'm only being used for my body —but I'm willing.
(He tries to kiss her.)

CECILIA: Not today. Your hat, Don Pablo.

DON PABLO: I'm not leaving yet.

TITO: Is it true men can be fertile till their nineties?

DON PABLO: I'm not quite up there yet, little boy.

CECILIA: Don't forget your gun.

DON PABLO: What about the flag?

CECILIA: Let Digna take care of it, she's got this thing about the flag.

TITO: Maybe she could expose herself again! It could be an annual event.

DON PABLO: Look, I get enough jokes at the station about her exposing her tits. So she got drunk during the coup, that's my daughter. I used to think she was just one of these modern women, but that poor soul is lost, so pray she'll join the Salvation Army or something. Young people—look at this one. *(Pointing at Tito who's slouching forward like Mick Jagger on acid.)*

TITO: Huh?

CECILIA: Sit up, Tito. He does that on purpose.

TITO: No, I don't.

DON PABLO: Now I asked a question, where is the flag? Why isn't it up?

CECILIA: I, ah, I just threw it in the washer to give it a rinse.

DON PABLO: And?

CECILIA: I accidentally bleached it, all right?

DON PABLO: What?
(She throws it at him, he unfolds it, it has white streaks and is a little torn.)

DON PABLO: Looks like a flag of surrender now!

TITO: Or peace.

DON PABLO: Peace? That's all we need. But not to worry, you bunch of subversives. I have a spare.

CECILIA: A spare?

DON PABLO: Yes, a patriot prepares!

TITO: For what?

DON PABLO: I wasn't about to get caught without a flag on September 11—it's the law!

(He opens a cabinet by the hallway full of old stuff, pictures, old campaign posters, soccer team banners, etc.)

TITO: I think this entire holiday is a glorification of fascist militarism.

DON PABLO: So be it! The general's a dictator, but at least he's our dictator!

TITO: Words to live by.

DON PABLO: Anyway, here it is—Nice and new!

CECILIA: All this fuss over a new holiday they throw at us. With no guidelines to the average housewife.

DON PABLO: Come on, help me.

CECILIA: I mean, it's been two years since the takeover, you'd think they'd order us to do a barbecue? A pastel de choclo? Empanadas? No culinary orders from above!

TITO: Try fried fish, it goes well with beer.

CECILIA: But you don't drink beer.

TITO: Let's not get started, mom.

DON PABLO: Help me put this up! My arthritis kicks up. *(She comes to help him.)* See? Let those Communists next door notice: a new flag.

TITO: They're not Communists, they're Socialists.

DON PABLO: You shut up. Pull the string, Cecilia! Come on. Pull it.

CECILIA: Yeh, yeh, yeh.

DON PABLO: More respect. There it goes, let the Andean breeze stroke its colors. *(The flag goes up. Don Pablo looks exhilirated, she's bored.)*

CECILIA: Time to go now. And don't worry, I'll get Digna to open the letter and—

DON PABLO: And answer it, I hope.

CECILIA: Of course. I've got her under my control.

DON PABLO: Are you sure?

CECILIA: I've planned out her day along with her life!

DON PABLO: Perfect, the wicked stepmother comes out in you at last, baby!

CECILIA: Always on the lookout for you, sir!

DON PABLO: Good! I'll see you at the rally.

CECILIA: I'm not going.

DON PABLO: Yes, you are, you'll see General Pinochet face to face.

CECILIA: His face doesn't do much for me, sorry.

DON PABLO: Just one glimpse, it'll help you conceive.

CECILIA: I'm not the one who needs help, now out! And don't you stop at Dona Conchita's for her famous brew—

TITO: It's the best booze in the country.

CECILIA: You're a bad influence on the boy.

TITO: I think you're great, Uncle Pablo.

CECILIA: He's not your uncle, it's time to call him dad.

DON PABLO: It's OK.

TITO: It's better than "Grandpa."

DON PABLO: As far as I'm concerned, you're my son no matter what you call me. You're a good kid most of the time, and I want you to watch what you say, especially out there, OK?

TITO: Alright, but I'm at that age where—

DON PABLO: I know all about that age, you just watch it, OK?

TITO: Fine, dad.

CECILIA: Good. *(To Don Pablo.)* You've done one good deed for the day now out! Out!

DON PABLO: Alright, alright!

(She chases him out as he laughs.)

TITO: Mom, I just want to let you know, that it's official—

CECILIA: What?

TITO: That I'm not going to the rally either.

CECILIA: I figured.

TITO: Listen! I'm making a statement, a declaration, a pronouncement.

CECILIA: I know, you do a lot of that.

TITO: We talk about it in class—

CECILIA: About what?

TITO: —not with the teachers, they keep quiet, they might lose their jobs—but among us students, we took a poll. We've decided that dictatorship sucks.

CECILIA: That's nice, dear.

TITO: Whether it's a right-wing or a left-wing dictatorship, it's all the same. See? I'm a democrat—make that, a Social Democrat.

CECILIA: Most sixteen year olds worry about other things.

TITO: We talk about sex, too—and confession, of course—

CECILIA: I'm sure.

TITO: But the time has come to take a stand. Are you excited?

CECILIA: *(Not quite.)* Sure, very.

TITO: How can you say that?

CECILIA: I'm just tired of it. All these good intentions—there's only so much goodness a country can take.

TITO: Ma!

CECILIA: Just keep your room clean, and change your underwear every day—those are my politics!

TITO: But, Mom—

CECILIA: I don't want you ending up like that missing kid Benny.

TITO: Benny's not missing, ma, he's probably dead.

CECILIA: Now don't say that.

TITO: When we kids run away, we usually leave a note, that's how we do things. I'd say D.I.N.A. the Secret Police had something to do with it—you never know, the long hair, they singled him out.

CECILIA: Alright. So...Go buy me some...rice.

TITO: You have plenty of rice.

CECILIA: *(Pointing to Digna's room.)* I need to talk to someone.

TITO: I get it. Fine. Here, let's get the day started.

(He picks up an alarm clock and winds it.)

CECILIA: What are you doing?

TITO: Oh, just fun and games—

(The clock goes off. But nothing happens. No sign of Digna. One more time. But this awakens Dona Irma upstairs whose voice we hear.)

DONA IRMA: Turn that fucking thing off down there!

TITO: I gotta go now.

(Tito runs inside to get dressed.)

CECILIA: Sorry, Dona Irma!

DONA IRMA: It's bad enough you spend the whole day scrubbing and pounding away. What are you? A whore? Always scrubbing the sheets?

CECILIA: And you, I catch you sneaking in pets one more time, lady, and I'm gonna have them for dinner!

DONA IRMA: There's no respect! Cow!

(By then, Digna has walked in. She's got a hangover, but tries to smile it off radiantly. She wears a flowery robe and slippers.)

CECILIA: Lovely day for a hangover.

DIGNA: My body's a wreck, but my spirit soars.

CECILIA: Your face sags along with other things.

DIGNA: Cheap table wine for dinner and fish fried in pig lard do not ruin my essence.

CECILIA: Except you eat at 2 A.M.

DIGNA: The night was meant for illicit pleasures.

CECILIA: Just don't puke anywhere near me. Finish your father's tea. Come on, his germs are your germs. Sit down.

DIGNA: I demand a clean cup and saucer. Now!

CECILIA: Get it yourself, princess.

DIGNA: I want the head of John the Baptist!

CECILIA: Leftovers are good enough for you. And don't ignore my marmalade. I made it myself, country-style recipe. *(Digna spreads some marmalade a little intimidated.)* Look at you. Is this how you dress for September 11?

DIGNA: There is no tradition for September 11. Nobody knows how to celebrate a coup. We are pioneers!

CECILIA: Look at you, the past two years have been nothing but a hangover, haven't they?

DIGNA: Could I quote you?

CECILIA: What?

DIGNA: "The past two years have been nothing but a hangover." Sounds anti-government to me.

CECILIA: What are you? An informer?

DIGNA: You never know! Great marmalade!

CECILIA: Thanks. Now listen…I'm inviting Lautaro over for dinner tonight.

DIGNA: *(Not too thrilled.)* What? Again? Why?

CECILIA: I don't know, you sleep with him already, *(As she crosses herself.)* you might want a conversation out of it.

DIGNA: Or marriage.

CECILIA: Really?

DIGNA: *(Smiling playfully.)* Well, who knows?

CECILIA: There might be something to celebrate after all.

DIGNA: No, I had a dream: about Little Benny.

CECILIA: He's in the past.

DIGNA: I've tried to forget but it comes out in dreams—

CECILIA: Lautaro's in the future, I see it in my gypsy ring, my little "calli," you and he are about—

DIGNA: No, Benny was playing his guitar, very gently, a love ballad, "Love Me Tender," on top of a rock—no, it was something more glittery. A colorful mound of some kind. He had reached Tennessee.

CECILIA: What? Where?

DIGNA: The King's hometown.

CECILIA: King of Spain?

DIGNA: Elvis. His idol. As in Presley. Lives in Tennessee, the state where Las

Vegas is, don't you know anything? Now look into your ring, and concentrate, gypsy woman, don't you see him as I see him in my dreams?

CECILIA: He's…present—and, besides, if they haven't found a body, that means he's still—

DIGNA: Oh…this country's full of bodies that haven't been found.

CECILIA: Look…You're the patriot. You celebrated the coup. You exposed your breasts at the soldiers—

DIGNA: Becoming a "legend" in the process. I am just the Naked Maja of Chilean patriotism.

CECILIA: Huh?

DIGNA: Come on, the painting by Goya?

CECILIA: I've never seen it, but fine, you are "famous" now, and it's a good time to look ahead and plan for the future. There's Lautaro, beautiful, available, sensual Lautaro, future Olympic equestrian hero, prince of the Mapuches. Indian god!

DIGNA: And there's Benny, one of the Missing. You want me to forget him just like that.

CECILIA: No! Of course not. But there's also your sister's letter.

DIGNA: I know.

CECILIA: She deserves an answer.

(Tito comes running in, dressed in funky bell bottoms.)

TITO: Hey, I'm ready.

DIGNA: What is he wearing?

TITO: Latest bell bottoms, they help you do the hustle. Want me to show you?

DIGNA: *(Hangover's still kicking in.)* Not now, love.

CECILIA: That's right, not now.

TITO: Well, I'm making a run for rice. Need anything, Naked Maja?

DIGNA: See, Cecilia? He catches on.

TITO: Goya. Art History. Everybody knows that.

CECILIA: Well, I don't!

TITO: But you know what, to be more accurate about it, Delacroix works better for you.

DIGNA: What? Who?

TITO: Lady Liberty holding the flag as she leads the French troops into the battlefield with her tits up in the air, that's more like you.

DIGNA: Really? Delacroix! Yes, I feel it! I feel it!

TITO: She feels it!

DIGNA: I'm outsmarted again by a little gnome. Get me some cigarettes, boy.

CECILIA: No, no cigarettes.

TITO: Sorry, mom, necessities of life. And before I go, Lady Liberty, are you going to reenact your act of daring and expose yourself again?

DIGNA: I just might.

TITO: Wait till I get back. Bye, mom. *(Looks at his ridiculous bell bottoms and realizes mom is suffering.)* Poor mom. *(He exits.)*

DIGNA: I'm a good influence on him, aren't I?

CECILIA: Come on...Your sister's letter!

DIGNA: You want me to leave, don't you?

CECILIA: No, I want you to have choices. Lautaro is one choice, the United States is another.

DIGNA: Who wants to go to the U.S. on a tourist visa?

CECILIA: Fine, then sneak in like a gypsy.

DIGNA: More like an illegal alien! My tourist visa would expire and then what? No, when I go to Hollywood, I expect carpets to roll out for me, and I don't mean for vacuuming. I'll manage an all-girl rock band and we'll tour the world.

CECILIA: That sounds like fun. Go do it.

DIGNA: That would require work. I think I'll stay.

(They hear a rattling outside, then someone ringing the bell.)

DIGNA: What's that?

CECILIA: It's her again!

DIGNA: Who?

CECILIA: Don't move...she'll know we're here.

DIGNA: A ghost of September 11ths past.

CECILIA: No. This must be her new morning route. She rattles that tin cup at my face one more time and I... *(Calls out.)* I already gave you money last week, lady, don't insist, and please put away those dirty children you probably borrowed—I think she's deaf.

DIGNA: It's all an act. Call the cops.

CECILIA: We are the cops! Just stand still. She makes me nervous.

DIGNA: We bombed their shantytowns and they're still here.

CECILIA: She's gone.

DONA IRMA: Ceciliaaaaaaa! Who the hell was that?

CECILIA: Go back to sleep!

DONA IRMA: They should put those people away. In concentration camps!

CECILIA: We'll evict you, shut up! *(They hold still, then they laugh.)*

DIGNA: You know what? Could I borrow money?

CECILIA: I have things for you to do. Earn your money.

(She throws her some bags.)

DIGNA: What's this?

CECILIA: For Benny's mother.

DIGNA: She won't take old rags from me.

CECILIA: She sells them at the open market—I get a cut!

DIGNA: I need these old sunglasses—

CECILIA: You have new ones.

DIGNA: They're a memory of summers at the beach.

CECILIA: No, you wore those at your mother's funeral.

DIGNA: That, too. Maybe I don't need them.

CECILIA: This woman's expecting you.

DIGNA: Since when? She blames Benny's sexual awakening on me, which she should, of course—

CECILIA: The bags are ready, your day can start now—but not before opening your sister's letter, of course.

DIGNA: So many things to do, what should I do first?

CECILIA: Come on.

DIGNA: OK. I will open it…and I might even read it.

CECILIA: Open it!

DIGNA: Alright…I'm trying, it's fat.

CECILIA: So what is it?

DIGNA: Just a birthday card.

CECILIA: Your birthday? And you didn't tell me—

DIGNA: That's why I waited to open it today.

CECILIA: Well, Happy 33rd. *(Digna gives her a look.)* I thought we were the same age.

DIGNA: I'll be generous.

CECILIA: I don't care. Happy, Happy, Happy Birthday, my own Miss Chile, Miss Naked Maya! *(Hugs her, Digna doesn't hug back.)* Does Lautaro know about this?

DIGNA: Why should he?

CECILIA: I'll make sure he does.

DIGNA: Why did the military choose my birthday to take over the government?

CECILIA: Think of it. People put up the flag now on your birthday!

DIGNA: No, no, I've been overshadowed by events.

CECILIA: We'll have to organize something then.

DIGNA: No, we'll spend it in quiet dignity.

CECILIA: Right. But…what about the letter?

DIGNA: The letter?

CECILIA: Helena's letter. What does it actually say?

DIGNA: Oh, yes…well…She's bought me a one-way ticket to Los Angeles.

CECILIA: A ticket? Are you serious? Is it in here?

DIGNA: No, I have to go redeem it at the airline office.

CECILIA: *(Feeling hurt.)* And you weren't going to tell me this either?

DIGNA: I'm not going to the U.S. to be some cleaning woman.

CECILIA: Work would do you good, the more domestic the better.

DIGNA: Thanks.

CECILIA: Every animal that God created was meant to get up and hunt and scavenge for his food, but, honey, you do nothing.

DIGNA: I...I go out and I...I...I contribute to this country's sense of idleness, somebody has to.

CECILIA: Look, over there the maids don't work as hard as they do here. They have the latest washing machines. You just push buttons and read magazines while you wait for the spin cycle, and they're always out on the pool socializing with their movie star bosses.

DIGNA: Really? What kind of movie stars?

CECILIA: You take your pick, I'm sure. And I even read about this one maid whose boss got sick on Oscar night—and the maid went in her place. Her boss won for supporting actress and the maid picked up the Oscar on live TV.

DIGNA: Really?

CECILIA: Sure, a girl from Tegucigalpa, Honduras, about your age. And I'm sure it's all close to Las Vegas, Tennessee. Must be a short ride from Los Angeles.

DIGNA: I could drive over on the weekends, I suppose. They're into "weekend drives" over there.

CECILIA: And if you miss our quakes, they have their share in California.

DIGNA: Oh, great! Earth-shattering pleasures! You're insane, stepmother! I'm not going anywhere.

CECILIA: All these choices opening up for you—

DIGNA: Choices, what choices?

CECILIA: You'll see.

(Starts to leave.)

DIGNA: Come back here.

CECILIA: Excuse me, I have to—

DIGNA: I'll deal with Lautaro, you hear me?

CECILIA: It's all in the stars.

DIGNA: Don't give me that! Now listen!

CECILIA: Yes?

DIGNA: Listen closely. I've decided...since this is what you want me to do... I've decided that on my 30th birthday, I will...

CECILIA: You will...

DIGNA: I will...I will be decisive.

CECILIA: How?

DIGNA: After tea maybe, yes, after tea, tea's reflective, Oriental, karmic, reading-of-tea-leaves, that type of thing, I will make a decision to do something grand and decisive with my life.

CECILIA: What?

DIGNA: Well...I will plunge into the world and make fire and music, I will do wonders with the rest of my youth, I will break with the past, and I will chart a new path—something like that. That was tough.

CECILIA: Close enough! This is a wonderful birthday then. I never thought September 11 would turn out to be this festive, like a real holiday! You shouldn't have kept your birthday a secret, I would have known immediately what to do!

DIGNA: Like a dictator.

CECILIA: No, like a wicked stepmother. Now you do something about that hair, that face, that posture, everything. *(Calling up.)* Hey, Dona Irma. It's Digna's birthday, and the horoscope points to many great things, like marriage to Lautaro maybe!

DIGNA: Oh, no, she doesn't have to know!

CECILIA: I'll never forget this September 11.

DIGNA: Get used to them, there's many more to come.

CECILIA: Whatever you say, my Little Naked Mayan!

DIGNA: Maja!

CECILIA: Whatever! Here's a ten thousand

DIGNA: Inflated money!

CECILIA: Still buys a match and a pack of cigarettes for our Precious' lips. See ya, sweetie.

(Cecilia grabs her purse and a light sweater. By then, she's done with the sheets which she leaves hanging on a wire, creating a line-up of whites that engulf the stage.

Digna's left alone. She looks into the bags meant for Benny's mother. She takes out the sunglasses and puts them on. She stares at the Chilean flag. She approaches it wearing her sunglasses, trying to look cool. She lowers the flag. She plays with it as she wraps herself around it and recalls that special day two years previously. She waves at imaginary audience and hears cheers and applause as she did that day.)

Suddenly, out of this fantasy emerges Lautaro, the handsome hero in his equestrian gear. He reaches out to her and pulls her to him as they do a little dance, maybe a tango combined with a little merengue and salsa.

Suddenly, the window in Dona Irma's room opens and Digna sees Benny with his long hair to his shoulders. He's tied down to a chair as a white interrogation light beams on him. This image scares the hell out of her. The window shuts itself. Lautaro is gone.

Reality is restored. She runs out leaving the flag at half mast.
She picks up bags and exits.)

END OF SCENE

(During the transition, we see a radio out of which emerges General Pinochet's nasal voice.)

PINOCHET'S VOICE: My fellow Chileans, compatriots, the nation celebrates its second anniversary of freedom! Freedom from Marxism-Leninism. Freedom from the agents of atheism. And let us not forget. They are still with us, the enemy, everywhere. We must be on the lookout for them. We are under internal siege, but we will eliminate them. We will leave no stone unturned, until they are forever exterminated as the parasites, the cancer they represent! We have no problem with unarmed citizens, peaceful, God-fearing citizens. People like you! *(Roar of the crowd.)* That's right, you! The nation must now light a torch. A torch of Liberty that will blaze into the night as the world watches in awe of our Liberation!…And for those fellow Chileans who couldn't make it to the rally, I will have our planes deliver to you…*(We hear planes again.)*…flyers carrying the picture of your leader to help you celebrate on this glorious anniversary of Freedom.
(Flyers blanket the stage bearing General Pinochet's face. They make a mess. Roar of crowds, as we proceed.)

Scene Two

Later that afternoon. Cecilia enters burdened down by packages. She's angry to see the flag at half mast.

CECILIA: Digna…Digna. Where are you, you shithead? *(Sees flyer.)* Look at this! Who gets stuck cleaning up the dictator's mess—the average housewife! *(She puts down packages, and then goes to put up the flag again. Without her noticing, Lautaro enters and is standing there looking at her, calmly. He's a man in his mid-20s. He wears his green "carabinero" uniform. He smokes quietly using the cigarette as a form of defense. Cecilia finally turns around and sees him.)*

CECILIA: Oh, hi, sweetie.

LAUTARO: Busy again, "sweetie"?

CECILIA: I tried calling you at the station, Lautaro, nobody's seen you all day.

LAUTARO: People don't need to know my whereabouts all the time.

CECILIA: You were riding one of those smelly horses again, weren't you?

LAUTARO: Key to my future glory.

CECILIA: Yeah, yeah. Why aren't you at the rally?

LAUTARO: I had the curfew shift, I slept in today. Anything else, oh, Grand Inquisitor?

CECILIA: You of all people should be at the rally. It's very suspicious. You're up to something.

LAUTARO: I skipped it, all right? I'm still a patriot.

CECILIA: Then you clean up this mess! Look at it!

LAUTARO: To help us remember this glorious day!

CECILIA: *(Meaning flyers.)* They'll come in handy when we run out of toilet paper. Look…I was just going to invite you to dinner, and it's too early, so go home and take a nap, honey.

LAUTARO: I'm not sleepy, honey.

CECILIA: Digna's not here.

LAUTARO: That's all right.

CECILIA: Nothing's ready.

LAUTARO: You look ready. Get me some brandy or something—

CECILIA: Table wine's good enough for you, peasant.

LAUTARO: Be good to me, I'll be good to you.

CECILIA: Well, you caught me at a bad time. I took the bus downtown and I bought all these nice pastries and this imported tea, and a few gifts, and finally I got a new tablecloth for this table, oh, it's been bugging me for so long, all these cigarette burns on it, careless people around here, how have they survived without me? And then I come home and the flag is at half mast.

LAUTARO: *(Laughing.)* Digna?

CECILIA: Who else? And it's not funny. People wonder.

LAUTARO: What's all this fear? Your husband's a cop for goddsake. You're one of us.

CECILIA: Nah, gypsies are never "one of us." *(She sees a huge bag of rice on one of the shelves.)* Oh, and look at this!

LAUTARO: What? It's just a bag of rice.

CECILIA: Not just a bag, but the biggest bag he could possibly find—why does that boy do things like that?

LAUTARO: He's a kid.

CECILIA: He does it on purpose—you carry it, in there. Come on!

LAUTARO: Anything for you, love.

CECILIA: Move it.

(He takes bag of rice inside, she continues to pick up flyers, he runs back out.)

LAUTARO: Yeah, hard labor! We have that in common, too.

CECILIA: We're country trash, is that it?

LAUTARO: Yeah.

CECILIA: In you it shows.

LAUTARO: And proud of it, love!

CECILIA: Whatever, love…look, make yourself at home, don't mind if I ignore you.

LAUTARO: No, don't do that. I don't want to be ignored.

CECILIA: Go look for Digna, flirt with her.

LAUTARO: Is that what I'm doing?

CECILIA: What?

LAUTARO: Am I flirting?

CECILIA: Save it, and come back later.

LAUTARO: I'm staying right here. This is my chair. The Andes look good from this angle. Not just good—imposing, tremendous, overpowering!

CECILIA: They just look bloody, all that sunlight on them. The snow will melt, we'll have a flood, we'll all drown.

LAUTARO: What's wrong? Don Pablo not keeping you happy?

CECILIA: My business, boy.

LAUTARO: Or…you miss the countryside?

CECILIA: No. I like my TV and my phone—though I have to share it with that she-devil renter up there—and when my washing machine gets fixed, I'll be living in style.

LAUTARO: Big dreams, huh?

CECILIA: No, just little, realistic ones.

LAUTARO: Not me! When I'm riding on one of those horses, I become one of them—no, I transform myself into one of those beasts with wings and fire spewing out their mouths. A dragon, that's it, that's what it feels like to be me. Sometimes it's hard to find the words to describe my natural magnificence. Call me Lancelot.

CECILIA: More like Don Quixote. Or Sancho Panza.

LAUTARO: Thanks.

CECILIA: Look, hero…you know she needs you.

LAUTARO: Who?

CECILIA: Digna, who else? Concentrate! She needs someone to tame her.

LAUTARO: Well, you're the stepmother.

CECILIA: I'm not wicked enough. Look…Help me with this cloth, make yourself useful—come on—(*He comes near.*)—from the other end, you fool.

LAUTARO: Sure, boss me around, I don't mind.

CECILIA: I'll get my brothers to come rough you up.

LAUTARO: See? We have lots in common, rough killer brothers. It runs in our blood.

CECILIA: Gypsy, too.

LAUTARO: Not me though, just Spanish and Indian here.

CECILIA: Calli! (*Pronounced "catchee".*)

LAUTARO: What's it mean?

CECILIA: You're an "alangari."

LAUTARO: What?

CECILIA: As in, you're an "alangari" in the butt. Now go buy Digna a present. It's her birthday, gentile.

LAUTARO: Really?

CECILIA: See? That's why I was trying to reach you. You still have time to go buy her something.

LAUTARO: If I buy her something, she might think I like her.

CECILIA: But you do, you just don't know it yet. Now here…(*Meaning wrapped gift.*) Take this one, we'll make believe you bought it. Play along. What's wrong with you? A kid like you, a widower already.

LAUTARO: I know, it's unfair.

CECILIA: Time has passed, Lautaro. Mariana was a wonderful little thing, so frail and—if I may say so—conceited. I don't mean to be disrespectful to the dead, but move on. You're not the type who mourns anyway. I know your type, never shows the pain inside or outside, you're perfect for Digna.

LAUTARO: Cecilia, I don't want you putting ideas into Digna's head.

CECILIA: It's the natural convergence of Virgo and Taurus.

LAUTARO: Oh, all right, in that case—

CECILIA: Help her forget that rock singer kid.

LAUTARO: He was a minor, you know. *(Playful, in a sick way.)* You have a son, keep an eye on him around her.

CECILIA: You're sick. Is this the type of respect women who sleep with you get?

LAUTARO: Excuse me?

CECILIA: Would you be surprised to find out she actually felt something for you?

LAUTARO: Feelings? Her?

CECILIA: I realize she is trouble. She's spoiled, she's even disgusting at times, but that's exactly what you like in women.

LAUTARO: What do you know about what I like in women?

CECILIA: I watch from a distance. I know what you've been up to since Mariana's death.

LAUTARO: Are you spying on me?

CECILIA: I observe with my gypsy third eye—and I don't approve.

LAUTARO: I like the idea of you quietly observing me.

CECILIA: Stick to Digna.

LAUTARO: Yes, Digna. Well, Helena wants her in the U.S. So we'll put her on a plane to Hollywood.

CECILIA: You're some lousy suitor, you know.

LAUTARO: Deport the bitch.

CECILIA: That's disgusting! You're disgusting.

LAUTARO: How come we've never talked before?

(He grabs her hand.)

CECILIA: What's this?

LAUTARO: Don't push it away.

CECILIA: I wasn't about to, it's a nice hand really, but I think I better—

LAUTARO: Why are you married to that man?

CECILIA: What? Don Pablo? He's the kindest old fool—

LAUTARO: I'm sure he's kind. But why the hell marry him? Why aren't you just his maid? Why isn't Dona Irma up there married to him? Why you? And why call him "Don" Pablo? Too reverential. Call him Pablo, call him asshole, call him anything, just don't call him "Don." It bothers the hell out of me to see a young woman like you—

CECILIA: Look, I know what you're up to. You're only doing this because I'm married.

LAUTARO: That's only one of the reasons.

CECILIA: Don't play with me. I've only made one mistake—

LAUTARO: Only one? No room for more?

CECILIA: I've had to live with it since. I've had to feed "it."

LAUTARO: The kid, you mean? Was a it horny landowner? A priest? A general?

CECILIA: No, only a peach picker who made too many promises he couldn't keep—I was seventeen, and he was married... That's all you need to know.

LAUTARO: That's it? After luring me into your secret web—

CECILIA: Lure you? I don't think so.

(She gets up to fold her sheets.)

LAUTARO: Need help with that?

CECILIA: You stay away from my sheets, honey.

(Tito comes in, he's still wearing his bell bottoms, but also a sports jacket and tie.)

TITO: Hello....*(Mockingly.)* Happy Holidays!

LAUTARO: *(Ironically.)* You sound like you mean that.

CECILIA: What's with the tie and everything?

TITO: I got you a good deal on the rice, didn't you notice?

CECILIA: Thanks, I noticed alright. And what is this? Lipstick? You have lipstick on your cheek.

TITO: Really? Sorry.

LAUTARO: What's happening to you, brother?

TITO: *(To Lautaro.)* I only went to your mom's tavern—

CECILIA: Why is Dona Conchita's tavern open on a holiday?

LAUTARO: People drink on holidays—*(Meaning Tito.)* Perfect example right there.

TITO: That place is jumpin'.

CECILIA: You've been smoking, too, haven't you?

TITO: I know that, mom. I told you a long time ago that it was time for me to make these types of decisions—

CECILIA: It is not time, dear.

TITO: In the countryside, wouldn't I already be a married man with kids, which means I'd be, you know, sexually active?

CECILIA: Even people in the country are waiting longer these days to get married.

LAUTARO: But he's got something there—the modern world has ruined teenage sex, delaying it forever, making a big deal out of it.

TITO: Nobody slows you down, Lautaro, you're my hero.

CECILIA: You know, I'm trying to be a mother here—

TITO: But it's true, mom. In the medieval world, everyone got married in their teens and then died in their early 30s, so teenage sex and pregnancy were not an issue. Those people were in sync with nature.

CECILIA: I think I know enough about teenage pregnancy to recommend waiting.

TITO: Don't worry, we talk about contraceptives in "my crowd," and the threat of marriage after pregnancy especially in a country like this one where divorce and abortion are both illegal so you're stuck for life if you do marry. So I will make responsible decisions, and then there's always the recommended minimum dosage for a kid my age to masturbate four times a day.

LAUTARO: Beware of tendonitis.

CECILIA: Lautaro!

LAUTARO: Sorry.

TITO: I will avoid the typical mistakes, mother. That is what you want me to do, isn't it?

CECILIA: It's a deal.

TITO: I'll go lie down now before dinner—I mean because of the hangover. *(To Lautaro.)* Oh, and did you know that Digna is our own Delacroix Lady Liberty and all her sins will be washed away the moment she finds someone to share her life with?

LAUTARO: Really?

TITO: Just thought I'd let you know, man to man.

(Tito exits.)

CECILIA: Hollywood movies! *Shampoo, Carnal Knowledge, The Graduate, Easy Rider*—he's seen them all.

LAUTARO: He plays with fire alright. But you'll have other kids.

CECILIA: Yes, but I don't want to give up on this one yet. I don't want to give up on any of you. It's as if I've adopted you all, bunch of kids every single one of you.

LAUTARO: Why does Don Pablo need more kids anyway?

CECILIA: They're not just for him, they're for me, too.

LAUTARO: You never answered my question, you know.

CECILIA: Which one?

LAUTARO: Don Pablo? Why Don Pablo?

CECILIA: Why do I call him that?

LAUTARO: No, why did you marry him?

(Digna walks in. Her hair has been neatly done, and she's dressed up in an elegant dress. Lautaro and Cecilia look surprised to see her this way.)

DIGNA: *(Deeper voice, trying to play sophisticated.)* Good evening.

CECILIA: My! What happened to you?

LAUTARO: Yes, you look decent.

DIGNA: Radiant maybe?

LAUTARO: Decent.

DIGNA: I went to see Benny's mother just like you told me to, stepmother.

CECILIA: And she did all that?

DIGNA: I look respectable, isn't it godawful?

CECILIA: You don't sound very grateful.

DIGNA: I sound like I usually sound.

CECILIA: Did she lend you the dress?

DIGNA: I gave her your old rags, she gave me hers. Something she wore twenty years ago at some party where she conceived Benny.

LAUTARO: Make that seventeen years, he was a minor.

DIGNA: He was almost eighteen—and in some Scandinavian countries, the age of consent is fourteen.

CECILIA: Swedish movies.

DIGNA: I'm not a molester, contrary to popular myth. But Myths die hard when a woman is sexually active, don't they, especially in a country ruled by the Mafia?

CECILIA: Ah…

DIGNA: Look, I must admit though, I behaved in her presence, I was charming. We had tea—

CECILIA: Tea? Did you say tea?

DIGNA: Now, don't read into it. I haven't made any earth-shattering decisions yet. You're assigned to read the tea leaves later, Cecilia, I don't want to take my chances on a misreading.

CECILIA: Any news on Benny?

DIGNA: No. All a mother can do in that position is talk about how much she misses him, we had a little cry. Then his little sister arrived, she did my nails, see? She had a cry, too. Then some old fuddy-duddy arrived, a granduncle, he gave me home-made brandy, and then he did my toenails. See? We all had a little cry. After meeting me, they agreed that if Benny was meant to be corrupted, it might as well be done by someone of my caliber.

LAUTARO: Did they say that in so many words?

DIGNA: I'm paraphrasing, asshole!

LAUTARO: I figured.

DIGNA: His mother has become fond of me! You see, in her youth, she was — shall we say—loose?

CECILIA: Trash!

DIGNA: You said it, I didn't. The church was after her to annul her first communion, my type of woman. Benny was a love child, I didn't know this!

LAUTARO: There's a lot of that going around.

CECILIA: Very avoidable these days.

DIGNA: She realized that I wasn't the devil, just a youthful reflection of herself.

LAUTARO: You have that effect on people.

DIGNA: It's refreshing to meet people who can appreciate your vices. We parted on good terms, she gave me two friendly pecks on the cheek and said we'd meet again when Benny returned.

CECILIA: What if he doesn't?

DIGNA: Oh, I don't know. We didn't discuss that. Thank you for sending me over though.

CECILIA: You needed to get out of the house, that's all.

DIGNA: I needed a little cry.

LAUTARO: I can't quite see you cry.

DIGNA: Look, pig! I'm a sensitive woman with feelings of genuine tenderness and compassion!

LAUTARO: I believe you!

DIGNA: I just don't get a chance to show it, not when I have to hang out with fascists like you.

LAUTARO: Nobody's forcing you to. And I'm not a fascist.

CECILIA: *(To Digna.)* It's not as if you don't enjoy being seen with Lautaro, our national equestrian hero.

LAUTARO: Add future Olympic hero to the list.

DIGNA: I'm not in the mood for adding to his list of conquests.

LAUTARO: I should get a medal for sleeping with you, yes.

DIGNA: The test of endurance was all mine.

CECILIA: Excuse me, I think we—

DIGNA: I could be accused of bestiality.

LAUTARO: I am a bull, I admit.

DIGNA: Good, he admits it! Now is that for me, champ?

LAUTARO: What?

CECILIA: The gift, Lautaro.

LAUTARO: I guess it's for you, take it.

DIGNA: How did you know it was my birthday?

LAUTARO: A lucky guess.

DIGNA: May I open it?

CECILIA: Go ahead, open it. I mean, Lautaro thinks you should.

LAUTARO: I don't give a damn.

DIGNA: I guess he means yes. *(She tears it open, finds lingerie inside.)* Oh, Lautaro, baby—who would have guessed?

LAUTARO: Oooh-la-la.

DIGNA: Why wear this if the man's just going to tear it apart with his teeth?

CECILIA: And if you don't like it, dear, you could always hang it at half mast.

DIGNA: It's the height of bad taste, and I'm into bad taste—and when I find a man worthy of it, I'll wear it.

CECILIA: Time for tea.

LAUTARO: Let Digna serve it. It'll help her prepare for the U.S.

DIGNA: I ask you, who's preparing the U.S. for me? Stand back, California!

LAUTARO: See? She is going!

DIGNA: Maybe. Maybe not.

CECILIA: I'll prepare the tea. And, oh, Helena called from Los Angeles.

DIGNA: Again?

CECILIA: It's your birthday after all! And while I'm gone, I don't want any horseplay. I want business, you hear me? Business!

DIGNA: I notice somebody put the flag back up again.

CECILIA: That's what I mean, business! *(She exits.)*

LAUTARO: Now is she really a gypsy?

DIGNA: I don't know, why?

LAUTARO: What does "gachi" mean?

DIGNA: Who cares?

LAUTARO: I'm just curious. So when are you leaving?

DIGNA: Lautaro...somebody might think you were trying to get rid of me.

LAUTARO: *(Obnoxiously.)* I just want what's best for you always.

DIGNA: Since when? People stop me in the streets to find out when I'm leaving. I think they're lighting candles to pray for my departure.

LAUTARO: The entire neighborhood cares about you.

DIGNA: Some people think you're about to ask for my hand.

LAUTARO: Your hand?

DIGNA: As in holy matrimony?

LAUTARO: You're the one who said marriage is up there with dictatorship.

DIGNA: But when I said it, I still admired dictatorship.

LAUTARO: And you don't now?

DIGNA: Come on, you're supposed to propose. I'd like the satisfaction of rejecting you.

LAUTARO: What if you accept? Then I'd be stuck.

DIGNA: Take your chances, soldier boy.

LAUTARO: Why would a soldier marry some radical? Some bohemian?

DIGNA: I'm no bohemian, I'm the Naked Maja of Patriotism.

LAUTARO: The what?

DIGNA: Meaning my "unveiling" two years ago—

LAUTARO: You exposed your tits. You were a true nationalist then!

DIGNA: It's true I "celebrated" the coup. I was drunk; it was my birthday. I had to celebrate something. I really believed the military had saved us from Communism. Only to wake up and face what? A right-wing hangover?

LAUTARO: Let's not talk politics, I'd rather propose.

DIGNA: Then do.

LAUTARO: Get me really drunk first. Then maybe, who knows?

DIGNA: I see. Well, this is that special awkward moment—

LAUTARO: What do you mean?

DIGNA: This is the moment I've read about.

LAUTARO: What? Where?

DIGNA: In an article in my endless research on human passion.

LAUTARO: The Spanish version of Cosmopolitan.

DIGNA: Right. This is where the groom-to-be plays it cool, and hesitates and makes believe he is above this. The bride-to-be doesn't want to seem too eager, she has doubts herself—

LAUTARO: Not about me—him?

DIGNA: Because she couldn't do better than him?

LAUTARO: You said it.

DIGNA: See? It's that moment when he has to pull back to make himself seem tough, but the truth is, she is too strong for him.

LAUTARO: Is she?

DIGNA: She intimidates.

LAUTARO: You intimidate!

DIGNA: He admits it!

LAUTARO: I do not—he does not!

DIGNA: She outwits him every time, so he has turn her down, otherwise his pride will hurt, but what he doesn't know is she'll turn him down before he gets a chance to do so.

LAUTARO: Fine, let's try it. You turn me down! I dare you.

DIGNA: She can't turn anyone down before he proposes.

LAUTARO: Really?

DIGNA: In so many words, on his knees!

LAUTARO: No way!

DIGNA: What's he afraid of?

LAUTARO: Who's afraid?

DIGNA: Somebody is.

LAUTARO: Alright—I'll take my—

DIGNA: He—

LAUTARO: He'll take his chances—*(On his knees, laughing through it.)* Digna—would you marry me?

DIGNA: *(Surprised.)* He said it!

LAUTARO: Come on, you're supposed to turn me down now.

DIGNA: There's another article.

LAUTARO: What?

DIGNA: "Women Over 30: Grab Him While You Can."

LAUTARO: Oh, come on, that's not fair, you didn't say anything about this other—

DIGNA: It's so cute when you pout.

LAUTARO: I don't "pout!" Turn me down already.

DIGNA: I have choices now.

LAUTARO: Let's not play this any more. *(She's laughing.)* Stop! Right now! I mean it! Look, what if the groom is in love with someone else?

DIGNA: Oh…like whom?

LAUTARO: Or the memory of someone else.

DIGNA: She's feeling the same way then!

LAUTARO: What? Like who?

DIGNA: A minor maybe?

LAUTARO: Oh…I don't know where Benny is, Digna. You're a cop's daughter yourself—

DIGNA: Dad won't talk either. He has his own secrets, you all do. We've become a nation of secrets. Is this my cause then? Am I supposed to become some activist or something? Me? An activist? I thought I was above it all once, welcomed to any party, Left or Right, booze was booze anywhere. Yet I wake up now feeling this hangover—you people are pushing me in the direction of, heaven help me, having a social conscience.

LAUTARO: *(Ironically.)* You poor thing!

DIGNA: I dread the thought, too, but you people are pushing me.

LAUTARO: No need to go that far. Benny's somewhere in the U.S. snorting coke and getting a record deal.

DIGNA: That's what I'd like to believe, too. Otherwise, what would be the point of him missing? He wasn't even involved in politics—

LAUTARO: Exactly, so people like you shouldn't worry so much about him.

DIGNA: So we should just keep our mouths shut, and wait, is that what you're saying?

LAUTARO: We have enough trouble dealing with real terrorists, your Benny's not on anyone's list.

DIGNA: Then why can't you people share your "lists?"

LAUTARO: You're making stupid allegations now and—*(Very sincere.)* Digna, this is getting out of hand, all these rumors, we are not the enemy, we are your military, we are your family—we have a duty to restore order after years of chaos.

DIGNA: I know, I've heard it nonstop for two years now. Then again, I also worry about you.

LAUTARO: What about me?

DIGNA: I'd wish you'd get out before it's too late.

LAUTARO: Too late for what? And you haven't officially rejected me yet—I can't believe I just proposed! You're supposed to reject me and we can end this game—

DIGNA: I don't want to end it. I want you agree to run away from it all.

LAUTARO: What are you talking about now?

DIGNA: Desertion.

LAUTARO: Let's not play this.

DIGNA: People keep telling me to go to the U.S. But I'm not the one who needs to run away the most. You are. *(As she digs through her purse.)* In fact, you might as well have it then.

LAUTARO: Have what?

DIGNA: A little birthday surprise.

LAUTARO: But it's your birthday.

DIGNA: And I can give away my gifts if I want to. *(She hands him envelope.)* I went downtown to get it. They were closing early because of the holiday and I got there just in time.

LAUTARO: This is your…

DIGNA: Helena bought it for me, but I have decided to let you take my place on that plane to California.

LAUTARO: What the hell are you talking about now?

DIGNA: Simple. You'll desert the Chilean National Police, avoiding in the process becoming one of "them."

LAUTARO: You fool, I joined to become one of "them."

DIGNA: You joined because of the equestrian team, you're an athlete not a mass murderer.

LAUTARO: I've had enough of your jokes! Where's the damn tea? Cecilia! Where's—

DIGNA: Think about it, with your connections, you could get a tourist visa in no time, you go as a tourist, you stay as a refugee.

LAUTARO: Only Communists do that!

DIGNA: I'm just asking you to dream a little, to have some imagination, to grab a chance when you see one.

LAUTARO: People want you to leave, and you're not listening!

DIGNA: There's no future for you here—

LAUTARO: I have a future in the military—

DIGNA: What type of future is that?

LAUTARO: Some people are proud to serve their country.

DIGNA: I exposed myself once for the troops, where did that get me?

LAUTARO: You're the neighborhood easy woman, that's all you are.

DIGNA: In that case, let me help you change your mind.

    (She puts her arm around him.)

LAUTARO: We always end up like this.

DIGNA: Because we communicate so well, face to face.

LAUTARO: Come on—*(Trying to move away.)*

DIGNA: No, stay. *(Stroking his face.)* Why didn't Benny have this stubble?

LAUTARO: Because he was a kid!

DIGNA: And you're not, that's for sure.

LAUTARO: If you leave, I'd miss the disgusting feeling I get every time we end up naked.

DIGNA: Abroad. It sounds so good. It melts in your mouth.

LAUTARO: How can I go abroad? I've got everything going for me here?

DIGNA: Then don't let it, don't let it happen. Take the ticket, use it. You're young. This country's not about to let you enjoy your talents without strings attached. This country's going to destroy you.

LAUTARO: More respect for the country!

    (Cecilia is walking in quietly for this final speech. She carries a tray with tea cups, tea kettle, and birthday cake. She has changed into a modest, new getup that makes her look more charming, a dress with flowery embroideries, very old-fashioned. They don't notice her as Digna continues.)

DIGNA: *(To Lautaro.)* By the time I get through with you, soldier boy, you'll be a pacifist!

(She kisses him all of a sudden, surprising him. He has a hard time resisting this. Cecilia witnesses this kiss and is left looking mesmerized, surprised, and delighted as the lights go off.)

END OF ACT ONE

ACT TWO

Same setting. The action resumes as we left it in Act One. Digna pushes him away satisfied with her kiss. The two lovers notice Cecilia standing there, holding her tray.

CECILIA: Hi.
> *(Cecilia puts down the tray, all self-conscious.)*

DIGNA: *(Pulling away.)* Hi yourself.

LAUTARO: Cecilia to the rescue!

DIGNA: *(As a put-down.)* You look respectable!

LAUTARO: Very pretty actually.

CECILIA: *(As she serves them.)* Oh, you two. Stop it!

DIGNA: *(Making fun of her.)* "Us two."

CECILIA: You behave, city trash.

DIGNA: That's more like it, I want sugar on this tea, stepmother. Now!

LAUTARO: Leave the woman alone—

DIGNA: Shut up! In our home, Cinderella calls the shots, stepmother obeys.

CECILIA: So she thinks. Well, I was listening to the radio and there's hundreds of thousands of people in front of the Presidential palace.

DIGNA: Don't they have anything better to do like dig a few mass graves?

LAUTARO: *(Ironically.)* You're very charming.

DIGNA: No, just perceptive.

LAUTARO: That could be dangerous.

DIGNA: To those with something to hide, yes.

CECILIA: We should all be there, but of course, we're not.

DIGNA: Nope, we're not. This is hot, you're evil.

CECILIA: Sorry. Now why didn't you go again, Lautaro?

LAUTARO: Yes, again. Just let me drink.

CECILIA: Now you notice I brought out the birthday cake.

DIGNA: Very nice.

CECILIA: Notice I didn't sing or light candles. I figured she'd do something nasty to me.

LAUTARO: She's nasty alright.

CECILIA: It's her birthday, let her call the shots.

DIGNA: Fine by me.

LAUTARO: No, I say, we really need to celebrate. To a Happy September 11.

CECILIA: Of course. Happy Holidays, Happy Birthday, Happy Futures together, and not alone....And General Pinochet was delivering his speech to great acclaim from hundreds of thousands of people around him. They've lit a torch, a torch of liberty, in commemoration of September 11, 1973. It's only a second anniversary—

DIGNA: With many more to come, I'm sure.

CECILIA: And now I know how to celebrate it, with a birthday cake, it just fits in so nicely. So anything going on on the home front?

(Silence. Lautaro and Digna are angry, and don't say anything.)

CECILIA: I interrupted something, I get the point.

LAUTARO: Nothing of importance.

CECILIA: But it must have been, I thought I saw some tongues. It looked passionate to me. What happened? A brief summary and then I'll go.

DIGNA: As if you weren't listening from the kitchen.

CECILIA: I had the radio on...come on, what's going on? I want good news for a change. I want a true celebration for good times to come. I was thinking we could combine the wedding with the anniversary of the War of Pacific—you know, the Battle of Iquique—

DIGNA: Try September 18.

LAUTARO: Really?

CECILIA: But that's Independence Day, there are too many things going on on that day—

DIGNA: That's when he'll desert.

CECILIA: He'll do what?

DIGNA: Escape to freedom. I might join him in the process—we'll see the world, marriage might follow. See? Cinderella rules. Drink up, enjoy, it's on the house.

CECILIA: But desertion—that's nothing to joke about.

LAUTARO: That's what I say.

CECILIA: One doesn't ask for such things. I guess she would, but she can't be serious. Lautaro came here to talk about, you know, ah, coupling.

LAUTARO: That's for sure.

CECILIA: Look at him, he'd make a cute, angelic, little husband—when he's not whoring around, that is.

DIGNA: How cute is he gonna look in front of a human rights tribunal?

LAUTARO: Fighting terrorists is not a crime, it's a duty.

CECILIA: Well, this isn't proper tea-time conversation!

DIGNA: Oh, for godssake, people are getting killed all around us so if I want to have a human rights talk along with my tea on my fucking birthday, I will, thank you so much!

CECILIA: Well, now we know.

LAUTARO: She's really become one of "them," hasn't she?

DIGNA: So have you.

CECILIA: *(Still trying to make light of it all.)* Digna, I don't want to see you on TV getting gunned down on a holdout or kidnapping a millionaire, or *(A little titillated.)* living on a mountain hideout with hairy horny rebels.

DIGNA: You never know. What about him, Cecilia? I offered him my spot on the plane.

CECILIA: I don't understand. What for?

DIGNA: Isn't it obvious?

CECILIA: What about the engagement?

LAUTARO: There was never going to be any wedding, Cecilia.

CECILIA: You say that now, but you love each other—you really do, you must— I mean, there's enough love in the two of you to say such cruel things to one another. Hatred is a sign of something intimate. Don't ruin it, Digna! And don't you follow along, Lautaro. Save your marriage! Save it now before it happens!

DIGNA: Don't be such a cow.

LAUTARO: Don't you call her names.

CECILIA: She calls me cow, I call her whore!

DIGNA: My life is not about pleasing you, alright?

CECILIA: Then get the hell out of mine, and get the hell out of my house!

DIGNA: Her house? She said it, her house!

LAUTARO: Why don't we just eat the damn cake or something!

DIGNA: *(At Cecilia.)* I look at you and I see the living nightmare of what this country wants to turn me into. A smiling, yet bitter, nurturing, repressed mooing little peasant cow! Mooooo!

CECILIA: I'm not like that at all!

LAUTARO: She didn't mean it.

DIGNA: Of course I meant it!

CECILIA: There is a wild side to me, too, you know.

DIGNA: Mooooo!

CECILIA: I read the tea leaves—and your future is clouded by your tits!
    (She runs out, crying.)

DIGNA: Okay, so my future is…cloudy.

LAUTARO: You made her cry.

DIGNA: There are people hurting a lot more in this country—

LAUTARO: There's no point in being cruel to her though, she's…she's harmless.

DIGNA: That's just the problem, that's all she is. She gets on my nerves, she won't shut up!

LAUTARO: Neither will you!

DIGNA: Why are you defending her? She's trying to shove this marriage down your throat, too. It's the only thing she understands, marriage.

LAUTARO: She means well—

DIGNA: What's this? A soft spot for that pathetic creature in there.

LAUTARO: You might say I like her!

DIGNA: Like her? You like her tea, you mean.

LAUTARO: No, I happen to lust after her.

DIGNA: Her? Lust after her? If there were anybody around here to lust after, that would be me.

LAUTARO: No. In fact, she's hot!

DIGNA: What a disgusting thought! Did you hear that in there?

CECILIA: *(Offstage.)* No!

LAUTARO: You're jealous.

(She slaps him good and hard, almost surprising herself, as well as catching him off guard. The slap has reverberated in the other room. Cecilia comes running out.)

CECILIA: What was that? Lautaro, you didn't.

LAUTARO: No, I didn't!

CECILIA: Because you can't do that in my house, hit a woman, no matter how deserving she might be in this case—

LAUTARO: Cecilia, I—

CECILIA: We kicked our own father out of the house once, we women had had enough of his violent drunken fits, and the moment we stood up to him, he was out the door, you hear? We never saw that old drunk peasant again! Nobody hits a woman around here, I won't have you or anybody else do that, I won't tolerate it in my house!

DIGNA: That's all right, I enjoyed it.

CECILIA: What?

(Tito comes in with a hangover.)

TITO: Excuse me….I'm trying to recover—

DIGNA: See what it's like trying to sleep through a hangover in this house?

TITO: I heard people proposing, and then beating each other up—I couldn't make sense of it.

DIGNA: Sit down and shut up! Alright, everybody, I—I apologize—I mean to you, dear *(Meaning Cecilia.)*, but not to you! *(Meaning Lautaro.)*—I'm thirty years old today, my mom's dead, my sister's gone, and I'm ruled over by a stepmother and a dictator, I'm a national scandal and my future looks unglamorous, Hollywood without the lights, Hollywood with a mop and a bucket all because I wasn't born a general's daughter. That's all I need to become: a damn immigrant! I'm in love, too, I admit it! Yeah, I'm in love— I may care about a minor, but I'm actually in love with the asshole, yes, him! *(Meaning Lautaro who looks away, a bit panicky.)* So cut a woman some slack here and forgive her for not settling down into an everyday routine and baptizing more babies—thank you all for listening, you've been very kind, forgive my trespasses and FUCK YOU ALL!…that felt good.

(She sits, highly relieved she's said what she's had to say. There's a look of sudden peacefulness that lights up her face. There's also shock and silence around her.)

TITO: Happy Birthday. *(No answer.)* Well… I could go to the U.S. for you!— Go surfing and—

CECILIA: Shut up, Tito. *(To Lautaro.)* See? Real feelings. And you don't even deserve it.

LAUTARO: Damn!

(Don Pablo coming in, helped in by Dona Conchita, Lautaro's mother.)

DON PABLO: Hello.

CECILIA: He's early.

DONA CONCHITA: Why are you all out in the patio?

LAUTARO: My mom…what is she doing here?

TITO: Conchita, my heroine!

DONA CONCHITA: My favorite customer!

DIGNA: This oughta be fun.

LAUTARO: He's bleeding.

DIGNA: What? Bleeding?

CECILIA: What happened, Don Pablo?

LAUTARO: One of those Communist kids must have thrown a rock at him.

CECILIA: Sit down, sit down now.

DIGNA: Yes, please, daddy, sit.

DONA CONCHITA: Over here, come on.

DON PABLO: Calm down, and shut up! Everybody! Please, I just slipped on one of those General Pinochet flyers. I hit my head on the curb…They let me go for the day and they even offered me early retirement. Is dinner ready?

CECILIA: You've been drinking again, haven't you?

DON PABLO: It's a holiday, isn't it?

CECILIA: But you're on duty.

TITO: He's off now.

DIGNA: Let him drink.

DON PABLO: Get me some Chilean wine, Tito.

DONA CONCHITA: Not wine! You haven't finished my—I mean—I'm sorry, I must admit, I already gave him a taste of my homemade Pisco.

LAUTARO: Then let's all have some pisco. Have a party!

DONA CONCHITA: Wait! Cecilia, lady of the house, I present you with Dona Conchita's homemade brew, open it.

CECILIA: It's already open!

DONA CONCHITA: I meant—that was a gesture.

DON PABLO: Great recipe!

DONA CONCHITA: Oh, thank you, Don Pablo! My mother shared it with me on her deathbed—our ancestors brought it from Andalusia, Spain, our children don't appreciate that.

LAUTARO: I appreciate it, momma. Now you should go please.

DONA CONCHITA: What? Are you ashamed—You're ashamed of me. Say it!

LAUTARO: No, it's just that—

DON PABLO: The good Samaritan helped me home, she stays.

DIGNA: (Pouring a little pisco into her tea.) We like you, Good Samaritan!

TITO: Good Samaritan's a lifesaver!

CECILIA: They should shut down all the taverns.

DONA CONCHITA: Very funny—so when the hell's the wedding?

LAUTARO: What?

DONA CONCHITA: I wasn't even told! Dona Irma had to call me to tell me.

CECILIA: (Sarcastically.) She's spreading the news! Wave to Dona Irma. Wave everyone!

LAUTARO: She's hiding from us.

DIGNA: Yeh, hide away, Dona Irma! Hide away!

DONA CONCHITA: So is it true or not? To be honest, Digna, I'm worried about your reputation, poor girl.

LAUTARO: Mother—

DONA CONCHITA: You offended both the communists and the fascists—how does one do that with a simple pair of breasts?

LAUTARO: Mom, go home, I'll deal with this.

DONA CONCHITA: Nothing personal, Digna, but there are too many rumors about you. We may be poor, but we have our pride.

LAUTARO: Since when do you get to decide?

DONA CONCHITA: Since you made a lousy choice last time, may she rest in peace, that snot you married! If she'd had real money, I could have lived with it, but she was all manners and pretenses—I say no cash, no snot!

DON PABLO: But Digna here is our own flag-waving heroine, she'll go down in history! We could create a true legend, woman bearing the flag during the coup—children will learn about her in the schools—

TITO: Yes, and your grandchildren, Dona Conchita, will be sons and daughters of a true patriot.

DIGNA: I do wake up these days feeling heroic.

LAUTARO: Little do they know!

DIGNA: And they will know!

DON PABLO: People throughout the country—throughout the world—will come to see the place where she lived out her epic heroic life. We could charge admission!

DONA CONCHITA: Well, she looks like a true legend now like this, hair tied back, pretty dress, the fabric seems old, but well-kept. The shoes…never mind those. But for the most part, she has improved her look overnight, I've never seen her quite like this, so graceful, so adorable. Where have you been hiding, you little jewel?

DIGNA: Somewhere undiscovered, like a pearl at the bottom of the ocean.

CECILIA: Oh, brother.

DONA CONCHITA: *(To Cecilia.)* Shhh—learn some manners, Cecilia. She's got gut and soul. *(Turning to Lautaro.)* And besides, Lautaro, it's time to end this endless mourning for that Mariana—I couldn't stand that poor girl.

LAUTARO: Mother, she's dead.

DONA CONCHITA: Let her stay that way, poor dear!

LAUTARO: I realize I should have married a nice country girl, mother—

DONA CONCHITA: Or a rich city one, but nothing in between, I say.

CECILIA: Are you staying for dinner or not?

DONA CONCHITA: *(Flattered.)* What? Are you inviting me?

CECILIA: You're popular among the alcoholics here, I just need it confirmed.

DON PABLO: Just set up more places.

CECILIA: It's not that simple! I don't just set up places.

LAUTARO: She has a right to know how many people to cook for!

DON PABLO: You stay out of this!

CECILIA: Maybe I'm not cooking at all.

DONA CONCHITA: I can help you, my child, I've got recipes engraved right here. *(Meaning in her mind.)*

CECILIA: No one comes near my kitchen, thank you! We're in the city now, we should learn formalities, people shouldn't just invite themselves in.

DONA CONCHITA: Oh, who says you can cook anyway! (To Digna.) Now come here, girl! *(To Digna.)* Why have I always dismissed you as a lost soul, poor dear, why?

DIGNA: I don't know.

DONA CONCHITA: People can be so cruel, calling you a whore and a slut and—

DIGNA: I'm a modern woman!

TITO: No, classic art woman.

DONA CONCHITA: He's so cute.

(She kisses his cheek, that's where the lipstick came from.)

DON PABLO: Lautaro, please—let's get to it—

LAUTARO: To what?

DON PABLO: What have you chosen to do with our grand national heroine?

DONA CONCHITA: I say he gets no choice! I mean, how indecisive these young people can get! In my time, you got married because parents said so and that was that! What else is the dictatorship for? To make sure husbands come home on time and children do as their parents tell them! What other purpose could it serve? I say, Lautaro, my own national champion, tamer of stallions, you're going to marry this poor young soul, save her from a life of sin, and if not, you are not worthy of your uniform! Patriot without a wife, it's unheard of! Drink some more!

LAUTARO: I'm alright.

DONA CONCHITA: Finish it!

(He obeys reluctantly.)

CECILIA: Don Pablo, are we having officers over tonight?

DON PABLO: What? We're in the middle of noble pronouncements!

CECILIA: The hell with your noble pronouncements. I just want to know how many people I need to cook for.

DON PABLO: She's obsessed! Just cook enough for an entire regiment like you always do!

LAUTARO: Leave Cecilia alone!

(They all turn around, rather surprised at his outbreak. Even he seems surprised at the severity of the outbreak.)

DON PABLO: What's wrong with you all of a sudden?

LAUTARO: Nothing. Maybe I should go—

DON PABLO: I just got here, boy. Relax.

DONA CONCHITA: Lautaro, look, stand here and stare at this precious little jewel...from her profile.

LAUTARO: (Tired.) Very nice, sure.

DIGNA: It's been the most colorful birthday ever.

DONA CONCHITA: Oh, it's even her birthday!

DON PABLO: Perfect timing, Lautaro! My boy, I say these are the best of bad times.

LAUTARO: The what, Don Pablo?

DON PABLO: We must cope. Coping requires military endurance. In bad times, one gets married and has a few kids. Better sow your seeds now. Seven years of drought, seven years of plenty—

DIGNA: But we're only on the second year of "drought."

DON PABLO: As a wedding gift, I'll buy you a new TV to cope with the other five years. We get "Bonanza" and "Gilligan's Island."

CECILIA: And Venezuelan soap operas.

TITO: A few documentaries on the destruction of the environment?

DON PABLO: Some other time, boy! We're all in this together, one big family united behind our military leader to ward off the forces of atheism. As Mussolini might have said, the tanks run on time, right?

DONA CONCHITA: Without dictatorship, the world would be chaos.

DIGNA: Such tender harmonious thoughts!

DONA CONCHITA: Ah, she's so perky.

DON PABLO: So what's going on, Lautaro? Have you and my daughter come to any earth-shattering conclusions that will change the course of history?

LAUTARO: You don't know your daughter, do you, Don Pablo?

DON PABLO: Look, Lautaro. What's it gonna be, boy? Are you or are you not dying to go off with my daughter? Tie the knot? Beget a little policeman or two? Otherwise, why bore me with all your visits? Why keep coming here? What are your plans? Talk them out now, man to man!

DIGNA: He plans to become one of you.

DON PABLO: That's a good thing, isn't it?

DIGNA: You know what I mean.

DON PABLO: But not like any other cop, I hope. I'm sure with his looks and his training, he can go higher.

DONA CONCHITA: My son is headed for the Olympics.

TITO: Our very own!

DON PABLO : No need to chase after a bunch of Communist kids at the age of 60.

CECILIA: Sixty-five and a quarter.

DON PABLO: Well, who's counting? Besides, he'll be our own gold medalist. The nation needs more like him. He's the pride of our country. Well, Lautaro, just remember, last time we had this little talk, you bypassed my beautiful Helena for that uppity girl—may she rest in peace, of course—

CECILIA: Don't disturb the memory of the dead, no matter how uppity and conceited, I say.

LAUTARO: I appreciate that, Ceci.

DON PABLO: Ceci. Since when does he call you "Ceci?"

(Everyone gives Cecilia a funny look, she looks uncomfortable.)

DON PABLO: Never mind. This time, Lautaro, you get a second chance to choose right.

LAUTARO: With all due respect—

DON PABLO: Forget respect, get married! Get her out of my sight, she's getting old, the old hag! Hah!

DIGNA: I love drunks who laugh at their own jokes.

CECILIA: He's not drunk, he only thinks he's funny.

LAUTARO: Everybody please, shut up! I'm sorry, Don Pablo, let's make this clear. I can't, I won't, I have no desire to marry your daughter. That is definite and that is final!

DIGNA: Now wait, this violates my—

LAUTARO: I'm not playing along any more! You were supposed to reject my stupid proposal long ago.

DONA CONCHITA: See? He did propose!

CECILIA AND TITO: What?

DONA IRMA'S VOICE: He proposed! He proposed!

DIGNA: He did! In so many words! Right there! On his knees!

DONA CONCHITA: Of course on his knees!

CECILIA: Wonderful!

DIGNA: And I was about to reject him, too—!

DON PABLO: What was that?

LAUTARO: See what I mean?

DONA CONCHITA: I don't understand!

DON PABLO: You can't take it back, boy! We won't let you!

TITO: And divorce is illegal in Chile!

LAUTARO: That's right. I'll never marry again, Don Pablo!

DON PABLO: I've been there myself, boy. We'll give you time to think about it.

DONA CONCHITA: How about five seconds? Hah!

(She and Don Pablo both laugh.)

CECILIA: *(To Digna.)* What was that about rejection?

DON PABLO: Everyone beware! Love and spring, it's a recipe for foolishness!

DIGNA: What about my offer, Lautaro?

DONA CONCHITA: Oh, so she has an offer. What? What offer?

TITO: I think that was the part I dreamed.

DON PABLO: Quiet. So, Digna, what offer have you made to Lautaro, our glorious national hero, equestrian master of the Olympiad?

CECILIA: She wants him to desert!

DON PABLO: What? But that doesn't sound right...*(Laughs.)*

DONA CONCHITA: She's a jokester, our Little Naked Maja!

DIGNA: It's no joke actually.

LAUTARO: That's right, it's not, that's the problem.

CECILIA: She even gave him her plane ticket.

DON PABLO: What plane ticket?

CECILIA: The one Helena sent her—

DON PABLO: Oh, in the letter. She opened it?

TITO: She gave it to him just like that?

DON PABLO: For honeymoon purposes, I'm sure.

DONA CONCHITA: Of course, they'll go to California for their honeymoon—go to Hearst castle! Ah, there's a man who would have appreciated home-made brew.

LAUTARO: Don Pablo, Mother: Digna and I really can't stand each other.

DIGNA: That's not true, we may hate things about each other—

DONA CONCHITA: All right, so there's some things to iron out.

LAUTARO: There's nothing to compromise about.

DON PABLO: So you hate each other, fine. But do it under the safety of holy matrimony.

DIGNA: I've done my best, daddy, he knows I'm serious about my offer.

DONA CONCHITA: But, little girl—

DIGNA: I'm a 30-year-old woman secure in what she no longer believes in!

DONA CONCHITA: She's fiery, I don't know what she's talking about, but she's fiery!

LAUTARO: What would I do in the United States, fool?

DON PABLO: Who's talking about the United States?

DIGNA: I am!

LAUTARO: Some of my friends have left, you know. Some of them have given up careers to bus tables abroad. Helena was lucky to get a green card, most people have to overstay their tourist visas. Don't think I haven't thought about it—

DIGNA: Good for you!

DONA CONCHITA: Hey, we could use some dollars. Hard currency. *(Realizing she's straying from the argument.)* Oops, sorry.

LAUTARO: Maybe the kid could take the ticket if you don't want to go.

TITO: Led Zeppelin's having a concert in Anaheim, CA.

DONA CONCHITA: What is he talking about?

DIGNA: It's rock 'n' roll, Conchita, wise up.

CECILIA: My son's not going to any rock concert, thank you.

TITO: You can kill socialism, but not rock 'n' roll.

CECILIA: Don't dare me.

LAUTARO: You caught me at the wrong time, Digna.

DIGNA: What do you mean by that?

LAUTARO: Who knows, a few days ago, the offer might have sounded great, seeing Helena again, but...I have news of my own.

DONA CONCHITA: How nice.

LAUTARO: I didn't want to talk about this yet, but looks like I have to.

DON PABLO: About the equestrian team going to the Olympics? Everyone knows that.

LAUTARO: Yes, that's old news. I meant something else.

DIGNA: Like what?

DONA CONCHITA: Like marriage and happiness.

LAUTARO: No...I know we're living in difficult times, and it's a touchy issue for some of you, but I'm not satisfied where I'm at—and I am committed to the full restoration of order everywhere in this country...I mean...I've just been offered a job with "Inteligencia." Better known of course as D.I.N.A. Similar to your name, by the way—

DIGNA: Shut up, that's not funny.

LAUTARO: Born September 11, so the secret police is named after you, naked patriot!

DIGNA: Asshole!

DONA CONCHITA: I don't understand, why's the secret police named after Digna! I'm confused.

CECILIA: You've had a bit too many, old lady!

DONA CONCHITA: But I don't want Lautaro to—I don't understand anything anymore! What's going on?

LAUTARO: You should be in bed, mother.

DIGNA: You're not going to accept this job, are you?

LAUTARO: We'll see.

TITO: Great, he might dig up Benny's corpse himself.

CECILIA: Tito, we really don't need that type—

TITO: He was a friend of mine, you know.

LAUTARO: I'll do what I can to help you people find him.

DIGNA: The hell with your generosity!

DONA CONCHITA: It's as if I don't know you any more. I don't know you! This isn't what I was expecting to hear.

DON PABLO: How come I didn't know about this?

LAUTARO: I didn't either until today.

CECILIA: I knew it, I knew something was up.

LAUTARO: Aren't you proud of me, Don Pablo?

DON PABLO: Have you given them a firm answer?

LAUTARO: No. I told them I'd think about it.

DON PABLO: Then, it's not too late to turn them down, is it?

LAUTARO: Why would I?

DONA CONCHITA: Just listen to Don Pablo and don't make a fool of yourself.

CECILIA: Don't you get involved any more, old man.

TITO: We see nothing, we hear nothing, is that it?

CECILIA: Leave me alone, kid.

DON PABLO: Sit down, Lautaro. Have some more wine. Be merry. Enjoy your holiday, then just go back, be polite about it, oh, they're very polite, but tell them no.

LAUTARO: I thought you'd be happy for me.

DON PABLO: These people are dangerous, Lautaro.

LAUTARO: These are dangerous times, Don Pablo. Besides, it's better to be on the inside than the outside, don't you think?

DON PABLO: Look, you're an athlete first, a cop second. Don't get more involved than you have to....Do what you do best, be young, give him more wine, Cecilia. Fuck this tea!

CECILIA: No, no more wine for any of you.

LAUTARO: And why not? It's a day for celebrations. Back in Linares, nobody puts an end to an honest gathering of good-for-nothing drunks.

DONA CONCHITA: This party's over.

DON PABLO: No, not necessarily. It's OK, Lautaro, you party on, leave the job of cleaning up this country's mess to others. Stay out of it. Be low key, your pension won't suffer by keeping quiet.

LAUTARO: I'm not thinking about retirement so far in advance.

DON PABLO: Maybe you should.

LAUTARO: Maybe you should retire.

DON PABLO: That's not for you to say, is it?

LAUTARO: Then don't tell me what to do. Any of you!

CECILIA: You get a choice of pig's feet or brains tonight.

LAUTARO: I've had enough of this! *(Starts to leave.)*

DON PABLO: I order you to stay away from these people.

LAUTARO: And end up what? An old cop on the beat like you?

DIGNA: Better a cop than a secret police pig.

DON PABLO: I don't care what he thinks of me, Digna, it's his future that's at stake.

LAUTARO: Well, the hell with you! All of you! We are at war with international communism!

DON PABLO: How many times can you kill the same terrorist?

LAUTARO: I thought you were a patriot, Don Pablo.

DON PABLO: Nobody questions my patriotism!

LAUTARO: The war's not over, you know, it goes on and on, and damn you all, comfortable little people, letting others do the dirty work and you getting upset because people get killed. None of you have your asses on the line, yet you want the cops to be polite, and help old ladies cross the street, get kittens off trees, pass out balloons to sick kids on Easter, and come to the rescue every time your car breaks down—Well, fuck you all!

DONA CONCHITA: Don't you use that tone of voice on Don Pablo.

DON PABLO: That's OK, Dona Conchita, that's just cop talk.

DONA CONCHITA: Honor your elders, I say, even if they're drunks and fools.

DON PABLO: Sure, Dona Conchita. Now look...I never thought I'd be saying this, Lautaro, but take my daughter's advice.

TITO: Her advice?

DIGNA: My advice?

DON PABLO: Her offer, I mean. At thirty—more or less, right?

DIGNA: On the dot.

DON PABLO: She seems to have learned some wisdom from me, the kid.

DIGNA: I have, haven't I?

DON PABLO: Strange outfit, by the way. But you look terrific in it—as I was saying...(To Lautaro, insinuating desertion without saying it.) Maybe the two of you could go away on a long, very long, extended honeymoon.

DONA CONCHITA: That would be romantic.

LAUTARO: Only those poor Cubans defect like that, and they have good reasons to—I'm staying put.

DON PABLO: No, we could just say you're going abroad for a little while.

LAUTARO: Don Pablo...desertion is not a joke.

DON PABLO: No, I could be shot for saying it, but what the heck, I'm desperate.

LAUTARO: Don Pablo! Really, that's enough. You've all made so many plans for my life, I'd wish you gave me a say. I can't believe you people would start believing this Communist terrorist propaganda against our government. Nobody, nobody has anything to fear in this country except them—

DIGNA: Or innocent bystanders like Benny?

LAUTARO: (Comes out without thinking.) When they get involved in things they shouldn't!

DIGNA: I see. Is that how it happened?

CECILIA: Lautaro, watch what you say.

TITO: No, say it! Say what you've got to say.

LAUTARO: I haven't even started working there yet, so don't any of you judge me.

DIGNA: You're lying through your ass.

LAUTARO: I can be of service—

DIGNA: To your generals.

LAUTARO: To my country! I can do something with my life other than becoming a goddamn servant abroad, or an illegal alien, or some nobody busing tables in California. I've got a future here in the armed forces. Since when is that shameful? It was good enough for you, Don Pablo, wasn't it?

DON PABLO: Yes, it sure was. Once.

LAUTARO: So what's changed since? Isn't it even more honorable now to serve the nation, in times of crisis? Especially now? Isn't it? You're not gonna tell me, now that I joined, that it's become less honorable. What's changed?

DON PABLO: You know what's changed, you know damn well!

LAUTARO: And you, mother, you who swear by the dictatorship day and night—

DONA CONCHITA: Sure, but that doesn't mean we can't criticize a few things.

LAUTARO: Like what?

DONA CONCHITA: Like that secret police, you fool! Why can't we just have a regular good ol' dictator?—why this secret police where the scum of the earth—thugs—rapists—assassins—people who can't get a job anywhere else go to. Not my son, you hear? He was only supposed to serve his country and that used to be an honorable profession, our military! An honorable, decent way to get ahead in this world! What's become of it? God help us all if, if—

LAUTARO: God doesn't put away terrorists, mother.

DONA CONCHITA: Then heaven protect us from our protectors.

LAUTARO: You make no sense.

DONA CONCHITA: Get married then, just get married! See? There are worse things in this world than getting stuck in an unhappy marriage. Lautaro, don't...

LAUTARO: Don't what, mother?

DONA CONCHITA: Just don't! Don't! Don't!

LAUTARO: You, Cecilia? Gypsy woman? What's my future?

CECILIA: Pigs' feet with the nails on.

LAUTARO: Talk to me!

DON PABLO: She's no gypsy, I'm not married to no damn gypsy.

CECILIA: We're only domesticated gypsies. We've lost our powers. We can no longer help you gentiles.

LAUTARO: *(Still insisting with Cecilia.)* One word. One sentence.

CECILIA: At the banquet, some eat, others get eaten.

(She exits quickly to go to the kitchen.)

LAUTARO: Come on, everybody! Why should I have to apologize for what's happening? This is the mess that I came into. Why do you all look at me that
way? I haven't done anything wrong. I don't come from a rich family or
anything. How am I supposed to get to the Olympics? Just by being a great
athlete? No, you play the game! Whatever it is you're supposed to join, you
join! Where's the harm in that? I don't need you people to judge me and…

*(There's rattling outside again. The beggar woman is back. The rattling seems
louder. It startles Lautaro. Cecilia runs out again.)*

LAUTARO: What the hell is that?

CECILIA: Ignore her, she'll go away.

LAUTARO: They're everywhere!

(He pulls out gun.)

DON PABLO: What are you doing?

LAUTARO: Just practicing for the Olympics.

TITO: Wrong team.

DONA CONCHITA: You put that away!

LAUTARO: Just trying to give her a little scare.

TITO: Our hero—look at him!

DONA IRMA'S VOICE: What's going on down there!

LAUTARO: *(Startled by voice.)* They're everywhere! Coming at us from all directions—the enemy!

(Digna intervenes.)

DIGNA: I got it, Dad. *(To Lautaro.)* Come on, give it to me. We've all had a bit
too much—I'll get rid of the beggar. *(To beggar.)* Excuse us—but we have
more pressing issues right now than your bout with starvation. Thank you.

(Beggar's gone.)

DIGNA: See? Now here….come on. Baby. Sugar. Give it here.

*(She takes the gun from him. She gives it to Don Pablo. Lautaro breaks down
into tears.)*

DON PABLO: It's loaded, too. You're not on duty, it shouldn't be.

LAUTARO: The country's under martial law! We don't follow your rules, old man!

DIGNA: Quiet! Put it away, Cecilia, where he won't find it…

(Cecilia rushes out with it.)

DIGNA: *(To Lautaro.)* Simmer down, hero.

TITO: I've decided, dad: I'll be a draft resister!

DON PABLO: Don't you get started now.

TITO: That's it, every September 11, every military holiday like this, I'll go out and face up to them, and even throw rocks at the cops!

DON PABLO: We are the cops, we're in your family!

TITO: I don't care any more—if this is Civil War, so be it.

DON PABLO: Fool!

TITO: We'll have a riot every September 11 until they cancel the holiday, until they turn it into a day of mourning—with the flag at half-mast like Digna had the brilliant idea of doing.

DON PABLO: What?

DIGNA: Yes, I'm guilty of that, too.

TITO: We won't rest until it ends!

DON PABLO: Don't forget, we are your family, not them…not the type of people who put ideas into…*(As Tito is leaving.)* Where are you going?

TITO: I told you—time for a little action, riot!

DON PABLO: Tito!

TITO: This isn't the country I was proud of once!

(Tito runs out, angry, defiant, leaving him in mid-sentence.)

CECILIA: Tito. How could you let him go?

DON PABLO: He can take care of himself.

CECILIA: No, not today…

DON PABLO: Let him go, he's no longer your little boy.

CECILIA: I just wanted a celebration in my home, away from everything that goes on outside—and yet it keeps slipping in, I can't control it any more. I'm a failure as a stepmother!

DIGNA: *(To Lautaro.)* And you, sober up!

LAUTARO: I got no limits, hear that? No limits.

DONA CONCHITA: I didn't teach him to drink like this—I only brew the stuff—

DIGNA: Be quiet everyone! We're not gonna stand here comparing notes on boozing 'cause I can outdrink any of you any day, hear me? Now you listen—you all want to see me in the U.S., fine, maybe that's where I'll end up one day, but I'm not going anywhere yet. I'm asking you instead: look at yourself, like a drunk in the gutter and ready to shoot. Some patriot! A real patriot would know when the nation's being screwed! It's bad enough you cops have to bury the corpses, now you want to join the department that makes them, and that's a promotion! We might as well all pick up a shovel. Because that's what we've become. The regime's gravediggers. All of us! You too, Conchita! *(Pause.)* Benny is dead, isn't he?

LAUTARO: Don't ask me. I'm new around here.

DON PABLO: You answer my daughter, take her seriously.

DIGNA: What about you, old man? You're in the police, too—

DON PABLO: Don't get me involved, I'm retiring to make babies.

CECILIA: Yeh, devote time to the house.

DIGNA: And you won't talk?

DON PABLO: What would that change, honey?

DIGNA: We keep their secrets, we're all in this together!

LAUTARO: I have horses to ride. *(Starts to leave.)*

DIGNA: No. You don't walk out on me like this.

LAUTARO: I have no answers for you, Digna. We had a good time, why not just leave it at that?

DIGNA: Why do you think I've followed you to all those seedy hotels by the Mapocho River with paint peeling off the walls? Why would I crawl into rotting beds at all, and play your games, you fascist drunk? I thought you were the only one who could match my contempt for all this. We were so neatly perverse together—that's romance, isn't it?—I love you, and I couldn't bear to see you getting up at 2A.M. to go off and knock on doors and pull people out of their homes, people we wouldn't see again. People like Benny. Look at me, look at me, baby. How beautiful you are, yet how rotten you've begun to look these days.

DONA IRMA'S VOICE: *(Interrupting suddenly.)* It's Helena—Helena—long distance!

DON PABLO: Go talk to your sister.

DONA CONCHITA: I miss Helena, too, I want to stop missing people.

DIGNA: You talk to her.

CECILIA: Answer it, Digna.

DONA IRMA'S VOICE: It's costing her money.

CECILIA: It's time for you to make your own choices. For you and you alone!

DONA IRMA'S VOICE: Digna!

DON PABLO: She's coming, you old hen!

(Digna is still staring at Lautaro. He straightens up and goes to get the plane ticket, which he's left on the coffee table, to give to her.)

DONA CONCHITA: Don't let her go!

LAUTARO: Digna…your sister.

(She looks around her, everyone staring at her. She knows that by taking the plane ticket, she'll be doing what's supposed to be impossible to her: making a decision. He's daring her. He knows he'll lose her. It has to hurt him as well, but he's determined to stay the course, be stubborn, and carry on. As if plunging into the unknown already, she takes the ticket. Turns around, sees the flag.)

DIGNA: Well…I'll see the world, the poor world gets no choice!

(She runs out.)

LAUTARO: What happened to the patriotism!

DONA CONCHITA: Don't you lecture me on patriotism. You listen here, because if you join that secret police, I'll be there every morning to remind you, as your mother, to never let you forget that you're going straight to hell!

LAUTARO: I'll move out then! I'll get a place of my own.

DONA CONCHITA: I'll haunt you to your grave, you hear that, boy? Till you can no longer stop hearing your mother's voice! To your grave!

LAUTARO: That's no worse than what I've already had to put up with, you old hag!

DONA CONCHITA: Well…*(Hurt, but keeping back the tears.)* I just wanted a decent daughter-in-law, someone I can pass my pisco recipes to, not like my other daughters-in-law who sit around chewing gum watching reruns of "Bewitched." Such wasted lives, wasted lives…

DON PABLO: I'll walk you home, Dona Conchita.

DONA CONCHITA: Yes, yes, and stay with me for a while, Don Pablo. We'll look at the moonlight.

DON PABLO: Yes and pray for the best. *(To Lautaro.)* And you, good luck in your new job, you'll need it.

LAUTARO: I hope…I hope I can always count on you for advice.

DON PABLO: Don't ever speak to me again.

(They exit, arm in arm. Lautaro and Cecilia are left alone in an awkward moment for them both.)

CECILIA: He asked me to.

LAUTARO: What?

CECILIA: The reason I married him, he asked me to.

LAUTARO: But other men must have asked.

CECILIA: No one with a military pension. It seemed to matter once. Besides, I could tell you stories about the ideal men who got away.

LAUTARO: Tell me everything.

CECILIA: Let's get something straight. I love Don Pablo in my own special way. He's the kindest of the older men with a pension who proposed, someone honest enough to understand that my feelings for him are not romantic. We make a good marriage, in other words in spite of all the other temptations in the world—and yes, I will have his children.

LAUTARO: You'll have all the children you need, I'm sure.

CECILIA: Now that his daughters seem to have left him, somebody around here should keep her commitments. That's what I intend to do: honor my commitments.

LAUTARO: You don't hate me, do you?

CECILIA: I should.

LAUTARO: No.

CECILIA: If it did any good, I should.

LAUTARO: But you can't. You can't hate me.

CECILIA: Maybe not.

LAUTARO: Good. Same time tomorrow?

CECILIA: What?

LAUTARO: I'll come at four.

CECILIA: It won't be the same.

LAUTARO: Four fifteen? Maybe three-thirty, 'gives you thirty minutes before the four o'clock soap opera.

(She touches his face very lightly, and kisses him on the face. She pulls back making it clear that's it for now, and forever.)

CECILIA: This isn't fun anymore.

(He withdraws, looking defeated, but defiant. He puts on his jacket, then his hat with great determination. Then he salutes the flag, as he exits. She's left alone.

She goes about her chores again, picking up used glasses. Then she sees it, that flag again.

With great misgivings, but very respectfully, she pulls it down. She folds it carefully, and then, as if another day has ended, she goes inside, holding the flag close to her chest, and a repressed tear of lament sneaking into her eyes.)

END OF PLAY

Missing Marisa
and
Kissing Christine
by John Patrick Shanley

BIOGRAPHY

John Patrick Shanley is a writer and director from the Bronx. He was last at Actors Theatre of Louisville for the premiere of his *Danny and the Deep Blue Sea* in the 1984 Humana Festival. Another new play, *Psychopathia Sexualis*, was produced at Seattle Repertory Theatre and the Mark Taper Forum, and *Four Dogs and A Bone* was produced at Manhattan Theatre Club, the Lucille Lortel Theatre and David Geffen Playhouse in Los Angeles. Other full-length plays include: *The Big Funk, Beggars in the House of Plenty, Italian American Reconciliation, The Dreamer Examines His Pillow, Savage in Limbo, Women of Manhattan* and *Welcome to the Moon*. Mr. Shanley's screenplays include *Five Corners* (Barcelona Film Festival Special Jury Prize), *Moonstruck* (Academy Award for Best Original Screenplay), *Joe Versus the Volcano* (also directed), *Alive* and his adaptation of Michael Crichton's *Congo*.

ORIGINAL PRODUCTION

Missing Marisa was first performed at the 1996 Humana Festival of New American Plays, March, 1996. It was directed by Douglas Hughes with the following cast:

Terry	Christopher Evan Welch
Eli	Daniel Oreskes

Kissing Christine was first performed at the 1996 Humana Festival of New American Plays, March, 1996. It was directed by Douglas Hughes with the following cast:

Larry	Christopher Evan Welch
Christine	Laura Hughes
Server	Elaine C. Bell

Both plays used the following production staff:

Scenic Designer	Paul Owen
Costume Designer	Jeanette deJong
Lighting Designer	T.J. Gerckens
Sound Designer	Michael Rasbury
Properties Manager	Ron Riall
Stage Manager	Janette L. Hubert
Assistant Stage Manager	Susan M. McCarthy
Dramaturg	Val Smith
New York Casting Arrangements	Laura Richin Casting

CHARACTERS

Missing Marisa
TERRY
ELI

Kissing Christine
CHRISTINE
LARRY
SERVER

PLACE

Missing Marisa
Eli's kitchen, end of day — some daylight, some twilight.
Kissing Christine
A Thai restaurant, the present.

NOTE

This published version of these scripts premiered at Actors Theatre of Louisville. The scripts have been revised for subsequent productions. For the revised script, contact George Lane at the William Morris Agency, 1325 Avenue of the Americas, New York, NY 10019.

MISSING MARISA

When the lights come up, we discover two men, Terry and Eli.

Terry sits at a coffee counter on a high stool in Eli's kitchen. He has a cup of coffee. He's about 35. He's flushed with drink, though he's not at all drunk. He's handsome and maybe a little dissipated. His hand shakes a little. His clothes are fancy and casual and he wears them well.

Eli is sitting lower and slightly more Down Front, at a card table in a folding metal chair. He also has a cup of coffee. He's a little older or younger than Terry. He wears a somewhat rumpled businessman's shirt and trousers.

It is end of day. Some daylight, some twilight.

Both of these guys are tired.

ELI: Cake?

TERRY: No. No cake.

ELI: It's good to see you, Terry.

TERRY: It's good to see you, Eli.

ELI: How's the coffee?

TERRY: Black.

ELI: How's Marisa?

TERRY: I stopped seeing her. She stopped seeing me. She's gone. I don't know where she is. I just bought some land.

ELI: Where?

TERRY: Up in the Hudson River Valley.

ELI: The Mesopotamia of New York State!

TERRY: Yes. 13 acres.

ELI: 13! The number of guests at the Last Supper!

TERRY: Well actually, it's 12.84 acres.

ELI: Good. That destroys the negative significance.

TERRY: There's a stream down the middle of the property. Hemlock trees.

ELI: Hemlock!

TERRY: That's what the realty guy told me, but don't take it to heart.

ELI: Don't take it internally, that's the point.

TERRY: I planted tulip bulbs I bought at a state fair I fell into while wandering upstate, looking for a life that makes sense to me.

ELI: Are you alright?

TERRY: WHAT DOES THAT MEAN?! *(Silence.)* I'm grateful you could meet me for coffee, have me for coffee, have coffee with me.

ELI: It's fun for me, too.

TERRY: Any kind of contact is hard now.

ELI: You mean, for you?

TERRY: No. I mean any kind of contact is hard now. Do you think I'm wrong?

ELI: No.

TERRY: The coffee's enjoyable. It's good. It's serviceable. It's the better for me being able to tell somebody it's good. And it's almost gone.

ELI: I feel like the depth of your...You're speaking from a different head than I'm at.

TERRY: Can you get this head?

ELI: No. I have my own head.

TERRY: This coffee's unusual. This coffee's weak *at the bottom*.

ELI: Should we speak of something obvious? Obviously, we have something new in common.

TERRY: What?

ELI: Marisa.

TERRY: We already had Marisa in common.

ELI: Yeah, but now we have her more deeply in common. For now, not only have we both loved her, now we've both lost her. Lost her irrevocably.

TERRY: I took her away from you.

ELI: Understandably, Terry, that's how you've always seen it. But you didn't take Marisa away from me.

TERRY: Then what happened?

ELI: Did she leave you for somebody else?

TERRY: No.

ELI: Is she with someone else?

TERRY: No. I don't know. I don't think so. It's unlikely.

ELI: Why?

TERRY: It's highly unlikely.

ELI: Why?

TERRY: Because she has the clap.

(Pause.)

ELI: She has the clap?

TERRY: Yes.

ELI: Do you have the clap?

TERRY: Yes.

ELI: You do?

TERRY: Yes, I've got it alright.

ELI: So she got it from you?

TERRY: No, she gave it to me.

ELI: You're sure?

TERRY: Yes.

ELI: Where'd she get it?

TERRY: Well, that's where it gets tricky.

ELI: She won't say?

TERRY: Oh, she'll say, but what she says is, she says it's not the clap. But there on the other hand is my doctor. And my doctor would beg to differ. My doctor says it is most definitely the clap. He says me and her, we're applause. You haven't got the clap, have you?

ELI: No.

TERRY: I'm hungry.

ELI: Do you want me to get you something?

TERRY: That'd be very kind of you.

ELI: What do you want?

TERRY: If I knew that I wouldn't be SO FUCKING HUNGRY!

ELI: Marisa didn't jump off you for somebody?

TERRY: Not to my knowledge.

ELI: And you didn't give her the clap?

TERRY: She gave it to me!

ELI: Then where'd she get it from?

TERRY: She says she doesn't have it.

ELI: But she does.

TERRY: How the fuck do you know?

ELI: Because you told me.

TERRY: She's got it.

ELI: Then who gave it to her and how do you know she didn't go to that guy?

TERRY: Outta what, gratitude?

ELI: Outta just, you know, the inevitable.

TERRY: Everything's outta the inevitable.

ELI: Alright, alright, have your caveats. Then outta her hunger.

(Pause.)

TERRY: My goal is to be empty and say a prayer that something comes. But every time emptiness draws nigh, I get clawed open by this like Bengal Tiger— Hunger and I end up…begging.

ELI: Begging what?

TERRY: At the foot of some stone Madonna. The desperate man shuns the quiet, Eli. Shuns the quiet like Dracula shunned the sun. Life was death to him. Life is death to me. That's the hunger that sucks my own blood and makes me weak and weaker as I feed.

ELI: She left us both. I've been offered a job.

TERRY: So what?

ELI: Well, that's a big area arena of life.

TERRY: Not to me.

ELI: Hmm.

TERRY: Are you gonna take it?

ELI: Don't you want to know what it is?

TERRY: A job is what you make it.

ELI: Don't you want to know what I'd make it?

TERRY: No.

ELI: Jump back! Do you have any interest in me?

TERRY: I don't know.

ELI: Can you really see me? Do you even know I'm here?

TERRY: Alright, what's the job?

ELI: A teacher for musically gifted people who've been overlooked by the school system of Southern New England.

TERRY: That job, that job'd be totally quality dependent on the performance of the recruitment person who finds the students who you would subsequently teach.

ELI: That's true.

TERRY: Is that job open?

ELI: The recruitment person job?

TERRY: Yeah.

ELI: Are you looking for a job?

TERRY: I am noticing opportunities. If you got me a job, if you *wanted* to get me a job, I would know that you were inherent in, to, Marisa leaving me.

ELI: Do you have any experience in the musical area?

TERRY: It would be guilt help.

ELI: I mean, I've been to your apartment, Terry. You don't have a piano.

TERRY: The goodness of Judas.

ELI: I'm sure Mr. Iscariot had his points.

TERRY: I would know that you gave Marisa the clap. So I would know that you gave me the clap. Did you give me the clap?

ELI: No.

TERRY: Have you got the clap?

ELI: No.

TERRY: Have you recently been cured of the clap?

ELI: No. *(Pause.)* Not recently. But you say Marisa says she doesn't have the clap?

TERRY: But she gave it to me!

ELI: You're sure you've got it?

TERRY: I've been diagnosed! I'm under treatment.

ELI: For the clap?

TERRY: For the clap. Not recently. So you've had the clap?

ELI: In my life.

TERRY: Really?

ELI: Uh-huh.

> *(The phone rings.)*

TERRY: Aren't you going to get that?

ELI: I have a service.

TERRY: But you're here.

ELI: I'm talking to you.

TERRY: I've been here when you've answered the phone. Your service isn't picking up.

ELI: They will.

TERRY: Do you know who's calling?

ELI: No.

TERRY: Do you have a suspicion?

ELI: What's your point?

TERRY: Could it be Marisa?

ELI: Why would it be her?

TERRY: Why would it? Unless it is!

> *(Terry grabs the phone.)*

TERRY: Hello? *(Listens.)* Hang up.

ELI: I have a proposition for you.

TERRY: What?

ELI: Answer my phone again and I'll punch you right in the mouth.

TERRY: That's the most direct thing you've ever said to me. I stole your wife and you weren't that direct.

ELI: Nobody steals anybody's wife.

TERRY: I stole yours.

ELI: She left me. She didn't even leave me. It wasn't about me anymore than it was about you.

TERRY; Oh, it was about me. She came to me.

ELI: We're just egomaniacs. She was living her life. We were like two trees out her train's window. Scenery. You think too much of yourself. I used to do the same thing.

TERRY: And now?

ELI: My insignificance has found its voice. It's like Galileo testifying, saying very softly but firmly: It's not you, chump, it's the sun. We had it wrong for so long. Tell the Pope. It's the sun.

TERRY: You tell the Pope! What's this got to do with Marisa?

ELI: Not much. There are stars governing Marisa no doubt, but they're not our stars. We're on our own. We can make ourselves believe that everything we do or say is about this person who isn't here and doesn't give a damn about us, or we can face up. It's just you and me, buddy. And about the one thing you're right. In effect. If I ever gave Marisa the clap and she turned around and gave it to you. And now she's gone and it's just you and me. Then forget Marisa. She was just the telephone we talked through. I gave you the clap.

TERRY: You did?!

ELI: No, no. Man! I am just so fucking bored with you! You're like forcing me to live in a shoebox and talk in the lint and dust about some truant shoe. Cracks in the ceiling. What do they remind you of? Did you start off this way?

TERRY: Now wait a minute!

ELI: Everything boils down to something you call Marisa. Marisa? What is Marisa?

TERRY: No! Who is Marisa!

ELI: No! What is Marisa! Because you use this name to reduce all experience between us to like the squeakings of mice!

TERRY: There isn't much between us anyway. I haven't got any feeling. Not really.

ELI: How could you, buddy? You never bothered to ask who I am.

TERRY: I know you as well as I want to.

ELI: That's not saying much. I've always had this problem with enthusiasm and force. Did you know that? I've always had this problem, when I liked somebody, that I'd grab their hand and run them down the street. But in my joy of having connected with someone, found someone, I would always run too fast, and they would fall, and I wouldn't stop fast enough, and this person of whom I had become enthused would get bloody. Would GET VERY BLOODY. And look up at me in shock. What had I done? And my reaction was always this homocidal kind of embarrassment where I just wanted to beat this person to death. UNTO DEATH! And live thereafter alone in the woods and know no one. Forget my identity. Sometimes I wish, I honestly wish, that I had never met another person. That I was raceless, nameless, that I had no rap sheet with anybody, that I did not have this blood on my hands!

TERRY: What blood? Wait a minute! What...Have you done something to Marisa?

ELI: CHEESE AND RICE! WHAT'S WRONG WITH YOU?!

TERRY: I guess not.

ELI: This has nothing to do with your precious Marisa!

TERRY: I just wanted to make sure.

ELI: If you didn't know me at all. If I was a stranger and I stepped up to you and slapped your face, and didn't answer you when you asked me why, we would be further along then we are having known each other for years, slept with the same woman, etc.

TERRY; There's something sort've infantile about that fantasy.

ELI: Sophomoric, maybe. Not infantile.

TERRY: It's unmodern.

ELI: It's worse if they're fat.

TERRY: What?

ELI: If I accidentally injure someone who's fat, that's worse.

TERRY: Just exactly how many people have you injured?

ELI: I don't know. That's like, How many women have you slept with?

TERRY: No, it's not.

ELI: Well then, how many?

TERRY: That's...

ELI: Do you know?

TERRY: Exactly?

ELI: Yes.

TERRY: No.

ELI: You've never sat down and figured it out?

TERRY: No.

ELI: Well then, why should I know how many people I've accidentally injured? I remember a few vivid scenes. Bloody knees, bloody hands, bloody lips on astonished faces. A few sounds I'll never forget but... Knowing the exact number I've injured? That'd be kind of creepy.

TERRY: Actually, I do know the exact number of women I've slept with.

ELI: You do?

TERRY: Yeah.

ELI: So did I, Sport, but it's none of your business.

TERRY: Eighteen.

ELI: Eighteen!

TERRY: What? Is that a lot or a little?

ELI: Compared to what? Zeus?

TERRY: Compared to you.

ELI: My mother told me I was going to be fat when I grew up. I think that's why I have a horror of injuring the fat. It's like savaging myself. I sliced this fat girl's knee in a head-on bicycle thing and I remember looking into her knee through this gaping slice and blood and I remember thinking: Look at that white layer of fat there. I remember thinking: That's her fat. Am I going to wear a bloody thick white coat of fat like that? Like some kind of lardy mattress pad? Or for me will it be some other kind of extra useless thing? Like insanity? Will that be my unshuckable aspect of wardrobe? Terry, look at me! Where's the meat? Or is it like Marisa? Where all you see is the fat?

TERRY: Marisa's not fat.

ELI: She's fat! She's just fat!

TERRY: You sound like her.

ELI: I am not Marisa!

TERRY: Just as dissatisfied as you are with me, that's how dissatisfied I am with you. I bet that's like a general equation you could make about any encounter between two people. Unless of course...

ELI: But what about friendship?!

TERRY: What friendship?

ELI: Ours.

TERRY: You'd cut my throat if you had the shot.

ELI: There's ten things I'd do if you trusted me. Only one in ten would be the throat-cut-thing. Think of the other nine alternatives.

TERRY: You think of them.

ELI: O.K. The hand clasp. Contact. If you trusted me.

TERRY: That's a *mere* one.

ELI: Oh, you're counting. Advice good, advice bad.

TERRY: A paltry three.

ELI: Count silently. I might make you take yourself less seriously. Take me more seriously. I might educate you about a third party.

TERRY: Who?

ELI: Never mind who!

TERRY: You couldn't tell me anything about her!

ELI: I could accuse you of something.

TERRY: What?

ELI: Forgive you.

TERRY: Forgive me what?!

ELI: That's nine alternatives to cutting your throat, Terry.

TERRY: That's eight.

ELI: That's nine, Terry, give or take. If you trusted me.

TERRY: What could you forgive me, Eli?

ELI: The fact that, potentially, you could block my reading light. But let's stop these oblique thrusts and parries.

TERRY: That's fine with me.

ELI: It's exhausting.

TERRY: I wasn't doing it. It wasn't me. I try to bluntly step forward and blurt.

ELI: Let's talk about Marisa if Marisa's what you want to talk about.

TERRY: I don't need to talk about her.

ELI: Let's just talk about her till there's nothing left of her.

TERRY: I could talk about something else.

ELI: She had big eyes.

TERRY: I don't need to talk about this.

ELI: She had great big eyes.

TERRY: Yes, she did. She had great big eyes. They were like hubcaps. And they were red.

ELI: They were red a lot. Were they always red?

TERRY: The hubcaps were red.

ELI: She had great energy.

TERRY: Yes, she did. Lots of energy.

ELI: And a certain ability to bust your balls.

TERRY: Well, she was a bitch.

ELI: She had a bitchy side.

TERRY: She was a howling bitch. She could clear a restaurant.

ELI: I got along with her though.

TERRY: I never did.

ELI: I have this ability to abandon my point of view which worked pretty well with her.

TERRY: She was sexy though. Sometimes. When the mood was on her. Like a voluptuous slinky.

ELI: I have this ability to abandon my body, too, if necessary. And it was necessary, on occasion, with Marisa.

TERRY: You know, I take it back. I take it all back. She wasn't a bitch. I miss her.

ELI: That's human, and by that I mean, chaotic and twisted.

TERRY: When I told her that I had the clap, it was a very emotional scene.

ELI: I bet.

TERRY: She denied that she'd given it to me. She accused me! But there was no way that was going to stick. I had the bottom line fact of monogamous certainty. She burst into tears. I found myself comforting her.

ELI: What man hasn't been that idiot.

TERRY: Then the whole thing turned a corner. She fanned open those thighs. I was like a monkey seeing aluminum foil for the first time. From that point on, of course, she could say that I gave it to her. The clap, that is.

ELI: Did she?

TERRY: No. She still said she didn't have it!

ELI: Well that's... Then you're...obtuse!

terry: She had this position, has this position, wherever the hell she is, and she won't give it up!

ELI: She thinks the earth's axis goes right up her dress and pops out the top of her head.

TERRY: She should have road signs leading to her saying *this street does not go through.*

ELI: Well. The chicken must be ready.

TERRY: The chicken? What chicken?

ELI: I've been baking a chicken. Let's take a look at it.

(Eli opens the oven and takes out a baked chicken.)

TERRY: I smelled it, but I thought it was coming in the window.

ELI: No, it's my chicken.

TERRY: It's big.

ELI: Not that big.

TERRY: It's a roaster. Big enough for three anyway.

ELI: Two.

TERRY: But I thought we were just having coffee?

ELI: We are. This is for later.

TERRY: After I go.

ELI: That's right.

TERRY: Dinner for two.

ELI: I read this book, Bartlett's Quotations.

TERRY: Dinner for two.

ELI: This guy Bartlett had an incredible mind.

TERRY: She's coming here, isn't she?

ELI; And he had a tremendous sensitivity to attention span. Never goes on at any length. Just a little something, pithy, and moves on.

TERRY: That was her on the phone. She heard me and hung up. It was her, wasn't it?!

ELI: Now Terry, what if it was?

TERRY: Was it?

ELI: Isn't she my wife?

TERRY: Hasn't the divorce gone through?

ELI: Wouldn't it be alright for her to call me?

TERRY: No.

ELI: And even if I wanted to make her dinner. Wouldn't that be alright, given that she was once my spouse?

TERRY: So the divorce has gone through.

ELI: And even if we slept together, and I had previously consoled myself with a girl of such loose habits that contracting the clap, or worse, was not out of the question. Wouldn't that be understandable?

TERRY: I can understand it.

ELI: And human?

TERRY: Yes.

ELI: And forgivable?

(Terry struggles with the question.)

TERRY: Is that what you want from me?

ELI: Have we never been friends?

TERRY: You were married.

ELI: Yes.

TERRY: By comparison, I'm just an aging eternal boy. My quality, what was beautiful and natural about my quality, the years have made grotesque. That will always be in the way. Between us.

ELI: Make a wish, Terry.

TERRY: I wish I was alone and liked it.

ELI: Make another wish.

TERRY: I wish I was with somebody and liked it.

ELI: I see you're at home with contradiction.

TERRY: Better than being home with my mother.

ELI: That's two wishes. Make it three. That's the formula. What's the third wish?

TERRY: Serve me that chicken.

ELI: Oh, ask anything of me but that, and I will prove my friendship.

TERRY: Serve me that chicken, Eli.

ELI: I can't do that.

TERRY: I've been smelling unconsciously. It's affected me without my knowing it. I'm starving for chicken. There's enough for three. It's a roaster.

ELI: You're not thinking of the repercussions. I can't serve someone a mutilated chicken for dinner.

TERRY: Why can't we connect?

ELI: I don't know.

TERRY: I'd like to believe it's Marisa.

ELI: It's not.

TERRY: Give me some fucking chicken!

ELI: Why did you never marry?

TERRY: Why *did* you marry?

ELI: I wanted a home!

TERRY: *I* have a home!

ELI: I wanted children.

TERRY: You don't have children!

ELI: I *thought* I wanted children!

TERRY: I've had bastards.

ELI: I wanted love.

TERRY: You wanted Marisa.

ELI: I did want Marisa.

TERRY: Did you get love?

ELI: Some. Not enough. A ration. A half ration.

TERRY: What do you know about getting by on very little?! I'm the expert on starvation! Now. If you pick a small piece of meat off the bird's bottom—there's little pockets of dark meat under there—if you do that, no one would ever know.

ELI: No.

TERRY: Please.

ELI: No.

TERRY: Please.

ELI: No.

TERRY: Please, please, please!

ELI: Alright, alright.

   (*Eli carefully spoons a small piece of meat from under the bird.*)

TERRY: Be careful to leave no trace! Use a spoon.

ELI: "The flea, though he cannot kill, does all the harm he can."

TERRY: What are you talking about?

ELI: That's Bartlett!

TERRY: "Nothing emboldens sin so much as mercy." That's Shakespeare.

ELI: No, that's Bartlett, too. But everybody stole from him. Alright, blow on it. It's hot.

(Terry blows on it repeatedly.)

TERRY: I'm getting dizzy.

ELI: The earth's rotation will do that. Open and receive.

TERRY: And when I eat this, and when I eat this, and when I eat this...

ELI: Oh, would you eat it before the sun goes down on us!

(Terry eats.)

ELI: What do you think?

TERRY: It's good.

ELI: You think so?

TERRY: It's moist.

ELI: That's what I was after.

TERRY: It is good! Was this a chicken that had a good life?

ELI: As a matter of fact, this was a chicken... Oh, he was the Richard Corey of chickens. But then he became despondent, went in the coop. There was a shot.

TERRY: When will they give us gun control?

ELI: Everyone was shocked. Not that chicken. Nobody could believe it.

TERRY: Maybe he knew Marisa?

(Savage laughter from both.)

ELI: Oh, maybe he did! I'm glad we've got a sense of humor about it. At last.

TERRY: Oh, I see the humor in too many things. Privation does that to a man. I see the humor in the mirror.

ELI: You're like a skeleton!

TERRY: That's it! I'm like a rattling around skeleton, rattling around, grinning, hoping if not to frighten than at least amuse.

ELI: Oh, you frighten me.

TERRY: Do I? What is it? Is it my ruined youth?

ELI: No.

TERRY: The absence of future in my squeeze-toy heart?

ELI: No.

TERRY: How much I've stolen from you, beaten you, circumvented you, forced you into emotional perjury?

ELI: No, it's none of those things, my friend.

TERRY: Do you fear that I'll take Marisa away from you again?

ELI: There is no Marisa.

(Terry takes up a knife.)

TERRY: Tell me! What is it about me frightens you? Am I missing my own greatness? Are you dwarfed by my grand good fortune that I cannot know? Am I deaf to my own poetry, afraid of my courage, numb to my own fine feelings? Or am I dangerous to you in the old original way? Are you terrified that I may replace you, kill you, that I am your murdering twin?! Or is it that I'm an animal! Just an animal. And so revolt your basic humanity? Is it because I wear makeup? Just a little. To hold off the inevitable a few more days. I remember when we were equals.

ELI: Yes. I remember when we thought we were equals.

TERRY: I remember when my terror did not outweigh my optimism.

ELI: I remember when I was optimistic about you. But then, then, you were truly young.

TERRY: What about me could possibly frighten you, old comrade?

ELI: That look of hope in your eyes. Your hope.

TERRY: Alright. I am failing at life.

ELI: No. Don't say that.

TERRY: I am failing at life, and you are not.

ELI: Terry, I'm sorry.

TERRY: Eli, in this brief moment before my guardians close ranks around me for the remainder of my days, I forgive you.

ELI: Why?

TERRY: For the sake of friendship. We were friends back before the forking of the road. And for the sake of the ghostly gossamer Marisa, who softened my hatred of you, and eased my love.

ELI: Thank you.

TERRY: It's the least I can do. The chicken, the little I am allowed, was very, very good.

ELI: You're welcome.

TERRY: I am welcome nowhere.

END OF PLAY

KISSING CHRISTINE

Larry and Christine are eating in a Thai restaurant. They're sitting at one of those low tables, in chairs without legs.

They're eating with chopsticks. They have beers. They're nicely dressed. He sports hair tonic. She has a little bow in her hair.

CHRISTINE: One, two, three, four.

LARRY: Yeah. We are surrounded by the Buddha.

CHRISTINE: Comforting. That's a comfort.

LARRY: Single. Singleness. What is "single"?

CHRISTINE: You mean like, I'm single? As opposed to married or significantly entangled?

LARRY: Beer.

CHRISTINE: Isn't beer beautiful?

LARRY: Yeah.

CHRISTINE: There are different kinds of intelligence.

LARRY: Sure.

CHRISTINE: What kind am I?

LARRY: Quick.

CHRISTINE: I'm quick?

LARRY: That's the gloss anyway. Under that is something quite different again. Your, you know, the actual way you are. There's the gloss which really probably reflects back aspects that are coming at you. Right now: me. Like you're a fielder. Dealing with the balls that come your way. And you're a quick fielder. You're good. But under that, the other kind of intelligence, that's when you're at bat. And you're the pitcher. And the ball.

CHRISTINE: You know, originally I'm from Queens.

LARRY: I didn't know that.

CHRISTINE: Yeah. So that part of me wants to say, What the fuck are you talking about?!

LARRY: I'm talking about whatever comes into my head.

CHRISTINE: I know. And another part of me wants to have this kind of conversation because it's different from when I grew up, WHICH WAS SO STULTIFYING? You know, I lived with a guy, he knew me like a book. If I needed a pillow behind me in my chair when I sat down he had the pillow there. He knew my thoughts. He knew my music. He could work me like the bar sharpie works the shuffleboard machine. Do you know what that's like?

LARRY: I think it'd give me the creeps.

CHRISTINE: No. It's pretty nice. It's very complete. It has a lot of good points.

LARRY: So what happened?

CHRISTINE: I left him.

LARRY: Why?

CHRISTINE: I was getting bored. I was starting to feel sadistic.

LARRY: You don't mean sadistic.

CHRISTINE: Alright, what do I mean?

LARRY: I don't know.

CHRISTINE: Did you ever have an event, a single event, that changed everything like that?!

LARRY: Well, I'm sure I have, but… I mean I'm sure I've had a few…

CHRISTINE: I fell in a hole.

LARRY: You fell… You what?

CHRISTINE: I fell in a hole. I was in a deli. I turned a corner. There was nothing there. It was a hole. And I fell in.

LARRY: There was a hole in a deli?

CHRISTINE: It was a trapdoor in the floor. Somebody left it open. It was late. I fell through. I fell fifteen feet. Landed on my head. Got a bad concussion. Messed up my face.

LARRY: Really.

CHRISTINE: I was paralyzed for six months.

LARRY: Jesus.

CHRISTINE: When I could walk again, and after the reconstructive surgery, and after the speech therapy…

LARRY: What did you need that for?

CHRISTINE: I forgot how to talk. My brain was affected.

LARRY: So you were like completely destroyed.

CHRISTINE: Yeah. My speech therapist was from the Midwest so now I have a slight Midwestern accent. I lost my Queens accent while I was still in Queens. And my face. I used to have a round face. Now it's long.

LARRY: I don't know what to say.

CHRISTINE: You want to hear the strangest thing?

LARRY: What?

CHRISTINE: I used to be... I used to have a different personality.

LARRY: What do you mean?

CHRISTINE: A lot of people who knew me before have commented on it. Even my mother says it's true.

LARRY: You mean the experience changed you.

CHRISTINE: I mean I got hit on the head and before that I was different than I was after.

LARRY: What were you like?

CHRISTINE: Oh, I was sly, you know? Always looking for the opportunity. Always had something to say. People looked scared when I showed up. I liked that. And I had this very specific laugh. You know, nasty, at-the-expense-of kind of laugh.

LARRY: So you looked different and you talked different and you *were* different.

CHRISTINE: Yes.

LARRY: How long ago did this happen?

CHRISTINE: Little over three years ago.

LARRY: You know I invited you to dinner, I thought it might be fun to go out and get to know each other a little bit...

CHRISTINE: Me too.

LARRY: I wish you were going to have amnesia tomorrow.

CHRISTINE: Why? Do you have a secret?

LARRY: Sure. Why did you tell me?

CHRISTINE: I felt you were starting to assume a huge number of things about me that weren't true, and before you dug yourself in too deep... Anyway, a revelation's always fun, right?

LARRY: Your face is so beautiful. I can't imagine that it was ever damaged.

CHRISTINE: All that stuff, it's not that important.

LARRY: What is important?

CHRISTINE: Nothing.

LARRY: What do you mean?

CHRISTINE: You asked me what's important. I can't think of anything.

LARRY: I can.

CHRISTINE: What?

LARRY: I think it's important that this minute I can't remember your name.

CHRISTINE: It's Christine.

LARRY: Of course it's Christine. How could that have happened, how could I have forgotten?

CHRISTINE: And your name's Larry.

LARRY: I remembered my name. What you're saying disturbs me very much.

CHRISTINE: What did I say?

LARRY: Nothing's important.

CHRISTINE: Oh don't let me bother you. Just forget it.

LARRY: It upsets me because I find myself agreeing with you!

CHRISTINE: You don't think anything's important either?

LARRY: Why couldn't I remember your name?!

CHRISTINE: I'm not offended.

LARRY: It's just, I mean, I find it strange. That's not like me!

CHRISTINE: We've only known each other a week.

LARRY: But to ask a woman on a…and not be able to remember her *name*?! I've never had that experience. Before.

CHRISTINE: Good.

LARRY: But that's not like me.

CHRISTINE: Think of my situation. Everything I do is not like me. I've become very comfortable with that. Larry.

LARRY: I just, I'm, I, it's, not to be melodramatic but… Married.

CHRISTINE: Married. You're married.

LARRY: Yes.

CHRISTINE: You're married.

LARRY: Yes.

CHRISTINE: You didn't tell me that.

LARRY: No. I neglected…

CHRISTINE: Well. And you asked me on a date.

LARRY: Yes.

CHRISTINE: And your wife is where?

LARRY: Home.

CHRISTINE: *(Simultaneous.)* Home.

LARRY: I'm sorry.

CHRISTINE: You're sorry what? You're sorry that you're married?

LARRY: Yes. Naw, I'm sorry that I've been duplicitous.

CHRISTINE: To me?

LARRY: Yes.

CHRISTINE: To your wife?

LARRY: Yes.

CHRISTINE: To yourself?

LARRY: Yes.

CHRISTINE: So you're REALLY sorry.

LARRY: I don't know what to do.

CHRISTINE: Eat something.

LARRY: I really don't know what to do.

CHRISTINE: I feel sorry for all men.

LARRY: That's nice. Why?

CHRISTINE: They suffer like dumb beasts.

LARRY: So you're alone.

CHRISTINE: That's right. I'm single.

LARRY: What's that like?

CHRISTINE: Being single is mysterious. It's silent. You live large parts of your life unobserved. There's no one there saying, That's the third time you've gone to the bathroom. Why do you laugh like that? Are you going to do anything today? There's no one saying, You look unhappy. What is it? I find for myself that when I live with someone, my life lacks depth. It has scope, it has activity... I don't know what I'm trying to say. Single, married, both ways are hard. Sometimes you want to suffer and not be seen. Then it's better to be single. Sometimes you don't even suffer unless there's someone there seeing you. Then it's much better to be single. It's better to be married when it's better to be married. For a woman, it's great when you're checking into a hotel and you're Mrs. Whatever. Very solid feeling. I guess it doesn't matter whether you're married or not. I guess I don't think it matters very much one way or the other.

LARRY: What if you have children?

CHRISTINE: That's more than I know about. I don't have children.

LARRY: I do. Two girls. The twins.

CHRISTINE: Look, Larry, why don't you just go home.

LARRY: I can't go home. I've lost my dignity. If I say I'm upset, my wife says she's more upset. If I say, I'm scared. She says she's terrified. Whatever I am, she's more, so I must be less. I am diminished. I am vanishing.

CHRISTINE: That's a lot.

LARRY: And why couldn't I remember your name?

CHRISTINE: Maybe my name isn't important.

LARRY: Oh, I just ate a whole hot pepper! Wow! Boy, that's hot!

CHRISTINE: Have some water.

LARRY: She's not bad, my wife, I just want her to disappear.

CHRISTINE: What about the kids?

LARRY: Oh, I love them but I can't take care of them, I don't want to take care of them, but if I didn't see them, I would miss them right away. Right away. They're beautiful.

CHRISTINE: You can't control your nature.

LARRY: I know. That's what scares the shit out of me. Like you. You fell in a hole. It's like that.

CHRISTINE: So here we are.

LARRY: Right. Eating Thai food, sitting on the floor. I like this.

CHRISTINE: Having a truthful conversation.

LARRY: Truth! Truth and spicy food.

CHRISTINE: The truth can be used as a spice. But that's perhaps…

LARRY: So this guy you left, the one who could read your every mood, were you with him before or after you fell in the hole?

CHRISTINE: After.

LARRY: Was your relationship, did it have a feeling like he was your nurse?

CHRISTINE: Yeah.

LARRY: Were you still messed up when he met you?

CHRISTINE: Not so you could see.

LARRY: Are you still messed up now?

CHRISTINE: Yes.

LARRY: You are?

CHRISTINE: Yes.

LARRY: How? Do you know?

CHRISTINE: I don't know. I just know something's still wrong.

LARRY: Before I was married, I was a different person.

CHRISTINE: What were you like?

LARRY: I don't know. I couldn't even tell you what I'm currently like, no matter what I was like in some bygone time slot. So what were you doing at that meeting?

CHRISTINE: I saw a flyer by a phone in a restaurant and I wrote down the number. I don't know why. I think I must have felt the subject was so specifically esoteric that, well, it made me curious.

LARRY: I picked up a leaflet in a Jungian bookstore.

CHRISTINE: I didn't' even know there was such a thing as a Jungian bookstore.

LARRY: You're kidding. I know of two purely Jungian bookstores. And several Jung slash flako, occult, Dolphins are Citizens of Atlantis bookstores.

CHRISTINE: New York.

LARRY: New York. What did you think of the lecture?

CHRISTINE: Well, I thought she was a little heavy.

LARRY: She made some witty comments.

CHRISTINE: I mean her weight. She was fat.

LARRY: Oh. Yeah.

CHRISTINE: So I thought, what does she know? She can't even diet. But then I thought she started to make some very good points. I didn't understand the box with the numbers.

LARRY: The Chinese Divination Box.

CHRISTINE: Yeah.

LARRY: I felt like I understood it while she was explaining it, but I didn't take away an understanding.

CHRISTINE: What a subject. The Study of Meaningful Chance. I think the most amazing thing about the lecture is that I went.

LARRY: I've never gone to anything like that before.

CHRISTINE: Oh God!

LARRY: What?

CHRISTINE: I just ate one of those peppers! Oh my God they're hot! Really wakes you up.

LARRY: It's the shriveled little ones. You should fish them out. There's about ten of them in there. Have some water.

CHRISTINE: Thanks.

LARRY: I feel it. The fatefulness of things. I have a very strong fate.

CHRISTINE: What do you mean by that?

LARRY: I feel like the whole world tells me what to do. Not people. Not in the social sense. The whole living world. Strangers are part of that. Strangers saying things to you that have meaning for you. Signs. Scraps of newspaper. A drop of water hitting you on the head in a very particular way that makes you feel the presence of meaning.

CHRISTINE: Did you read The Celestine Prophecy?

LARRY: Yeah. Total bullshit. Nancy Drew goes to Peru.

CHRISTINE: I couldn't put it down.

LARRY: Me neither. Basically, the guy's a paranoid. It's just that he's a positive paranoid. He writes positive conspiracy theories. Those guys can flip though. Those guys have a tendency to flip. Cat Stevens? The trick is to start from an experience that people have had, get them nodding, saying Yeah, that's happened to me, and then take them, walk them, talk them to some Egyptian Sci-Fi, flako, occult, Dolphins are registered to vote in Atlantis scenario. That's not to say I haven't had a psychic experience.

CHRISTINE: I've had them. But I've only had them when I wasn't trying to have them.

LARRY: What am I going to do about my life?

CHRISTINE: Are things bad?

LARRY: Things are bad. Things are very bad. My life has stopped working. It's only a matter of time before I stop working.

CHRISTINE: Did you read about the cop who talked a guy out of committing suicide and then committed suicide himself?

LARRY: I did read about that! Why would he do that!

CHRISTINE: It's like he made a deal with Death.

LARRY: I feel like there was a period when there was a lot of stories like that. Deals with Death or the Devil.

CHRISTINE: Right. Like the Devil and Daniel Webster.

LARRY: Yeah, that kind of thing! There were all these things about the power of eloquence. Daniel Webster can save your life by out-talking the Devil.

CHRISTINE: Cyrano can talk and make a woman fall in love with you.

LARRY: *Inherit The Wind*. You can turn a bunch of yahoos around, Clarence Darrow.

CHRISTINE: Right, right. And Brutus was an honorable man.

LARRY: Maybe he was.

CHRISTINE: That cop made a speech and turned a man around from taking his own life.

LARRY: Paid a big price.

CHRISTINE: Yes. Do you believe that somebody could say something to you that would make your whole life better or work or improve in some important way?

LARRY: Yes.

CHRISTINE: What could someone say to you?

LARRY: I don't know. Exactly what I haven't thought of, I guess.

CHRISTINE: After my accident, when I was lying paralyzed for six months, I had a lot of time to think. I thought about all the cruel things I'd done in my life. I tried to remember every generous thing I'd ever done. Moments of insight, of terrible pain, of pleasure. I tried to see patterns in my lists. I saw some things. I made some connections. But after a while it all began to dissolve away like a lace cookie dissolves away in your mouth. Some sweetness, then all gone like a dream. At first it felt like I was wearing an iron hat that was just a little too small. That was the concussion. My brain was actually swollen, pressing against my skull. After a time, that lessened. The feeling of the hat. But I could feel myself then like a tiny object caught in a great flood. I still have that feeling. Like I'm bound up, a little splinter, pitching along in a black rush. People said I was different after the accident. That the blow to my head had hurt me. Maybe. Six months to think about things changed me. Banging my brain changed me. But I look at people and people change. Don't you agree?

LARRY: Sometimes. Most of the time, no. I don't know.

CHRISTINE: People change. People do. I mean think of evolution. We crawled up out of the sea. We rejected life underwater. It's just that nobody notices. I noticed my change. It had a sudden look. People were looking to see if I'd been affected and I had been. And they shook their heads, my own mother shook her head and said, Christine has changed.

LARRY: What am I going to do about my life?

CHRISTINE: I don't know, Larry.

LARRY: I know it's a terrible thing to say but I wish in a way that I had fallen in a hole, and that everybody knew to expect that I was going to be different afterwards.

CHRISTINE: Why was that woman fat, do you think?

LARRY: You mean the woman who gave the lecture?

CHRISTINE: Yeah.

LARRY: She probably sits around reading her books and talking to people on the phone and, you know, she's sedentary and...she eats!

CHRISTINE: Yeah. She eats.

LARRY: It's funny how the circumstances of your life can build up into a kind of infernal machine. Kids are huge that way. You have kids. One change to the circumstances of your life, but that one change engenders ten thousand little slavey tasks that must be done. Suddenly all the time is eaten up. There's no time! You've got to give up everything. You can't read, talk on the phone, look out the window, stay up late, have a conversation. You get married, that's one changed circumstance. You have children, I'm telling you, you get married, your entire universe is destroyed. Your rules are hollow broken signs, your love life is a vacant gutted ghost town. Your finer feelings, you don't have any finer feelings. You have shredded electrical wiring jutting out of a busted box like so much smoking spaghetti. A burning radio picking up a non-stop station of accusations. Your life, MY LIFE, has become a stupid contest of pain with my wife who used to be a woman, but now is my demented screeching other half. Did I do this to her? She says I did. If I did, and there's a Hell, they will put me there.

(A Thai server, a lovely woman of I don't know what age, appears, smiling. The two diners notice her and fall silent. They smile, as if on cue, after a moment.)

SERVER: Hiii. How are you doing today? Okay?

CHRISTINE: Good.

LARRY: Very good. Fine.

SERVER: Need anything?

LARRY: No, thanks.

SERVER: More beer? More water?

LARRY: Actually.

CHRISTINE: I would have another beer.

LARRY: Me too.

SERVER: And why don't you have the water, too? It's free.

LARRY: That's true.

CHRISTINE: Actually I'd love some water.

SERVER: Good. The best things in life are free, right?

CHRISTINE AND LARRY: Right.

SERVER: Easy to say, hard to remember. Water. My mother used to say, You want water around. You got water around, everything's going to be okay. You okay?

LARRY: I'm alright.

SERVER: But there's bad news too. The bad news is my sister lives in the desert.

CHRISTINE: I'm sorry.

SERVER: No water. Her boyfriend took her there. This guy Freddie. Nevada. She called me today. She's on my mind. She asks me, how can it be, that love can take you to a bad place? She's conflicted. I told her she should come work with me, but the manager here is a strange man. He keeps going up on the roof. I think he's on drugs. He's Portuguese.

CHRISTINE: Excuse me. Enough.

SERVER: Two beers and two waters.

CHRISTINE: Thanks.

(The server goes.)

LARRY: Thank you.

CHRISTINE: I can't tell you how many times that's happened to me in New York.

LARRY: What?

CHRISTINE: Somebody shows up like…The Annunciation. A person appears like a messenger from Divinity. They say something that absolutely, it's just right. Their words, their aura, it reminds you of this other level you could be on. They take you to that other level. And then they start bitching about the Portuguese.

LARRY: I have an idea about that.

CHRISTINE: What?

LARRY: Aspects of the Divine. All these gods. There used to be all these gods. And they used to impersonate people. Odysseus arrives home and Athena impersonates a guy he knows. Nestor. Odysseus runs into he thinks Nestor, who tells him something he needs to know. He goes on his way. He thinks he talked to Nestor. But he wasn't talking to Nestor. He was talking to a god inhabiting the appearance of Nestor. He was talking to a god. And you recognize it. I've seen it. You're talking to a woman, a woman you know, you've known her forever. And one night, you see her, look into her face. The Goddess of Love. The eyes, the skin, the hair, the Goddess of Love. You kiss her. It's like tumbling down a wild Irish mountain and the wolves are howling and stars are crashing into the earth. But the next day, the next minute sometimes, it's just a woman again. The Goddess has fled. Gone into some other girl. Or hidden her light beneath the ocean or something. Or she starts bitching about the Portuguese. I've felt it in myself. Moments when I give over to something else. A natural sudden certainty of bravery, or romantic love, or intellectual clarity. And afterwards I think, that was Ares, or Aphrodite, or grey-eyed Athena. Never at the time. Always afterwards. A truly peculiar delightful feeling of humility. Of who was that man? It is sort've a Lone Ranger feeling. Who was that man, that mask? Who did that deed that needed to be done? And I think, why, it was a god. They're hiding. They're still here. Just like they always were. So you work in publishing?

CHRISTINE: What? No. I'm a receptive, excuse me, I'm a receptionist in a thing they call an executive tower in Long Island City. And I'm a proofreader for an obscure financial newspaper on Wall Street. And you? I know you work in an office.

LARRY: You know what I used to be?

CHRISTINE: What?

LARRY: I used to be a bond salesman.

CHRISTINE: That's...?

LARRY: A financial instrument. I was the guy who handled the old ladies. Old ladies love bonds.

CHRISTINE: They do?

LARRY: Yes. I made a lot of money doing that for a while. A lot of money. That's when I met my wife. She was married to a commodities trader from Chicago who I knew. We used to have drinks when they came to New York at Christmas.

CHRISTINE: You stole the guy's wife?

LARRY: No. When he stopped drinking it turned out that the reason he was drinking was he was gay.

CHRISTINE: Oh.

LARRY: He stayed in Chicago, she moved to New York. She was still only twenty-five. We started going out...While we were still going out, this thing happened that's always haunted me. I'm ashamed about it.

CHRISTINE: You don't want to go home, do you?

LARRY: This customer, bonds you know, her husband was dead. She was one of these women with nothing to do but rearrange her portfolio. She was a very good customer. She invited me to the Caribbean, San Juan. I was seeing Babette. And I went. Babette knew about it. And I went with this fifty-five-year-old fur coat — I didn't sleep with her. But I went with her. The place we were at had this little casino filled with only other women like her. They had these handbags stuffed with chips. And this woman, this customer, she towed me in there. See I was a trophy. And my wife, Babette, she wasn't my wife then, but my wife Babette, that was alright with her. Because it was a customer. Whenever I hear the word "sleazy" I think of those women, that casino, their handbags croaked open with chips. I don't think a god was co-starring with me then. I don't think there's a god of sleaze.

CHRISTINE: There's the Devil.

LARRY: You think there's a Devil?

CHRISTINE: There's something about the way you see things, it's…

LARRY: Overblown?

CHRISTINE: If every great moment in your life, if the way you see it is, it wasn't you that was doing it, then what are you going to think of yourself? You're left with the sleaze, and the gods did everything else.

LARRY: Huh. I still think that's the way it is. Jesus!

CHRISTINE: What?

LARRY: I must be cracking up. I've forgotten your name again!

CHRISTINE: Christine.

LARRY: Christine. Christine. Beautiful name.

CHRISTINE: Thank you.

LARRY: You're a proofreader.

CHRISTINE: Yes.

LARRY: And a receptionist in an executive tower.

CHRISTINE: In Long Island City. Very good. I don't really give a shit if you can remember my name. I don't really care if you can remember my face tomorrow. What does it matter? I'm your company for this meal. This conversation.

LARRY: So I bought an apartment and I paid off the mortgage and Babette got pregnant and I quit my bond job and I got a thing selling memberships at a Greenwich Village Health Club.

CHRISTINE: Why are you telling me all this…garbage.

LARRY: I don't know. Because it's my life.

CHRISTINE: I feel like you're just telling me THINGS.

LARRY: Alright, let's talk about you.

CHRISTINE: I'm not interested in that, either.

LARRY: Well, what are you interested in?

CHRISTINE: Nothing.

LARRY: Nothing?

CHRISTINE: I have a burning interest in nothing.

(The server appears with the tray of beverages.)

SERVER: Stop the clock. *(Sings.)* I dream of Jeannie with the light brown hair. Beer, beer. Water, water.

LARRY: Spiseba. That's Russian for thanks.

CHRISTINE: Thanks.

SERVER: You want new glasses for your beer?

CHRISTINE: We can use the ones we have. Spiseba.

SERVER: You're not finished with anything, are you?

LARRY AND CHRISTINE: No.

SERVER: You were talking. Big conversation, huh? That's good. Talk everything over. You've gotta run down the rabbit. A lot of times people sit here and don't talk to each other. It's depressing. Everybody should talk, don't you think? Really talk. If you talk about everything, turn it over, turn it over…

CHRISTINE: Excuse me?

SERVER: I know. Enough. Sorry.

CHRISTINE: Forget it.

SERVER: Need anything else right now?

CHRISTINE: No.

LARRY: Tea. Hot tea.

CHRISTINE: Oh, I'll have tea.

SERVER: Hot?

CHRISTINE: Yeah.

SERVER: *(Sings.)* I dream of Jeannie with the light brown hair. Start the clock.

(The server goes.)

LARRY: She's a character.

CHRISTINE: I am not distracted. I will not be distracted. Listen. For a while there I got you were really telling me something, but then I felt you were just mindlessly dredging up dead information and dumping it on me. Now I don't mind, NO, I'm grateful for when you or anybody actually speaks to me, but I will not just be a garbage can while you automatically dispose.

LARRY: I'm sorry if I crossed some line of yours.

CHRISTINE: And don't appease me. You can't appease me.

LARRY: I'm trying to get along with you.

CHRISTINE: You've gone on automatic pilot and you're trying to put me in a certain box.

LARRY: I am not.

CHRISTINE: Yeah. I'm the whore with a heart of gold rubbing your feet while you bitch about your wife. It's like that sculpture, the Pieta. The wounded man, the nurturing woman.

LARRY: As I recall, the man was dead.

CHRISTINE: Point taken, and so what?

LARRY: You're a receptionist and a proofreader?

CHRISTINE: So?

LARRY: You're too smart to be a receptionist and a proofreader.

CHRISTINE: Oh, those ideas don't apply anymore, don't you know that? There's incredibly educated people all over this city doing unbelievably strange tiny things to get by.

LARRY: I want to cry.

CHRISTINE: So cry. I didn't mean to say it that way, but why not cry?

LARRY: I can't. I've had times when I could let go, but not now.

CHRISTINE: Why not?

LARRY: Oh, I don't know. It's not safe.

CHRISTINE: I'm sorry I've been, I don't know how to put it, repulsing you.

LARRY: You don't repulse me.

CHRISTINE: I didn't mean it like that.

LARRY: I like you.

CHRISTINE: I was a double major in college. Philosophy and Dance. I was a dancer till I was injured. I couldn't be after that.

(The server returns. She's wearing a coat.)

SERVER: Hot tea. Hot tea.

LARRY: Why is it dark like that?

SERVER: It's Thai tea. Very good. It's different that Tetley. You put this sweet milk in it, it's very good. Anything new's scary at first, but how scary can you get of a cup of tea? May I give you your check? I'm going home.

LARRY: Sure.

(She puts the check on the table.)

SERVER: There's no hurry to pay. The man up front will take it whenever you want. Take your time. Talk forever.

(The server goes. Christine says after her.)

CHRISTINE: Good night.

(Christine looks after the departed server. Larry looks at Christine. Neither of them moves for a long time. Then Larry reaches over, pulls Christine gently but firmly to him in a single motion, and kisses her. She is not surprised. She kisses him back. He suddenly stops the kiss.)

CHRISTINE: What is it?

LARRY: I just got a little nervous.

CHRISTINE: What do you need?

LARRY: I wouldn't know where to begin.

CHRISTINE: Because if you told me what you needed, you might get it.

LARRY: I need to be accepted completely.

CHRISTINE: This table accepts you completely. That's not a lot to ask. In a way.

LARRY: Oh look, forget it. I'm just a ridiculous person. My problems are ridiculous and boring TO ME!

CHRISTINE: You're unhappy.

LARRY: Yeah.

CHRISTINE: Why did you kiss me?

LARRY: I couldn't think of anything else to do.

(She looks at him. She leans over and she kisses him.)

CHRISTINE: Your lips are soft.

LARRY: I'm upset.

CHRISTINE: You're scared.

LARRY: Yeah.

CHRISTINE: So what. It's alright.

LARRY: What are you thinking about?

CHRISTINE: I was thinking about, what am I going to do in my life now?

LARRY: Don't worry. I'm not going to make some kind of demand on you.

CHRISTINE: I wasn't thinking about you. You're like a dream to me. This restaurant is like a dream to me. I was thinking about my life. My experience. It's extremely difficult for me to really know you're here. I know you're married. You're unhappy. You've gotten into appeasing your wife, who can't be appeased. You're a man, whatever that is. Men are so different. My father was a man. He's dead. When men died, women used to wash them. I wish I'd washed my father's dead body. Been allowed that tenderness. I think it would be easier to express physical tenderness to a dead man than any man I've ever dated.

LARRY: Do you know how to make love?

CHRISTINE: No. Not really.

LARRY: Me neither. Not really.

CHRISTINE: I've done it.

LARRY: You have?

CHRISTINE: But it just happened to work out that way.

LARRY: I know what you mean. It's happened to me, too.

CHRISTINE: You're an interesting man, Larry.

LARRY: I am?

CHRISTINE: Yeah.

LARRY: I don't feel interesting. I feel like a fool. I feel like I don't have anything to offer except my confusion, my clownish agonies, my needs whatever they are, my…I don't know. What do you find interesting about me?

CHRISTINE: Your kiss. I felt something in my bowels when I kissed you.

LARRY: In your bowels?

CHRISTINE: Yeah.

LARRY: Wow, that's…I guess that's really something. I don't know what I feel. I'm upset. Let me try this tea. So I didn't tell you what I do now for a living.

CHRISTINE: I thought you sold memberships in a health club.

LARRY: No, I quit that job. You know, I…This is how I quit it. A guy came in, an old man. He had high blood pressure and his doctor had said, join a gym. So I was giving him my spiel about the place and he looked at me. He had these penetrating eyes, almost like he was surprised to see me there, and very surprised by what I was telling him. And right in the middle of my pitch, he blurted: What are you doing here?! And I went to answer him, it seemed so obvious, I had this job and I was doing my job, but I couldn't answer him. I didn't know why I was there. I didn't know. He made me see myself in my situation because he had this incredulity.

CHRISTINE: You are nervous.

LARRY: So I quit that job.

CHRISTINE: You're a salesman.

LARRY: Not now.

CHRISTINE: I think I could be a very good salesman except there's nothing I believe in.

LARRY: Now I'm running the New York office of an arts colony in Italy. They're going to do a play on a mountaintop in Umbria next August.

CHRISTINE: Why?

LARRY: Because this guy, he's actually a big baker here in New York, he got this vision of doing this project in Italy, he's Italian, and he's raising the money. He's raised a lot of it already.

CHRISTINE: What do you mean, he's a big baker?

LARRY: He bakes. He's got like five bakeries in and around New York. He's very successful. He does the cakes for all the biggest society people in New York. He's very well connected. But he's, well, he's an artist. I mean if you saw the way that he decorated these cakes it would remove any doubt from your mind. And he was frustrated because it wasn't enough.

CHRISTINE: Making cakes.

LARRY: The whole baking thing, it didn't satisfy the artist in him, so he got this idea of starting an arts colony in this ancient Etruscan town on a mountain in Umbria, and he started a New York office to coordinate the fundraising…See, he was the old man! Who came to the gym. And asked me why I was there! His doctor said he had high blood pressure and he realized he wasn't going to live forever, and that if he was going to ever make his dream a reality, it had to be now!

CHRISTINE: What does your wife think of this?

LARRY: Well, it's a finite job. It ends when the colony cranks up. Or at best it's seasonal. And it doesn't pay much. I've had to take a loan against the apartment to pay tuition. Two daughters in school. My wife thinks everything I've done for the last several cycles has been the wrong thing.

CHRISTINE: Why doesn't she leave you?

LARRY: She can't leave me. We're chained together like galley slaves. We're in debt together. We have the kids to think of. She believes that she has lost her looks and she couldn't get another man.

CHRISTINE: Has she lost her looks?

LARRY: She looks alright.

CHRISTINE: Have you had affairs before?

LARRY: Never! That kiss was the first kiss I ever had out of the house.

CHRISTINE: I wish you hadn't told me that.

LARRY: Well, I did.

CHRISTINE: It puts a lot more responsibility on the situation.

LARRY: Good! Why shouldn't you feel responsible? The fact of the matter is as soon as you realize that I am not a dream, that I'm really here, and who I really am, at that moment you will head for the door!

CHRISTINE: I don't know about that.

LARRY: I do.

CHRISTINE: Do you think you know who I really am?

LARRY: No. But if I did, or when I do, I would still want you to kiss me.
    (It dawns on him what he said. He smiles.)

CHRISTINE: What a thing to say. Me to kiss you.
    (He looks at her and kisses her.)

LARRY: That was a wonderful wonderful…kiss.

CHRISTINE: Why do I like you?

LARRY: I don't know. Do you really like me?

CHRISTINE: Yes.

LARRY: You really do?

CHRISTINE: Yes.

LARRY: That makes me very happy. Confide in me. Confide in me something.

CHRISTINE: Alright. What? Alright. I've only been really satisfied by one man.

LARRY: That guy you left because you were starting to feel sadistic?

CHRISTINE: No. No, he could get me where I wanted to go, but I always felt his mind, that I was being worked on, played. No, this was another man. He was a little older than me. He had a very affected way of talking. He was totally materialistic. And a drunk, pretty bad drunk. He had a completely deluded idea of who I was. I don't think he could really see any woman. His mother was this kind of Auntie Mame type. I never met her. He talked about her. She'd abused him, deserted him. He thought she was IT. He smoked, reeked of this horrible cologne, wore these big double-breasted pin stripe suits. But he had a touch with me, he didn't have to think about it, he didn't have to work at it, he just had it. He could take me to the moon. He could take me to the Amazon. I saw visions with that man. His name was Dennis.

LARRY: So?

CHRISTINE: It was a trade-off that could only go on for so long. I dumped him.

LARRY: I notice it's always you who dumps them.

CHRISTINE: I hadn't really thought. But yes.

LARRY: This is the strangest conversation I've ever had.

CHRISTINE: This is the strangest conversation I've ever had.

LARRY: Do you think it's because we went to that lecture with that strange fat woman? Do you think it affected us?

CHRISTINE: Maybe. Are you trying to hatch some alibi for your wife. The fat lady defense?

LARRY: But why couldn't I remember your name, Christine?

CHRISTINE: Why can you remember it now?

LARRY: You're a receptionist?!

CHRISTINE: A very busy receptionist. Headset and a microphone. I just hear voices and respond in this very automatic way all day long.

LARRY: And you like that?

CHRISTINE: It's great. I don't exist. I'm a piece of wire. It takes all my time and all my attention and it means absolutely nothing.

LARRY: I don't understand you. I know you're saying something that's at the core of something, but what is it?

CHRISTINE: What's so great about being you, Larry?

LARRY: Nothing.

CHRISTINE: Exactly. Exactly. Exactly.

LARRY: You said there's still something wrong with you.

CHRISTINE: Yes.

LARRY: I think I know what it is.

CHRISTINE: What?

LARRY: You've had some kind of experience and nobody can know what it is because it has nothing to do with words so you can't share it, and that makes you lonely.

CHRISTINE: No, that's not it.

LARRY: That was a little close, wasn't it?

CHRISTINE: What do you mean?

LARRY: What kind of dancer were you?

CHRISTINE: Modern. Abstract. We used video.

LARRY: Do you still see the other dancers?

CHRISTINE: No. The language of dancers is dance. I couldn't talk to them anymore.

LARRY: Do you miss them?

CHRISTINE: No.

LARRY: Do you miss dancing?

CHRISTINE: Yes. Yes.

(He takes her hand. She is sad.)

LARRY: Look at all these fingers.

CHRISTINE: Do you love your wife?

LARRY: Of course.

CHRISTINE: In proofreading, one proofreader reads against the other. They watch out for each other. Their object is to agree. But each of them must listen very carefully to the other. The agreement must be real.

LARRY: I don't really care, at this moment, how my story turns out. I'm deeply, deeply bored with my own story. But I like being alive. I like being here with you.

CHRISTINE: Is your wife's name really Babette?

LARRY: Yes. (They laugh.) I'm not laughing at her expense.

CHRISTINE: I know.

LARRY: There are so many jokes in my life. If I say my life out loud, I see it's full of jokes. But you know the whole story of my life, if I said the whole story of my life out loud, all the events, I don't think it has anything to do with who I am.

CHRISTINE: Oh, I bet it does.

LARRY: No, no. It doesn't. *Your* life, yes. The events of your life strike me as having something to do with your true story. You fell in a whole. It's so graphic! But me selling bonds, selling health, mortgaging the apartment, the twins…

CHRISTINE: Babette…

LARRY: Babette, Umbria, my medical problems…

CHRISTINE: What medical problems?

LARRY: Oh, I didn't mention that? I have a lazy eye. I HAD a lazy eye, a wandering eye. Six operations later it doesn't wander anymore and who gives a shit?

CHRISTINE: You mean it didn't look at you?

LARRY: Exactly! It didn't look at you. NOW it looks at you! The pain, the money that went into that…Well, it was worth it. I felt bad about it. Vanity.

CHRISTINE: I can understand that.

LARRY: I wanted to look attractive.

CHRISTINE: You are attractive.

LARRY: I am?

CHRISTINE: Whatever that means. Yes.

LARRY: You really think so?

CHRISTINE: I wouldn't have kissed you.

LARRY: If I had the wandering eye.

CHRISTINE: You do have the wandering eye.

LARRY: True! Before it was on the outside, now it's my character! Now I truly do have the wandering eye and you'd never know it to look at me. Six operations later.

CHRISTINE: They pushed it in.

LARRY: That's right. They shoved the wandering eye in. My third eye. The one that drifts. Like one of those space telescopes. Now it's at my core.
(He struggles with an emotion.)

CHRISTINE: Hey. That's right.

LARRY: I'm sorry. Emotion.

CHRISTINE: No, it's good.

LARRY: I'm okay now.

CHRISTINE: Why bother to be?

LARRY: I just sometimes feel this thing rise. It's like Hawaii being born. Except it doesn't get born. It sinks again. Until some other day. Some Supreme Court keeps it down. The weight of some authority. I have all this feeling, but the days are small. They're too small. It's like I'm smelting. But I have so much more bronze than I need to fill the form, lose the wax, make the life. But I hate to just spill it!

CHRISTINE: Come here.

LARRY: I'm useless.

CHRISTINE: I doubt that.

LARRY: Don't.

CHRISTINE: What upset you?

LARRY: I was upset. It's when I feel a little good that I know how bad I feel. You provided a little…easement, so now I feel really lousy.

CHRISTINE: Think about nothing.

LARRY: I can't think about nothing. That's not a skill of mine. I guess I can't be in the club. Can you do that?

CHRISTINE: Me? I'm the Queen of Nothing.

LARRY: Is that by blood or marriage?

CHRISTINE: Accident of nature.

LARRY: You mean the accident? That accident you had.

CHRISTINE: Yeah. At first I didn't know I was, but I was. And then after a time, I knew I was being in a bed. For a long time that's all I knew. I could hear my breathing which to me seemed like the universe through which I passed. My body, which had been everything to me, was gone. No memories, not for a long time. Then just pictures without language. Then my body came back. And pain. Struggle. Other people. Language. Life is very hard. Very, very hard. You shouldn't feel bad you suffer. Why wouldn't you? It breaks your heart. The tyranny of the body. These outward appearances. What we do for show. All these temporary situations and arrangements we have to believe are permanent. The emotion underneath everything is so strong. Like the power of the sea striking the immobility of a cliff.

LARRY: I don't know what you mean.

CHRISTINE: Yes, you do. The only thing you don't understand is the power of surrender and the freedom of nothing. I felt it when I came back. I saw how hard it is. It made me feel for people. It made me feel for myself. I used to think if I could pull the bread out of someone else's mouth I wouldn't starve, and I lived my life like that. Mean. I had some things then, some things I don't have now. I could dance. But I wouldn't go back, I wouldn't want to go back. It was an illusion anyway. A bunch of empty coconuts. We're turning in the dark, in the depths of the ocean. Luminous creatures looking for food in a world of spirit. When my mother looked at me and said: Christine, you've changed. You've changed, Christine. It made me shiver. Like that old man's incredulity made you see yourself and stop your selling.

LARRY: But the old man didn't stop me, he didn't change me. Yes, he changed what I was doing, and yes, that's something. And things are a little better, I believe, though, and if you asked my wife would agree, they look a little worse. I mean as a result of this encounter with this maker of cakes my outer landscape isn't as completely unlike my inner landscape as it was when I was a seller of bonds. Or at the health club answering questions about pool rules. But my apparent biography is still a crock of hypocrisy and shit.

CHRISTINE: I don't think things are as bad as you think they are.

LARRY: They're pretty bad. Now I'm out on dates. I'm going to crackpot lectures. Did I tell you I tried to take up painting?

CHRISTINE: No.

LARRY: Well, I can't paint! That much I know.

CHRISTINE: What did you paint?

LARRY: Doors! I just painted doors! But the doors never opened. And the doors were…Well, I can't paint! And I can't be married! And I hate being single! And though I have made some money in my life, and known some success, had some pleasure, perhaps been a good father once or twice…

CHRISTINE: Do you feel like you just haven't lived?

LARRY: No, I've lived. I've lived. But it's a train wreck. It's a pointless jig. I have danced a pointless jig. And under that, almost like a mockery, I see this, feel this vasty pattern, this gargantuan book of meaning. Like the plates that slide under the crust of the earth, like the pattern in the swirl of the Milky Way. It's there! That's clear to me! But it's there and I'm here and never the twain shall meet.!

CHRISTINE: That's funny.

LARRY: Is it?

CHRISTINE: Yeah.

LARRY: I guess my line is Why?

CHRISTINE: Because all these things you see out there, I see in here. But I don't see them out there like you do.

LARRY: You don't?

CHRISTINE: No. Out there, well, that's where I see the train wreck. I think Give up on out there. It's senseless. Whatever order there is, whatever meaning, whatever goodness, evil, strength, beauty, whatever makes sense comes from the inside.

LARRY: HOW CAN YOU SAY THAT?!

CHRISTINE: Do you remember my name?

LARRY: CHRISTINE?

CHRISTINE: Very good.

LARRY: Meaningful Chance. That was the fat woman's subject. And beyond that, if you recall, Divination. Reading into what's right here. The cards, the bones, the dice. Seeing the Future folded into the Present. I know that if I had the skill, I could read the Future in the stars tonight.

CHRISTINE: And I know that if I had the ability, I could see the Future in you.

LARRY: Do you really feel when you look at me that I make sense?

CHRISTINE: Yes.

LARRY: Like the Milky Way makes sense?

CHRISTINE: Well, I wouldn't know about that. To me the Milky Way is gibberish.

LARRY: Amazing. And I thought you were smart.

CHRISTINE: Oh, so now you know something?

LARRY: Some few things are obvious to me. Like perhaps it would be for the best if I were blotted off the face of the earth. And that the earth is good.

CHRISTINE: You are good. And I'll tell you, that's a dangerous line of thinking.

LARRY: Why's that?

CHRISTINE: When people get into their heads that the earth is good and they are shit, the next thing you know they become a certain kind of fanatic.

LARRY: What kind of fanatic?

CHRISTINE: A save the planet, kill the people kind of fanatic. The only thing wrong with the environment is that I'm in it kind of thinking.

LARRY: Well, I'm not that deep into the idea.

CHRISTINE: You can't hate yourself and love.

LARRY: I see what you're saying.

CHRISTINE: You can't even dislike yourself and love.

LARRY: Huh. Then I never loved and I never shall love. But I have loved.

CHRISTINE: You have?

LARRY: I did like myself then though.

CHRISTINE: So why don't you now?

LARRY: When I liked myself I didn't know myself very well. Now that I've gotten to know the man, I don't care for him.

CHRISTINE: Then you can't love.

LARRY: Can you?

CHRISTINE: I don't know.

(They kiss.)

LARRY: I feel something.

CHRISTINE: Me too.

(They kiss again.)

CHRISTINE: What do you feel?

LARRY: I'm not dead. Life. I feel life.

CHRISTINE: Yes. I guess I'll return to it.

END OF PLAY

One Flea Spare
by Naomi Wallace

BIOGRAPHY

Naomi Wallace is a native of Prospect, Kentucky, whose plays have been produced in both the U.S. and Great Britain. Her play *In the Heart of America*, set during the Gulf War, has been produced at the Bush Theatre, the Long Wharf Theatre and in Dortmund, Germany. It was recently published in *American Theatre* magazine and was awarded the 1995 Susan Smith Blackburn Prize. *Slaughter City* had its world premiere in January at the Barbican in London by the Royal Shakespeare Company and Faber and Faber will publish it this year. Her first book of poems, *To Dance a Stony Field*, was published in the U.K. by Peterloo Poets. At present, she is under commission by the Royal Shakespeare Company, BBC Radio and West End producers.

ORIGINAL PRODUCTION

One Flea Spare was first performed at the Bush Theatre, London on 18 October, 1995. Song lyrics by Naomi Wallace in collaboration with Bruce McLeod, music by Robert Lockhart. Presented by special arrangement with Alternative Theatre Company Ltd. (Bush Theatre). It was performed at the Humana Festival of New American Plays in 1996. It was directed by Dominic Dromgoole with the following cast:

Morse	Erin F. Joslyn
Bunce	Richard Thompson
Mr. William Snelgrave	William McNulty
Mrs. Darcy Snelgrave	Peggy Cowles
Kabe	Fred Major

and the following production staff:

Scenic Designer	Paul Owen
Costume Designer	Nanzi Adzima
Lighting Designer	T.J. Gerckens
Sound Designer	Michael Rasbury
Properties Manager	Mark J. Bissonnette
Stage Manager	Julie A. Richardson
Assistant Stage Manager	Susan M. McCarthy
Production Assistant	Brad O. Hunter
Dramaturg	Michael Bigelow Dixon
Dialect Coach	William McNulty
New York Casting Arrangements	Laura Richin Casting

CHARACTERS

MORSE: A girl of twelve.

BUNCE: A sailor in his late twenties.

MR. WILLIAM SNELGRAVE: A wealthy, elderly man.

MRS. DARCY SNELGRAVE: An elderly woman.

KABE: A watchman and guard.

PLACE

A comfortable house in Axe yard, off King Street, Westminster, in London, 1665.

> Oh stay, three lives in one flea spare,
> Where wee almost, yea more than maryed are.
> This flea is you and I, and this
> Our mariage bed, and mariage temple is;
> Though parents grudge, and you, w'are met,
> And cloysterd in these living walls of Jet.
> Though use make you apt to kill mee,
> Let not to that, selfe murder added bee,
> And sacrilege, three sinnes in killing three.
> —John Donne

> "Corruption is our only hope."
> —Bertolt Brecht

ONE FLEA SPARE

ACT ONE
Scene One

Morse locked in an empty room or cell. Alone. She wears a dirty, tattered, but once fine dress. She stands center stage with the dress pulled up to hide her face. She is wearing a torn pair of boys britches or long underwear under her dress. She is just barely visible in the dim light. She repeats the words that her interrogator might have used earlier.

MORSE: What are you doing out of your grave? *(Beat.)* What are you doing out of your grave? *(Beat.)* Speak to me.
(We hear the sound of someone being slapped, but Morse remains still and does not react.)
Speak to me, girl, or you'll stay here till it's know.
(Another sound of a slap, harder. Morse still does not move.)
What happened to the Gentleman?
(Another slap.)
What happened to his wife?
(Another slap.)
Whose blood is on your sleeve? *(Beat.)*
(Morse drops her dress down to reveal her face.)
The blood of a fish. Is on my sleeve. Because. The fish. The fish were burning in the channels. Whole schools of them on fire. And the ships sailing and their hulls plowing the dead up out of the water. And the war had begun. The war with the Dutch had begun. *(Beat.)* It was March. No, it was later. In summer. A summer so hot vegetables stewed in their crates. The old and the sick melted like snow in the streets. At night the rats came out in twos and threes to drink the sweat from our faces. *(Beat.)* And it had finally come. *(Beat.)* The Visitation. We all went to sleep one morning and when we awoke the whole city was aglow with the fever. Sparrows fell dead from the sky into the hands of beggars. Dogs walked in the robes of dying men, slipped into the beds of their dead Masters' wives. Children were born

with the beards of old men. *(Beat.)* They were locked in their own house, the two of them. All the windows, but one, nailed shut from the outside. They'd waited out their time of confinement. Three more days and they could escape. But then we came. In through the basement and across the roofs. One of us died. In that room. Two of us died. *(Beat.)* It was night. Yes. At night. He moved as though invisible. Gliding through the empty streets.

(Bunce, making a fair amount of noise, tumbles into the cell, which has now become the Snelgraves' room. He stands facing into a corner.)

He came in through the cellar. He thought the house was empty and so he made himself at home.

(Mr. and Mrs. Snelgrave enter their bare room.)

But his timing was off. Mr. and Mrs. Snelgrave caught him in the act of relieving himself into one of their finest vases.

(Morse joins the scene, but hiding in the corner. Everything freezes. Then lights go up on Bunce in the Snelgraves' house. Bunce is looking over his shoulder at the Snelgraves', who remain in the shadows, almost invisible.)

BUNCE: *(Producing the vase, with a genuine embarrassment.)* Thought I'd. Save my piss. It's got rum in it. Might be the last I'll have for weeks.

Scene Two

Lights up on the Snelgraves' room. Morse is still hiding. Mr. and Mrs. Snelgrave jump back, terrified of contact with Bunce.

BUNCE: I'm a poor man looking for shelter.
SNELGRAVE: My God! Lord have mercy on us!
BUNCE: I thought everyone died in this house.
SNELGRAVE: Help! Someone help us!
BUNCE: Shhh. I mean no harm.
DARCY: He's relieved himself. In my vase.
(Bunce holds out the vase, offering to give it back to her.)
Get out of our house.
SNELGRAVE: He has the infection!
BUNCE: Not I.
SNELGRAVE: He's lying. He stinks. And sick. Look at his eyes.
BUNCE: I'm not sick. Just hungry.
SNELGRAVE: The guards. What if they saw you enter?

DARCY: They have no mercy; it's the law.

SNELGRAVE: Open your shirt. Stay! Open! Prove there's no marks on you.

(*Bunce opens his shirt. With his cane, Snelgrave pokes at Bunce, moving the shirt this way and that to have a better look. We see a bandage around Bunce's waist and a spot of blood.*)

What? There's blood. My God! Blood!

BUNCE: It's years old.

SNELGRAVE: (*Brandishing his cane.*) Get back! Get back!

BUNCE: Still bleeds.

SNELGRAVE: Your arms, then. Show us your arms!

(*Bunce pulls up his sleeves and Snelgrave examines his arms.*)

No other marks. He's clean.

(*Morse comes out of hiding. All three of them jump back.*)

MORSE: I am Morse Braithwaite.

SNELGRAVE: There's another! God have Mercy.

MORSE: Sole daughter to Nevill and Elizabeth Braithwaite.

SNELGRAVE: Back, vile trespasser!

DARCY: Sir Nevill Braithwaite and his wife. We know them.

SNELGRAVE: Dead of the plague last Tuesday. Man, wife and daughter.

MORSE: It's true my father fell on me in a fit of fever and there I lay beneath him for two nights and a day. It's terrible to smell such things from a father. But I finally dug my way from under him and up on the roofs I went. To hide. To hide from the plague. I saw no light in this house. I came in through the window. I'm not a thief.

SNELGRAVE: Open your collar. Let's see your neck.

(*Morse opens her collar.*)

DARCY: Sleeves.

(*Morse pulls up her sleeves and they examine her.*)

SNELGRAVE: Shame. Shame on you both. You could have infected this house.

(*Banging at the window.*)

Both of you. Quickly! Crawl back out of this house, whatever way you came in. Hurry. Hurry! Before you're known.

(*Banging at the window again. Morse and Bunce hide. Kabe, the guard, peers in, thrusting half his body through the small window.*)

KABE: Good morning, Mr., Mrs. Snelgrave. Have a good sleep, did you? It stinks in here, it does.

SNELGRAVE: We've washed the floors with vinegar.

KABE: And stripped the room bare, I see. Well, the less the nasty has to hide in.

SNELGRAVE: We've boarded up the other rooms, except for the kitchen.

KABE: Ah. Shame it is. Such fine rooms, some of the finest in town maybe, empty but for stink. Bit cramped this one though?

DARCY: This is the only room where someone hasn't died.

KABE: Ah yes. Two maids and a houseboy, carted and pitted. And the canary too, Mrs. Snelgrave?

(He makes the sound of a canary.)

Shame. *(Beat.)* Will you be needing any provisions from the market this morning, Madame? Plenty of corn but cheese there's none. Butter, none. Some fruit but it's got the hairs.

DARCY: No, thank you, Kabe. That will be all.

KABE: The whole town's living on onions. You can smell it in the evenings. It's all that farting that's killed the birds.

(Sound of hammering on boards.)

DARCY AND SNELGRAVE: Kabe?

KABE: Sorry. Fellow across the way saw you let in a couple of guests last night.

DARCY: No. No.

SNELGRAVE: You can't do this. You can't—

DARCY: Please. Kabe. We beg you.

KABE: Can't have that. They might be carrying.

SNELGRAVE: They broke in. They were uninvited.

KABE: We're doubling up the boards.

DARCY: We are innocent.

SNELGRAVE: We have good health.

DARCY: We've held out in here alive.

SNELGRAVE: Alive, damn you, for almost four weeks! We are clean!

KABE: Sorry.

BUNCE: *(Appearing.)* Then why didn't you lot try and stop us?

KABE: Not our job. We're just the guards. We make sure no one gets out. If they get in, well, that's just luck. So, twenty-eight days again for the lot of you. Just enough time to get snug. I don't mind. I like this house. Pretty as a bird, it is, heh, Darcy?

(He tweets again.)

DARCY: How dare you!

KABE: Does stink, though. I get paid twice as much to guard a proper house like this. Could I have one of your gloves today, Mistress? Won't you show us your pretty white hands?

(Kabe shrieks with laughter.)

SNELGRAVE: I'll have you in the stocks when I'm out of here, Kabe.

KABE: I've been wanting to ask her that for years. Never could 'til now. *(To Morse.)* Why don't you ask her? Ask her to show you her pretty, white neck! *(Sings.)*

One o'clock, Two o'clock, Three o'clock, Four

Here's a red cross for your door.

Where's my enemy?

Flown to the country!

Never mind that, coz'

DARCY: Someone should shoot him.

KABE: One o'clock, Two o'clock, Three o'clock, Four

I've got the key to your locked door!

(Shrieks again with laughter and is gone.)

SNELGRAVE: Come here, child.

(Morse approaches him. Snelgrave slaps her.)

You would have been better off if you'd stayed put. Sir Braithwaite's daughter doesn't climb over roofs. Sir Braithwaite's daughter doesn't enter uninvited. Your father is dead. Give me your hand. In the Snelgrave house, we behave like Christians. Therefore, we will love you as one of our own.

MORSE: Why?

(Darcy takes the girl's other hand and the three of them stand together. Bunce stands alone.)

DARCY: Because you're one of us.

Scene Three

Bunce sitting alone in the bare room. A key turns in a lock and an apple rolls across the stage towards him. He picks it up, smells it with ecstasy. Snelgrave enters.

BUNCE: I haven't seen one of these in weeks.

SNELGRAVE: Something special I have Kabe bring in now and then.

BUNCE: The three of you in the kitchen?

SNELGRAVE: For the time being.

(Bunce holds up the apple, admires it, then begins to eat.)

I'm not a cruel man, Bunce. But even under these conditions I can't just let you walk about. This is my home. Under my protection. The problem is you have the only suitable room in the house because it has a door that I can lock and now we must sleep on the kitchen floor. *(Beat.)* And you smell awfully.

BUNCE: It's the tar, sir.

SNELGRAVE: Ah ha! A sailor. I knew it! It keeps the water out, the tar. And your buttons, of cheese or bone?

BUNCE: Wood, sir.

SNELGRAVE: That's unusual. I know a bit about the waters myself. I work for the Navy Board, just down the lane, on Seething. My friend Samuel and I, we control the largest commercial venture in the country, hmm. The Royal Dockyards.

BUNCE: They're as good as closed, sir.

SNELGRAVE: That's the curse of this plague. It's stopped all trade. There's not a merchant ship that's left the main port in months. Rats eating at the silks, damp at the pepper. You fellows out of work, selling spice and nutmeg on the streets. And starving. The lot of you.

(Bunce eats the apple core as well.)

BUNCE: I sailed three cats and a hag before we unloaded at the main port. Half of the crew got sick and died. A crowd set fire to three flys unloading beside our rig. They said the ships were carrying the plague. The crew had to swim to shore. Those that weren't burned.

SNELGRAVE: What were your routes? Did you ship to Calcutta? Bombay?

BUNCE: Green waters of the Caribbean and back, mostly. Green water, green islands, green air and all the colors of Port Royal.

SNELGRAVE: Port Royal. They say the women there are masculine, and obscene.

BUNCE: Salt Beef Peg.

SNELGRAVE: Your wife, certainly?

BUNCE: Not married.

SNELGRAVE: *(Enjoying this.)* Shameful.

BUNCE: She had nothing on Buttock-de-Clink Jenny.

SNELGRAVE: Not in this house.

BUNCE: Old Cunning-finger Nan. As sweet and sour as...ah well. Sorry, sir. There's not a lot of good memories a sailor has and them he has he carries tucked deep in.

SNELGRAVE: I've heard the stories at the coffeehouse. You know, I often dream of the sea but if I step my foot in a boat, the world goes black before my eyes. My body can't abide it, but my heart. Well. *(Beat.)* I'm a rich man, Bunce, and you a common sailor yet—look at the two of us—we have the sea between us. The struggle, the daring, the wrath. Cathay's lake of rubies. The North-West passage. Ice monsters fouling the sea—that angry bitch that'll tear you limb from limb. Man against the elements.

BUNCE: Mostly for us sailors it was man against the Captain.

SNELGRAVE: *(Begins to rock back and forth, eyes closed, living in the moment of a sea story.)* And the winds, how they blow like a madness and the sea leaps up like a continuous flame. The hideous, howling wilderness that stabs at the hull, that would rend flesh from bone. Sea spouts the size of cities. The cargo shifting and tumbling below deck and water casks rolling from side to side. One terrible cry after another pierces the air as the crew is swept overboard. *(Motions for Bunce to stand beside him and rock back and forth with him. After some initial hesitation, Bunce does so.)* To lessen the resistance to the fiendish wind and keep her from capsizing, three of our best crawl on deck with axes and climb aloft to cut away the fore top mast and the bowsprit ropes.

BUNCE: And as they hack at the mast, a monstrous wave, three times the size of the rig, whacks the starboard and snaps the foremast like a stick, and carries it with one of the sailors into the sea. The second is crushed.

SNELGRAVE: *(Continues for Bunce.)* Between the mast and the side of the ship.

BUNCE: The third is hung by his boot in the ratline.

SNELGRAVE: *(Holds out some nuts to Bunce, who takes them.)* The sea has no mercy and smashes all who try to rule her beneath her foul and lecherous waves.

BUNCE: Smashing, smashing.

SNELGRAVE: *(Continues.)* Smashing the small vessel like egg shells against a stone. Oh death, death, death.

(Snelgrave whacks his stick on the floor furiously a few times.)

And scurvy. Did you get the scurvy?

BUNCE: Many a time.

SNELGRAVE: Knots. You can do knots?

(Takes out a piece of rope. Knots it.)

What's that?

BUNCE: That's a bowline. But your tail's too short.

SNELGRAVE: Is it?

(Bunce takes the rope and reties the knot.)

Hmmm. Show me another.

(Bunce does a series of knots, one after the other as they speak.)

BUNCE: Butterfly knot.

SNELGRAVE: *(Indicating a scar on Bunce's neck.)* How'd you get that scar? Spanish Main pirates?!

BUNCE: *(Another knot.)* Lighterman's hitch. *(Meaning his neck.)* Sail hook.

SNELGRAVE: In a drunken brawl?

BUNCE: We were a short ways outside Gravesend. Our fly was carrying sugar and rum. The press gangs were looking for fresh recruits and boarded us just as we came into port. *(Another knot.)* Half hitch with seizing. *(Beat.)* To keep from the press, sometimes we'd cut ourselves a wound and then burn it with vitrol. Make it look like scurvy. They wanted whole men so I stuck myself in the neck with a sail hook. They passed me over when they saw the blood.

(Snelgrave hands Bunce some more nuts. Bunce eats. Snelgrave watches him eat.)

Scene Four

Morse, Bunce, Darcy Snelgrave and Snelgrave in their room. Darcy reads, but more often just stares. Snelgrave sits with an unopened book. Morse sits and stares. Bunce sits in the corner on a dirty mat, making himself small. A sense of boredom, tedium inside a house where no one can leave.

SNELGRAVE: Did you vinegar the corner, under your mat, as well, Bunce?
BUNCE: Yes I did, sir.
SNELGRAVE: Right. *(Long silence.)* The chairs as well?
BUNCE: Yes, sir.
SNELGRAVE: Right.
MORSE: Over and across the tall, tall grass
    They lay my love in the dirt
    He was just a kid and myself a lass
    If it'd bring him back I'd reconvert
    (Snelgrave whacks his cane.)
SNELGRAVE: Not in this house.
DARCY: Oh, let her sing.
MORSE: *(Continues.)* O fire of the devil, fire of love
    The truth is a lie and the pig's a dove
SNELGRAVE: She doesn't sing like a Christian child.
MORSE: *(Continues.)* The desert is cold and Hell is hot
    The mouth that kisses is sweet with rot
DARCY: I don't think I've heard song in this house since—
MORSE: Can't you sing?
DARCY: I don't like to. But I like to hear it. Sometimes.
MORSE: Are you not hot in all that dress?
DARCY: No, child. I never wear anything but this sort of dress.
MORSE: Can I see your neck?
DARCY: What? Why, child?

MORSE: Because I think you must have a beautiful neck and it's the time of the plague and there's not much of beauty left in this city but you.

DARCY: Who taught you to lie so kindly?

MORSE: Learned it myself. Can I see?

DARCY: I will get you a looking glass and you can look at your own neck, which is lovely. Mine is not. I am old.

MORSE: Please.

SNELGRAVE: Leave my wife in peace.

MORSE: Let me see.

SNELGRAVE: Sit back down.

MORSE: I think you have the scar of the hangman about your neck.

SNELGRAVE: I said leave her be.

DARCY: She means no harm.

MORSE: Or perhaps the finger marks of someone who hates you.

DARCY: *(Laughing.)* Perhaps the hole of a sword that went in here and came out there!

SNELGRAVE: Must you encourage such putrid imaginings? Enough. My head hurts from it.

(Snelgrave exits.)

DARCY: Stand here, child.

(Morse nears her.)

Closer. Let me feel your breath on my cheek.

(Morse moves closer.)

The breath of a child has passed through the lungs of an angel. That's what they say.

MORSE: My mother said to me that once a tiny piece of star broke off and fell from the sky while she slept in a field of wheat and it pierced her, here, *(Motions to Darcy's heart but doesn't touch her.)* and from that piece of star I was born.

DARCY: And your father. What did he say? That he molded you from a sliver of moon?

MORSE: My father is dead.

DARCY: I know. But what did he say about his little girl?

MORSE: My father was born dead. He stayed that way most of his life.

DARCY: I met your father, at the Opera, once. He seemed a decent man.

MORSE: My father hit the maids. I saw him do it. Sometimes twice a day.

DARCY: Well. Then he kept order. A household must have order.

MORSE: He used a piece of leg from a chair. He kept it in the drawer of his writing desk.

DARCY: Sometimes servants misbehave. That's not your father's fault.

MORSE: Do you hit your servants?

DARCY: My servants are dead.

MORSE: Did you hit them?

DARCY: No, I didn't. But when they did not listen, I told my husband and he dealt with them as was necessary.

MORSE: Can I see your neck now?

DARCY: No, you cannot.

MORSE: Can I see your hands?

DARCY: My hands are private.

MORSE: I'm not afraid to die.

DARCY: You don't have to be; you won't die.

MORSE: I already know what it's like. To be dead. It's nothing fancy.
(She moves away from Darcy. She takes the hem of her dress in her hands.)
Just lots of nothing to see all around you and nothing to feel, only there's a sound that comes and goes. Comes and goes. Like this:
(She slowly tears a rip in her dress, up to her waist. We hear the sound of ripping cloth.)
Have you heard that sound before, Mrs. Snelgrave?
(Darcy does not answer. Morse speaks now to Bunce.)
And you, sitting there on your lily pad like a frog? Have you heard it?

BUNCE: In Northumberland. Yeah. A coal miner I was, when I was a kid. We heard all sorts of things down in the earth. And when our lanterns went out, our minds went to hell.

MORSE: Did lots of you die down there?

DARCY: Morse.

BUNCE: Lost my baby brother in the mines. Well, he wasn't a baby, but he always was to us. Just thirteen, he was. We went deep for the coal. They kept pushing us. Pushing us deeper. The ceilings were half down most of the time. One fell in on top of us, six of us it were.

MORSE: Your brother was crushed?

BUNCE: Yes he was. And the Master, he kicked me 'cause I was cursing the mine. I jumped him and his men pulled me off. He kicked me again and I bit his ear in two. One of his guards popped a knife in my side. Never healed up right.

MORSE: What did he look like crushed up? Your brother.

DARCY: Stop it, Morse.

BUNCE: He looked like. Well. His face was the only part of him. Not crushed. His face looked. I don't know. What? Disappointed. I think.

DARCY: That's enough.

MORSE: *(To Bunce.)* And his body?

BUNCE: His body. It was like. What? Like water. What was left of him. I could-
n't take him up in my arms. He just. Spilled away.
(*Morse nears Bunce, kneels down and simply looks at him. After some moments,*
Bunce looks away from her and at Darcy.)

Scene Five

Outside of the Snelgraves' house. Just below the window. Kabe is guarding the house.

KABE: (*Calls.*) Bills. The Bills. Stepney Parish, Seven hundred and sixteen.
White-Chapel, three hundred forty six. The Bills. St. Giles's Cripplegate,
two hundred seventy-seven. St. Leonard Shoreditch—
MORSE: (*Pops her head out of the window above him.*) I got an uncle in St.
Sepulchers. How's it there?
KABE: Two hundred and fourteen dead this week. How's the Snelgraves?
MORSE: We're all right.
KABE: You a relative?
MORSE: Mrs. Snelgrave says you're a thief.
KABE: Does she now? And how old are you, sweetheart?
MORSE: Twelve. Mr. Snelgrave says you're the worst sort of rabble.
KABE: We're always rabble, we are, when we come out from our alleys and lanes
and rub shoulders with Snelgravys, hawk an innocent gob o' phlegm on
their doorstep. They're not much company, how 'bout you?
MORSE: Mr. Snelgrave says you're not much above vermin.
KABE: Does he now? And have you ever seen a little mousie?
MORSE: I seen rats.
KABE: Ever had a sweetheart?
(*Morse shakes her head "no."*)
Doctors say virgins ripe for marriage are ripe for the infection, their blood
being hot and their seed pining for copulation.
MORSE: Mr. Snelgrave says you want us to die. Then you can come in and loot.
KABE: I could show you a jewel that'd change your life.
MORSE: Go ahead then.
KABE: Don't know if you're grown enough.
MORSE: I'm old on the inside. Show me.
KABE: Hold onto that window.
(*Kabe stands directly under her and opens his pants. Morse looks. And looks.*)
Well!

MORSE: You're a man then?

KABE: Of course I'm a man. A bull of a man. A whale of a man.

MORSE: Sometimes people pretend.

KABE: *(Closing his pants.)* What you just saw wasn't pretending.

MORSE: Don't like all the strawy hairs on it.

KABE: Have you no manners, you Prince's whore? You should be beaten. Have you ever been beaten?

MORSE: *(Laughing at him.)* Lots of times. Can you get me a Certificate of Health from the Lord Mayor so I can pass out of the city?

KABE: *(Shrieks with laughter.)* You're a card, aren't you!

MORSE: I'm dead serious.

KABE: He's no longer in town.

MORSE: Yes he is. Lord Mayor of London. He's the only one who stayed.

KABE: Not counting the poor, child. The poor's all stayed. And what I hear tell, that's not the Mayor in the Mayor's house but a mad man who's broke in and jumps naked through the garden cawing like a crow at night. The rest of the Court's gone too. All that's got wealth has fled from the plague. And God's followed them.

MORSE: The Snelgraves haven't fled.

KABE: That's not for trying. They just got unlucky; their servants died before they could leave 'em behind to starve.

MORSE: Get me a Certificate so I can pass the blockades.

KABE: I got a hold of a few of those papers at the very start, but now. Well. They're as rare as...And what would you give me in return?

MORSE: Don't have much.

KABE: Let me have a feel of your leg. Go on.

MORSE: Why?

KABE: I've got an idea. Or two.

MORSE: *(Hangs a leg out the window.)* There's my leg.

KABE: *(Feeling her leg.)* A bit bony. I can't get you a Certificate even if I wanted but—

(Morse starts to pull her leg back in but he hangs on.)

Wait! I can get you some sugar knots. I know an old man who's got a bucketful.

MORSE: Got no money.

KABE: I'll make you a deal. You let me, ah, kiss your foot and for every kiss I'll get you a sugar knot.

MORSE: Deal.

(Kabe kisses her foot, twice. Then sucks on her big toe. Morse kicks him.)

You said kiss, not suck.

KABE: What's the difference?

MORSE: An apple. A suck is worth an apple.

KABE: Thief.

(He sucks on her toe. Then she pulls her leg up.)

That was a nibble, not a suck!

MORSE: Two sugar knots and an apple. And the worms in the apple better be alive!

KABE: You'll die by the plague, child. I feel it in me shins.

MORSE: Then I'll be good at being dead. My father and mother are already dead. Poor Daddy. Poor Mommy. Dead, dead, dead.

KABE: Stupid brat. What you lack is fear. This past week, I got the bodies piled so high in my cart I could hardly see over the tops of them. *(Beat.)* Hey. I know an old woman who's got tangerines, still good, that she wears under her skirts. She says they stay fresh down there because she's hot as the tropics.

MORSE: Get me a tangerine too.

KABE: Bring me a jewel of Mrs. Snelgrave's. Anything. Just make sure the gem's hard.

MORSE: I'm not a Braithwaite anymore, you know.

KABE: And I am not a guard at your door. But if you crawl out of that window, I will kill you and sleep well this night.

MORSE: Perhaps I'll kill you first.

KABE: *(Calling.)* The ninety-seven Parishes within the walls: one thousand four hundred and ninety three. Parishes on the Southwark Side: one thousand, six hundred and thirty six.

(Sings.)

We'll all meet in the grave
Then we'll all be saved.
You with your coins
Me with me scabs.
You with clean loins
Me with me crabs
We'll all meet in the grave
Then we'll all get laid
down, oh, down, deep down.

Scene Six

Bunce washes the floor with vinegar. He uses a small rag and a bucket. Snelgrave watches him.

SNELGRAVE: I heard the crier this morning. The Bills have almost doubled this week. Mostly the Out Parishes of the poor. But it's moving this way. A couple of persons I know personally have died. Decent people. Good Christians on the surface. But there's the key. On the surface. When the poor die, the beggars, it's no riddle. Look down at their faces and you'll see their bitter hearts. When the rich die, it's harder to tell why God took them; they're clean, attend the Masses, give alms. But something rotten lurks. Mark my words, Bunce. A fine set of clothes does not always attest to a fine set of morals.

(Bunce, wiping the floors, nears Snelgrave's shoes.)

Are you afraid, Bunce?

BUNCE: Sir?

SNELGRAVE: Are you afraid of the plague?

BUNCE: Who isn't, sir?

SNELGRAVE: It is written in the Ninety-First Psalm of the Book: "Thou shalt not be afraid for the pestilence that walketh in darkness...A thousand shall fall at thy side, and ten thousand at the right hand: but it shall not come nigh thee." That doesn't mean I don't ever doubt, Bunce. I use vinegar.

BUNCE: Those are fine shoes, sir. The finest I ever saw this close up.

SNELGRAVE: Cost me as much as a silk suit. A bit tight on my corns, but real gentlemen's leather. I would wager your life, Bunce, that you'll never wear such fine shoes as these.

BUNCE: I'd wager two of my lives, if I had them.

SNELGRAVE: A little learning, Bunce: Patterns will have it that you, a poor sailor, will never wear such shoes as these. And yet, the movement of history, which is as inflexible as stone, can suddenly change. With a flick of a wrist. Or, I might say, an ankle. Watch while I demonstrate.

(Snelgrave slips out of his shoes.)

Put them on, Bunce.

BUNCE: Sir?

SNELGRAVE: Put my shoes on your feet.

BUNCE: My feet are dirty, sir.

SNELGRAVE: Then have my socks on first.

(Bunce holds up the fine socks and examines them.)

Go on, then.

(Bunce carefully slips on the socks, then the shoes. The two men stand side by side looking back and forth at their own and each other's feet. Snelgrave wiggles his bare toes.)

Now, Bunce. What do you see?

BUNCE: I see the Master is without shoes. And his new servant. He is wearing very fine shoes.

SNELGRAVE: And history? What does history tell you now?

BUNCE: Not sure how that works, sir.

SNELGRAVE: Historically speaking, the poor do not take to fine shoes. They never have and they never will.

BUNCE: I'm wearing fine shoes now.

SNELGRAVE: Yes, but only because I allow it. I have given history a wee slap on the buttocks and for a moment something terribly strange has happened: you in my shoes. However, what we see here is not real. It's an illusion because I can't change the fact that you'll never wear fine shoes.

BUNCE: But I'm wearing them now, sir.

SNELGRAVE: Only because I gave them to you. In a moment I am going to take them back and then history will be on course again. As a matter of fact, it never strayed from course because what we're doing here is just a little game.

BUNCE: What if I kept the shoes?

SNELGRAVE: Kept them? You can't keep them. They're mine.

BUNCE: I know they're yours, sir. I'm just asking what if I kept them?

SNELGRAVE: That's not a historical question.

BUNCE: No. It's a game question. You said this was a game, sir.

SNELGRAVE: So I did. Well, if you kept them I would go and get another pair before my feet got cold.

BUNCE: Then we'd both have a pair.

SNELGRAVE: You're not attacking the problem correctly. If we both have a pair, how will people tell our feet apart? They'll look the same. That's not history, Bunce, that's obfuscatory.

BUNCE: May I have your cane?

SNELGRAVE: You most certainly may not.

BUNCE: I just want to hold it, sir. It's finely carved. I'll never hold a cane like that in my life.

SNELGRAVE: *(Snelgrave reluctantly hands it to him.)* I'm not a cruel man.

(Bunce takes the cane, tucks it awkwardly under his arm.)

Not like that. It's not a piece of firewood you're lugging for the stove.

(Snelgrave snatches it back. Delicately tucks it under his arm and walks this way and that.)

BUNCE: It doesn't look right on you without the shoes, sir.

(Bunce holds out his hand and after a moment's hesitation, Snelgrave hands the cane to him. Bunce carries the cane almost properly this time.)

SNELGRAVE: That's it. Elbow a bit higher. I always think of it as walking across the hands of children. You must do it lightly and carefully or you'll break their bones.

BUNCE: Is this it, sir? History?

SNELGRAVE: Certainly not. This is just practice.

BUNCE: Practice for what?

SNELGRAVE: Brrrrr. My feet are cold. The shoes, please.

(Bunce walks once more to and fro, then stops face to face with Snelgrave, close. Silence for some moments. He hands Snelgrave the cane and removes the shoes, slowly, then the socks. He sets the shoes carefully and neatly between them, laying out the socks one by one. The two men look at the shoes between them. They watch each other some moments, then Bunce returns to his bucket and rag. He cleans. Snelgrave picks up his shoes and socks.)

The Bills are up. Way up this week. We'll need to vinegar this room twice a day from now on. Starting tomorrow. One can't be too cautious. I'll send my wife in with some bread for you when you're done.

BUNCE: Yes, sir.

(Snelgrave begins to exit.)

Sir?

(Snelgrave turns to hear him.)

I'm not a cruel man, either, sir.

SNELGRAVE: I know that, Bunce. I wouldn't have taken you on as my servant if I had thought otherwise.

(Snelgrave exits. We hear the lock turn.)

Scene Seven

Bunce adjusting his wrappings under his shirt. Darcy enters, watches him some moments. He's unaware of her and curses the wrappings that are beginning to fall to pieces in his hands. We hear Kabe singing offstage.

KABE: *(Sings.)* Calico, silk, porcelain, tea
It's all the same to the poor man and me

BUNCE: Ah, fuck the Lord.

KABE: *(Sings, offstage.)* Steal it in the Indies, haul it cross the sea
And now it's nothing between the plague, you and me.

BUNCE: Ow! Fuck his angels too.

DARCY: I brought you some clean linen.

BUNCE: *(Backing into his corner.)* Beg your pardon, Mrs. I thought you three
were asleep.

DARCY: They are. Does it hurt all the time?

BUNCE: Only when I sit a lot. On the sea I'm standing most of the time and I
feel best.

DARCY: Here's a clean shirt. It belonged to our servant boy. I've soaked it in vinegar and cloves. It's safe.

BUNCE: *(He takes the shirt.)* Thank you, Mrs.

DARCY: I brought some clean strips too. So you can rebind it.

BUNCE: *(He takes them.)* You're kind.

DARCY: I don't want blood on my floors.

(They each wait for something from the other.)

BUNCE: Perhaps you should go back to the kitchen, Mrs.

DARCY: I will stay.

BUNCE: It's not pretty.

*(Darcy doesn't leave so Bunce shrugs and painfully takes off his old shirt. His
old bandage is still in place. He begins to wrap the new one over it.)*

DARCY: Take the old one off or it will do no good to put a clean one on.

BUNCE: It does no good anyhow but make it look better.

DARCY: I will do it.

BUNCE: No.

DARCY: *(Taking the new bandage from him.)* Yes I will.

BUNCE: *(Angry, holding the old bandage in place.)* I said no, Mrs.

DARCY: All right then. Do it yourself.

(She tosses the bandage at his feet so he must stoop to pick it up. He does so.)

BUNCE: *(Wanting her to turn away.)* Please.

*(She does so, annoyed. Turning his side with the wound away from her, he
rebinds it. We do not see the wound as he keeps it hidden.)*

DARCY: So you're a sailor. Merchant or Navy?

BUNCE: Merchant by choice. Navy by force.

DARCY: Then it's the sailor's life for you: Drinking, thieving, whoring, killing,
backbiting. And swearing.

BUNCE: *(Playing into the cliche.)* Yeah. Swearing. And once or twice we took hold
of our own fucked ship from some Goddamned Captain. We let our men

vote if the bloody prick lived or died. Mostly our men voted he died so first we whipped and pickled him, then threw the fat gutted chucklehead overboard. And because we couldn't piss on his grave we pissed on the bastard's back as he sank to the sharks below.

DARCY: A tongue that swears does not easily pray.

BUNCE: The times I was asked by my Captain or his mate to beat a fellow tar? I can't count them. The times I refused? Maybe less than one.

(Some moments of silence.)

DARCY: I've never sailed on a ship. I married when I was fifteen. *(Beat.)* Why did you come to our house?

BUNCE: The ships aren't sailing but the Navy's. I didn't want to get picked up again.

DARCY: Some would consider it an honor to serve the Navy.

BUNCE: Ay. Some would. Though I never met them.

DARCY: Do you have a wife?

BUNCE: I did for a little while, but I lost her. Was coming in to port at Liverpool, merchant ship. Making short trips. Got picked up for the second time to serve His Majesty's ships. Didn't get back to port for eight month and then my wife was gone. If she still lives, I don't know. The neighbors said she raved for months and went mad. Tick fever. But I don't believe it. She was a smart one. I think she just got tired of waiting and moved on.

DARCY: Did your wife have soft. Skin?

BUNCE: Soft skin? Well, no. It wasn't what you'd call soft. Her father was a ribband weaver and she worked by his side. Her hands were harder than mine.

DARCY: I'm sorry.

BUNCE: She used them well.

DARCY: Have you never touched a woman's skin that was soft?

BUNCE: Not a woman's, no. But I met a lad in the port of Bristol once and he had skin so fine it was like running your fingers through water.

DARCY: You speak against God.

BUNCE: I'm speaking of God's pleasure.

DARCY: *(Picking up the scraps of bandage he's discarded.)* And his. Breast. Was it smooth as well?

BUNCE: His breast. It was. Darker. Like the skin of an apple it smelled, and as smooth.

DARCY: Did you love him?

BUNCE: For those few months I loved him better than I could love another in years. His name was Killigrew. We got picked up off the streets and pressed onto the same ship. Warred against the Hollanders. He died.

DARCY: I'm sorry.

BUNCE: The bastard. Always had the luck.

DARCY: *(Taking off her earrings.)* When this is over and we're allowed to leave here, you'll have these. You'll be able to eat awhile and pay for shelter. They're real stones.

BUNCE: *(Accepting the earrings. Examining them.)* Why am I to be paid like this?

DARCY: It's not payment. It's charity.

BUNCE: I'm poor, Mrs., but not stupid. If your husband catches me with these I might as well jump into the pits.

DARCY: He won't find them if you keep them well hid.

BUNCE: Hid where? You keep 'em. When we're all out and by our own legs, if you still feel moved to charity, you can give them to me once more.
(He hands them back. She puts them on again.)

DARCY: And this man you loved. Killigrew. Were his.

BUNCE: What.

DARCY: *(She touches her own thighs. Not in a seductive manner, but as though she can't bring herself to say the word out loud.)* Here. Was he smooth here?

BUNCE: What do you want, Mrs.?

DARCY: For you to answer me.

BUNCE: And if I don't?

DARCY: We no longer lock you up. We trust you now.

BUNCE: All right. *(He nears her, close.)* Close your eyes. I'll do you no harm.
(Darcy closes her eyes. Bunce softly blows air across her face. When he stops, she does not open her eyes.) That's how it felt to touch him there.
(Some moments of silence.)

DARCY: I don't intend to die of the plague, Bunce. My husband has agreed to help me end my life if the tokens appear.

BUNCE: Not all that gets the plague dies.

DARCY: First the marks appear around the neck or groin. There's fever. Violent vomiting. The patient cannot control the body. The body fouls itself.

BUNCE: But if the swelling can be brought to break and run, sometimes a person can live. I saved a friend that way once. Cut the marks with a knife and bled them. He never could speak again, but he lived.

DARCY: No, no. The stench of the sores is unbearable. The body rots. And then the mind. Lunacy and madness is the end. I saw two of our servants die that way. Their screams are locked inside my head forever.

BUNCE: Would you like to know of any other parts of my lad Killigrew, Mrs.?

DARCY: No. Thank you. I've heard enough. Just bless the Lord He's brought you into this house. Against our will, certainly, but I assume not against His.

(*Beat.*) I could have you hanged for speaking of such matters to a married woman of my position.

BUNCE: (*Sings.*) Lust in his Limbs and Rust in his skin

A bear without, and a worse beast within.

DARCY: I'm just an old woman. That's what you think. Well. Smile as you like. I once had a lover and his arms were so strong that my skull was crushed in his grip. With his bare hands he plunged between my ribs and took hold of my heart. A wafer between his fingers it dissolved. Sometimes I wake up in the dark and stand in the hall and I can feel the cold draft pass freely through my chest as though there were nothing there.

BUNCE: I'll have those earrings after all.

(*Darcy is motionless, as though not hearing him. He gently slips the earrings from her ears .*)

I'll find a place. I'm a pirate.

Scene Eight

Darcy, Morse and Snelgrave in the room. Morse's wrists are bound with rope.

SNELGRAVE: The child's a thief, I tell you. What did I find in her pockets one morning last week? A set of my Spanish gold coins. "Just playing jacks with them," she says. She's got the manners of a servant and the tongue of a who—

DARCY: Don't you dare.

SNELGRAVE: That brooch belonged to my mother. Not you. The child will confess when I give her some of this.

(*Snelgrave brandishes his cane.*)

DARCY: I'll find the brooch. It's bound to have fallen when I was turning things out.

SNELGRAVE: The child will wear those ropes until we find it.

MORSE: I didn't steal your brooch.

SNELGRAVE: Hold your tongue.

MORSE: You belong in a cold, cold grave.

(*Snelgrave raises his cane to hit Morse. She runs to hide behind Darcy.*)

Help me, Mrs. Snelgrave.

DARCY: You did steal his coins.

(*Snelgrave whacks and misses.*)

MORSE: Yes I did. But you gave Bunce some of his gin.

SNELGRAVE: She did what?

MORSE: I saw it with my own eyes, sir. Mrs. Snelgrave thought I was asleep. You were, but I wasn't and she poured some of your gin into a bowl and she took it to him. She watched him drink it.

SNELGRAVE: Is this true?

MORSE: (*Makes the sound.*) Slurp, slurp.

DARCY: He asked me the other day if we might spare some spirits. I said no. Later, I changed my mind.

SNELGRAVE: In the middle of the night?

DARCY: I didn't want to wake you.

SNELGRAVE: (*To Morse.*) And what else did you see, Morse Braithwaite?
(*Morse raises her roped hands to him. After a moment he understands the deal and takes off the ropes.*)

MORSE: She asked him if the new bandage fit right. He said it felt a bit tight. He asked her to feel it.

SNELGRAVE: He asked her to feel what?

DARCY: This is ridiculous.

SNELGRAVE: You. Felt his bandage?

DARCY: I merely checked his bandage to make sure it wasn't pressing the wound.

SNELGRAVE: You did this. How?

MORSE: I can show you.

SNELGRAVE: (*To Darcy.*) How did you check his bandage?
(*Darcy doesn't answer, just shakes her head. Snelgrave calls Bunce.*)
Bunce. Bunce!
(*Bunce enters with the rag and pail.*)

BUNCE: I haven't finished the kitchen walls yet, sir.

SNELGRAVE: Put down the vinegar. I want you to stand there. Right here. Yes. Nothing else. Just stand.
(*Bunce stands with his back to the public.*)
Now, Mrs. Snelgrave. As my wife. As a Christian woman, show me how you checked that his bandage wasn't too tight. So that it wouldn't press the wound. (*Beat.*) Do it woman, or so help me what I do to him will not be worse than what I do to you.
(*Darcy slowly nears Bunce.*)
Just a minute, my dear. Surely, in the dark, his belly full of my gin, it would be difficult to feel the tension of his. Bandage. With your glove on. You must have taken off one of your gloves, didn't you? (*Shouts.*) Didn't you?!

MORSE: Yes she did. Because her glove dropped on the floor as he was slurping the gin. Slurp, slu—

SNELGRAVE: *(To Morse.)* You shut your mouth. *(To Darcy.)* Take off your glove. Let our good servant Bunce see what's touched him in the dark.

DARCY: William.

SNELGRAVE: Darcy?

(Darcy stands before Bunce and removes her glove. We cannot see her bare hand as Bunce is blocking our view.)

Have a look, Bunce.

(Bunce does not look down at her hand but looks at Snelgrave.)

BUNCE: If Mrs. Snelgrave wishes to keep her hands private, sir, it's—.

SNELGRAVE: *(To Darcy.)* Tell him you want him to look. Because you do, don't you? That's the nature of secrets. They yearn to be exposed.

DARCY: You may. Look.

BUNCE: If it pleases you, Mrs.

DARCY: It does.

(Bunce looks down at her hand. He does not react. Then he looks at Snelgrave, who deflates. Morse slowly gets to her feet and comes around Bunce to have a look. She's amazed rather than disgusted. She backs away and turns to Snelgrave.)

MORSE: You did this to her!

SNELGRAVE: It was an accident.

MORSE: You did this.

(Darcy puts her glove back on.)

SNELGRAVE: *(Calm now.)* No, child. It was the fire did it to her. When she was seventeen. Just two years after we married. We lived outside the city then. There was a fire in the stables. She insisted on saving her horse. It was a wedding gift.

MORSE: *(To Darcy.)* Did you save the horse?

DARCY: No.

SNELGRAVE: She burned. My beautiful wife, who only the night before I'd held in my arms. Naked, she was—

DARCY: Quiet, William.

SNELGRAVE: I used to kneel at your feet, by the bedside at night.

(Bunce steps back and stands beside Morse. They watch the Snelgraves.)

And you'd let your robe fall open. Your skin was like. Like. There wasn't a name for it on this earth.

(Darcy puts her gloved hand on his head, she comforts him almost automatically. He closes his eyes.)

For hours on end in the night. My God, how I loved you.

DARCY: *(Darcy moves away from Snelgrave.)* Some of the animals freed themselves. The dappled mare my father gave me broke out of her stall. Her mane was on fire. She kept leaping and rearing to shake it off but she couldn't shake it off. The mare ran in circles around the garden. Faster and faster she ran, the fire eating its way to her coat. Her coat was wet, running with sweat, but that didn't stop the flames from spreading out across her flanks. A horse on fire. In full gallop. It was almost. Beautiful. It would have been. Beautiful. But for the smell. I can still smell them. After thirty-six years. The horses. Burning.

(Morse puts her hand in Bunce's hand and the two of them stand watching the Snelgraves. This action should be a subtle, almost unconscious gesture, on both their parts.)

Scene Nine

Kabe outside on the street below the Snelgraves' window. He is half-naked and wears a pan of burning charcoal on his head. He is preaching.

KABE: A monster, last week, was born at Oxford in the house of an Earl. His name on fear of death I do withhold. One eye in its forehead, no nose and its two ears in the nape of its neck. And outside in the garden of that very same house, a thorn which bore five different fruits. And, good people of this city, if we must read these phenomena as signs—

SNELGRAVE: *(At the window.)* Kabe.

KABE: And we must. Listen not to the liars and hypocrites—

SNELGRAVE: Did you get the quicksilver?

KABE: For they will tell you that it is the wrath of God against an entire people, corrupt in both spirit and heart.

(Kabe stops preaching, steps back, and speaks to Snelgrave.)

Got it. Babel, Babylon, Sodom and Gomorrah, cow shit I tell you.

SNELGRAVE: And the walnut shell?

KABE: Had a little trouble with the walnut shell. Hazelnut is all I could come by.

SNELGRAVE: A hazelnut shell? Have you gone mad? Dr. Brook's pamphlet specifically states that the quicksilver must be hung about the neck in a walnut shell.

KABE: With the hazelnut, only five shillings.

SNELGRAVE: You said four yesterday.

KABE: That was before the Bills went up again. *(Turns back to preach.)* And I say to you if it is God's wrath, then why has he chosen Oxford for the birth of this monster?

SNELGRAVE: What about the oil and frankincense?

KABE: Because Oxford is where the Court has retired, the King and all his fancy, fawning courtiers. Because the plague—*(To Snelgrave.)* couldn't get any—*(Preaching.)* is a Royalist phenomena. Who dies? One simple question. *(To Snelgrave.)* But I do have a toad. *(Preaching.)* Who dies? *(To Snelgrave.)* Not dead two hours. *(Preaching.)* Is this not a poor man's plague? *(To Snelgrave.)* Bore a hole through its head and hang it about your neck.

SNELGRAVE: What if my wife spies it?

KABE: Keep it under your shirts. Should dry out in a day or two.

SNELGRAVE: Two shillings.

KABE: Right. *(Preaching.)* Go to the deepest pit near Three Nun's Inn, if you dare, and you will see who it is that dies, their mouths open in want, the maggots moving inside their tongues making their tongues wag as though they were about to speak. But they will never speak again in this world. The hungry. The dirty. The abandoned. That's who dies. Not the fancy and the wealthy, there's hardly a one, for they have fled, turned their back on the city. Clergymen, physicians and surgeons, all fled.

SNELGRAVE: Have you thought again about my little offer?

KABE: *(To Snelgrave.)* Sorry.

SNELGRAVE: I could make you rich.

KABE: As well as dead if I let you escape. *(Preaching.)* And here we perish on the streets in such vast number as much from lack of bread and wages as from the plague—

SNELGRAVE: Where are your clothes? And what's that you got on your head?

KABE: Pan of charcoal. Keeps the bad air from my head when I unplug my finger from God's arsehole.

SNELGRAVE: Blasphemer! Put on your clothes. You're a Snelgrave guard.

KABE: Not on Tuesdays I'm not. *(Nods to offstage.)* On Tuesdays old Stewart fills in for me.

SNELGRAVE: Why, you're behaving like one of those madmen. Those conjurers. Those dealers with the Devil.

KABE: Soloman Eagle, at your service.

SNELGRAVE: This is outrageous. I won't have a conjurer guarding our door! It's bad enough that I'm kept captive by you Kabe, but that you summon more scum from their hellholes to stand below my windows. My house. My street. My city!

KABE: *(Preaches again.)* —is on the verge of the eternal storm of chaos. Orphan's money is on loan by the Lord Mayor to the King, and Parliament takes no action. They stir their soup with our bones. The grass grows up and down White Hall court and no boats move on the river but to war. Dead as dung upon the face of the earth we all shall be if we do not resist. I say to you: Get off your knees. Rise up! Rise up! *(Beat.)* But how do we begin? With this. With this, my friends. *(Kabe takes out a small vial of liquid.)* The road to the Poor Man's Heaven: Only six shillings! Solomon Eagle's plague-water.

SNELGRAVE: Six shillings! That's robbery.

KABE: *(Preaching still.)* Is your dignity not worth six shillings? It's your duty to keep your body strong for this long and bloody struggle! Do not let the Monsters of Oxford beat you down. Arise, arise into all your glory! You, the mob! The dissolute rabble! Six shillings! Six shillings and the world is yours!

SNELGRAVE: I'll give you five. *(Drops the coins to Kabe, who catches them in a small jar of vinegar.)* Do I drink it?

KABE: One thimbleful each night before retiring. Also anoint the nostrils, ear holes and anus twice a day. *(Beat.)* Sir Braithwaite's girl. She died with her parents.

SNELGRAVE: How do you know?

KABE: Spoke to one of the maids that used to work there. Her husband did their garden. He found the family dead. They say there was something stuffed in the dead child's mouth. Some kind of animal.

SNELGRAVE: She can't be dead! She's alive and well and a pest in my house.

KABE: The maid used to bathe the Braithwaite girl. Maid said the girl had a scar the shape of a key 'cross her belly. Happened when she was a baby. Some kind of accident. *(Beat.)* I've been thinking, sir. If one of you dies in there, can we pull the body out the window? We doubled up the boards on your door and it will be a hell of a work to open it up again.

SNELGRAVE: The dying is done in this house, I thank the Lord. And when the dying is done in this city, Kabe, you better run because I smell a Leveller's blood in you, ringing loud and clear. I thought we buried the lot of you.

KABE: My father was a Leveller, sir. His son's just a poor man with a pan of charcoal on his head. And now the old man's dead.

SNELGRAVE: Plague?

KABE: One of my toads, sir. Had a dozen of them in a bucket at the bedside. One of them got out and well, my father, he snored and down one went and got stuck and the old man choked to death.

SNELGRAVE: A proper death for a man of his station. Levellers. Diggers. I say cut them to pieces or they will cut us to pieces.

KABE: Do you want the toad as it is, or do you want me to bore the hole?

SNELGRAVE: You do it. And get me a piece of string to hang it on as well.

KABE: Wife's piss also works wonders.

SNELGRAVE: *(Realizing he's being taken in.)* Vermin.

KABE: Use your wife's urine to purify, before that sailor does.

SNELGRAVE: You'll be dead soon . . .

KABE: But will she let you have it?

SNELGRAVE: And I'll find you in your lime pit and piss in your mouth.

Scene Ten

> *Snelgrave, Darcy, Morse and Bunce in the room. Boredom. Morse sits and ties figures out of cloth and sticks. Then she glances about the room. Her eyes rest on Darcy. She stands and goes to her.*

MORSE: I can smell your heart.

DARCY: Can you?

MORSE: It's sweet. It's rotting in your chest.

> *(Snelgrave snorts.)*

My mother didn't smell like you. She smelled like lemons.

DARCY: That's lovely.

MORSE: Because she was always afraid.

> *(Snelgrave snorts again.)*

Last night I dreamed that an angel tried to land on our roof. But he had no feet so he couldn't stand. He crawled in through the window, to touch our faces, but he had no hands. He said to me, "Come to my arms." But he had none. This morning I woke up and there was a feather in my mouth. Look. *(She shows Darcy a small, white feather. She runs the feather gently over Darcy's face.)*

SNELGRAVE: Must we listen to this senseless babble day in and day out. I'm sick of it. Bloody sick of it.

DARCY: Then pass your time in the kitchen.

SNELGRAVE: Kabe says Sir Braithwaite's daughter died in her own house. Says they found her naked. Naked and dead. Stripped.

DARCY: Kabe is a liar.

MORSE: He showed me his mouse.

SNELGRAVE: He says the daughter had a scar. Under her skirts.

DARCY: A scar?

SNELGRAVE: On her stomach.

MORSE: *(To Darcy.)* Is the rest of your body burned?

DARCY: Yes.

MORSE: What does it feel like?

SNELGRAVE: I think we should have a look.

DARCY: Feel like? Most of the places on my skin I can't feel.

(Morse runs her hand lightly down Darcy's arm, slowly.)

MORSE: Can you feel that?

DARCY: No. Yes. There. At the elbow.

(Morse caresses Darcy's neck through the cloth.)

SNELGRAVE: She's strong, but Bunce could manage.

DARCY: Yes. There. *(Beat.)* Not there. No. Maybe. No.

SNELGRAVE: Bunce could do it.

(Morse runs her hands slowly over Darcy's breasts. Darcy does not stop her. This action is no different from how Morse touched Darcy's arms. Snelgrave stands over them.)

MORSE: Can you feel this?

SNELGRAVE: A scar the shape of a key.

DARCY: *(Sincerely trying to answer Morse's questions.)* Not yet. Yes. There. Under your left hand. I can feel something there.

MORSE: What do you feel?

SNELGRAVE: We could all be in danger.

DARCY: I feel…I don't know. No one has touched me there. In years.

SNELGRAVE: *(Grabbing Morse's arm.)* It's about time we found out just who you are, young lady. Bunce!

DARCY: Let go of her.

SNELGRAVE: *(Shoving the child into Bunce's arms.)* You're the strongest, Bunce. Strip her.

BUNCE: I don't think I should be the one, sir.

SNELGRAVE: You do as I tell you.

BUNCE: Will you show him your belly, Morse?

(Morse shakes her head, but does not physically resist. She is calm.)
I'm sorry, then.

(Bunce begins to unbutton Morse's shirt buttons.)

DARCY: Bunce. Don't you dare.

(Bunce looks from Snelgrave to Darcy.)

SNELGRAVE: You cross me?

DARCY: I sponged the child. Twice. She has the scar. But your idiot Kabe is mistaken. It's not a key. The scar is like a spoon. *(To Snelgrave.)* After the fire. Not once. Not even to embrace me. I was. Even changed. I was still—

SNELGRAVE: *(Interrupts.)* How could I have loved you? It was never about who you were but about what was left of you.

(Morse, raising her skirts to reveal her stomach, which has no scar.)

MORSE: The angel took my scar.

(Snelgrave glares at his wife.)

In exchange for the feather.

BUNCE: I think I'll vinegar the kitchen walls again, sir.

(Snelgrave puts out his cane to stop Bunce.)

SNELGRAVE: Tell me something, Bunce. If you had a wife and she lied to you. Lied to you, in front of company. What would you do?

(Bunce is silent.)

You'll learn, Bunce.

(Snelgrave shoves Bunce towards Darcy, accidentally touching Bunce's wound. Bunce winces. Snelgrave looks at his hand in disgust and then wipes it off.)

Get that thing to stop oozing! There she is. The liar. And perhaps a whore. Though she'd have to do all her whoring in the dark because. Well. As a young woman she was rather large up top. How would you sailors say it?

BUNCE: Well-rigged, sir.

SNELGRAVE: Yes. As a young woman she was well-rigged. Let's just say that half her sails have been burned away and leave it at that *(Beat.)* As you stand there, Bunce, looking at your wife, you realize that she's not only a liar but unsound under all that linen. *(Beat.)* Strike her. *(Beat.)* I said strike her.

BUNCE: *(To Darcy, because he is going to hit her.)* I'm sorry, Mrs.

(He raises his arm to strike her.)

MORSE: *(Sinking to her knees, quietly.)* Mother? *(Beat.)* Hush, hush. Do not cry.

(The others look at her. Morse has wet herself. She is ill. The piss slowly makes a line across the floor between them.)

I am filled. With angels.

Scene Eleven

Morse still sitting on the floor, alone, in dim light. In the cell or place of confinement, as in Scene One.

MORSE: *(Whispers.)* I can't. I can't remember.

(Sound of a slap.)

She smelled. Of lemons.

(Another slap, harder.)

Maybe she was my age. No. She was. Lissa was. A year younger. She had brown hair as long as a horse's tail and like cakes her dresses were. Rimmed with yellows and blues. Lissa had a fat stick that she kept in her trunk of toys and she would sneak up behind me as I swept the floors and hit me across the back. When I cried, she'd let me hold the bird that her grandfather brought home with him from India. It was a green and black bird and it could sing a melody. When I held it I could feel its tiny heart beating inside its chest.

(Darcy enters and stands in the shadows of the cell.)

Sometimes when Lissa's father scolded her she would come running to me and fling herself into my arms and weep. Her tears soaked my dirty frock.

(After some moments Morse gets to her feet and feels her dress is wet.)

Ugh. I've wet myself.

(Morse takes the dress off and casts it in the corner. She is wearing long underwear, perhaps a boy's, underneath.)

And then I got sick and Mr. Snelgrave shouted, "Plague! Plague!," but I had no tokens.

(Darcy takes up the dress and holds it, then exits with the dress.)

My teeth swelled. I vomited. I had the spotted-fever. For three days, Mrs. Snelgrave held me in her arms. *(Beat.)* That week Kabe said the pits were near overflowing. But Kabe said it wasn't only the dead that went to the pits. Some of the living went to the pits to die of grief. More than once, he said, when he tried to pull the grievers out of the pits he heard a sound like a stick snapping in their chests. Lissa's father, Mr. Braithwaite, died first. Then the mother. They died quickly. In each other's arms. From inside out they rotted. Lissa died more slowly. We were alone in the house. She said, "Hold me." Her body was covered in tokens. *(Beat.)* But it wasn't Lissa's blood that was on my sleeve. *(Beat.)* Who was alive and who was dead? In the pits their faces looked the same. Dried out by grief. And their hearts snapping in two inside their chests. Such a sound, Kabe said. Such a small, small sound, like this:

(Makes a small sound.)

END OF ACT ONE

ACT TWO
Scene One

Snelgrave and Bunce in the room.

MR. SNELGRAVE: And what was the longest period you sailed without port?

BUNCE: Two years. Though we docked, we couldn't leave the ship, so afraid was our Captain that we'd not come back.

SNELGRAVE: You're still a young man.

BUNCE: I was never a young man, sir.

SNELGRAVE: Well, what did you do with your natural instincts while so long at sea?

BUNCE: Stayed alive. As best we could.

SNELGRAVE: I mean with your baser instincts. Those instincts against God.

BUNCE: Aboard the vessels I sailed, we never murdered our Captain. Though once we threw one overboard after he beat the cook with a pitch mop.

SNELGRAVE: Bunce. You are in my house. I come in contact with the Court and Parliament. I attend cabinet meetings. At this very moment the Dutch are nuzzling at our shores.

(Gives Bunce an orange, which Bunce takes but does not eat. Bunce lets out a whistle as oranges are a delicacy even in good times.)

On these long voyages, without the comforts of a wife, what did you do to satisfy your unseemly satisfactions?

BUNCE: Between the Devil and the deep blue sea, there's little satisfaction, sir.

SNELGRAVE: *(Whacks his cane.)* At night, Bunce. Packed in there man to man, God forsaken flesh to God forsaken flesh. You're half way to Madras and it's sweltering hot and you wake with the hunger of a shark. But not for food. The Devil is foaming at your lips. What do you do, man? You're frothing with desire. What do you do?

BUNCE: I don't know as I ever frothed with desire, sir.

SNELGRAVE: The Lord, may He be forgiven, Bunce, gave you a foul and fleshful instrument that resides in your loins. And though you may attempt to ignore this instrument of debasement, in the darkness of a ship, among the sweat of rats and tired men, this instrument certainly led you—

BUNCE: *(Interrupts.)* You mean my prick, sir?

SNELGRAVE: Not in this house.

BUNCE: It goes where I go, sir.

SNELGRAVE: Exactly. And where does it go when your body is snarling and gnashing and snapping like a wild dog and it must be satisfied or you'll die!? *(Bunce is silent.)*
God curse you! Speak!
(Bunce nears Snelgrave, close, too close. He takes Snelgrave's finger, examines it a moment, and then forces it through the rind of the orange. Bunce turns the orange on Snelgrave's finger, slowly, sensually. Then he pulls the orange off of Snelgrave's finger. Involuntarily, Snelgrave looks at his wet finger. Bunce raises the orange over his head, squeezes it and drinks from the hole in the rind.)
I issue commissions to the Navy Board. *(Beat.)* I draft resolutions to send to the King.
(They look at each other.)

Scene Two

Snelgrave, Darcy, Morse and Bunce in the room. Morse now sits on the mat in the corner with Bunce. Morse is in long johns. Darcy coughs once, twice.

BUNCE: Can I get you some water?
DARCY: No, thank you, Bunce.
SNELGRAVE: *(Mocking.)* Can I get you some water? Can I get you some water? What's happened to your manners? It's Mrs. Snelgrave. Mrs. Snelgrave. Can I get you some water, Mrs. Snelgrave. *(Beat.)* Bunce.
BUNCE: Mrs. Snelgrave.
SNELGRAVE: That's right. That's right.
DARCY: William.
SNELGRAVE: I'm an old man, Bunce. I sleep sound. Do you sleep sound?
BUNCE: Usually, sir.
SNELGRAVE: They say a man who'd put to sea for pleasure, would go to hell for pastime. *(Beat.)* What's your pastime, Bunce? Heh?
(He begins to poke at Bunce with his stick. Morse runs to Darcy.)
We'll be out of here one day. Never see each other's rotten faces again. But where will you go? What will you do? I have work. I have friends. Do you have work, Bunce? Do you have friends?
MORSE: I'm his friend.
SNELGRAVE: *(To Morse.)* Ha. *(Beat.)* Tell us another story, Bunce. A real brute of a sea story. We've got some time left. To kill. I'll give you two shillings if it's good.

BUNCE: No, sir.

SNELGRAVE: No?

MORSE: He said no.

SNELGRAVE: What's the matter, Bunce? What's got under your skin?
(Poking him again with his stick, harder.) What's on your mind?

BUNCE: I got four things on my mind, sir.

SNELGRAVE: *(Still poking him.)* Go on. I'm intrigued. Four things.

BUNCE: First is that stick you keep poking me with. Second is when I get out of
here, I won't sail for the Navy again. Ever. I'll kill somebody first, even if it's
me. Third is your wife, Darcy Snelgrave. And fourth is your wife as well. I
count her twice cause she's much on my mind—

SNELGRAVE: You filthy— How dare you think of my wife!

BUNCE: You don't, sir, so I thought I might.

SNELGRAVE: What? What? What do you think of my wife?

DARCY: Stop this, William.

SNELGRAVE: What do you think of my wife?

BUNCE: The way a tar thinks, sir, you don't want to know.

SNELGRAVE: *(Still poking him.)* No. I don't. You swine. Eat your words. Eat them.
(Snelgrave forces the stick in Bunce's mouth.)
Eat them.
*(Bunce firmly but calmly grabs the stick and walks Snelgrave backwards until
Snelgrave sits in his chair.)*

BUNCE: Move, sir, from this chair and I'll push this stick through your heart.

SNELGRAVE: Darcy?

DARCY: *(Calmly.)* Morse, bring me the rope.

SNELGRAVE: Darcy!
*(Morse gets the rope and they wrap it around Snelgrave and tie him in the
chair. Banging at the window. Bunce pulls a knife and warns Snelgrave. Kabe
pops his head in.)*

KABE: A morning to all, good neighbors. Mr. Snelgrave, Mrs. Snelgrave. Rabble.
Want the Bills this week? Not leveling out. God save the King I say. The
Devil won't have him.

MORSE: We're playing: we're going to cook Mr Snelgrave.

KABE: No harm done, heh? And here's something for your game, Morse.
(He throws her an orange.)
Mrs. Snelgrave? Need anything?
(There is no reply but an awkward silence.)
Well. I'm off, as the scab said. Working the pits. Deaf Stewart'll take over
for me tonight. Throw something at him when you want his attention.

MORSE: Can you get me some good linen from the pits? I want a new dress.

KABE: There's a king's ransom in them pits. And along the roads. Bodies just asking you to strip 'em. If the family ain't robbed them first. Probably before they died...

DARCY: Morse! Kabe! Have you no sympathy...

KABE: They don't need it anymore, do they, Mrs. Snelgrave. Mr. Snelgrave.

SNELGRAVE: Kabe...

KABE: *(Ignoring Snelgrave's plea.)* What's terrible at the pits isn't the dead. What's terrible is that there are persons who aren't dead but are infected with the plague and they come freely to the pit, shouting, delirious with fever, half-naked, wrapped in blankets, and they throw themselves into the pits, on top of the dead and expire there.

SNELGRAVE: Kabe!

KABE: Others are still dying. They leap about the pit, roaring, tearing the clothes from their bodies, taking up sticks and sharp stones and cutting open their sores to relieve the pain, some hacking away at their flesh until they fall down dead in their own blood. Ay, that's what's terrible. Not death, but life that has nothing left but won't give itself up.

(Kabe waves and is gone.)

SNELGRAVE: Let me go.

(Bunce begins removing Snelgrave's shoes.)

What in God's name are you doing?

(Bunce puts on the shoes.)

BUNCE: I'm practicing.

(Morse puts the orange in Snelgrave's mouth.)

Scene Three

Night. Bunce sits on his mat in the corner, watching over Snelgrave who sleeps, still tied to his chair. Darcy enters. They watch each other silently in the dark.

DARCY: He sleeps.

BUNCE: Yes.

(Ater some moments.)

BUNCE: What do you want, Mrs.?

DARCY: I want. To see it.

BUNCE: Why?

DARCY: I think about it. All the time. What it must. Look like.

BUNCE: That's what you think about?

DARCY: Please. Lift your shirt.

BUNCE: You know what I think about, Mrs. Snelgrave?

DARCY: Maybe it's a joke. A lie. And when you leave here you'll go out in the streets, and pretend you're Christ, with a wound that doesn't heal, and they'll give you alms.

BUNCE: Excuse me, but it's none of your damn business.

(Darcy turns to leave.) Darcy.

DARCY: You're not to call me that. Ever.

BUNCE: I don't want you to see it.

(He takes off his shirt. He doesn't remove the bandage.)

But you can touch it. If you must.

DARCY: Yes.

BUNCE: Give me your hand. *(She does so.)* Close your eyes, Mrs.

(Darcy closes her eyes.)

Keep them closed.

(She nods. He guides her hands under his shirt.)

Feel it?

DARCY: *(After some moments.)* There.

BUNCE: Yeah.

DARCY: Does it hurt?

BUNCE: I don't know. Some of the skin, it has feeling left. Go on. Some of it doesn't.

DARCY: It's a small. Hole. There.

BUNCE: *(Winces, almost imperceptibly.)* What?

DARCY: My finger. I've put my finger. Inside. It's warm. *(Beat.)* It feels like I'm inside you.

BUNCE: You are.

(After some moments, Darcy takes her hand out from under his bandage. There is blood on her fingers. She looks at her hand as though it might be changed.)

DARCY: You should have died from a wound like that.

BUNCE: It was an accident.

DARCY: An accident?

BUNCE: That I lived.

DARCY: Do you know I've hardly given you a thought in these weeks but every night I ravish you in my sleep. Why is that, Bunce? Can you tell me why that is?

BUNCE: It's nothing to worry over, Mrs Snelgrave. You people always want to fuck your servants.

(Darcy raises her arm to hit him but he stops her.)
You haven't an idea in hell who I am.

DARCY: You're a sailor. You steal. You kill.

(Bunce begins to run his hands along her arms, much as Morse did earlier, slowly, watching her face to see what she can feel.)

BUNCE: I worked the Royal Navy off and on for eleven years. Here?

DARCY: No.

BUNCE: Deserted when I could. In between I skulked the city. There?

(Darcy shakes her head "no." Bunce moves on slowly to touch her shoulders and neck.)

I got picked up on the waters—here?

DARCY: Yes.

BUNCE: —by the Spaniards and served them against the French. There?

(Darcy shakes her head "no.")

Then the Hollanders against the English.

(Bunce goes down on his knees. He puts his hands under her dress to touch her ankles. We cannot see his hands or her legs as her dress is long. She doesn't stop him, though she looks to see if Snelgrave is still sleeping. The rest of the scene should be very subtle. Darcy does her best to hide both her fear and pleasure and she hides them very well. Now and again she repeats his words.)

Then I was taken up again by the English out of Dunkirker and served against the Hollanders. *(Beat.)* There?

(Moving his hands higher up her legs.)

There?

DARCY: I don't know. Yes. I think so.

BUNCE: Last I was taken by the Turks—

DARCY: The Turks.

BUNCE: Where I was forced to serve them against the English, French, Dutch and Spaniards and all Christendom. The last time I got picked up, I was in church.

DARCY: Church.

BUNCE: In Bristol. The press gangs had orders to pick up all men without property, above fifteen. They must have raided half a dozen churches to get the men they needed. *(Moving his hands up further.)* And here? *(Beat.)* Most of those lads didn't know the first thing about sailing, let alone war. In the first hours we sailed, two of them got tangled in the jib boom and swept overboard. Another fell from the mizzen shrouds.

DARCY: The mizzen shrouds?

BUNCE: One boy took sick with the motion. His neck and face swelled with the retching. Then his tongue went black. He held out his arms to us. For mercy. Then he vomited his stomach up into his hands and died. *(Touching her.)* This? Yeah. Here. *(Beat.)* We sailed to battle the Dutch at Tescell.

DARCY: Tescell.

BUNCE: Over twenty ships went down on fire. And the gulls. Screaming above the cannons. They wouldn't fly from the ships. Here? *(Beat.)* Some of them. Their wings caught fire, so close did they circle the sinking masts. When the battle was over, half of the men. Dead in the water. Floating face down in the waves, still in the Sunday suits they'd been picked up in. *(Beat.)* I sailed ships for Navies most of my life. *(Touching her intimately.)* And here? Yeah. Right here. *(Beat.)* In all that time I didn't kill. *(Beat.)* Mrs. Snelgrave?

DARCY: *(Whispers.)* Yes.

BUNCE: I never killed. It was in me though. Do you want me to stop?

(Darcy does not answer him.)

Scene Four

Snelgrave still tied in his chair. Bunce curled up and asleep on his mat. He does-n't stir through the entire scene. Morse sits and plays with two small cloth and stick dolls. She is wearing one of Darcy's dresses, which doesn't fit her at all, but she is happy to be dressed in it.

MORSE: And the two lovers were happy and the sky a blue grape and the birds sang. *(To Snelgrave.)* Can you make the tweet of the birds?

SNELGRAVE: If you untie me.

MORSE: *(Uses the doll to speak.)* I can't, Mr. Snelgrave. If I let you go you will break me in half with your cane. *(Beat.)* If you don't want to play, then shut up. *(Beat.)* And the two lovers were happy and the sky a fat apple and the birds sang. And the world—
(Snelgrave begins to make bird sounds. Morse listens a moment. She approves.)
And the birds sang sweetly and the world was good and—
(She looks at Snelgrave's bare feet.)
—even the rich had shoes. But one day the world changed.
(Morse strikes a tinderbox.)
And it never changed back.
(She holds one of the dolls near the flame.)

SNELGRAVE: Don't do that. *(Beat.)* Please.

MORSE: The young man said. But the fire-angel would have her heart.

(She lights the stick doll on fire and sets it on the floor to burn. They watch it burn out.)

Even her voice was burned, but still he heard her say "Hold me" and the young man came to her and—

SNELGRAVE: No. He didn't come to her. He was a coward, your man.

(Darcy almost enters the room, but then stops and watches them. They are intent on the story and do not see her.)

MORSE: He knelt down beside her—

SNELGRAVE: He walked away.

MORSE: —and put his hand into the ashes that were her body.

SNELGRAVE: He turned his back.

MORSE: The young man sifted the ashes until he found what was left of her heart.

SNELGRAVE: Small and black and empty it was—

MORSE: But it was her heart.

SNELGRAVE: And the young man put the burnt organ—

MORSE: No bigger than a walnut shell—

SNELGRAVE: Into a glass of his own blood.

(While Morse speaks the following, Snelgrave again whistles softly as before.)

MORSE: And there the heart drank and drank until it was plump once more. And though the prince could never hold her in his arms again, she being now only the size of his palm, he could caress her with his fingers and when it was winter the heart lay against his cold breast and kept him warm.

(Darcy exits. They do not notice.)

SNELGRAVE: I'm an ordinary man. I never meant to be cruel.

MORSE: Neither did Sir Braithwaite. And yet when my mother, a maid in his house for fourteen years, came to him one morning with the black tokens on her neck, he locked her in the root cellar. He was afraid they'd close up his house if they found out someone had taken sick. Neither food nor water he gave her. I lay outside the cellar door. With the door between us, we slept with our mouths to the crack so that we could feel each other's breath.

SNELGRAVE: We didn't lock up our maids. We called for a surgeon.

MORSE: She said "Hold me" because she was cold but the door was between us and I could not hold her.

SNELGRAVE: Enough of this. Get me some water, child.

MORSE: Did you bring them water when they were dying?

SNELGRAVE: Yes.

MORSE: You lie. You sent your boy to do it. You never looked on them once they were sick.

SNELGRAVE: I couldn't help them. It was God's wish.

MORSE: You locked them in the cellar.

SNELGRAVE: That's not true.

MORSE: And they died in the dirt and filth of their own bodies. And their last cries blew under the door and found your fat mouth and hid inside it and waited for the proper moment to fill your throat.

SNELGRAVE: You are an evil, evil girl. If your mother were alive—

MORSE: My mother lives in your mouth and one day she will choke you.

SNELGRAVE: Who's your father, girl?

MORSE: I was born from a piece of broken star that pierced my mother's heart.

SNELGRAVE: More likely Sir Braithwaite. Masters make free with their maids. I'll be honest. I've done so myself. Perhaps this gentleman you despise and ridicule was your own father. Heh? How about that little girl? Ever thought of that?

(Morse stands staring at him some moments. Then she slowly, slowly lifts the long dress and flashes him. This action is not seductive. For Morse it is as though she were pissing on him. After a moment, he turns his head away. She picks up the doll that played the prince. The remains of the burnt doll on the floor she scatters with a kick.)

Scene Five

Darcy, Bunce, Morse and Snelgrave, still tied to his chair. Morse has taken off Darcy's dress and goes about in her long johns again. Snelgrave is dressed in Bunce's clothes, which fit poorly. Bunce is putting on Snelgrave's pants. The shirt doesn't fit him so he throws it aside.

SNELGRAVE: Ha! They're a poor fit. You see! Untie me, Darcy.

DARCY: Please stop asking me that. Tomorrow perhaps. Not today.

SNELGRAVE: Bunce. I'll pay you in gold if you let me go.

BUNCE: The child has already given me half your gold, sir.

SNELGRAVE: But I have more at the Navy Board. Much more.

MORSE: *(Brings the vinegar bucket and begins to wash Snelgrave. He pays no attention.)* First we clean the meat. Then we cook it.

SNELGRAVE: *(To Darcy.)* You do realize we can't go on after this as man and wife.

DARCY: We haven't gone on as man and wife—

SNELGRAVE: I'll put you out in the streets.

DARCY: —since I was seventeen.

SNELGRAVE: You'll be the shame of the city. Less than a whore. You'll live in the kennel, stink—

DARCY: La, la. And I will strip and walk naked to your Navy Board, and in the Court yard I will dance.

MORSE: Like a pinecone on fire she'll dance.

SNELGRAVE: There's no life for you outside of this marriage, outside of this house. Bunce can't take care of you.

MORSE: But Bunce can tie knots.

(She takes a piece of rope out of her pocket and ties knots.)

I can tie a catspaw best. Mrs. Snelgrave can do a flemish-eye faster than he can.

SNELGRAVE: Tying knots with Bunce now, are we? How sweet. How delicious. Tell me, Bunce, what's her cunny like?

(Bunce doesn't answer.)

Bread that's left too long in the oven?

DARCY: *(To Bunce.)* Why don't you answer him?

(Silence some moments. Bunce shrugs, then takes a drink of water. He leans over Snelgrave as though to kiss him, and almost kisses him but instead he lets the water trickle slowly out of his mouth across Snelgrave's mouth and face. Snelgrave is so shocked by the audacity and sensuality of this act that by the time he resists, Bunce is through.)

BUNCE: That's your wife, sir. Though I haven't yet had the pleasures you assume. Only with my left hand. My right hand aches with jealousy. *(Snelgrave closes his eyes and appears to be praying. Bunce looks at Darcy for approval. She blushes. Snelgrave opens one eye and sees her blush. He spits at her but misses.)*

SNELGRAVE: If all you needed was a man as low as this to bring you round, I could have paid Kabe to do it.

MORSE: I saw Kabe's mousie once. It's tail was long and skinny.

DARCY: No one brought-me-round, William. I've lain beside you like a piece of old charcoal most of my life and well, if that's what I am—

SNELGRAVE: *(Interrupts.)* I wouldn't expect much pleasure in return, Bunce. She's an old woman. Her mouth stinks. Her—

MORSE: *(Sticking her bare toe in his face.)* What will you pay me if I let you suck my toe?

SNELGRAVE: You foul child!

DARCY: It seems centuries ago, but you used to weep at the pleasure I gave you.

MORSE: Kabe paid me a sugar-knot for a kiss.

SNELGRAVE: *(To Darcy.)* You lie. *(To Bunce.)* I bet she hasn't pleased you, has she?

MORSE: Small fruits and berries for a suck on the little toes.

DARCY: Answer him, Bunce.

MORSE: Larger fruits for a suck on the big one.

BUNCE: No. She hasn't.

DARCY: *(To Snelgrave.)* He's never asked me to.

SNELGRAVE: You think a man needs to ask?! *(To Bunce.)* Listen to that! She says you've never asked her!

BUNCE: Well, sir. I just sort of expected she'd take what she wanted. It's always been that way between us kind, hasn't it?

SNELGRAVE: Ha!

MORSE: Ha!

BUNCE: What's changed?

MORSE: You're wearing new shoes.

BUNCE: That I am. And a man in these shoes should be able to ask...

SNELGRAVE: Go on.

MORSE: Yes?

BUNCE: Will you, Mrs. Snelgrave...

SNELGRAVE: Yes?

MORSE: Go on.

BUNCE: Bring. A poor sailor. And part time servant. To his crisis?

(Snelgrave bursts out laughing and Morse laughs too, copying Snelgrave. Bunce blushes.)

DARCY: I don't think I could—

SNELGRAVE: See? It wasn't only me. She didn't like it after the fire either.

DARCY: I don't know a great deal about—

SNELGRAVE: It was a horror even to lie beside her.

DARCY: Other people. Their bodies.

SNELGRAVE: For years, the smoke rose out of her mouth as she slept.

MORSE: But she could learn. Couldn't she, Mr. Snelgrave?

SNELGRAVE: Learn? Her? Never, child.

MORSE: Of course she could. If Bunce stands here. And Mrs. Snelgrave right there.

SNELGRAVE: What?

MORSE: Come on. Don't be stupid. *(They follow her orders.)* Mrs. Snelgrave puts her hands on his chest. Go on.

SNELGRAVE: His chest?

BUNCE: Isn't that my bit?

MORSE: Not this time, it isn't.

SNELGRAVE: You're all mad.

MORSE: Then she gives him a little kiss on the cheek.

(Darcy does so.)

SNELGRAVE: Mad!

MORSE: Then she takes off her glove. Mrs. Snelgrave?

(She takes off her glove.)

And she lets it drop to the floor. Like a leaf. Ha.

(Darcy lets the glove drop.)

Then Mrs. Snelgrave, she lets her hand slowly move down his chest, slowly, down. Yes. To there.

(Darcy's hand rests on Bunce's belt.)

SNELGRAVE: *(To Morse.)* Where were you schooled, slut?

MORSE: Keyholes. *(Beat.)* And now it's only polite to make sure Bunce is still with her, so she says "May I?"

(Darcy doesn't speak.)

SNELGRAVE: She can't say it! Ha.

MORSE: "Do you want me to touch you?" she says.

(Bunce doesn't answer.)

SNELGRAVE: "Yes, I do," he says.

MORSE: And then we do this.

(She blindfolds Snelgrave.)

SNELGRAVE: Hey! Devil's spawn. Take that off.

MORSE: And I go to the kitchen.

SNELGRAVE: Take it off!

(Morse takes the rag from the bucket and puts it in his mouth. She exits.)

DARCY: *(Wanting Snelgrave to hear them.)* Shhh. I don't want my husband to hear us.

BUNCE: We'll be as quiet as the dead.

(Snelgrave screams through his stuffed rag.)

Scene Six

Early morning light. Snelgrave slumped in his chair. Morse enters in a night-dress that is Snelgrave's shirt that Bunce discarded in the previous scene. Morse approaches him, closer, closer until their faces are almost touching.

MORSE: That wasn't a poor bird you did yesterday. It was quite good, really.

(She whistles like a bird, as he did, earlier, then she picks up his hand. He is dead.)

Where did you go, Mr. Snelgrave?

(She unbuttons his shirt and checks his chest and neck.)

You haven't even got the tokens.

(She whistles again.)

Sir Braithwaite's daughter had a bird. A green and black bird. Whack, whack went her stick on my back when I swept. Then she'd let me hold the bird so I'd stop my crying. The bird had a song like a long, long spoon and we could sip at it like jam. And the song put a butterfly inside our mouths and it opened its wings in there and made us laugh. *(Beat.)* But everyone died in that house. And then Lissa was dying too and we were alone and she lay on the floor with the tokens shining black on her neck. The tokens would not break and run and Lissa wept from the pain. She said "Hold me." *(Beat.)* She could no longer see and was blind. *(Beat.)* She said "Hold me" and I said "Give me your dress." She couldn't take it off because she was too weak so I undressed her. Lissa said "Hold me now." She was small and thin without her dress. I said "Give me your shoes" and she let me have them. I put on the dress and the shoes. I went to the looking glass. The silk of the dress lapped at my skin. The ruffles whispered hush, hush as I walked. Lissa said "Hold me, Morse. I'm so cold." I went to her then. *(Beat.)* But then she was. Dead. I sat beside her, holding the bird. It sang for her. It sang for hours and hours until its heart stopped in my hands. *(Beat.)* It was Lissa's bird. I could take her dress and shoes but I couldn't take the bird. Even dead, it was Lissa's bird. Not mine. *(Beat.)* I opened her mouth and put the bird inside. *(Morse touches Snelgrave's face.)* You are dead. I can hold you. *(She gently embraces his body.)*

Scene Seven

Below the window, outside, Kabe is singing.

KABE: Tyburn tree, Tyburn tree
Hang anybody but the poor man and me
(Bunce appears.)
BUNCE: Pssst.
KABE: Hang the King, Hang the Duke
If I survive you'll be the death of me
BUNCE: I got gold.
KABE: Says the man in chains.
BUNCE: I'm going out through the cellar.
KABE: *(Ignoring Bunce.)* The King's coming back.
BUNCE: I got gold to pay you.

KABE: Kabe and King don't see eye to eye. Hell'll break loose. No place for a man of ability.

BUNCE: I'll throw in a pair of shoes the likes you've not seen before. Gentlemen's leather.

KABE: Chaos. Destruction. Mammon's back. Swarms, Sodom and all. Maybe I'll off to Oxford. Pass the monster on the way. Bow and wave.

BUNCE: And a pair of earrings.

KABE: Living's a nasty business.

BUNCE: I think they're emerald.

KABE: How's Mr. Snelgrave this morning?

BUNCE: I'm not Snelgrave.

KABE: Yes you are. *(Beat.)* The gold and the silk suit. Put the earrings in the pocket. You keep the shoes. Dumb Samuel will be on some night this week. I can't tell you when. Keep watch. He can't shout, but be quick. They'll kill you.

BUNCE: *(About to thank him.)* Kabe—

KABE: *(Interrupts.)* I don't care enough about you to hate you, Rabble. *(Beat.)* Tell the girl she'll have to give me a suck, on the mouth this time, or no deal. Said the cock to the chicken.

BUNCE: I heard you.

KABE: *(Recites.)* I don't like sailors. They stink of tar.
But my lass she smells of the falling star.
(Bunce disappears from the window.)
(Sings.) Tyburn tree, Tyburn tree
Can't find work for any fee
The Plague's got your tongue, worm's at your bone
You're as near to me as the West Indy.
Tyburn tree, Tyburn tree.
Won't you, won't you make love to me!

Scene Eight

Bunce is putting a few spare items, a shirt, bread, onto a piece of cloth that he'll tie up as a sack. Morse watches him. Mr. Snelgrave sits dead in his chair, a small cloth over his face.

BUNCE: Don't know. Out of the city if I can. And find work. Back up North maybe. Some quiet parish that's not got too many poor. God willing.

MORSE: You don't believe in God.

BUNCE: If there's employment, I'll believe and more.

MORSE: You could stay.

BUNCE: Not now. I'd might as well rope myself and walk to Tyburn. Save them and me trouble.

MORSE: But my word and Mrs. Snelgrave's...

BUNCE: Her word? Can't trust that the right story would stick in her mouth. Who's to say she wouldn't be front row just to see me rise up in me britches after I drop down and into hell.

MORSE: Rise up in your britches?

BUNCE: It's the rush of blood to your...to me...I can't stay.

MORSE: (*Nodding towards Snelgrave.*) They'll have to come and get him. (*Beat.*) They'll throw him in the pits, though it wasn't plague, won't they?

BUNCE: He won't care.

MORSE: I don't mind him here. Now. He doesn't smell.

BUNCE: Not yet.

MORSE: And me?

BUNCE: Mrs. Snelgrave will care for you.

MORSE: She has no heart. That's what she told me.

BUNCE: Trust her; she's a liar.

MORSE: You didn't mind how she felt? Her skin.

BUNCE: You don't feel with your hands.

MORSE: (*Holding out her arms.*) Am I soft?

BUNCE: (*Touches her arms.*) You are. (*Beat.*) You feel. Alive.

MORSE: Everyone leaves.

BUNCE: Ay.

MORSE: Even when they stay.

(*Morse takes the stick doll she didn't burn out of her pocket and puts it on the small pile Bunce is about to wrap up.*)

It wants to go with you.

BUNCE: (*Picking up the stick doll and looking at it.*) Who is it?

MORSE: It's me.

(*Bunce puts the stick doll on his pile and ties it all into a bundle. Then he takes some rope from his pocket to show Morse one more knot. Darcy enters and stands watching them. They don't notice her.*)

BUNCE: I'll show you a last one, then I'm off. Thumb knot you use to tie the mouse and collar on the mast. You always go in here, not around. A good knot is like a dead man's heart; you can't break it.

(*Bunce notices Darcy standing there. She is quietly watching them. Her face and hair are wet with sweat.*)

MORSE: *(Making the knot.)* You can't break my heart. It's made of water.

(She shows him her knot. Then she too sees Darcy.)

BUNCE: Your dress is wet.

DARCY: That's because my head is full. Of ocean. And the shells are sliding back and forth in my ears. *(Touching her head.)* It's hot in here. Very hot.

BUNCE: *(To Morse.)* Get a blanket.

(Morse stands transfixed on Darcy.)

A blanket! And some towels.

(Morse gets them.)

DARCY: You mustn't bother.

(Bunce nears her.)

Stay back.

BUNCE: The tokens. Are they on your neck or thighs?

DARCY: They're in my mind.

BUNCE: We've got to make a fire. Are the botches hard yet?

(Darcy doesn't answer. He approaches her again.)

Take off your dress. Let me look.

DARCY: Never. *(Beat.)* You must get out. Take the child with you.

(She reveals a knife.)

I will not hesitate.

BUNCE: *(He moves close enough to her so she can cut him.)* Neither will I.

(She lowers the knife. Weakened by fever, she sits. Bunce drops to his knees and raises her skirts.)

BUNCE: *(To Morse.)* It's her thighs. Get some coals from the kitchen. And some wet cloth.

(Morse exits. Bunce puts his arms under her dress and begins to massage her thighs vigorously.)

We've got to soften the botches. With heat. Then we can lance them.

(Darcy sits in a daze. She stares at Snelgrave in his chair.)

DARCY: Take it off.

(Bunce starts to unbutton her dress. She stops him.)

The cloth.

(Darcy indicates Snelgrave. Bunce removes the small cloth that was covering Snelgrave's face. Morse returns with a bucket of coals and wet clothes.)

Is he laughing, Morse?

(Morse looks at Snelgrave's face.)

MORSE: No, Mrs. Snelgrave. He's weeping. But he's so far away we can't hear him.

DARCY: Is he cold?

(Morse touches Snelgrave's arm. Bunce rips up cloth.)

MORSE: Like snow, he is.

DARCY: I envy him.

MORSE: Does it hurt?

DARCY: Here. *(Indicating her stomach.)* As though I had swallowed. Large pieces of glass.

(Bunce takes up a hot coal and wraps it in the wet cloth.)

BUNCE: You'll feel this, Mrs. Snelgrave. *(He puts them under Darcy's dress, against her skin. Darcy flinches strongly at the heat.)*

MORSE: *(Morse attempts to distract her.)* Did you care for him?

DARCY: Who?

MORSE: Mr. Snelgrave.

DARCY: I knew him only as a boy. After the fire, he bore the same name but that was the only resemblance. Yes. As a boy. Perhaps I loved him. Look at him there. Can you believe it, Morse? We used to touch each other for hours. We thought we were remaking ourselves. Perhaps we were. For each morning we were someone new and the world was almost a surprise, like biting into a piece of fruit with your eyes closed. *(Beat.)* No more, Bunce. Please. It does no good.

(Bunce puts another wrapped piece of coal under her dress. Darcy stifles a scream.)

MORSE: *(Distracting Darcy.)* Did William kiss you many, many times, Mrs. Snelgrave?

DARCY: Many, many times. And his tongue. So cold. And it covered my skin with frost.

(Darcy screams again. Bunce takes the knife from her hand and begins to bring it under her skirt to lance the tokens. Suddenly Darcy is completely lucid. She stops Bunce's hand.)

No.

BUNCE: If I can make them run there's a chance.

DARCY: God damn you, Bunce. The life is pouring out of me. *(Shouts.)* Help me! *(Quietly.)* Help me.

BUNCE: I'm trying to save your life.

DARCY: That's not what I mean.

(Bunce shakes his head "no." Morse moves away and watches them.)

Do you love me?

(For a moment, Bunce laughs in a desperate manner.)

I said do you love me?

BUNCE: Not enough to kill you.

DARCY: Then. Let me.

BUNCE: Don't ask. Shhh. Please.

(Bunce lays his head in her lap. She takes the knife from his hand.)

I haven't the courage.

(There is silence for some moments.)

MORSE: I do.

DARCY: You're not afraid?

(Morse nods "no.")

Take my hand. Come then. Now squeeze it with all your might.

(Morse does so.)

MORSE: I'm strong. I am.

BUNCE: No.

DARCY: If you stop me you'll regret it. And I'll curse you the moment I die. *(Beat.)* You can leave the room, Sailor. I'm not asking you to stay.

(Bunce stares at her for what seems a long time. Then he kisses her, gently, on the forehead. As he begins to move away, she pulls him back and forces him to kiss her, hard, on the mouth. Then Bunce goes to his mat and kneels there, his face to the wall. Darcy speaks to Morse.)

So you will help me.

MORSE: *(Still holding Darcy's hand.)* What will you give me?

DARCY: Well, I don't think I have anything left.

MORSE: Your gloves.

DARCY: Alright, my gloves.

(Darcy removes her gloves. She puts Morse's hands on the knife and her own hands over Morse's.)

You must not waver, Morse. Not for one moment. Do you understand?

(Morse nods. Darcy places the blade point against her chest, over her heart. Darcy closes her eyes.)

MORSE: Don't close your eyes, Mrs. Snelgrave. All you'll see is blackness. *(Morse puts her face close to Darcy's face.)*

Look at me. At my face.

(Darcy opens her eyes.)

DARCY: Yes.

MORSE: The breath of a child has passed through the lungs of an angel. You said that.

(Darcy nods.)

So the breath of an angel now covers your face. Can you feel it?

(She blows on Darcy's face.)

And I will hold you, hush, hush. The angel's tongue is so cold it covers your

skin with snow as the flames, like scissors, open your dress. And my kiss is a leaf. It falls from the sky and comes to rest on your breast. And my kiss is strong and pierces your heart—
(Morse helps Darcy drive the knife into Darcy's heart.)
Like a secret from God.
(Morse pulls out the knife. Darcy is dead. Morse holds the knife out to Bunce. Morse is completely still, perhaps in shock. Finally Bunce turns around.)
It is done. We are dead.

Scene Ten

Music of a funeral procession, Gregorian chants. Darkness. In the cell or place of confinement as in previous scenes. In the shadows we see the dead Snelgraves, still in their chairs. Nothing of Bunce or of Bunce's presence remains. Morse stands center stage, again in her dirty dress.

MORSE: Can I go now? *(Beat.)* There's nothing more to tell of them.
   Years it was. Or weeks and days, by the time the doors were opened. The city was empty. The air was sweet with sugar and piss. And it was quiet. So quiet. And I walked down to the quay side. The boats were still. There was no wind. The river was not moving. Everyone had gone. One way or another.
   (Kabe enters in the shadows. He covers Mr. Snelgrave with a cloth.)
   I stood by the banks and looked in the water. There were no fish. There was nothing but water. Water that didn't move. But then, I saw a child floating there. On her back. She rose so close to the surface I could have touched her. A girl of nine or ten. Pale and blond she was. And naked. She had no marks. In each hand she clutched a fist of black hair. Her mouth was open and filled with the river. As I reached in the water to touch her, a ship hoisted its sail. A door slammed in the street. One, two, three voices called out to one other. A bell rang. And the city came alive once more.
   (Sings.) Oranges and lemons
   Sing the bells of St. Clements
   (Kabe covers Mrs. Snelgrave with a cloth.)
   When I looked down in the water again for the body of the child, it was gone. And I was glad. I was glad it had gone.
   (Kabe exits.)

Kabe once said to me, "Our lives are just a splash of water on a stone. Nothing more."

(Morse kneels, as though in prayer.)

Then I am the stone on which they fell. And they have marked me. So beware. Because I loved them, and they have marked me.

(Morse sits and takes the orange from her pocket. She holds the orange in her lap, looking at it, her head bowed. We hear Kabe singing, offstage, though his voice fills the entire cell.)

KABE: Farewell said the scab to the itch
Farewell said the crab to its crotch
Farewell said the plague to death's ditch
Farewell said the dead to their watch.

(Morse tosses the orange high into the air. Just as she catches it, the lights go black.)

END OF PLAY

Humana Festival History
compiled by Joel A. Smith

First Festival of New American Plays (1976-77)

THE GIN GAME by D.L. Coburn: 2 acts. In a letter, Flaubert wrote, "We laugh with pity at the vanity of the human will." One hundred years later it is this laughter that we celebrate, as Weller Martin tries desperately to retain some control over his life despite falling into ill health and becoming a reluctant resident of a nursing home. Fonsia Dorsey serves as the symbol of all gone wrong, and his battles with her, though over a simple game of gin, become not only a conflict with the woman but with divine will itself. 1m, 1f. Winner of 1978 Pulitzer Prize. Published by Samuel French, Inc. and selections published by Dodd, Mead & Company in *The Best Plays of 1977-1978*.

INDULGENCES IN THE LOUISVILLE HAREM by John Orlock: 2 acts. Two spinster sisters in turn-of-the-century Louisville decide to escape from their protective solitude and write to a mail-order catalogue for companions. When a professor of mesmerism and his assistant arrive, the results are not what the sisters had expected. 2m, 2f. Contact Actors Theatre of Louisville.

Second Festival of New American Plays (1977-78)

THE BRIDGEHEAD by Frederick Bailey: 2 acts. In 1970, a reconnaissance squad is sent into Cambodia looking for North Vietnamese bases. Surrounded on all sides by their own troops, but isolated from them, they discover that their native guide is a traitor. 11m, 1f. Contact Actors Theatre of Louisville.

DADDIES by Douglas Gower: 2 acts. The Christmastime meeting between a man and his former wife's new lover. They question one another's motivations, testing gracious behavior with their various fears and needs. 2m. Published by Dramatists Play Service, Inc.

DOES ANYBODY HERE DO THE PEABODY? by Enid Rudd: 2 acts. A fast-talking ex-dancer wins the heart of a woman who has always dreamed of a show business career, despite the objections of her irritable mother and stoical sister. 2m, 4f. Contact Flora Roberts, 157 West 57th St., New York, NY 10022.

GETTING OUT by Marsha Norman: 2 acts. A young woman struggles to re-enter the world after eight years in prison, contending with environmental forces as she attempts to assimilate her former and present selves. 6m, 6f. Published by Dramatists Play Service, Inc.; by TCG in *Marsha Norman: Four Plays*; by Broadway Play Publishing in *Plays from Actors Theatre of Louisville*; by Smith & Kraus in *Marsha Norman Volume I: Collected Plays*; selections published by Dodd, Mead & Company in *The Best Plays of 1977-78*.

AN INDEPENDENT WOMAN by Daniel Stein: 2 acts. The self-exploration of a social/political activist of the late 1800s; the struggles, accomplishments, and frustrations of having a voice and daring to use it. 1f. Contact Actors Theatre of Louisville.

THE LOUISVILLE ZOO by Anonymous Authors: A collection of scenes and monologues satirizing political and social life in Louisville. Contact Actors Theatre of Louisville.

Third Festival of New American Plays (1978-79)

CIRCUS VALENTINE by Marsha Norman: 2 acts. An exploration of the private struggles facing a small family circus in its final days perfoming in a shopping mall parking lot. 5m, 3f. Published by Smith & Kraus in *Marsha Norman Volume I: Collected Plays*.

CRIMES OF THE HEART by Beth Henley: 2 acts. Three sisters from a small Southern town are reunited when the youngest of them is released on bail after shooting her husband. Together, they break from their equally painful pasts and look toward the future with new strength. 3m, 4f. Winner of the 1981 Pulitzer Prize. Published by Dramatists Play Service, Inc. and by Broadway Play Publishing in *Plays from Actors Theatre of Louisville*.

FIND ME by Olwen Wymark: 2 acts. A sensitive examination of the disruptive force a seriously disturbed child creates within her family. 3m, 5f. Contact Gil Parker, William Morris Agency, Inc., 1325 Avenue of the Americas, New York, NY 10019.

HOLIDAYS: a compendium of short plays

BAR PLAY by Lanford Wilson: An argument occurs when one of the regular customers at a neighborhood bar makes insinuations about the bartender's daughter. 3m, 1f. Contact ICM, 40 West 57th St., New York, NY 10019.

FIREWORKS by Megan Terry: During an Independence Day celebration, two children learn of their parents' impending divorce. 2m, 1f. Published by Smith & Kraus in *20/20: Twenty One-Act Plays from the Twenty Year History of the Humana Festival of New American Plays*.

THE GREAT LABOR DAY CLASSIC by Israel Horovitz: People with different backgrounds compete in a marathon. 3m, 3f. Contact Writers and Artists Agency, 19 W 44th St, New York, NY 10036.

I CAN'T FIND IT ANYWHERE by Oliver Hailey: On Memorial Day, a mother and father try to visit the grave of their son who was killed in Vietnam. 1m, 1f. Contact Actors Theatre of Louisville.

INDEPENDENCE DAY by Tom Eyen: Three couples release their hostilities during a fireworks display on the 4th of July. 3m, 3f. Contact Bridget Aschenberg, ICM, 40 West 57th St., New York, NY 10019.

IN FIREWORKS LIE SECRET CODES by John Guare: While watching the 4th of July fireworks, an Englishman announces his desire to return home. 3m, 3f. Published by Dramatists Play Service, Inc.

JUNETEENTH by Preston Jones: A newcomer to a small Texas town is the object of a practical joke involving Juneteenth, the celebration of the emancipation of the slaves. Contact ICM, 40 West 57th St., New York, NY 10019.

MERRY CHRISTMAS by Marsha Norman: A family copes with their mother's sudden deafness when she is released from the hospital for Christmas. 3m, 3f. Contact Jack Tantleff, The Tantleff Office, 375 Greenwich St., Suite 700, New York, NY 10013.

NEW YEAR'S by Ray Aranha: Death comes calling for a prostitute with a "heart of gold." 1m, 2f. Contact Actors Theatre of Louisville.

REDEEMER by Douglas Turner Ward: A diverse group of people gather for the "second coming." 3m, 3f. Contact The Negro Ensemble Company, 133 Second Ave., New York, NY 10003.

LONE STAR by James McLure: 1 act. A humorous look at a Vietnam War veteran's attempt to adjust to life in his hometown in Texas. 3m. Published by Dramatists Play Service, Inc.

MATRIMONIUM by Peter Ekstrom: (retitled **CLOSE YOUR EYES AND THINK OF ENGLAND**) 2 acts. A stylized musical based on George Bernard Shaw's indulgent one-acts, *Overruled*, 2m,2f; and *Passion, Poison, and Petrifaction*, 4m, 2f. Contact Peter Ekstrom, 128 West 82nd Street, New York, NY 10024.

FOURTH FESTIVAL OF NEW AMERICAN PLAYS (1979-80)

AGNES OF GOD by John Pielmeier: 2 acts. A psychiatrist becomes obsessed with an unusually mystical nun who has been charged with murdering her child at birth. 3f. Published by Samuel French, Inc.

THE AMERICA PROJECT: a compendium of short plays
    AMERICAN WELCOME by Brian Friel: A foreign writer arrives in the U.S. and is greeted by a loquacious American director. 2m. Published by BARC Publishing and by Samuel French, Inc. in *More Ten-Minute Plays From Actors Theatre of Louisville*.

    THE DRUMMER by Athol Fugard: A streetperson in New York City finds a pair of discarded drumsticks and proceeds to drum a variety of objects creating a world full of rhythm. 1m. Published by Samuel French in *Twenty-Five Ten-Minute Plays from Actors Theatre of Louisville*.

    THE GOLDEN ACCORD by Wole Soyinka: A couple wins a game show prize when the husband breaks a very private trust. The wife responds with vengeance. Published by Samuel French, Inc. in *More Ten-Minute Plays From Actors Theatre of Louisville*.

    HOORAY FOR HOLLYWOOD by John Byrne: A writer's first collision with tinsel-town machinery. 5m, 2f. Contact Actors Theatre of Louisville.

    SAN SALVADOR by Keith Dewhurst: A debate relating to cannibalism and cultural prejudice. 2m, 1f. Contact Alexandra Cann, London Management, 235 Regent St., London, England W1A 2JT.

    THE SIDE OF THE ROAD by Gordon Dryland: The conflict between a woman's sensitivities and her husband's insecurities. 1m, 1f. Contact Esther Sherman, William Morris Agency, 1325 Avenue of the Americas, New York, NY 10019.

    STAR QUALITY by Carol Bolt: Backstage moments at the Miss Teenage Manitoba Contest. 2m, 2f. Contact the Great North Agency, Suite 500, 345 Adelaide Street W., Toronto, Ontario, Canada M5V 1R5.

    SWITCHING by Brian Clark: A series of brief scenes depicting the conflicts of human relationships. 5m, 2f. Contact Judy Daish Associates, 122 Wigmore St., London, England W1H 9FE.

    TALL GIRLS HAVE EVERYTHING by Stewart Parker: A quick-witted American woman inspects an Irish musician's flat for possible accommodation and challenges his various cultural biases. 3m, 1f. Contact Alexandra Cann, London Management, 235 Regent St., London, England W1A 2JT.

    VICKI MADISON CLOCKS OUT by Alexander Buzo: A young reporter watches or commits an assassination from her high-rise office. 1f, 1m (voice). Contact June Cann Management, 283 Alfred St., North Sydney, Australia.

DOCTORS AND DISEASES by Peter Ekstrom: (Additional lyrics by Kay Erin Thompson) A cabaret-type entertainment featuring songs about health ranging from death to hypochondria. 1m, 1f. Contact Peter Ekstrom, 128 West 82nd Street, New York, NY 10024.

POWER PLAYS by Shirley Lauro: Two one-acts.
THE COAL DIAMOND A group of women face the fact that years of dedication to work and the mundane provide little insulation from the past. 4f. Published by Dramatists Play Service, Inc.

NOTHING IMMEDIATE An Eastern socialite checks into an empty motel in Iowa. A conflict of values flares as she attempts to deal with the manager, a stern and aggressive fundamentalist. 2f. Published by Samuel French, Inc. and by Applause in *Best Short Plays 1980*.

REMINGTON by Ray Aranha: 1 act. A one-man show based on the life and work of Frederic Remington. The audience is Mr. Remington's guest for a night of story-telling and philosophizing about the changing Old West. 1m. Published in TCG's *Plays in Process* series.

SUNSET/SUNRISE by Adele Edling Shank: 2 acts. An over-the-fence look at the confusion of suburban lifestyles and relationships as illuminated by a backyard party. 6m, 7f. Published in *West Coast Plays*.

THEY'RE COMING TO MAKE IT BRIGHTER by Kent Broadhurst: 2 acts. On Christmas Eve, the art deco lights of an old building in New York City are replaced by modern glaring globes. The employees and other people passing through the lobby have mixed reactions to the new replacing the old. 8m, 4f, extras. Published by Dramatic Publishing.

TODAY A LITTLE EXTRA by Michael Kassin: 1 act. The threat of cultural disintegration is apparent when a man sells the neighborhood kosher butcher shop that has been his life for 40 years. 2m, 1f. Published by Applause in *Best Short Plays 1982*.

WEEKENDS LIKE OTHER PEOPLE by David Blomquist: 2 acts. After their hope for advancement is destroyed, a lower-middle class couple recognizes that they must accept their way of life. 1m, 1f. Published by Dramatists Play Service, Inc.

FIFTH FESTIVAL OF NEW AMERICAN PLAYS (1980-81)

THE AUTOBIOGRAPHY OF A PEARL DIVER by Martin Epstein: 1 act. A negligent husband and his alcoholic buddy belittle his totally suppressed wife. A Triple-A mechanic shows her the strength and hope she needs to change her bleak situation. 4m, 1f. Contact Actors Theatre of Louisville.

EARLY TIMES: a compendium of short plays
THE A**HOLE MURDER CASE by Stuart Hample: Three drama majors create a hilarious scene for their professor. 3m, 1f. Published by Samuel French, Inc. in *Twenty-Five Ten-Minute Plays from Actors Theatre of Louisville*.

CHAPTER TWELVE—THE FROG by John Pielmeier: While dissecting a frog, a babbling young girl stops talking long enough to discover she is losing her boyfriend to her lab partner. 2f. Contact William Craver, Writers & Artists Agency, 19 W 44th St, Ste 1000, New York, NY 10036.

PROPINQUITY by Claudia Johnson: An assistant professor learns about love from a college freshman. 3m, 1f. Contact Howard Rosenstone, Rosenstone/Wender, 3 East 48th St., 4th floor, New York, NY 10036.

QUADRANGLE by Jon Jory: A terse confrontation between the victims of a one-night stand which resulted in a pregnancy and a subsequent abortion. 1m, 1f. Published by Dramatic Publishing in *University*.

SPADES by Jim Beaver: Two medics playing cards are surprised by the appearance of a soldier who has been pronounced dead. 2m. Published by Samuel French, Inc. in *Twenty-Five Ten-Minute Plays from Actors Theatre of Louisville*.

TWIRLER by Jane Martin: A former twirler reveals the ritual of baton twirling. 1f. Published by Applause in *Best Short Plays 1982*; in *Esquire Magazine* (Nov. '82); and by Samuel French, Inc. in *Talking With*.

WATERMELON BOATS by Wendy MacLaughlin: The audience watches two friends grow from girls to women against the background of a watermelon regatta. 2f. Published by Samuel French, Inc. in *Twenty-Five Ten-Minute Plays from Actors Theatre of Louisville* and by Smith & Kraus in *20/20: Twenty One-Act Plays from the Twenty Year History of the Humana Festival of New American Plays*.

EXTREMITIES by William Mastrosimone: 2 acts. During an attempted rape, a woman captures her attacker and proceeds to torture him. Her roommates return home and struggle to determine who is guilty of a crime, the woman or her would-be rapist. 1m, 3f. Published by Samuel French, Inc.

A FULL LENGTH PORTRAIT OF AMERICA by Paul D'Andrea: 2 acts. A black New Orleans jazz musician in her eighties is transformed by the news that she will bear a child if her husband's music is freed from its captivity. 4m, 2f. Contact Paul D'Andrea, Theater of the First Amendment, Institute of the Arts, Rm A407, George Mason University, Fairfax, VA 22030.

FUTURE TENSE by David Kranes: Two one-acts.
  AFTER COMMENCEMENT A recent graduate thinks he is alone in an empty fraternity house until he comes upon an acquaintance contemplating suicide. 2m, 1f. Contact Robert Freedman, Robert A. Freedman Dramatic Agency, 1501 Broadway, Suite 2310, New York, NY 10036.

  PARK CITY: MIDNIGHT An unexpected encounter with her estranged father causes a young woman to re-evaluate what she wants from life. 3m, 2f. Contact Robert Freedman, Robert A. Freedman Dramatic Agency, 1501 Broadway, Suite 2310, New York, NY 10036.

MY SISTER IN THIS HOUSE by Wendy Kesselman: 2 acts. When two emotionally abused servant-sisters respond to their pent-up hostilities, brutal murder of their mistress is the result. Based on a historical incident in Le Mans, France in 1933. 1m, 5f, voices. Published by Samuel French, Inc.

SHORTS: three one-act plays
  CHOCOLATE CAKE by Mary Gallagher: Two women meet at a career conference and spend the evening in a motel room comparing their fears and compulsions. 2f. Published by Dramatists Play Service, Inc. and by Applause in *Best Short Plays 1982*.

  CHUG by Ken Jenkins: A southern Indiana man's frog-breeding Midas scheme falls just short of success. He discusses the situation and how he can "handle it." 1m. Published in *Rupert's Birthday* by Dramatists Play Service, Inc. and by Applause in *Best Short Plays 1984*.

FINAL PLACEMENT by Ara Watson: A natural mother attempts to retrieve her formerly abused son who has been placed in an adoptive home, resulting in a trying review for the responsible caseworker. 2f. Published by Dramatists Play Service, Inc. and in *Louisville Today Magazine*.

SWOP by Ken Jenkins: 2 acts. A rural mystic in his late 80's becomes the nemesis to his self-centered and frustrated son-in-law. When the struggle between the two intensifies, the former prevails. 7m, 2f. Contact Robert Freedman, Robert A. Freedman Dramatic Agency, 1501 Broadway #2310, New York, NY 10036.

SIXTH HUMANA FESTIVAL OF NEW AMERICAN PLAYS (1981-82)

CLARA'S PLAY by John Olive: 2 acts. The story of a reclusive old woman and her hot-tempered Norwegian handyman. 3m, 1f. Published by Samuel French, Inc. and by TCG in *Plays in Process* series.

A DIFFERENT MOON by Ara Watson: 2 acts. A small-town family in the mid-1950's redefines its parameters when faced with a dilemma resulting from an absent son's ingenuous love. 1m, 3f. Published by Dramatists Play Service, Inc.

FULL HOOKUP by Conrad Bishop and Elizabeth Fuller: 2 acts. A drama detailing relationships with no strings, and violence without conscience. 2m, 3f. Published by Dramatists Play Service, Inc.

THE GRAPES OF WRATH by Terrence Shank: 2 acts (Adaptation of the John Steinbeck novel) A powerful chronicle of the displaced farmers of the Dust Bowl and their torturous journey toward the mirage of the West. 22m, 7f. Contact Actors Theatre of Louisville.

THE INFORMER by Thomas Murphy: 2 acts. (Adapted from the novel by Liam O'Flaherty) A suspenseful and intimate view of Ireland's poor, caught in the maelstrom of revolution. 16m, 10f. Contact Bridget Aschenberg, ICM, 40 West 57th St., New York, NY 10019.

OLDTIMERS GAME by Lee Blessing: 2 acts. A wild, rowdy — and honest — look at the high pressure, high stakes realities of baseball, as new ownership upsets the status quo in a struggling AAA team. 9m. Published by Dramatists Play Service, Inc.

SHORTS: three one-act plays
> **THE EYE OF THE BEHOLDER by Kent Broadhurst**: This comic farce about definitions of art is set in a painter's studio where two artists and an intellectual model resort to paint-slinging to settle their debate. 3m. Published by Dramatists Play Service, Inc. and by Smith & Kraus in *20/20: Twenty One-Act Plays from the Twenty Year History of the Humana Festival of New American Plays*.

> **THE NEW GIRL by Vaughn McBride**: Two women in a nursing home accomplish the impossible and create a new dignity as they confront their limitations. 2f. Published by Samuel French, Inc.

> **THE GROVES OF ACADEME by Mark Stein**: The development of a special relationship between an enthusiastically inquisitive student and his patient and inspiring professor. 2m. Published by Dramatists Play Service, Inc.

SOLO: a compendium of seven monologues

BUTTERFLY, MARGUERITE, NORMA... & IRMA JEAN by Trish Johnson: A character study of a woman who stands through hundreds of performances at the Metropolitan Opera House each season. Contact Actors Theatre of Louisville.

CEMETERY MAN by Ken Jenkins: A gravedigger, who has received his notice of employment termination from the city, tells a series of stories about the people he has helped bury. Published by Dramatists Play Service, Inc. in *Rupert's Birthday and Other Monologues*.

RUPERT'S BIRTHDAY by Ken Jenkins: A farm woman recalls a mystical evening when, while her mother gave birth to her brother, she helped to deliver a calf, and became a woman. 1f. Published by Dramatists Play Service, Inc. and by Applause in *Best Short Plays 1983*.

SIDEKICK by Jim Beaver: A man relates his experiences as a supporting actor during the heyday of Western filmmaking, chronicling his work as a "sidekick." Contact Sam Adams, TRIAD Artists, Inc., 10100 Santa Monica Blvd., Los Angeles, CA 90067.

SLOW DRAG, MAMA by Dare Clubb and Isabell Monk: An old black woman relives the final moments of her mother's life, vacillating between her own voice and that of her dying mother. Contact Actors Theatre of Louisville.

THE SUBJECT ANIMAL by Larry Atlas: An army officer tries to explain why it is necessary to use animals in medical experiments. 1m. Contact George Lane, William Morris Agency, 1325 Avenue of the Americas, New York, NY 10019.

THE SURVIVALIST by Robert Schenkkan: A man's lecture at a seminar on survival stresses the importance of preparing ourselves individually for the impending disaster of war. Published by Dramatists Play Service, Inc.

TALKING WITH by Jane Martin: monologues for eleven women

AUDITION: An actress auditions for a role she covets in a new play.

CLEAR GLASS MARBLES: A young woman reminisces about her mother's courageous encounter with death.

CUL-DE-SAC: A potential rape victim turns on her assailant and forces him to perform self-emasculation.

DRAGONS: A woman in labor speculates about dragons and her soon-to-be-born child.

FIFTEEN MINUTES: As an actress prepares for a performance, she ponders her position as an entertainer and her relationship with an audience.

HANDLER: A young country woman, having lost faith in God's role in the act of snake-handling, relies on her own spirit to protect her.

MARKS: A woman covers her body in tattoos commemorating the major events in her life.

RODEO: A cowgirl comments on commercialism's destruction of the rodeo.

SCRAPS: A young housewife escapes the tensions and confinements of her life by dressing as the Patchwork Girl of Oz while doing her housework.

TWIRLER: A former twirler reveals the ritual of baton twirling.

Published by Samuel French, Inc.; by Smith & Kraus in *Jane Martin Collected Works: Vol I*; and by Applause in *Best Short Plays 1982*; selections published by Samuel French, Inc. in *What Mama Don't Know*; in *Esquire Magazine* (Nov. '82); and by Dodd, Mead & Company in *The Best Plays of 1981-1982*.

SEVENTH HUMANA FESTIVAL OF NEW AMERICAN PLAYS (1982-83)

COURAGE by John Pielmeier: 2 acts. This sensitive close-up of J.M. Barrie, creator of Peter Pan, is drawn from Barrie's famous 1922 commencement address at St. Andrew's Academy in Edinburgh. 1m. Contact William Craver, Writers & Artists Agency, 19 W 44th St, Ste 1000, New York, NY 10036.

EDEN COURT by Murphy Guyer: 2 acts. In a low-rent trailer park, Shroeder Duncan faces his 30th birthday frustrated by an elusive mouse, tormented by neighborhood dogs, and embroiled in marital conflict with his Elvis-worshiping wife. 2m, 2f. Published by TCG in *Plays in Process* series.

FATHERS AND DAUGHTERS: two one-act plays
A TANTALIZING by William Mastrosimone: A lonely professional woman brings a once-elegant tramp to her home. She offers him charity, but instead, he teaches her a lesson in self-respect. 1m, 1f. Published by Samuel French, Inc.

THE VALUE OF NAMES by Jeffrey Sweet: An actor who was blacklisted in the Fifties faces hard choices when his daughter considers working with the director who named him to HUAC. 2m, 1f. Published by Dramatists Play Service, Inc.; by Mentor in Fruitful and Multiply; and by Smith & Kraus in *20/20: Twenty One-Act Plays from the Twenty Year History of the Humana Festival of New American Plays*.

FOOD FROM TRASH by Gary Leon Hill: 2 acts. A prophetic Indian shows a garbageman how to transform trash into energy, and toxic waste becomes a metaphor for the poverty and sexual anger that paralyze people's lives. 7m, 4f, 1 boy. Published by TCG in *Plays in Process* and *New Plays USA 2*, and by Broadway Play Publishing in *Plays from Actors Theatre of Louisville*.

IN A NORTHERN LANDSCAPE by Timothy Mason: 2 acts. Against the background of a harsh Minnesota landscape in the 1920's, a couple returns to their burned-out farmhouse and recalls the events that led to the destruction of their family: the breaking of a powerful taboo by their children and the subsequent retribution by the community. 7m, 2f. Published by Dramatists Play Service, Inc.

NEUTRAL COUNTRIES by Barbara Field: 2 acts. During World War I in Belgium the dangers of emotional neutrality become apparent when a young man becomes the prize in a three-way struggle among his revolutionary mother, his academic father, and an apolitical mercenary. 4m, 2f. Contact Lois Berman, 240 West 44th St., New York, NY 10019.

SANDCASTLES by Adele Edling Shank: 2 acts. On a California beach, two vacationing couples, one about to break up, one stable but dispassionate, interact with a bizarre collection of characters: a prostitute, her streetwise business-manager daughter, a young surfer bum, a crazed dope-dealing surfer, and a mysterious paraplegic. 4m, 6f. Published in *West Coast Plays 15/16*.

SHORTS: three one-act plays

BARTOK AS DOG by Patrick Tovatt: An out-of-work photographer searches for a job. As he sinks deeper into guilt and self-loathing, his girlfriend becomes fed up and exits, leaving him to chat with the ghost of his dog Bartok, the one thing in his life that provided him with continuity. Published by Dramatists Play Service, Inc.

THE HABITUAL ACCEPTANCE OF THE NEAR ENOUGH by Kent Broadhurst: A hard-nosed art dealer is confronted by a talented young painter. As the dealer considers the worth of the painter's work, they lock horns in a discussion of style, integrity, and the necessity of commercialism in art. 2m. Published by Dramatists Play Service, Inc.

PARTNERS by Dave Higgins: A peg-legged cocaine runner struggles to survive in the world of organized crime, where suspicious, uneasy alliances and grisly murders are commonplace. 4m. Published by Applause in *Best Short Plays 1984*.

THANKSGIVING by James McLure: 2 acts. Three couples, casualties from the "Me"generation, gather over turkey and drinks only to discover that little lies and infidelities have kept them together. 3m, 3f. Contact Mary Harden, Bret Adams, Ltd., 448 West 44th St., New York, NY 10036.

A WEEKEND NEAR MADISON by Kathleen Tolan: 2 acts. Old college friends from the 60s reunite after a five-year separation and confront each other with their choices of political involvement, careers, sexuality, and parenthood. Published by Samuel French, Inc.

EIGHTH HUMANA FESTIVAL OF NEW AMERICAN PLAYS (1983-84)

007 CROSSFIRE by Ken Jenkins: 1 act. Within the context of the Korean Airline tragedy, a theatrical company debates artistic responsibility, the political nature of theatre, and the ability of the citizens to affect events. 12m, 6f. Contact Robert Freedman, Robert A. Freedman Dramatic Agency, 1501 Broadway, Suite 2310, New York, NY 10036.

COURTSHIP by Horton Foote: 1 act. Two young sisters dream of the world of romance and freedom that awaits them beyond the sheltered life of Harrison, Texas, 1914. 5m, 7f. Published by Dramatists Play Service, Inc.

DANNY AND THE DEEP BLUE SEA by John Patrick Shanley: 1 act. Two urban outcasts in a South Bronx bar make a war of romance in a desperate struggle for affirmation and change. 1m, 1f. Published by Dramatists Play Service, Inc.

EXECUTION OF JUSTICE by Emily Mann: 3 acts. The controversial killing of San Francisco's mayor George Moscone and City Supervisor Harvey Milk by Daniel James White is examined in the courtroom, reflecting conflicting social and political ideals. 14m, 6f. Published by Samuel French, Inc. and by TCG in *New Plays USA 3*.

HUSBANDRY by Patrick Tovatt: 1 act. A son must weigh his obligation to return to the land against the economic reality of the American family farm. 2m, 2f. Published by Samuel French, Inc.

INDEPENDENCE by Lee Blessing: 2 acts. The eldest daughter's return to her small town Iowa home prompts examination of a demanding mother's pattern of manipulation. 4f. Published by Dramatists Play Service, Inc. and by Methuen in *Lee Blessing Four Plays*.

LEMONS by Kent Broadhurst: 2 acts. Private enterprise, shiny new cars, and once-solid friendships all turn sour when a son takes over the family car dealership. 8m, 5f. Published by Dramatists Play Service, Inc.

THE OCTETTE BRIDGE CLUB by P.J. Barry: 2 acts. Set in the 1930's and 40's, two evenings of Bridge—occurring ten years apart—illuminate the inevitable changes in the lives of eight high-spirited sisters. 1m, 8f. Published by Samuel French, Inc.

THE UNDOING by William Mastrosimone: 2 acts. A woman's journey through guilt to truth and ultimate redemption is orchestrated by the stranger who comes to work for her in a poultry slaughtering house. 1m, 4f. Published by Broadway Play Publishing in *Plays from Actors Theatre of Louisville*.

NINTH HUMANA FESTIVAL OF NEW AMERICAN PLAYS (1984-85)

AVAILABLE LIGHT by Heather McDonald: 2 acts. In a poverty-ridden French village in the 1880's, amidst famine and hardship, a young boy studies sparrows and learns to fly, transcending his desperate circumstance. 10m, 5f. Contact Helen Merrill, 435 West 23rd St., New York, NY 10011.

DAYS AND NIGHTS WITHIN by Ellen McLaughlin: 1 act. In a prison in East Berlin in 1950, a woman accused of spying matches her intellect and determined strength against the full power of the state and the keen insights of her interrogator. 1m, 1f. Published by TCG in *Plays in Process* series.

RIDE THE DARK HORSE by J.F. O'Keefe: 2 acts. A family's inner resources are severely tested when one of their member falls ill and all are confronted with own mortality. 5m, 3f. Contact Actors Theatre of Louisville.

SHORTS: four one-act plays
    ADVICE TO THE PLAYERS by Bruce Bonafede: Two black South African actors struggle against the politics of their country when their performance at an American theatre festival is suddenly in danger of being banned. 4m, 1f. Published by Samuel French, Inc. and by Applause in *Best Short Plays 1986*.

    THE AMERICAN CENTURY by Murphy Guyer: A returning World War II veteran and his new wife find their rosy dreams compromised when their son visits them from the future and reveals the truth of what's to come. 2m, 1f. Published by Dramatists Play Service, Inc. and by Smith & Kraus in *20/20: Twenty One-Act Plays from the Twenty Year History of the Humana Festival of New American Plays*.

    THE BLACK BRANCH by Gary Leon Hill with Jo Hill: The inhabitants of a state-run mental home, who are at the mercy of the system that condemns them, fight for dignity and power. 3m, 3f. Published by Smith & Kraus in *20/20: Twenty One-Act Plays from the Twenty Year History of the Humana Festival of New American Plays*.

    THE ROOT OF CHAOS by Douglas Soderberg: This black comedy takes place in Centralia, Pennsylvania. As the underground fire gets closer, a family fights to maintain the aura of normalcy. 3m, 2f. Published by Dramatists Play Service, Inc. and by Applause in *Best Short Plays 1986*.

TENT MEETING by Larry Larson, Levi Lee & Rebecca Wackler: 2 acts. The Reverend Ed Tarbox leads his son and daughter on a mission, believing his illegitimate grandchild is actually a gift from God. The journey culminates in a hilarious, irreverent revival meeting. 2m, 1f. Published by Dramatists Play Service, Inc.; by The University Press of Kentucky in *By Southern Playwrights: Plays from Actors Theatre of Louisville*; by TCG in *New Plays USA 4*; and by TCG in *Plays in Process* series.

TWO MASTERS by Frank Manley: Two thematically linked scenes explore Southern hospitality and the performing of Good Works. The first concerns the confession of a rural couple who entertain a murderer, and the second reveals the awkward attempt of two well-intentioned women who try to comfort a bedridden hospital patient. 1m, 2f. Published by Samuel French, Inc.

THE VERY LAST LOVER OF THE RIVER CANE by James McLure: 1 act. A beautiful woman who runs the Tranquility Lounge near Muleshoe, Texas, is the cause of a yearly barroom brawl between her suitor of 15 years and any available member of the local Pike family. 7m, 2f. Contact Mary Harden, Bret Adams, Ltd., 448 West 44th St., New York, NY 10036.

WAR OF THE ROSES by Lee Blessing: (now titled RICHES) 1 act. A couple returns to the inn where they spent their wedding night 25 years earlier and confronts the troubling truth of their marital state. Published by Dramatists Play Service, Inc. and by Methuen in *Lee Blessing Four Plays*.

TENTH HUMANA FESTIVAL OF NEW AMERICAN PLAYS (1985-86)

ASTRONAUTS by Claudia Reilly: 2 acts. A male teacher at a Catholic psychiatric home conducts a frantic search for a "major" singing talent for the annual fundraiser while his female colleague tries to avoid a psychopathic student she secretly believes is an aeronautical genius. 2m, 3f. Published by Heinemann in *A Decade of New Comedy: Plays From the Humana Festival*.

HOW TO SAY GOODBYE by Mary Gallagher: 2 acts. The friendship of three women is chronicled over an eight-year span. The severe illness of one woman's child cracks the foundation of her marriage and she flees, leaving one friend to fulfill the role of mother and the other to act as a buffer between them. 1m, 3f, 1 boy. Published by Dramatists Play Service, Inc.

NO MERCY by Constance Congdon: 1 act. A man who witnessed the first testing of the atom bomb at Trinity Site struggles to find faith and meaning in the modern world while Robert Oppenheimer examines the consequences of his own experimentation. 5m, 3f, 1 boy. Published by Broadway Play Publishing in *Seven Different Plays* and by TCG in *Tales of the Lost Formicans and Other Plays*.

THE SHAPER by John Steppling: 1 act. The grim underworld of California surfers is detailed in this story of a man who, having just been released from jail, returns to his surfboard shop and convinces his buddy and step sister to attempt another robbery. 3m, 3f. Contact George Lane, William Morris Agency, 1325 Avenue of the Americas, New York, NY 10019.

SMITTY'S NEWS by Conrad Bishop and Elizabeth Fuller: 2 acts. A divorced mother is forced to confront her troubled past when she tries to prosecute the two boys who beat and raped her teenage daughter in this portrait of the violence that permeates modern society. 5m, 4f. Contact Lucy Kroll, 390 West End Ave., New York, NY 10024.

SOME THINGS YOU NEED TO KNOW BEFORE THE WORLD ENDS: A FINAL EVENING WITH THE ILLUMINATI by Larry Larson and Levi Lee: 2 acts. A hilarious look at the result of blind faith in organized religion. The obsessed Reverend Eddie experiences an increasingly maniacal series of hallucinations and visions, culminating in a game of basketball with the grim reaper. 2m. Published by Dramatists Play Service, Inc., and by Heinemann in *A Decade of New Comedy: Plays From the Humana Festival*.

TO CULEBRA by Johathan Bolt: 2 acts. Ferdinand de Lesseps, the charismatic Frenchman who successfully built the Suez Canal, attempts to repeat his "miracle" in Panama, resulting in one of the greatest financial scandals of all time. 9m, 2f. Published by Gibbs-Smith Publisher (Peregrine Plays) and represented by Dramatists Play Service, Inc.

TRANSPORTS: two one-act plays
   21A by Kevin Kling: A wild tour-de-force in which one man portrays a busload of eccentric characters on a city route in Minneapolis. 1m. Published by Samuel French, Inc.; by Playsmith Publishers, Inc.; and by Smith & Kraus in *20/20: Twenty One-Act Plays from the Twenty Year History of the Humana Festival of New American Plays.*

   HOW GERTRUDE STORMED THE PHILOSOPHER'S CLUB by Martin Epstein: The sanctity of an all-male club dedicated to quiet thinking is violated when a softball-playing mother of three plops herself down in the Wittgenstein chair. 3m, 1f. Published by Applause in *The Best Short Plays 1987* and by Smith & Kraus in *20/20: Twenty One-Act Plays from the Twenty Year History of the Humana Festival of New American Plays.*

Eleventh Humana Festival of New American Plays (1986-87)

DEADFALL by Grace McKeaney: 3 acts. In 1938, in a run-down roadhouse near Waycross, Georgia, two sisters who have retreated from the world are shaken out of their placidity by the arrival of four men, who remind them that love is still possible. 4m, 2f. Contact Mary Meagher, William Morris Agency, 1325 Avenue of the Americas, New York, NY 10019.

DIGGING IN by Julie Crutcher and Vaughn McBride: 1 act. This docu-drama, which examines the plight of rural America, is a compendium of Kentucky farmers' stories taken from actual interviews and juxtaposed with bankers' and politicians' views. Together they form a frightening and understandable picture of the farm crisis. 8m, 3f. Published by The University Press of Kentucky in *By Southern Playwrights: Plays from Actors Theatre of Louisville.*

ELAINE'S DAUGHTER by Mayo Simon: 2 acts. In this modern day comedy, a daughter comes to grips with the resemblance her life bears to her mother's, despite her desperate attempts to have it otherwise. 3m, 2f. Published by Dramatic Publishing.

GLIMMERGLASS by Jonathan Bolt: 3 acts. Suggested by the characters and events in James Fenimore Cooper's *Leatherstocking Tales*, this epic adventure follows Natty Bumppo, Harry March, and the Indian Chingachgook through 50 years of early American history. As the American wilderness retreats westward, the friendship among the three men disintegrates, for Natty and Chingachgook resist colonization while Harry profits from it. 12m, 2f, plus extras. Contact Robert Freedman, Robert A. Freedman Dramatic Agency, 1501 Broadway, Suite 2310, New York, NY 10036.

GRINGO PLANET by Frederick Bailey: 2 acts. This comically crazed sci-fi spoof parodies B movies when five chess-mad mechanics fall prey to alien infiltration. When a mysterious Soviet journalist arrives shortly after a UFO crash, the mechanics' eccentricities begin to run amuck. 5m, 1f. Contact Actors Theatre of Louisville.

SHORTS: three one-act plays
   CHEMICAL REACTIONS by Andy Foster: A black comedy in which two men, illegally dumping barrels of toxic waste for a violent underworld kingpin, pit the possible loss of their own lives against the life of a man they discover inside one of the barrels. 3m. Published by Smith & Kraus in *20/20: Twenty One-Act Plays from the Twenty Year History of the Humana Festival of New American Plays* and by Applause in *Best Short Plays, 1989.*

FUN by Howard Korder: One night in the lives of two teenage boys, whose search for "fun" takes them through the American suburban landscape. A disturbing portrait of the artificiality of modern life and adolescent isolation within it. 5m, 1f. Published by Dramatists Play Service, Inc. and by Smith & Kraus in *20/20: Twenty One-Act Plays from the Twenty Year History of the Humana Festival of New American Play*s.

THE LOVE TALKER by Deborah Pryor: A mystical and mythical examination of a young girl's coming of age, and her introduction to the frightening but enticing world of male sexuality. 3f, 1m. Published by Dramatists Play Service, Inc. by Smith & Kraus in *20/20: Twenty One-Act Plays from the Twenty Year History of the Humana Festival of New American Plays*; and by Applause in *Best Short Plays 1988*.

T BONE N WEASEL by Jon Klein: 2 acts. In this comic adventure of life on the lam, T Bone and Weasel, inept partners in petty crime, careen down the back roads of South Carolina until one of them ends up in jail and the other vows to mend his ways. 3m. Published by Dramatists Play Service, Inc., and by TCG in *Plays in Process* series and *New Plays USA 4*.

WATER HOLE by Kendrew Lascelles: 2 acts. An explosive drama in which lust, greed, jealousy and pride do battle on an oasis in Africa, as a murderous but charming slave trader butts heads with a beautiful Hollywood actress full of Good Samaritan resolve. 2m, 2f. Contact Robert Goldfarb, Sy Fischer Company, 10960 Wilshire Blvd., Ste. 924, Los Angeles, CA 90024.

Twelfth Humana Festival of New American Plays (1987-88)

ALONE AT THE BEACH by Richard Dresser: 2 acts. Six lonely strangers, an ex-husband and a dog turn a carefree vacation into a hilarious summer of discontent. Frustrated by computerized work shifts, bed-hopping and torrential rains, these miserable Manhattanites finally overcome their fear of friendship in this desperate search for meaningful weekends. 4m, 3f. Published by Samuel French, Inc.

CHANNELS by Judith Fein: 2 acts. A sophisticated mind and spirit begin to disconnect. Jennifer Bassum resigns her university position to give herself time to think. Depression blossoms into surreal hilarity as Jennifer reprograms her existence, casting husband, mother, lover and best friend into nightmarish episodes on the TV screen of her mind. 2m, 5f. Contact Dan Halsted, The Bauer-Benedek Agency, 9255 Sunset Blvd., Los Angeles, CA 90069.

LLOYD'S PRAYER by Kevin Kling: 2 acts. Raised by raccoons, Bob learns he's a boy when his arm gets caught in a trap and he's spirited away by the huckster Lloyd, who hustles for the boy's salvation at sideshows and revival meetings. When a beautiful angel is sent to stop Lloyd's blasphemy, a struggle for Bob's soul ensues, shaking heaven and earth and leaving Bob out on a limb. 3m, 1f. Published by Samuel French, Inc. and by TCG in *American Theatre* magazine.

THE METAPHOR by Murphy Guyer: 1 act. When a strange interrogation is derailed by a prisoner's defiance, the interrogator pulls out all the stops—outrageous, absurd and theatrical. But the prisoner's resistance ultimately disrupts everything, even the performance! 4m, 1f. Contact Murphy Guyer, 100 E. 31st Street, New York, NY 10016.

THE QUEEN OF THE LEAKY ROOF CIRCUIT by Jimmy Breslin: 2 acts. On the eve of eviction from her New York tenement, a black welfare mother decides to challenge the system and save her children. Her crusade against corruption and prejudice leads her through a series of startling confrontations with a judge, the police and James Boy—the man who abandoned her. 6m, 4f. Contact Barry Weiner, Artists Agency, 230 West 55th St., Suite 17D, New York, NY 10019.

SARAH AND ABRAHAM by Marsha Norman: 2 acts. Day one, we begin the rehearsal process of an improvised drama based on the Biblical story of Sarah and Abraham. Conflicts intensify as the lives of the performers and those of their Biblical counterparts begin to intersect. 5m, 3f. Published by Smith & Kraus in *Marsha Norman Volume I: Collected Plays*.

WHEREABOUTS UNKNOWN by Barbara Damashek: 2 acts. A requiem for the forgotten: lost people who roam the netherworld of our city streets. Her work, based on direct testimony collected in Louisville's missions, day centers and soup kitchens, and echoed by the voices of transients from other parts of the country, is a resonant tribute to our indomitable will to survive. 13m, 5f, 3 children, 4 extras. Contact Richard Krawetz, Agency for the Performing Arts, 888 Seventh Ave., New York, NY 10106.

THIRTEENTH HUMANA FESTIVAL OF NEW AMERICAN PLAYS (1988-89)

AUTUMN ELEGY by Charlene Redick: 2 acts. For over 50 years, Ciel and Manny have lived in rural isolation. Retreating from a world destroyed by the Crash of '29, they built a home and evolved between them elegant rituals centered on work, shared possessions and individual involvement. But Ciel is dying. She faces incapacity and must seek the help of strangers or surrender dignity and independence to the husband who would become her caretaker. At what point can a relationship no longer change? With lyrical emotional ferocity, *Autumn Elegy* explores the outer boundaries of human intimacy and leave-taking. 2m, 2f. Published by Samuel French, Inc.

BLOOD ISSUE by Harry Crews: 2 acts. Joe returns home with a case of Jack Daniels in his trunk and questions of blood on his mind. Unearthing buried truths, he digs beneath the surface landscape of horseshoes, dumplings, and time-worn stories to the unmarked graves of his family history. 5m, 3f. Published by The University Press of Kentucky in *By Southern Playwrights: Plays from Actors Theatre of Louisville*.

BONE•THE•FISH by Arthur Kopit: (retitled: **ROAD TO NIRVANA)** 2 acts. When a film producer offers his best ex-friend, Jerry, the chance to co-produce a hot new movie, the deal turns out to be not only raw but raunchy. But Jerry endures the onslaught of hilarious humiliations to get his one shot at fame and fortune. In a land where the deal justifies the means, there's apparently no part of Jerry's body or soul which is not negotiable. 5m, 2f. Published by Samuel French, Inc.; by Heinemann in *A Decade of New Comedy: Plays From the Humana Festival*; and by TCG in *American Theatre* magazine.

THE BUG by Richard Strand: 2 acts. The trouble in corporate paradise begins at Jericho Inc. with an employee's simple question, which cannot be answered simply or otherwise. The ensuing confusion shifts the employee's hyperactive imagination into comic overdrive, and the result is a farce of multi-national proportions. As this Everyman of the 1980s faces off against a faceless bureaucracy, he discovers a bug in the system that threatens to tumble the pre-fab walls of Jericho Inc. 3m, 2f. Published by Heinemann in *New American Plays Vol. I*.

GOD'S COUNTRY by Steven Dietz: 2 acts. In September of 1983 members of a racist organization known as The Order began robbing, counterfeiting and murdering so-called "enemies of the white race" in an effort to ignite a "white revolution." The crime spree ended one year later in a fatal shoot-out followed by an explosive courtroom drama. By documenting the facts and fallacies of the white supremacists movement, *God's Country* traces the brutal rise and fall of The Order. 8m, 3f. Published by Samuel French, Inc.

INCIDENT AT SAN BAJO by Brad Korbesmeyer: 1 act. An eccentric, humorous and spellbinding tale of seven people who survive a mystical mass murder in the American southwest. 6m, 3f. Published by Samuel French, Inc.

STAINED GLASS by William F. Buckley Jr.: 2 acts. CIA operative Blackford Oakes is sent into deep cover as an architect rebuilding a bombed-out chapel in 1952 West Germany. When the cold war heats up because of a charismatic German leader who promises to reunite the Fatherland, Oakes becomes a pawn in Washington-Moscow détente strategies. 10m, 2f. Published by Samuel French, Inc.

TALES OF THE LOST FORMICANS by Constance Congdon: 2 acts. Trapped in a planned community where nothing works as planned, the characters search for explanations in their dreams and in the artifacts around them—for even in Formica there may be a fleck of God. In *Tales of the Lost Formicans*, we finally meet the aliens, and they are us. 4m, 3f. Published by Broadway Play Publishing; by TCG in *American Theatre* magazine; by TCG in *Tales of the Lost Formicans and Other Plays*; and by Broadway Play Publishing in *Plays from Actors Theatre of Louisville*.

FOURTEENTH HUMANA FESTIVAL OF NEW AMERICAN PLAYS (1989-90)

2 by Romulus Linney: 2 acts. Nuremberg, Germany: 1945-46. Inside the Palace of Justice, Hermann Goering defends himself and his Führer against charges of war crimes and crimes against humanity. Defiant in the face of evidence documenting Nazi atrocities, Goering emerges from courtroom battles as a fierce, brilliant and conscienceless manipulator who very nearly sabotaged the Nuremberg trials. This explosive drama raises provocative questions about responsibility in the German and American chains of command. 9m, 1f, 1 child. Published by Dramatists Play Service, Inc. by The University Press of Kentucky in *By Southern Playwrights: Plays from Actors Theatre of Louisville* and by TCG in *Romulus Linney—Six Plays*.

IN DARKEST AMERICA by Joyce Carol Oates: Two one-acts.
  THE ECLIPSE: an aging woman's fantasies perplex and amaze her daughter. 1m, 3f. Published by Samuel French, Inc.

  TONE CLUSTERS: a father and mother endure an unnerving, often absurd interview with a disembodied voice that pries into secrets of a family tragedy. 2m, 1f. Published by Samuel French, Inc. and by Smith & Kraus in *20/20: Twenty One-Act Plays from the Twenty Year History of the Humana Festival of New American Plays*.

INFINITY'S HOUSE by Ellen McLaughlin: 2 acts. As Oppenheimer and his colleagues await the detonation of the first nuclear warhead, specters of past American pioneers converge in a desert dreamscape. This provocative play is an epic exploration of humanity's ceaseless struggle to control the world, tracing our uncertain progress in the journey toward infinity. 13m, 3f, 1 child. Published by TCG in *Plays in Process* series.

THE PINK STUDIO by Jane Anderson: 2 acts. Sometimes artists walk a tightrope between life and art, as is the case with Henri Matisse. In this fantasy journey through Matisse's mid-life crisis, the great Fauvist painter (fauve is French for "wild beast") experiences passions as extreme as the colors on his canvas. Desire, jealousy, confusion and love imbue the Matisse paintings that introduce each scene of this whimsical, sensual comedy. 2m, 4f, 1 child. Contact Martin Gage, The Gage Group, 9255 Sunset Blvd., Ste. 515, Los Angeles, CA 90069.

THE SWAN by Elizabeth Egloff: 1 act. A swan collides with Dora's house. She drags it inside and takes care of it. Problems: It can't do anything right. It keeps killing the neighbor's rabbits. Plus, Dora already has a boyfriend. This dark comedy explores the transforming power of love and sex. 2m, 1f. Published by Dramatists Play Service, Inc. and by TCG in *American Theatre* magazine.

VITAL SIGNS by Jane Martin: 2 acts. From the author of Talking With: new signs of off-beat humor, rage and imagination in the female voice. Jane Martin proves again the infinite resonance of monologue form. Moving in new directions, she introduces a gallery of characters who shatter expectation, reinvent the ordinary and dignify the bizarre. 2m, 6f. Published by Samuel French, Inc. and by Smith & Kraus in *Jane Martin Collected Works: Vol I*.

ZARA SPOOK AND OTHER LURES by Joan Ackermann: 2 acts. Three women drive into the Land of Enchantment to compete in the annual Bass'n Gal Fishing Tournament, but, before they even cast a line, two men get hopelessly hooked. With the World Championship and two marriages at stake, the anglers pull out their trickiest lures to match wits with lovers and fish. Confronted by beanie-shooters, rifles and rattlesnakes, the women discover that men are more difficult than fish to unhook. 2m, 4f. Published by Samuel French, Inc. and by Heinemann in *A Decade of New Comedy: Plays From the Humana Festival*.

FIFTEENTH HUMANA FESTIVAL OF NEW AMERICAN PLAYS (1990-91)

CEMENTVILLE by Jane Martin: 2 acts. Championship wrestling comes to Cementville, Tennessee, and then all hell breaks loose! Set in the locker room of a decaying coliseum, this wicked comedy tests the limits of self-control, as sex and pseudo-sport inflame the passions of the fans. Wrestling may be fantasy entertainment, but, as a satire of vicarious violence, this play pulls no punches. 5m, 9f. Published by Samuel French, Inc; by Smith & Kraus in *Jane Martin Collected Works: Vol I*; and by Heinemann in *A Decade of New Comedy: Plays From the Humana Festival*.

THE DEATH OF ZUKASKY by Richard Strand: 2 acts. Welcome to the circus of corporate politics! In the center of this three-ring farce, competing managers—working without a net! —attempt to climb a single career ladder. Marvel as they juggle ethics, tumble over one another, and jump through the boss's hoops! Oh sure, not everyone who wants a promotion gets this crazy...or do they? 4m, 1f. Published by Dramatists Play Service, Inc. and by Heinemann in *A Decade of New Comedy: Plays From the Humana Festival*.

DOWN THE ROAD by Lee Blessing: 1 act. When a married couple accepts an assignment to write the authorized account of a convicted serial killer, they face an ethical dilemma: When does a fascination with evil become an exploitation of horror? This riveting drama examines the haunted relationship of an imprisoned murderer with his biographers. 2m,1f. Published by Dramatists Play Service, Inc.

IN THE EYE OF THE HURRICANE by Eduardo Machado: 2 acts. Caught in the storm of revolution, three generations of a Cuban family declare themselves against the enemy—but is that Castro, the Cuban people or themselves? This tragicomedy about family business, love and buses is set amidst the Cuban crisis of 1959. As the family defends its bus company against nationalization, tempers flair, passions soar and blood proves thicker than gasoline. 7m, 4f. Published by TCG in *The Floating Island Plays* and by Heinemann in *A Decade of New Comedy: Plays From the Humana Festival*.

NIGHT-SIDE by Shem Bitterman: 1 act. Memories, ghosts and strange encounters guide a woman down a path of dark discovery. Does she witness a murder in the park, and is she now being followed, or does she imagine it all? Set in a surreal landscape of dreams and sexual fantasies, this one-character mystery is an acting tour de force! 1f. Contact Scott Hudson, Writers & Artists Agency, 19 W. 44th St., Ste. 1000, New York, NY 10036.

OUT THE WINDOW by Neal Bell: 10-minute play. Pandora's box is opened when a young man awakens in a wheelchair atop a kitchen table. How did he get there? What happened last night? And will his girlfriend tell him the truth? This comic tale of hope and devotion is co-winner of the 1990 Heideman Award for ATL's "best of the shortest" National Ten-Minute Play Contest. 1m, 1f. Published by Samuel French, Inc. in *More Ten-Minute Plays from Actors Theatre of Louisville* and by Smith & Kraus in *20/20: Twenty One-Act Plays from the Twenty Year History of the Humana Festival of New American Plays*.

A PASSENGER TRAIN OF SIXTY-ONE COACHES by Paul Walker: 1 act. Just a century ago, Anthony Comstock rose from his position as a U.S. postal clerk to lead a crusade against obscenity. Operating under laws written expressly for his cause, Comstock destroyed 160 tons of literature, imprisoned countless writers, publishers and artists, and declared the plays of George Bernard Shaw "smut." Based on the writings of Comstock and his victims, this performance art piece refracts the issues of our times through the mind of a fanatical puritan. 6 actors, non-traditional casting. Contact Actors Theatre of Louisville.

A PIECE OF MY HEART by Shirley Lauro: 2 acts. In this powerful and profound remembrance of Vietnam, six courageous women struggle to make sense of a war that irrevocably changed them and a nation that shunned them. Inspired by stories of valiant nurses and entertainers, this stunning drama about heroism, ideals and sacrifice continues Actors Theatre of Louisville's exploration of theatrical documentary, and offers a timely reflection on America and war. 6 f, 1m. Published by Samuel French, Inc.

WHAT SHE FOUND THERE by John Glore: 10-minute play. When Alice went through the looking-glass, her mirror-image, Celia, entered our world. Now Celia's shacked up with a truck-driver named Lou, and after making love they talk of many things, "of ships—and shoes—and sealing wax"—and new beginnings. This magical return to innocence is co-winner of the 1990 Heideman Award for ATL's National Ten-Minute Play Contest. 1m, 1f. Published by Samuel French, Inc. in *More Ten-Minute Plays from Actors Theatre of Louisville* and by Smith & Kraus in *20/20: Twenty One-Act Plays from the Twenty Year History of the Humana Festival of New American Plays*.

SIXTEENTH HUMANA FESTIVAL OF NEW AMERICAN PLAYS (1991-92)

BONDAGE by David Henry Hwang: 1 act. When a man and woman meet for games of dominance and power in an S&M parlor, ethnicity becomes their instrument of pleasure. Yet what the couple finds beneath the leather, under the hoods, lurking just below the spikes is skin that is human. This eccentric romance, commissioned by Actors Theatre of Louisville, examines the politically incorrect ways in which race and sexual attraction remain bound, despite these pluralistic '90s. 1m, 1f. Published by Dramatists Play Service, Inc; by Applause in *Best Short Plays of 1993*; and by Smith & Kraus in *20/20: Twenty One-Act Plays from the Twenty Year History of the Humana Festival of New American Plays*.

THE CARVING OF MOUNT RUSHMORE by John Conklin: 1 act. Stamping human likenesses on nature's enduring greatness—was it a brilliant vision or arrogant folly? Now four men of stone—imagined by the artist, carved by the worker, and observed by us all—dominate impressions of the Black Hills. Commissioned by Actors Theatre, this evening of poetry, music and performance illuminates myriad public and personal issues embedded in that "Shrine of Democracy." 5 actors, 1 pianist. Contact Actors Theatre of Louisville.

D. BOONE by Marsha Norman: (retitled **LOVING DANIEL BOONE**) 2 acts. In a cluttered historical museum, a cleaning woman disillusioned in love seeks romance and adventure with a mythic hero. Leaving her dustpan, broom and several men behind, the woman pursues her historic fantasy by fighting Indians and British alongside Daniel Boone—but she finds herself pursued by her most unlikely lover. This magical comedy travels the timewarp of love to put a human face on heroics—then and now. 7m, 2f. Published by The University Press of Kentucky in *By Southern Playwrights: Plays from Actors Theatre of Louisville* and by Smith & Kraus in *Marsha Norman Volume I: Collected Plays*.

DEVOTEES IN THE GARDEN OF LOVE by Suzan-Lori Parks: 1 act. As a bride-to-be and her mother watch from atop a hill, two suitors vie in bloody combat for the lady's hand in marriage. Meanwhile, the young lady prepares her heart and trousseau for the victor—until news from her matchmaker reveals just how deadening romantic illusions can be. This tragicomedy of courtly ritual is an Actors Theatre commission. 3f. Published by Smith & Kraus in *20/20: Twenty One-Act Plays from the Twenty Year History of the Humana Festival of New American Plays* and by TCG in *The America Play and Other Works*.

EUKIAH by Lanford Wilson: 10 minute play. Butch's haunting call for Eukiah to come out of the shadows echoes through an abandoned airplane hangar. What does Eukiah know, and what does he think he knows about a plot to kill racehorses? This brooding exploration of power lures us into a dimly lit corridor where truth and trust lean precariously against one another. 2m. Published by Samuel French, Inc. in *More Ten-Minute Plays from Actors Theatre of Louisville*; by Smith & Kraus in *20/20: Twenty One-Act Plays from the Twenty Year History of the Humana Festival of New American Plays*; and in the journal *Art Teatral: Cuadernos de Minipiezas Ilustrades*.

EVELYN AND THE POLKA KING by John Olive: 2 acts. Music by Carl Finch and Bob Lucas, Lyrics by Bob Lucas. Bad times are the best times for polka—and things could not be worse for a dethroned "polka king" who's coming off a 25-year bender. When Evelyn appears, claiming she's his daughter, his blurred life slowly comes back into focus. Together they search for her birth mother, revive his band (The Vibra-Tones!), and rediscover the outrageous joys of polkamania. 1m, 2f, + polka band. Published by Samuel French, Inc. and by TCG in *Plays in Progress* series.

HYAENA by Ross MacLean: 2 acts. A failing patient shuttles across his final perceptions of the world around him. Nearing cessation, his family and friends pull away. Into this twilight zone comes the Hyaena, a spiritual carnivore, who devotes himself to the dying man. A disturbing and seductive drama of mortality, surrender and irrepressible life. 5m, 2f. Contact Michael Traum, Don Buchwald and Associates, 10 East 44th Street, New York, NY 10017.

LYNETTE AT 3AM by Jane Anderson: 10 minute play. Things are not going well for Lynette and Bobby; she's contemplating the abyss and he's asleep. As Bobby snores the Brooklyn night away, Lynette turns her restless thoughts to salsa music, a gunshot, and the mystical appearance of a kindred soul. For her, if not for Bobby, it's a night to remember. 2m, 1f. Published by Samuel French, Inc. in *More Ten-Minute Plays from Actors Theatre of Louisville* and in the journal *Art Teatral: Cuadernos de Minipiezas Ilustrades*.

MARISOL by José Rivera: 2 acts. Armageddon in the heavens—the angels go to war! Apocalypse on earth—cities self-destruct! Seen through the eyes of Marisol Perez, an Everywoman on a journey through a surrealistic Bronx, this miraculous drama pins the destiny of our planet on the outcome of revolution on renewal. 1m, 3f. Published by Dramatists Play Service, Inc.; by TCG in *American Theatre* magazine; and by Penguin USA in *Nuestro New York*.

OLD LADY'S GUIDE TO SURVIVAL by Mayo Simon: 2 acts. A very independent old lady, Netty is surviving quite nicely, thank-you, until her eyesight fails. Pragmatically, Netty adopts the not-quite-so independent old lady Shprintzy as a surrogate pair of eyes but gets more than she bargained for. This honest portrait of aging considers the balance between self and selfishness, dependence and connection. 2f. Published by Dramatic Publishing.

PROCEDURE by Joyce Carol Oates: 10 minute play. By adhering to strict hospital procedures, an experienced nurse helps a novice prepare a patient's corpse for its journey to the morgue. This riveting confrontation of body and soul explores the many-layered mechanism which protects the human psyche. 1m, 2f. Published by Samuel French, Inc. in *More Ten-Minute Plays from Actors Theatre of Louisville*.

SEVENTEENTH HUMANA FESTIVAL OF NEW AMERICAN PLAYS (1992-93)

DEADLY VIRTUES by Brian Jucha: 1 act. The seven Deadly Sins threaten damnation. The seven Moral Virtues promise transcendence. Brought together as Deadly Virtues, this high-energy performance, conceived by Brian Jucha in collaboration with actors Regina Byrd Smith, Tamar Kotoske, Barney O'Hanlon, Steven Skybell and Andy Weems, enlists dance, torch songs and film noir to deconstruct the battleground of human conscience. 3m, 2f. Published by Smith & Kraus in *Humana Festival '93, The Complete Plays*.

THE ICE FISHING PLAY by Kevin Kling: 2 acts. In the middle of a frozen lake, a chilly Minnesotan baits his fish hook to catch The Big One. Suddenly his ice hut is overrun by family, friends...and apparitions in search of a beer? As comaraderie melts back into solitude, this winter comedy brings the lonely fisherman cheek-to-gill with destiny. 6m, 1f, voices. Published by Smith & Kraus in *Humana Festival '93, The Complete Plays*.

KEELY AND DU by Jane Martin: 1 act. From the author of Talking With and Vital Signs, a volatile full-length drama about abortion. Du, a radical Right To Life activist, and Keely, the pregnant rape victim she confines, transcend their circumstances and the ideological issues that separate them. Jane Martin develops their unlikely bond with a deeply felt humanity that refuses to become political. 2m, 2f, extras. Published by Samuel French, Inc. by Smith & Kraus in *Humana Festival '93, The Complete Plays*; and by Smith & Kraus in *Jane Martin Collected Works: Vol I*.

POOF! by Lynn Nottage: 10 minute play. What's that heap of smoking ash where her husband used to be...a magic trick, the wrath of God or evil mojo maybe? As two friends work out the boundaries of personal rights and social consequence, this surprising comedy raises a novel question: Is spontaneous combustion illegal? *POOF!* is co-winner of the 1992 Heideman Award for ATL's National Ten-Minute Play Contest. 2f. Published by Broadway Play Publishing in *Facing Forward;* by Smith & Kraus in *Humana Festival '93, The Complete Plays*; in the journal *Art Teatral: Cuadernos de Minipiezas Ilustrades*; and in the journal *American Voice*.

SHOOTING SIMONE by Lynne Kaufman: 2 acts. As young lovers, Simone de Beauvoir and Jean-Paul Sartre promised to tell each other everything—and then Olga arrived. Forty years later, that erotic visitation is scrutinized by an American film-maker, who's come to Paris with her boyfriend to "shoot" Simone. By examining the changing face of feminism, this romantic comedy explores the politics of love, creativity and commitment. 2m, 2f, posssible extras. Published by Dramatic Publishing and by Smith & Kraus in *Humana Festival '93, The Complete Plays*.

STANTON'S GARAGE by Joan Ackerman: 2 acts. "Things fall apart," wrote William Butler Yeats—and he never worked on a car! When their Volvo conks out in the wilds of Missouri, a Chicago doctor and her stepdaughter-to-be find themselves stranded in a repair shop for broken hearts. Ex-husbands and estranged wives drive in for emotional tune-ups, and the women from Chicago become mechanics of their own destiny — in a high octane comedy that proves, "Things also fall together." 4m,4 f. Published by Samuel French, Inc. and by Smith & Kraus in *Humana Festival '93, The Complete Plays*.

TAPE by José Rivera: 10 minute play. If we suspected everything we said was being recorded, would we act differently? Like Nixon's drama of deceit with the White House tapes, Rivera's surreal and haunting play examines the links between technology and conscience when a lifetime of betrayal is uncovered. 2 characters (gender unspecified). Published by Smith & Kraus in *Humana Festival '93, The Complete Plays* and by Samuel French, Inc. in *Ten-Minute Plays: Volume 3 from Actors Theatre of Louisville*.

VARIOUS SMALL FIRES by Regina Taylor: Two one-acts.
    JENNINE'S DIARY: Vivid tales of family, career and romance illuminate the journey of Jennine through a maze of self-discovery and love. As she travels to "a dream called Venice," voices from her African-American past open cages within cages and find freedom within. 5f. Contact Mary Harden, Bret Adams, Ltd., 448 West 44th St, New York, NY 10036.

    WATERMELON RINDS: What happens to a dream deferred? Some pretty wild things, suggests this serio-comic exposé of African-American family politics. As the folks salute Martin Luther King Jr.'s birthday, talk of the past heats up until Mama's repast explodes —literally! And all the while a young girl watches, struggling to understand a society that demands sacrifice but offers only promises in return. 3m, 5f. Published by Smith & Kraus in *Humana Festival '93, The Complete Plays*; by Applause in *Best Short Plays of 1993*; by Dramatic Publishing in *Ties That Bind*; and by Heinemann in *A Decade of New Comedy: Plays From the Humana Festival*.

WHAT WE DO WITH IT by Bruce MacDonald: 10 minute play. Disagreement leads to bitter accusations in this father-daughter battle for the truth. Ten years ago Cheryl started to remember, and now her nightmare has become his. 1m, 1f. Published by Smith & Kraus in *Humana Festival '93, The Complete Plays* and by Samuel French, Inc. in *Ten-Minute Plays: Volume 3 from Actors Theatre of Louisville*.

EIGHTEENTH HUMANA FESTIVAL OF NEW AMERICAN PLAYS (1993-94)

1969 by Tina Landau: 1 act. 1969 captures the horror of high school and the chaos of the late 1960s. In a swirl of images, events and music of that year, a lonely high school senior takes a psychedelic journey towards sexual and political identity. Unable to conform and needing to escape, he travels along a Yellow Brick Road of the mind, encountering such personalities as Dr. Timothy Leary, Janis Joplin and Neil Armstrong—he is propelled headlong into the terrifying, hot center of the counterculture. Here, in the collective hallucination of the revolution, he embraces the possibility of reinventing himself and discovers the quirky spirit which will lead him into the gay Greenwich Village of the early 1970s. 1969 captures a generation's yearning to expand outward—into psychedelia, over the rainbow, to the moon. 5m, 2f. Published by Smith & Kraus in *Humana Festival '94, The Complete Plays*.

BETTY THE YETI by Jon Klein: 2 acts. In this comic Call of the Wild, a disgruntled logger heads for the woods after losing his job and his wife. Hounded by environmentalists, treed by his family, and baited by the lumber industry, it takes a lonely yeti to finally touch this logger's heart. But what's a mister to do with his myth when everyone wants her—alive or dead? With an acid wit that could strip the bark from a yew tree, Jon Klein weaves this woolly new fable about the ferocious tug of war taking place in Northwest forests. 2m, 3f, 1yeti. Published by Dramatists Play Service Inc. and Smith & Kraus in *Humana Festival '94, The Complete Plays*.

JULIE JOHNSON by Wendy Hammond: 2 acts. Julie Johnson has had enough. Filled with passions that sometimes terrify her, she embarks on a journey to the ends of the universe—without ever leaving Hoboken, New Jersey. In this fiercely comic tale of extraordinary courage, one woman explores love and physics in her overwhelming need to expand inward. 2m, 3f. Published by Dramatists Play Service, Inc. and by Smith & Kraus in *Humana Festival '94, The Complete Plays*.

THE LAST TIME WE SAW HER by Jane Anderson: 10-minute play. Does personal prerogative end when company policy begins? That's the delicate question at hand when a valued employee seeks her supervisor's approval to share a long-kept secret with her staff. The ensuing discussion illuminates the value systems of those who make the rules and those who must live by them—or not. 1m, 1f. Published by Samuel French in *Ten-Minute Plays: Volume 3 from Actors Theatre of Louisville* and Smith & Kraus in *Humana Festival '94, The Complete Plays*.

MY LEFT BREAST by Susan Miller: 1 act. A scar marks the transformation of a body—Susan Miller records the transcendence of a soul. With generous humor, surprising sensuality and unflinching perception, one woman reconstructs a journey through loss. A breast may be removed, love may be relinquished, but the greater part of life survives irreducible. My Left Breast is a passionate redefinition of self when "all definitions are off." 1f. Published by Applause in *The Best Short Plays of 1994* ; and by Smith & Kraus in *Humana Festival '94, The Complete Plays*.

SLAVS! (Thinking About the Longstanding Problems of Virtue and Happiness) by Tony Kushner: 1 act. *Slavs!* is a fantastical / political / historical exploration of life in the Soviet Union in the earliest dawn of Perestroika. In scenes ranging from the inner chambers of the Politburo to a secret chamber beneath Lenin's Tomb to a medical facility near a radioactive disposal site in Siberia, *Slavs!* considers the difficulty, the failure and the abiding importance of Socialism and of ongoing efforts towards building collective societies and a more just world. 3m, 3f, 1girl. Published by Smith & Kraus in *Humana Festival '93, The Complete Plays* and by TCG in *Thinking About the Longstanding Problems of Virtue and Happiness (Essays, a Play, Two Poems and a Prayer)*.

SHOTGUN by Romulus Linney: 2 acts. "Whose tongue was peace, while his heart was colored with blood?" A passage from The Last of the Mohicans begins one man's retreat to the wilderness of his lost boyhood. In a lakeside cottage, this habitually compliant son and husband brings together his long divorced parents, his wife and his best friend to face the disintegration of his marriage. Civility and enlightenment inevitably fall prey to the ferocity of his unexamined resentment. In the hands of Romulus Linney, a simple story of betrayal becomes a masterly parable of spiritual damage. 3m, 2f. Published by Smith & Kraus in *Humana Festival '94, The Complete Plays*.

STONES AND BONES by Marion McClinton: 10-minute play. In the ever present now, machismo and misogyny meet hip-hop and attitude when two couples struggle to relate. By distending the jargon of two distinct strata of the African-American community, Marion McClinton's *Stones and Bones* paints the ecstasy of connection and the agony of estrangement. 2m, 2f. Published by Samuel French in *Ten-Minute Plays: Volume 3 from Actors Theatre of Louisville*; Smith & Kraus in *Humana Festival '94, The Complete Plays*; and by Smith & Kraus in *20/20: Twenty One-Act Plays from the Twenty Year History of the Humana Festival of New American Plays*.

THE SURVIVOR: A Cambodian Odyssey by Jon Lipsky: 2 acts. Dr. Haing S. Ngor, a survivor of the Cambodian holocaust, won an Academy Award for his role in The Killing Fields. Since he wasn't an actor, all he could do was remember. A story of unspeakable struggle and unwavering hope, Dr. Ngor's metamorphosis is hauntingly dramatized through interwoven elements of Eastern and Western theatre. A saga of war and lost humanity, *The Survivor* reveals the spirit of a man tempered by hate and sustained by love. 3m, 3f. Published by Smith & Kraus in *Humana Festival '94, The Complete Plays*.

TRIP'S CINCH by Phyllis Nagy: 1 act. A wealthy man. A working-class woman. A random meeting over a pitcher of gin and tonics. When these worlds collide, a controversial scholar tries to exploit the politics of sexual pursuit. Caustic and wry, this uncompromising drama pushes the William Kennedy Smith and Mike Tyson trials one step further—Phyllis Nagy gives us both the truth and the lie. 1m, 2f. Published by Dramatic Publishing and by Smith & Kraus in *Humana Festival '94, The Complete Plays*.

NINETEENTH HUMANA FESTIVAL OF NEW AMERICAN PLAYS (1994-95)

BELOW THE BELT by Richard Dresser: 2 acts. Is there more to happiness than misery? That's the paradox in this labor of laughs, when three men grab for all the gusto their meaningless jobs can brew. Stationed in a remote industrial outpost, these pixilated fellows are rewarded for teamwork with loneliness, boredom, ennui, back-stabbing, jealousy and revenge. Yes, many are the benefits of working for a faceless corporation that sucks life from all it touches—including a front row seat when Mother Nature vents her towering rage! 3m. Published by Smith & Kraus in *Humana Festival '95, The Complete Plays* and by Heinemann in *A Decade of New Comedy: Plays From the Humana Festival*.

BEAST ON THE MOON by Richard Kalinoski: 2 acts. In 1921, an Armenian mail-order bride is shipped to Milwaukee to begin a new life with her photographer husband. Both yearn to emerge from the dark shadows of the Armenian holocaust. As they struggle to redefine family amidst grief and displacement, these kindred strangers realize a love deeper than ever imagined. 2m, 1f, 1boy. Published in *Dramatics Magazine* and by Smith & Kraus in *Humana Festival '95, The Complete Plays*.

BETWEEN THE LINES by Regina Taylor: 1 act. After graduating from college, Becca and Nina set off on an unpredictable journey. While Nina stays home to pursue a career, Becca empties her trust fund to travel the globe. Soon Becca's adventures fuel Nina's discomfort with a life devoid of real passion, intimacy and romance. So when Becca returns, Nina's already primed to make a few radical—and violent—changes. 3m, 5w, 2 extras. Published by Smith & Kraus in *Humana Festival '95, The Complete Plays*.

CLOUD TECTONICS by José Rivera: 1 act. On a stormy night in Los Angeles, a lonely man picks up a pregnant hitchhiker and welcomes her into his home. Clocks stop, visitors materialize and love ticks toward its inevitable climax. In a magical world where two years can pass in a night, Cloud Tectonics asks if there ever exists a "right time" for love. 2m, 1f. Published by Smith & Kraus in *Humana Festival '95, The Complete Plays*.

HEAD ON by Elizabeth Dewberry: 10-minute play. Only minutes before an appearance on The Oprah Winfrey Show, a therapist specializing in multi-orgasmic sex must find a common ground with a woman who's witnessed a head-on collision. In this age of sensational media disclosures, it's surprising to watch what can happen off-camera when real intimacy is given a chance. 2w. Published by The University Press of Kentucky in *By Southern Playwrights: Plays from Actors Theatre of Louisville* and by Smith & Kraus in *Humana Festival '95, The Complete Plays.*

HELEN AT RISK by Dana Yeaton: 10-minute play. Helen takes her ideals to prison along with her workshop in creative mask-making. When a wise-guy inmate starts acting up, however, self-expression takes a nasty turn, and art provides the imprimatur for deadly craft. 1w, 2m. Published by Samuel French in *Ten-Minute Plays: Volume 3 from Actors Theatre of Louisville*; by Smith & Kraus in *Humana Festival '95, The Complete Plays* and in the journal *Art Teatral: Cuadernos de Minipiezas Ilustrades.*

JULY 7, 1994 by Donald Margulies: 1 act. Capturing a recent day of disturbance and fear, Donald Margulies' play, set in an inner-city clinic, charts the vital signs of our society. As a woman physician struggles to reconcile the extremes of hope and despair that define a typical day in her life, we are given a unique window on the way we live now. 4f, 2m. Published by Smith & Kraus in *20/20: Twenty One-Act Plays from the Twenty Year History of the Humana Festival of New American Plays*, and by Smith & Kraus in *Humana Festival '95, The Complete Plays.*

MIDDLE-AGED WHITE GUYS by Jane Martin: 1 act. Meeting in one of this country's finer landfills, three middle-aged white guys discover they've got one last chance to salvage their slice of American culture. But salvation can be painfully funny when God gets really angry. By airing America's dirty laundry, this hilarious satire probes the most sensitive place—what it means to be a member in the white guy club. 4m, 3w. Published by Samuel French, Inc.; by Smith & Kraus in *Jane Martin Collected Works: Vol I*; and by Smith & Kraus in *Humana Festival '95, The Complete Plays.*

TOUGH CHOICES FOR THE NEW CENTURY: A Seminar for Responsible Living by Jane Anderson: 1 act. If natural disaster struck your homestead, would you know what to do? Sign up for a seminar with Bob and Helen Dooley who, with a nationally recognized authority on personal defense—Arden Shingles—take the idea of "preparedness" to its funniest and darkest conclusion. 1m, 1w. Published by Smith & Kraus in *20/20: Twenty One-Act Plays from the Twenty Year History of the Humana Festival of New American Plays* and by Smith & Kraus in *Humana Festival '95, The Complete Plays.*

TRUDY BLUE by Marsha Norman: 1 act. Determined not to submit to mid-life malaise, a successful writer named Ginger embarks on a wildly irreverent spiritual journey. Her traveling companion and guide is Trudy Blue, the main character from her new novel. This comic, sexy, revisionist Doll's House for the 90s investigates what happens after "happily ever after." Published by Heinemann in *A Decade of New Comedy: Plays From the Humana Festival*; by Smith & Kraus in *Marsha Norman Volume I: Collected Plays*; and by Smith & Kraus in *Humana Festival '95, The Complete Plays.*

YOUR OBITUARY IS A DANCE by Benard Cummings: 10-minute play. Returning to his Texas hometown, a young man dying of AIDS attempts to say goodbye. Unable to overcome his own and his family's prejudices, his pain goes unresolved until he's reunited with another outsider who was his childhood friend. 1m, 1f. Published by Samuel French in *Ten-Minute Plays: Volume 3 from Actors Theatre of Louisville* and by Smith & Kraus in *Humana Festival '95, The Complete Plays.*

TWENTIETH HUMANA FESTIVAL OF NEW AMERICAN PLAYS (1995-96)

THE BATTING CAGE by Joan Ackermann: 2 acts. The last wishes of an extraordinary young woman have a secret design. At a Florida Holiday Inn, two estranged sisters struggle to carry them out, each marooned in a deep state of despair. A sip from the Fountain of Youth, speeding hardballs and bicycle couriers, a semi-gallant conquistador and a bouquet of roses all conspire to lead a brilliant engineer and her recently divorced sister to a new sense of themselves. And to each other. In this charming offbeat comedy, a family that has lost its bearings is restored. 2m, 2f. Published by Smith & Kraus in *Humana Festival '96, The Complete Plays*.
CHILEAN HOLIDAY by Guillermo Reyes: As Santiago celebrates the second anniversary of Pinochet's coup d'etat in 1973, one Chilean family marches to its own Latin rhythms. Romance, a birthday and plenty of homemade brew make theirs a festive backyard soiree—until plans to emigrate are revealed and collaborators are confronted. At a time when the darkest secrets are known only to secret police, this political-romantic comedy pries into the future of two cynics who are hatefully in love. 2m, 3f, female voice. Published by Smith & Kraus in *Humana Festival '96, The Complete Plays*.

CONTRACT WITH JACKIE by Jimmy Breslin: 10 minute play. What would happen in America if politicians first tested their schemes for our nation at home? Turns out some have, according to playwright/journalist Jimmy Breslin, in this high-spirited send-up of politics brought down to their most personal and revealing level. 1m, 1f. Published by Smith & Kraus in *Humana Festival '96, The Complete Plays*.

FLESH AND BLOOD by Elizabeth Dewberry: 2 acts. When Crystal commits the social indiscretion of the year, her astounded Southern clan can't figure out why—or can they? Unanswered questions abound in this comedy macabre, as sibling passions get channeled into culinary misadventure. Rattling the closet skeletons of "The New South," playwright Elizabeth Dewberry pushes her gothic rivalry to a shattering conclusion. 1m, 3f. Published by Smith & Kraus in *Humana Festival '96, The Complete Plays*.

GOING, GOING, GONE by Anne Bogart & The Saratoga International Theater Institute: Erratic quantum physics mix with torrid sexual gambits at the ultimate cocktail party of the century. As the social occasion unravels over too many martinis, so too do the absolute truths of Newtonian physics, leaving two couples to play out their dangerous games in a world of uncertainty, relativity and parallel universes. Inspired by recent scientific writings, this expressionist peformance explores our perilous balancing act between salvation and destruction. 2m, 2f. Contact Ruth Nightengale, Saratoga International Theater Institute, 236 W 78th St, New York, NY 10024.

JACK AND JILL by Jane Martin: 2 acts. In her newest work, Jane Martin mines the subtle and often treacherous depths of modern wedlock. To love, honor and cherish—those are the easy parts of the union. It's where one person leaves off and the other begins that proves the stumbling block. By turns funny, sensual and fierce, this poignant drama captures the essential humanity of relationship—for better or worse. 1m, 1f. Published by Samuel French, Inc.; and by Smith & Kraus in *Humana Festival '96, The Complete Plays*.

ONE FLEA SPARE by Naomi Wallace: 2 acts. Fleeing plague in the streets of 1665 London, a poor sailor and a waif steal indoors, only to discover themselves quarantined for a month with the Master and Mistress of the house. As fears of the outside world turn inwardly to jealousy and suspicion, the gentry and underclass boarded in together wait for either freedom or death. This searing and lyrical drama explores the politics of compassion within the shadow of the grave. 3m, 2f. Published by Smith & Kraus in *Humana Festival '96, The Complete Plays*.

REVERSE TRANSCRIPTION by Tony Kushner: 10 minute play. At midnight in a cemetary on Martha's Vineyard, six moderately inebriated playwrights prepare to bury the remains of a seventh— illegally. Countering despair with wit, these bandit dramatists revel in their mad adventure and muse against the dying of the light. Published by Smith & Kraus in *Humana Festival '96, The Complete Plays*.

MISSING MARISA AND KISSING CHRISTINE by John Patrick Shanley: Two one-acts.
MISSING MARISA Two men engage in a madcap wrangle over a woman who has left them both. Funny and scary and downright mysterious, Terry and Eli are rivals and friends. They speak in the raunchy shorthand of people who have too much history and no inhibitions. An outrageous play about men alone together, their bizarre transactions and their chaotic humor. 2m. Published by Smith & Kraus in *Humana Festival '96, The Complete Plays*.

KISSING CHRISTINE By turns romantic, fiercely introspective, and very, very funny, John Patrick Shanley zooms in on a very unusual first date. Two extremely individual people battle their way from hilarious self-disclosure to startling self-discovery. Valiantly working through "the strangest conversation of their lives," Christine and Larry manage to transform a chance encounter into a fateful affair. 1m, 1f. Published by Smith & Kraus in *Humana Festival '96, The Complete Plays*.

TRYING TO FIND CHINATOWN by David Henry Hwang: 10 minute play. Ronnie is a rock 'n' roll violinist, street-smart hipster and (only incidentally) Chinese-American. Benjamin is blonde, square, wide-eyed, Midwestern and (only incidentally) Caucasian. Their confrontation on the Lower East Side of Manhattan sparks a riff on race that swings to the very heart of identity. 2m. Published by Smith & Kraus in *Humana Festival '96, The Complete Plays*.

WHAT I MEANT WAS by Craig Lucas: 10 minute play. An American family sits down to dinner, and out pours more pain and comfort, admissions and understanding than most families experience in a lifetime — all in ten minutes! This comic yet rueful remembrance of the way things weren't offers at least a ray of hope for the way things still might be. 2m, 2f. Published by Smith & Kraus in *Humana Festival '96, The Complete Plays*.